MIAMI &
MIAMI BEACH
5TH EDITION

Where to Stay and Eat
for All Budgets

Must-See Sights
and Local Secrets

Ratings You Can Trust

Fodor's Travel Publications New York, Toronto, London, Sydney, Auckland
www.fodors.com

MIAMI & MIAMI BEACH

Editor: Andrea Lehman

Editorial Production: Tom Holton

Editorial Contributors: Collin Campbell, Viviana Carballo, Kathy Foster, Satu Hummasti, Carolyn Keating, Karen Schlesinger, Patty Shillington, Lisa Simundson

Maps: David Lindroth, *cartographer*; Rebecca Baer and Bob Blake, *map editors*

Design: Fabrizio La Rocca, *creative director*; Guido Caroti, *art director*; Melanie Marin, *senior picture editor*

Production/Manufacturing: Angela L. McLean

Cover Photograph (Art Deco on South Beach): Annie Griffiths Belt/Corbis

SPECIAL SALES

This book is available for special discounts for bulk purchases for sales promotions or premiums. Special editions, including personalized covers, excerpts of existing books, and corporate imprints, can be created in large quantities for special needs. For more information, write to Special Markets/Premium Sales, 1745 Broadway, MD 6-2, New York, New York 10019, or e-mail specialmarkets@randomhouse.com.

AN IMPORTANT TIP & AN INVITATION

Although all prices, opening times, and other details in this book are based on information supplied to us at press time, changes occur all the time in the travel world, and Fodor's cannot accept responsibility for facts that become outdated or for inadvertent errors or omissions. So **always confirm information when it matters,** especially if you're making a detour to visit a specific place. Your experiences—positive and negative—matter to us. If we have missed or misstated something, **please write to us.** We follow up on all suggestions. Contact the Miami editor at editors@fodors.com or c/o Fodor's at 1745 Broadway, New York, New York 10019.

PRINTED IN THE UNITED STATES OF AMERICA

10 9 8 7 6 5 4 3 2 1

DESTINATION MIAMI

M iami and Miami Beach may be the most exotic cities Americans can visit without a passport. On a typical evening in South Beach you'll witness the energy and passion of Rio, Monte Carlo, Havana, and Hemingway's Paris. Downtown Miami's glass, steel, and stone skyscrapers reach high into the blue, telling of a bustling city alive with commerce. Miami Beach's art deco beauties wink at the wide blue of the ocean, choosing not to tell the secrets of the revelers within and without. Other neighborhoods, such as Coral Gables and Little Havana, show off architecture and cultural events derived from their own distinct historical legacies. Born as a tourist spot in the 1920s, raised as a southern metropolis in the 1960s, Greater Miami has become one of the country's sexiest, though still evolving, destinations.

Tim Jarrell, Publisher

CONTENTS

Maps

CloseUps

ABOUT THIS BOOK

The best source for travel advice is a like-minded friend who's just been where you're headed. But with or without that friend, you'll be in great shape to find your way around your destination once you've learned to find your way around your Fodor's guide.

SELECTION

Our goal is to cover the best properties, sights, and activities in their category, as well as the most interesting communities to visit. We make a point of including local food-lovers' hot spots as well as neighborhood options, and we avoid all that's touristy unless it's really worth your time. You can go on the assumption that everything in this book is recommended wholeheartedly by our writers and editors. Flip to On the Road with Fodor's to learn more about who they are. It goes without saying that no property pays to be included.

RATINGS

Orange stars ★ denote sights and properties that our editors and writers consider the very best in the area covered by the entire book. These, the best of the best, are listed in the Fodor's Choice section in the front of the book. Black stars ★ highlight the sights and properties we deem Highly Recommended, the don't-miss sights within any region.

SPECIAL SPOTS

Pleasures & Pastimes and text on chapter title pages focus on experiences that reveal the spirit of the destination. Also, watch for Off the Beaten Path sights. Some are out of the way, some are quirky, and all are worthwhile. When the munchies hit, look for Need a Break? suggestions.

TIME IT RIGHT

Check On the Calendar up front and the Exploring chapter's Timing sections for weather and crowd overviews and best times to visit.

SEE IT ALL

Use Fodor's Great Itineraries as a model for your trip. Good Walks and Good Tours guide you to important sights in each neighborhood; ☛ indicates their starting points in text and on maps.

BUDGET WELL

Hotel and restaurant price categories from ¢ to $$$$ are defined in the opening pages of those chapters—expect to find a balanced selection for every budget. For attractions, we always give standard adult admission fees; reductions are usually available for children, students, and senior citizens. Want to pay with plastic? AE, D, DC, MC, V following restaurant and hotel listings indicate whether American Express, Discover, Diner's Club, MasterCard, or Visa are accepted.

BASIC INFO

Smart Travel Tips lists travel essentials for the entire area covered by the book. We assume you'll check Web sites or call for particulars.

ON THE MAPS

Maps throughout the book show you what's where and help you find your way around. Black and orange numbered bullets ❶ ① in the text correlate to bullets on maps.

BACKGROUND	We give background information within the chapters as well as in CloseUp boxes and in Understanding Miami at the end of the book. To get in the mood, review Books & Movies.
FIND IT FAST	Within the Exploring Miami & Miami Beach chapter, sights are grouped by neighborhood, and neighborhoods are arranged roughly north to south. Where to Eat and Where to Stay are also organized by neighborhood—Where to Eat is further divided by cuisine type. The Nightlife & the Arts chapter is split into those two related genres of entertainment, and Sports & the Outdoors is arranged alphabetically by activity type. Within Shopping, a description of the city's main shopping malls and districts is followed by a list of specialty shops grouped according to their focus. Heads at the top of each page help you find what you need within a chapter.
DON'T FORGET	Restaurants are open for lunch and dinner daily unless we state otherwise; we mention dress only when there's a specific requirement and reservations only when they're essential or not accepted—it's always best to book ahead. Hotels have private baths, phone, TVs, and air-conditioning and operate on the European Plan (a.k.a. EP, meaning without meals). We always list facilities but not whether you'll be charged extra to use them, so when pricing accommodations, find out what's included.
SYMBOLS	

Many Listings

- ★ Fodor's Choice
- ★ Highly recommended
- ⊠ Physical address
- ✦ Directions
- ⌂ Mailing address
- ☎ Telephone
- 🖷 Fax
- ⊕ On the Web
- ✎ E-mail
- 🎫 Admission fee
- ☉ Open/closed times
- ▶ Start of walk/itinerary
- Ⓜ Metro stations
- ▭ Credit cards

Outdoors

- 🏌 Golf
- ⛺ Camping

Hotels & Restaurants

- 🏨 Hotel
- ➦ Number of rooms
- ☌ Facilities
- ❍ Meal plans
- ✕ Restaurant
- ⌂ Reservations
- 🏛 Dress code
- ⚲ Smoking
- 🍸 BYOB
- ✕🏨 Hotel with restaurant that warrants a visit

Other

- ℭ Family-friendly
- 🛈 Contact information
- ⇨ See also
- ⊠ Branch address
- ☞ Take note

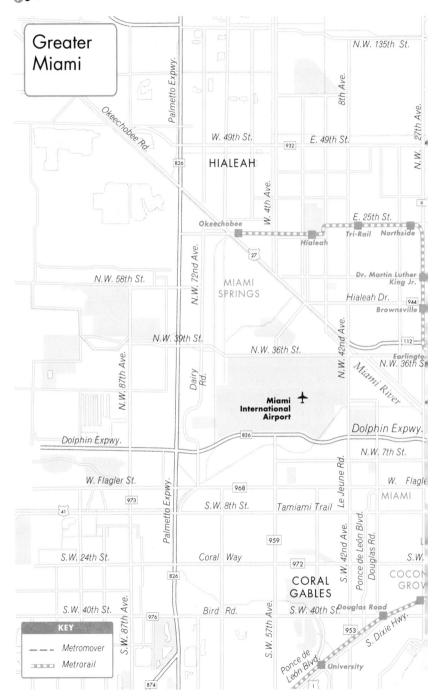

Greater Miami

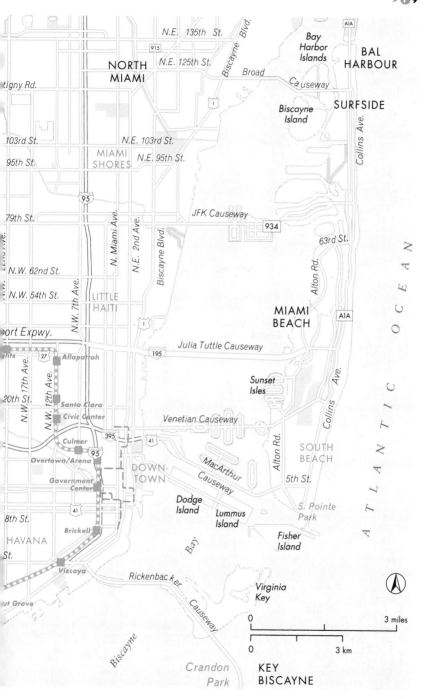

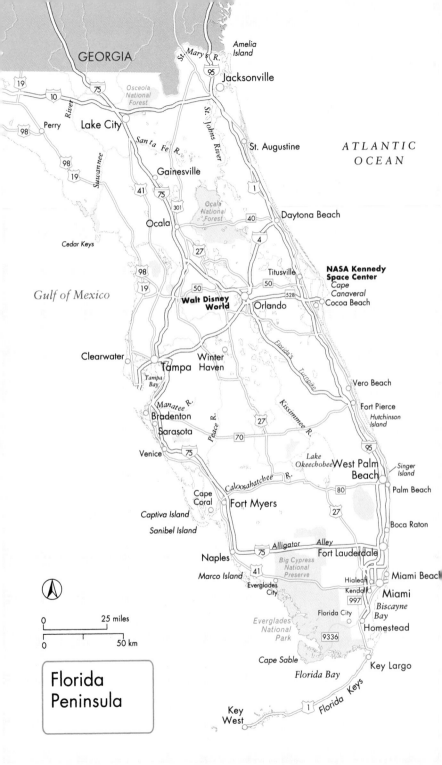

GEORGIA

St. Mary R.

Amelia
Island

95

Jacksonville

19

10

75

Osceola
National
Forest

River

98

Perry

Lake City

Santa Fe R.

St. Johns River

St. Augustine

*ATLANTIC
OCEAN*

Suwannee

98

Gainesville

19

41

75

301

Ocala
National
Forest

Ocala

40

Daytona Beach

Cedar Keys

27

4

98

19

50

Titusville

50

**NASA Kennedy
Space Center**
*Cape
Canaveral*
Cocoa Beach

**Walt Disney
World**

Orlando

528

Gulf of Mexico

Clearwater

Winter
Haven

Florida's Turnpike

Vero Beach

Tampa

*Tampa
Bay*

Manatee R.

Bradenton

Sarasota

Peace R.

70

Kissimmee R.

Fort Pierce

*Hutchinson
Island*

Venice

75

27

*Lake
Okeechobee*

West Palm
Beach

95

*Singer
Island*

Caloosahatchee R.

80

Palm Beach

Cape
Coral

Fort Myers

27

Boca Raton

Captiva Island

Sanibel Island

75

Alligator

Alley

Fort Lauderdale

Naples

*Big Cypress
National
Preserve*

41

Hialeah

Miami Beach

Marco Island

Everglades
City

Kendall

Miami

997

*Biscayne
Bay*

Florida City

Homestead

*Everglades
National
Park*

9336

Cape Sable

Key Largo

Florida Bay

Florida Keys

Key
West

1

0   25 miles

0   50 km

Florida
Peninsula

ON THE ROAD WITH FODOR'S

A trip takes you out of yourself. Concerns of life at home completely disappear, driven away by more immediate thoughts—about, say, what marvels will beguile the next day, or where you'll have dinner. That's where Fodor's comes in. We make sure that you know all your options, so that you don't miss something that's around the next bend just because you didn't know it was there. Because the best memories of your trip might well have nothing to do with what you came to Miami to see, we guide you to sights large and small all over the metro area. You might set out to laze on the beach or dance the night away, but back at home you find yourself unable to forget swimming in the Italian village that is the Venetian Pool or viewing of the Miami skyline from Bill Baggs Cape Florida State Park. With Fodor's at your side, serendipitous discoveries are never far away.

The more you know before you go, the better your trip will be. Miami's most fascinating small museum (or its hottest new restaurant) could be just around the corner from your hotel, but if you don't know it's there, it might as well be on the other side of the globe. That's where this book comes in. It's a great step toward making sure your next trip lives up to your expectations. As you plan, check out the Web as well. Guidebooks have been helping smart travelers find the special places for years; the Web is one more tool. Whatever reference you consult, be savvy about what you read, and always consider the source. Images and language can be massaged to make places appear better than they are. And one traveler's quaint is another's grimy. Here at Fodor's, and at our on-line arm, Fodors.com, our focus is on providing you with information that's not only useful but accurate and on target. Every day Fodor's editors put enormous effort into getting things right, beginning with the search for the right contribu-

tors—people who have objective judgment, broad travel experience, and the writing ability to put their insights into words. Although there's no substitute for travel advice from a good friend who knows your style, our contributors are the next best thing—the kind of people you would poll for advice if you knew them.

Born in Cuba, food writer and critic **Viviana Carballo** has written countless food articles and restaurant reviews for the *Miami Herald* and several national magazines (in English and Spanish). She updated the Where to Eat chapter.

Travel writer **Kathy Foster,** who has explored almost every spot from Miami to the Keys via bicycle, updated the Sports & the Outdoors chapter. When not biking, she's at work as an editor for the *Miami Herald*'s feature section.

Carolyn Keating is a Miami Beach native and freelance travel writer who updated the Nightlife & the Arts and Smart Travel Tips chapters. She has written about boating and fishing for the *Miami Herald* in addition to general-interest stories about unusual places in Florida.

Freelance writer **Karen Schlesinger** has been exploring South Florida shopping for more than a decade. She's a local expert and regular contributor to newspapers, magazines, books, and her Web site (theysay.cc)—a source for what's hip and haute in South Florida shopping and fashion.

A former *Miami Herald* editor and writer, **Patty Shillington** lives in Coral Gables with her daughter. Having covered everything but sports for the *Herald,* she covered the Exploring and Understanding Miami chapters of this guide.

A lifelong Miami resident, **Lisa Simundson** is a freelance travel writer who has written extensively about Miami and was previously the editor of a local visitors' guide to Greater Miami. She updated the chapter on where to stay.

Miami is a lot like New York City, except that here cops swab zinc oxide on their noses. Its neighborhoods are also as distinct as the Big Apple's five boroughs.

Coconut Grove

Not just a commercial outpost of manufactured charm, the quirky Grove really does have a history of its own. Under the guidance of Ralph Munroe, Coconut Grove established a yacht club, library, post office, churches, and a school for the New England intellectuals, Bahamian blacks, and Key Westers who settled in the neighborhood. Although today's artists and writers keep a lower profile than their predecessors, there's still a creative energy here generated by the mingling of carefree young people and the older, wealthier residents who like being considered slightly off center.

Coral Gables

In the 1920s George Merrick envisioned an American Venice, and then he built it. Canals, stunning homes, the majestic Biltmore Hotel, and the most beautiful municipal swimming pool in America are all right here. Sadly, Merrick's work was halted by the 1926 hurricane and ensuing Depression. Still, what he built set the stage for a bustling shopping district (Miracle Mile) and the University of Miami. Fine restaurants, a thriving arts scene, and a well-behaved nightlife are turning the Gables into a delightful destination.

Downtown Miami

After winter freezes obliterated much of Florida's orange crop in 1894–95, Miami landowner Julia Tuttle mailed some fresh orange blossoms to railroad developer Henry Flagler to prove that sunny Miami was worth a stop on his line. Flagler built the railroad, and in its wake came hotels, businesses, and people looking for winter warmth. Although Downtown has gone through some hard times, it's definitely rebounded with the arrival of the AmericanAirlines basketball arena, shopping mall, and major financial institutions. Downtown is now remarkably vital, with lots of small shops and restaurants, particularly in Brickell Village independent merchants; the gorgeous Gusman Center; and the Miami-Dade Cultural Center.

Key Biscayne & Virginia Key

Perhaps the best-preserved section of Miami, this pair of islands south of Miami Beach are part residential, part recreational, and primarily natural. At the public beaches, windsurfers dart about the waves and picnickers park beneath Australian pines to enjoy the bay. Two large and beautiful parks, Bill Baggs Cape Florida State Park and Crandon Park, have beaches, walking and skating trails, and golf courses. Crandon Park also has courts aplenty at the Tennis Center, home of the NASDAQ-100 Open.

Little Havana

In the 1960s the aging neighborhood west of Downtown first became a magnet for refugees fleeing Castro's Cuba. Today Little Havana, home to Spanish-speaking refugees from Cuba and Central America, seems every bit as Cuban—and in some places as destitute—as the original. It's intriguing to visit cigar shops where the product is hand-rolled by a Cuban-trained master and to glimpse a separate world whose residents seem entirely self-sufficient.

Mid-Beach & North

Miami Beach encompasses 17 islands east of Miami, stretching from South Beach (on the south) to North Beach, and west to exclusive private islands such as Palm, Star, and Hibiscus. The central and northern beaches have an identity all their own, separate from the trendy frenzy of South Beach. Mid-Beach, for example, has huge, throwback resort hotels like the Fontainebleau. Farther north you'll hit Bal Harbour. Although it occupies only a third of a square mile, Bal Harbour glitters with businesses like the Bal Harbour Shops and the Sheraton Bal Harbour. The northernmost reaches of oceanside Miami still resemble the Florida of the 1950s and '60s, complete with tacky souvenir shops and motels. But they're rapidly being bulldozed to make way for huge condos.

North Miami-Dade

The mainland towns and neighborhoods that make up the northern end of the county have a diverse ethnic makeup. An influx of Asian, Russian, and other immigrants has added spice to the mix, bringing Asian eateries to North Miami Beach and tiny East Indian and Jamaican restaurants to North Miami. Aventura has a popular mall and the terrific contemporary Allen Susser eatery, Chef Allen's. The area is also home to some peaceful nature preserves.

South Beach

South Beach, the shiniest jewel in the Miami Beach strand, is where you'll find sun worshipers, tourists, conventioneers, hippies, club hoppers, fashionistas, and supermodels. Look a little closer and you'll also find residential neighborhoods, city parks, and a surprisingly enjoyable "walking town" hidden in the middle of the city. Its epicenter is the Art Deco District, called by some "America's Riviera." Fronted on the east by Ocean Drive and on the west by Alton Road, the heart of the district runs from 5th to 17th streets. Cafés, shops, nightclubs, the fabled art deco hotels, and the glorious beach make the area pulse with possibility.

South Miami

South Miami is only a few miles away from Downtown, but it's worlds away in attitude. Tree-lined Sunset Drive threads its way through this suburb of fine old homes and an old-fashioned commercial district. Quiet parks, a popular annual art show, and good local restaurants like Two Chefs have long drawn tourists, and the arrival of the Shops at Sunset Place, a huge shopping and entertainment complex, hasn't diminished its small-town friendliness.

Miami in 5 Days

In a city with as many indoor intrigues and outdoor oases as Miami, you risk seeing half of everything or all of nothing. So use the efficient itineraries below to keep you on track as you explore both the famous sights and those off the beaten path.

Day 1 To recuperate from your journey to paradise, grab a towel and your suntan lotion, and head for the sand in South Beach to catch some rays. Afterward, take a guided or self-guided tour of the Art Deco District to see what all the fuss is about. Keep track of where you've been so you can later revisit the places that piqued your interest. Chances are one place will be the Lincoln Road Mall, where shops and sidewalk cafés spread for several blocks along a pedestrian mall. Take time to hit Collins Avenue between 6th and 8th streets for some traditional shopping. Have a quiet dinner at one of the grand hotels of Collins Avenue (the Delano or the National), and complete the night with a drink or two at the sidewalk cafés of happening Ocean Drive.

Day 2 Swing through Little Havana for a taste of Miami's Cuban culture (and to snag a stogie). At the Venetian Pool in Coral Gables, lay out a towel, swab on the sunscreen, and ponder that the lushly landscaped waterfalls were formed out of a rockpit. If you prefer to do something, head to the Gables' incredible Fairchild Tropical Garden. Or if you have children in tow you might want to check out Parrot Jungle Island and the new, interactive Miami Children's Museum. After a dip or a look at parrots and exotic flora, try one of the area's fine restaurants for lunch. In the afternoon, take in some window-shopping along Miracle Mile and then hop in the car to get lost in the Coral Gables neighborhoods, working your way over to the grand Biltmore Hotel. That evening, cruise over to Coconut Grove. At night the village is jumping along Main Highway, especially around mall magnets like CocoWalk and the Streets of Mayfair. Movie theaters, rowdy bars, smoky dives, and the traditional tourist fare of chain restaurants are at your service. The festive atmosphere should drain the last ounce of energy from your body and prepare you for a good night's sleep.

Day 3 On day three, sleep in and then pamper yourself with a trip to the beaches of Key Biscayne. Just before the William T. Powell bridge, pull off to take windsurfing lessons or just park and enjoy the tranquillity of this laid-back slice of Miami. Key Biscayne is one very large beach, and you can keep driving to reach Bill Baggs Cape Florida State Park, where you'll find more beaches and tackle stores; pick up gear for pier fishing. A fleet of deep-sea charters is moored at Crandon Marina for more adventurous sport fishing. Keep in mind that half-day charters don't come cheap, but if this is a once-in-a-lifetime trip, anchors aweigh! Whether you lounge on the shore or sail on the sea, that evening you can return to your favorite nightspot in South Beach, Coconut Grove, or Coral Gables.

Day 4 Use the morning to visit Coconut Grove's Italian Renaissance–style villa, Vizcaya Museum and Gardens. Afterward, head to burgeoning Brickell Village for lunch; it's a relaxed area with shops and restaurants between the Miami River and Downtown. If you're here on the right evening, take in a performance at the ornate Gusman Center for the Performing Arts. Even if the theater's dark, the bayfront should still be going strong. Join the throng over at Bayside Marketplace or the nightspots at the dazzling high-tech AmericanAirlines Arena. Another option is to board a gambling cruise and live the high life at sea.

Day 5 On your final day head north on Collins Avenue to explore mono-lithic tourist hotels such as the Fontainebleau Hilton and Eden Roc. Each has more restaurants, pools, and activities than many American towns. From here you're more than halfway to Bal Harbour, whose shops—Chanel, Tiffany & Co., Armani, Dolce & Gabbana—are simply among the finest in the world. That evening, return to South Beach for dinner and a walk up Washington Avenue, down Collins and back up Ocean Drive to return to your favorite deco hotels. Since you plan to call in sick when you get back home, pick a nightclub and party into the morning.

Miami in 2 Days

If 24 hours is your time limit for seeing the sights, head first to South Beach. Soothing pastel architecture, a soft sandy beach, and the sights and sounds of Ocean Drive will put you in a tropical frame of mind. Nearby Lincoln Road offers galleries, cafés, colorful shops, and more people-watching. When the sun sets, unwind with cocktails under the stars at the Sky-Bar at the Shore Club or the ever-trendy Delano. If late-night fun is part of the plan, options include a South Beach nightclub crawl or a gambling cruise or sunset sail from Downtown's Bayside Marketplace. Next day head for Parrot Jungle Island (great for kids) or Fairchild Tropical Garden (great for nature lovers), or wander around the shady streets of Coconut Grove (something for everyone). For dinner, go gourmet at one of Coral Gables' many upscale eateries or grab a fish sandwich at Monty's in the Grove or Scotty's Landing—both popular waterfront hangouts.

If You Have More Time

If you have more than five days, take a little more time in Little Havana, to explore the rich tapestry of culture there. Head to Máximo Gomez Park (known locally as Domino Park) for a glimpse of local color. Visit a cigar factory, browse a *botanica* (a spiritual kind of drug store selling statues of saints, herbal preparations, candles, and other Afro-Cuban religious items), and buy fresh fruit from a sidewalk vendor. Sample *arroz con pollo* (chicken and yellow rice) at a Cuban restaurant, or refuel with a quick *cafecito* at one of many café windows ladling out the potent local espresso. If it's the last Friday of the month, head over to 8th Street and 15th Avenue for Cultural Fridays, a nighttime party with art exhibits, music, and avant-garde street performances. Or visit a salsa club or other nightspot that offers live Latin music. Plan on staying up late.

Alternatively, spend more time on Miami's cultural treasures. The newly expanded Bass Museum of Art, on Miami Beach; the Lowe Art Museum, in Coral Gables; the Miami Art Museum, Downtown; or the Museum of Contemporary Art, in North Miami are all good choices. The amazing variety of art will remind you of Miami's prideful place as the crossroads of the Americas, where the best is yet to come—and what's already here is pretty darn enjoyable.

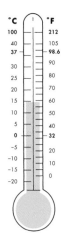

Miami and Miami Beach are year-round destinations, although most visitors come in October–April. Hotels, restaurants, shops, and attractions are busy then, and special events and the performing arts take center stage—so be prepared for in-season rates and low availability. Summer is a good time for budget-minded visitors; many hotels lower their rates considerably, and even nice restaurants may offer discounts (check newspapers). If you're traveling to other Florida destinations, you may also want to consider the fall and late spring, when many rates are as good as in summer—and rates plummet in the Keys and Orlando.

Climate

Miamians brag about South Florida winters—dry, clear blue skies, temperatures in the 60s and low 70s, and humidity-free, good-hair days. Even better, there's little difference between winter, late fall, and early spring. Good thing, since Greater Miami is often hot and humid in the summer, though temperatures rarely reach the high 90s. Along the coast ocean breezes make summer quite bearable, and afternoon thunderstorms disappear as quickly as they come. Hurricane season officially begins June 1 and ends on November 30. Severe storms can interrupt public services. In the rare instance of hurricane, Miami-Dade County may order evacuation of storm-surge areas. Most hotels have emergency plans to assist tourists, although if availability is scarce at inland hotels, you may find yourself at a shelter. If before you leave, you're advised South Florida is under a hurricane watch, consider postponing your plans.

Forecasts **Weather Channel Connection** ☎ 900/932–8437, 95¢ per minute from a Touch-Tone phone. **National Weather Forecast Service** ☎ 305/229–4522 offers local and marine conditions. **Miami-Dade Hurricane Hotline** ☎ 305/229–4470. You can also log on to ⊕ www.weather.com ⊕ www.intellicast.com is best for tracking severe weather systems.

GREATER MIAMI

Jan.	75F	24C	May	85F	29C	Sept.	88F	31C
	59	15		72	22		76	24
Feb.	76F	24C	June	88F	31C	Oct.	85F	29C
	60	16		75	24		72	22
Mar.	79F	26C	July	89F	32C	Nov.	80F	27C
	64	18		77	25		67	19
Apr.	83F	28C	Aug.	89F	32C	Dec.	77F	24C
	68	20		77	25		62	16

RAINFALL IN INCHES

Jan.	2.01″	May	6.21″	Sept.	7.63″
Feb.	2.08″	June	9.33″	Oct.	5.64″
Mar.	2.39″	July	5.70″	Nov.	2.66″
Apr.	3.03″	Aug.	7.58″	Dec.	1.83″

ON THE CALENDAR

Miami's famously fabulous weather makes festivals and events a year-round activity. While it's true that October through March reigns as high season for new works by major performing arts groups like the Miami City Ballet and Florida Grand Opera, as well as professional theater and classical music ensembles, it's also true that there is plenty of cultural activity to be found during the summer months. Film and dance festivals, heritage festivals like Miami/Bahamas Goombay, and only-in-the-tropics events like the International Mango Festival make spring and summer attractive to visitors—who can also take advantage of low- and shoulder-season rates at hotels and specially priced menus at some of Miami's pricier restaurants.

WINTER

Dec.

Culture vultures know to mark their calendars for the first week of December, when Art Basel–Miami Beach (☎ 305/674–1292 ⊕ www.artbasel.com) brings world-renowned galleries, dealers, and curators to the sunny shores of South Beach. The tennis careers of Seles, Agassi, and Evert were partly launched here, at the world's largest international youth sports-and-arts festival, Junior Orange Bowl Festival (☎ 305/662–1210 ⊕ www.jrorangebowl.com), held throughout Miami-Dade County. It begins in October and lasts through January, but most of its more than 20 events take place in December. Between Christmas and New Year's the youth-oriented Junior Orange Bowl Parade winds through downtown Coral Gables. The Junior Orange Bowl 5K race kicks off the festivities accompanying January's football classic. A hilarious cast of characters spoofs each year's local and national newsmakers as it sashays through Coconut Grove during the King Mango Strut (☎ 305/401–1171), a raunchy send-up of the Orange Bowl Parade.

Jan.

Miami rings in each new year with the FedEx Orange Bowl (☎ 305/371–4600 ⊕ www.orangebowl.org). The second weekend in January, Art Expo (☎ 305/666–7469)—with live concerts and 100 juried artists booths—takes over Sunset Drive from U.S. 1 to 62nd Avenue. More than 500,000 people flood the streets of South Beach for Art Deco Weekend (☎ 305/672–2014), a celebration of the Miami that put Miami back on the map. Art deco antiques sales, history lectures, and performances by jazz, swing, and big-band musicians make this perhaps the best time of year to see Miami. Usually held the third weekend of January, Art Miami (☎ 312/553–8928) fills the Miami Beach Convention Center with a massive art market that draws leading international collectors and exhibitors. Special exhibits showcase hot young talents from Latin America and the Caribbean. On the busy third weekend of January, the Lowe Art Museum presents the Beaux Arts Festival (☎ 305/284–3535 ⊕ www.lowemuseum.org) on the University of Miami campus, a family-friendly event that includes the works of 250 juried exhibitors. More than 150 artists from around the world head to the island for the Key Biscayne Art Festival (☎ 305/361–0049 ⊕ www.keyartfest.com). On a weekend at the end of January, it is held at the entrance to Cape Florida State Park, a gorgeous setting.

Feb.

The Miami International Map Fair (☎ 305/375–1492), held at the Historical Museum of Southern Florida the first weekend of February, brings together map dealers, collectors, and enthusiasts from around the world for a weekend of browsing and buying. Each Presidents' Day weekend, the Coconut Grove Arts Festival (☎ 305/447–0404 ⊕ www.groveartsfest.com) brings hordes of people to the bohemian community to participate in one of the country's top art festivals. For 10 days in late February and early March an excellent selection of 26 to 30 international films is screened at the Miami International Film Festival (☎ 305/348–5555). More than 45,000 people, including many actors and directors, descend on the eye-popping Gusman Center for the Performing Arts and attend scores of galas and midnight parties on South Beach.

Mar.

More than a million people attend the nine-day Latin blowout known as Carnaval Miami (☎ 305/644–8888 ⊕ www.carnavalmiami.com), which turns Little Havana into Little Rio. The week includes beauty pageants, cooking competitions, and Noche de Carnaval, a Downtown concert showcasing top international Latin performers. The nation's largest Hispanic celebration culminates in the 23-block-long one-day Calle Ocho Festival, with more dance, food, and top-notch entertainment. The Miami International Orchid Show (☎ 305/255–3656) brings more than a half- million blooms and spectacular botanical exhibits to Coconut Grove in early March. Dade Heritage Days (☎ 305/358–9572) ⊕ www.dadeheritagetrust.org) run from early March through the end of April; neighborhood associations organize tours, lectures, boat and trolley tours, nature walks, and canoe trips throughout the county. The Ford Championship at Doral (☎ 305/477–4653 ⊕ www.fordchampionship.com), typically held the last week in February through the first week of March, attracts 144 of the world's top golfers to the famed "Blue Monster" at the Doral Golf Resort. For 11 days each spring the NASDAQ-100 (☎ 305/446–2200 ⊕ www.nasdaq-100open.com) fills the Tennis Center at Crandon Park on Key Biscayne. The tournament is one of the world's largest in terms of attendance, and it has the cash clout to attract such international stars as Andre Agassi, Tim Henman, Anna Kournikova, and Serena Williams.

SPRING

Apr.

NASDAQ-100 excitement continues through the beginning of the month, as do the carnival rides and fun family atmosphere of the annual Miami-Dade County Fair & Exposition (☎ 305/223–7060 ⊕ www.fairexpo.com), which runs from mid-March through the first week of April.

May	CubaNostalgia (☎ 305/856–7595 ⊕ www.cubanostalgia.org) is an annual expo celebrating all things Cuban, with music, food, memorabilia, a fine art exhibit, books, and collectibles. The International Hip Hop Exchange/Miami (☎ 305/576-4350 ⊕ www.miamilightproject.com) is a late-May celebration of music, dance, theater, spoken word, and film focusing on the influence of Caribbean cultures on the evolution of Hip Hop in the United States. The festival features visiting artists, lectures, workshops, demonstrations, and performances.

SUMMER

June	Things slow down in Miami during the warmer months, but there's no better time for the Miami/Bahamas Goombay Festival (☎ 305/372–9966 ⊕ www.goombayfestival.com). The street party in the heart of Coconut Grove highlights the culture and contributions of Miami's early Bahamian settlers, with junkanoo parades, appearances by the Royal Bahamas Police Band, a golf tournament, and plenty of Bahamian food. With around 600,000 participants, the three-day festival claims to be the largest black heritage festival in the U.S. During the two-week Florida Dance Festival (☎ 305/867–7111 ⊕ www.fladance.org) at the end of the month, dance companies from all over the United States perform here. Catch local talent at the City Theatre company's very popular Summer Shorts Festival (☎ 305/755–9401 ⊕ www.citytheatre.com)—short plays, that is—held at the University of Miami in Coral Gables.
July	America's Birthday Bash (☎ 305/358–7550, ⊕ www.bayfrontparkmiami.com), in Bayfront Park, is an old-fashioned July 4th extravaganza with lots of rides, music, food, fireworks, and a petting zoo. Key Biscayne's 4th of July Parade & Fireworks Display (☎ 305/365–8901) is one of South Florida's longest and largest fireworks shows. The parade passes by the Village Green; a spot here or on the beach will give you a prime view of the action. The International Mango Festival (☎ 305/667–1651, ⊕ www.fairchildgarden.org), held the second weekend of July at Fairchild Tropical Garden, extols the king of tropical fruits with smoothies and other taste treats, plus mango medics, and a celeb-studded mango auction.

FALL

Sept.	As summer draws to a close, the University of Miami Frost School of Music hosts the six-week Festival Miami (☎ 305/284–4940 ⊕ www.music.miami.edu) from mid-September through the end of October. From jazz to flamenco and traditional Cuban music to chamber music recitals and symphony concerts, the festival brings together guest artists and award-winning student performers. Depending on the show, admission is free or runs up to $35—not bad when a musician like Wynton Marsalis shows up.
Oct.	The Hispanic Heritage Festival (☎ 305/541–5023 ⊕ www.hispanicfestival.com), one of the oldest Hispanic cultural festivals

in the United States, takes place throughout the month. A food fair kicks off the festivities; other highlights are Discovery of America Day (on Columbus Day weekend), a beauty pageant, and the Festival of the Americas, a huge street party.

Nov.

The first weekend of the month, the juried South Miami Art Festival (☎ 305/661–1621) brings more than 150 artists and craftspeople to Sunset Drive along the downtown business district. For the 11 days leading up to Thanksgiving, literary lions and book lovers gather for Miami Book Fair International (☎305/237–3258 ⊕www.miamibookfair. com), an international author's congress and book exhibition where top authors give nightly readings. A weekend street fair with more than 300 book exhibitors (including rare-book sellers) makes this one of Miami's most civilized and entertaining events. It's held Downtown at the Wolfson Campus of Miami Dade College.

PLEASURES & PASTIMES

Beaches

Greater Miami has numerous free beaches to fit every oceanfront mood. A sandy, 300-foot-wide beach with several distinct sections extends for 10 mi from the foot of Miami Beach north to Haulover Beach Park. Amazingly, it's all man-made. Seriously eroded during the mid-1970s, the beach was restored between 1977 and 1981, and restoration remains an ongoing project for environmental engineers, who spiff up the sands every few years. Between 23rd and 44th streets the city of Miami Beach built boardwalks and protective walkways atop a dune landscaped with sea oats, sea grapes, and other native plants whose roots keep the sand from blowing away. Key Biscayne adds more great strands to Miami's collection. Even if the Art Deco District didn't exist, the area's beaches would be enough to satisfy tourists.

Boating

It's not uncommon for traffic to jam at boat ramps, especially on weekend mornings, but the waters are worth the wait. If you have the opportunity to sail, do so. Blue skies, calm seas, and a view of the city skyline make for a pleasurable outing—especially at twilight, when the fabled "moon over Miami" casts a soft glow on the water. Key Biscayne's calm waves and strong breezes are perfect for sailing and windsurfing, and though Dinner Key and the Coconut Grove waterfront remain the center of sailing in Greater Miami, sailboat moorings and rental firms are located all along the bay.

Dining

Whether you've got a couple of bucks in your wallet or a couple of hundred, you can sample from such an array of dishes here that it's only fair to call Miami's culinary reaches global. Dishes native to Spain, Cuba, and Nicaragua as well as China, India, Thailand, Vietnam, and other Asian cultures create a veritable United Nations of dining experiences. The Miami-born New World Cuisine also blends culinary influences from throughout the Americas. Tropical combinations of fresh, natural ingredients—especially seafood—and classic Caribbean island flavors have yielded an American cuisine that is sometimes called Floribbean. Try the work of über-popular chefs or strike out on your own—you may come across your best Miami meal at a little ethnic eatery.

Nightlife

Fast, hot, and as transient as the crowds who pass through their doors, Miami's nightspots are as sizzling as their New York and L.A. counterparts. Clubbing is a 24-hour-a-day art form here. The densest concentration of clubs is on South Beach along Washington Avenue, Lincoln Road Mall, and Ocean Drive. Other nightlife centers on Little Havana and Coconut Grove, and on the fringes of downtown Miami. Miami's nightspots offer jazz, reggae, salsa, various forms of rock, disco, and Top 40 sounds, most played at a body-thumping, ear-throbbing volume. Some clubs refuse entrance to anyone under 21, others to those under 25, so if that is a concern, call ahead. If you prefer to hear what people are saying, try the many lobby bars at South Beach's art deco hotels. Throughout Greater Miami, bars and cocktail lounges in larger, newer hotels operate nightly discos with live week-end entertainment. Many hotels extend their bars into open-air courtyards, where patrons dine and dance under the stars throughout the year.

Shopping

Miami is a serious shopping city. Chichi shopping districts like Lincoln Road and come-spend-here enclaves like Coral Gables and Bal Harbour are rather astonishing sociological spheres, drawing locals day and night. Here, the question easily comes to mind, Does anyone work during the day? If your cold-weather hometown makes finding a bathing suit impossible, fret not. You'll find one here with ease.

Spectator Sports

Greater Miami has franchises in basketball, football, and base-ball. Fans still turn out en masse for the Dolphins, and—in the best fair-weather-fan tradition—show up for basketball's Heat and the 2003 World Series–champion Marlins. Miami also hosts top-rated events in boat racing, auto racing, jai alai, golf, and tennis. Each winter the FedEx Orange Bowl highlights college football.

FODOR'S CHOICE

$$$$ **Delano Hotel,** South Beach. Ian Schrager's Miami masterpiece is still the see-and-be-seen capital of South Beach style. The trend-setting (and smallish) stark-white rooms are really just a way station between trips to the pool and the hip bar, which is set off from the lobby by a huge, billowing curtain. If you go, bring your haute couture.

$$$$ **Four Seasons Miami,** Downtown. It's a business hotel. It's a vacation resort. It's a sculpture museum. Whatever it is, it doesn't feel like your average Downtown hotel.

$$$$ **Mandarin Oriental Miami,** Brickell Key. The location can't be beat, offering views of ocean and city skyline, and the spa, fusion restaurant (Azul), and luxurious details add to the opulence here.

$$$$ **Ritz-Carlton,** Key Biscayne. You'll find all the luxurious amenities and facilities you'd expect from a Ritz-Carlton plus a great location on Key Biscayne.

$$$-$$$$ **Biltmore Hotel,** Coral Gables. This 1926 palace offers large guest rooms with a Moorish air. The Biltmore chefs are constantly sharpening their skills, and a spa, tennis courts, and scenic golf course allow you to work off the fruits of their labor.

$$$-$$$$ **Loews Miami Beach Hotel,** South Beach. This new grande dame holds its own among Miami Beach's huge oceanfront resorts. With nearly 800 rooms and 85,000 square feet of meeting space, it could feel impersonal, but it manages to retain a young girl's charm.

$$$-$$$$ **National Hotel,** South Beach. The 205-foot pool is the most obvious bit of spectacle at this classic art deco gem, but it's not the only one. Preserved pieces of the past rub elbows with the latest gadgetry to create a modern period experience.

$$ **Hotel Place St. Michel,** Coral Gables. In the heart of town, this little inn has the intimate feel lacking in big resorts. Its restaurant is a reason to go in itself.

¢–$$ **Miami River Inn,** Little Havana. Miami's only remaining clapboard houses from the beginning of the 20th century are only a short walk from downtown. Antiques-filled rooms and warm hospitality make this place a bargain.

¢   **San Juan Hotel,** South Beach. Right across the street from the Delano but at half (okay, a tenth) the cost, this simple hotel offers basic rooms and friendly service at a price that can't be beat this close to the action.

RESTAURANTS	
$$$$	Timo, Sunny Isles. Robust Mediterranean flavors spring from chef Tom Andriola's attractive Italian bistro. Dark walls, brick, and an enormous wood-burning stove add to the warmth here.
$$$–$$$$	Blue Door at the Delano, South Beach. Claude Troisgros of the famous French culinary family is consulting chef at this hippest of South Beach hotels. Tropical and Asian flavors guest star on the soundly French menu.
$$$–$$$$	Chef Allen's, Aventura. Beyond a huge picture window, chef Allen Susser creates a different menu nightly. Try rock-shrimp hash with roasted corn, followed by the double-chocolate soufflé.
$$$–$$$$	Nemo, South Beach. Things are a little different here. The menu blends Caribbean, Asian, Mediterranean, and Middle Eastern influences. The pastries are a little funky. And the location is a little out of the way in SoFi. It's worth the detour.
$$$–$$$$	Norman's, Coral Gables. Considered by many to be Miami's best, this restaurant perfects the New World cuisine for which South Florida is famous.
$$$–$$$$	Pascal's on Ponce. Coral Gables. Unlike the capricious Miami that lives for the moment, Pascal Oudin's streamlined French cuisine disdains trends and discounts flash. Instead substantive delicacies are matched with proper service and just the right wine. And, ooh la la, les desserts.
$$–$$$$	Azul, Brickell Key. Hotel restaurants sure are better than they used to be. Chef Michelle Bernstein's exotically rendered French–Caribbean cuisine does wonders for redeeming the genre. Service is crisp and somehow comforting, with house pashminas for the sleeveless and reading glasses for the forgetful.
$$–$$$$	Chispa, Coral Gables. Latin flavors fuse thanks to the "spark" (Chispa's English translation) this place generates. Order lots of smaller portions and share the joy.
$$–$$$$	Pacific Time, South Beach. The happy bustle at this South Beach favorite attests to the beauty of chef-owner Jonathan Eismann's food, which simmers with magical American and Asian influences.
BUDGET RESTAURANTS	
$–$$	Havana Harry's, Coral Gables. If you want to eat traditional Cuban cuisine where Cuban families eat, this spacious restaurant is the place. And it offers great value for the money.
¢–$$	Big Pink, South Beach. This is a diner with a capital D. After making your way through the tome of a menu, dine on great all-American food in a setting that's vaguely roller rinkesque.

FUN IN THE SUN

Bill Baggs Cape Florida State Park. Great beaches, sunsets, board-walks, fishing piers, picnic shelters, and bike paths are all the reason you need to drive to Key Biscayne's southern tip. Plus, there's a lighthouse that's the oldest structure in South Florida.

Fairchild Tropical Garden. In the southern reaches of Coral Gables, the largest tropical botanical garden in the continental United States showcases orchids, bellflowers, coral trees, bougainvillea, rare palms, and flowering trees. Windows to the Tropics houses rare tropical plants, and a 2-acre exhibit displays tropical rain-forest plants from around the world.

Miami Dolphins. Do you dream in aqua and orange? Cheering for the Dolphins and hoping for a repeat of that perfect season is a tradition for Dol-Fans.

Ocean Drive beaches. There are gay stretches, topless stretches, and family stretches; a palm-lined park; volleyball courts; funky life-guard stands; and plenty of soft, white sand. And if you get bored just swimming and sunning, the wild world of South Beach is just steps away.

Oleta River State Park. Fish, bike, or rent canoes or kayaks at this largest urban park in Florida. There are 1,000 lush acres in which to forget you're so close to Miami.

Tennis Center at Crandon Park. You can play on grass, clay, or hard courts at this 30-acre tennis complex—unless it's during the NAS-DAQ-100 Open each spring. Then you'll have to be content to watch some of the greatest players in the world play.

Venetian Pool. Sculpted from a rock quarry in 1923 and fed by artesian wells, this fantastical municipal Coral Gables pool has secret caves, stone bridges, and a delightful wading pool. Spend an afternoon cooling off where Johnny Weissmuller and Esther Williams once swam.

FUN UNDER THE MOON

crobar. What doesn't happen at this South Beach outpost of a Chicago club? There's lights, sound, and action for straight and gay alike, but beware the carpeted dance floor.

Pearl. This combination restaurant-nightclub has pretty good food and a pretty great location on the ocean, at the southern end of South Beach.

Rose Bar at the Delano. The airy lobby lounge is the perfect spot to sip a drink and indulge in a quintessential South Beach experience.

SkyBar at the Shore Club. Lounge outdoors around the pool at this chic garden space. The Red Room and Nobu Restaurant and Lounge are adjacent.

Tobacco Road. This isn't some here-today, gone-tomorrow bar du jour. People have been coming to this Downtown joint since 1912—and still do for the great food, drink, cigars, and live blues and jazz.

SHOP TILL YOU DROP

Bal Harbour Shops. This is the swankiest shopping to be had in Florida outside of Palm Beach, with an open-air collection of 100 shops, boutiques, and department stores from Prada to Pratesi.

Books & Books, Inc. In this time of chains, it's nice to know there are some independents left. Like the chains, there are author readings and a café, but there's also a photography gallery and a courtyard to while away the time with a good book.

Brownes & Co. Indulge in upscale products for your face, hair, and body, or have someone else do the pampering at the in-house salon.

Epicure Market. This South Beach institution has gourmet treats, home-baked goodies, fresh produce, and the occasional celebrity.

Holly Hunt. This is the cream of the crop of Design District showrooms. Browse to your heart's content, but you'll need a designer if you want to buy.

Lincoln Road Mall. There is no wrong way to experience this open-air mall. Shop, sip a drink at an outdoor café, ride a skateboard, walk your dog, treasure-hunt at the antiques market, sample fresh fruit at the farmers' market, peek in at galleries, listen to the symphony, or just people-watch—the most popular Lincoln Road pastime of all.

Miami Twice. Vintage clothing, accessories, and furnishings can take you right back to the pastel '80s of Miami Vice. and beyond. It's a little out of the way—in South Miami—but it's worth it.

Village of Merrick Park. The style is Mediterranean, the location is Coral Gables, and the shopping choices are nearly limitless, from Neiman Marcus and Nordstrom to Jimmy Choo and Carolina Herrera. To recover, stop in at the day spa or one of the international food options, like Norman Van Aken's new New World café, Mundo.

SO YOU WANT SOME CULTURE?

Bass Museum of Art. Part of the Miami Beach Cultural Campus, this growing museum counts temporary exhibits of contemporary art along with a permanent collection of European art among the good reasons to visit.

Lowe Art Museum. Renaissance, baroque, American, Latin American, and Native American art are all represented at this museum at the University of Miami.

Miami City Ballet. Also located at the Miami Beach Cultural Campus, this professional classical ballet troupe has achieved international acclaim, thanks in no small part to its founding artistic director, Edward Villella.

New World Symphony. It's only fitting that such a young vibrant city as Miami Beach would have a young vibrant orchestra in residence. The training orchestra of recent conservatory graduates is under the direction of conductor Michael Tilson Thomas.

Vizcaya Museum and Gardens. Built by industrialist James Deering in 1914–1916, this neoclassical Coconut Grove residence is surrounded by 10 acres of formal gardens with fountains. It's filled with paintings, sculpture, antique furniture, and other fine and decorative arts in Renaissance, baroque, rococo, and neoclassical styles.

Wolfsonian–FIU museum. "Elegant" and "storage facility" sound almost as incongruous together as "modern design" and "propaganda arts." But they all blend together nicely at this museum showcasing the collection of Mitchell Wolfson Jr.

SMART TRAVEL TIPS

Finding out about your destination before you leave home means you won't squander time organizing everyday minutiae once you've arrived. You'll be more street-wise when you hit the ground as well, better prepared to explore the aspects of Miami that drew you here in the first place. The organizations in this section can provide information to supplement this guide; contact them for up-to-the-minute details. Happy landings!

ADDRESSES

Greater Miami (also referred to in this guide as Miami-Dade County) is made up of more than 30 municipalities, of which vacation favorites Miami and Miami Beach are only two. Within most of Greater Miami, addresses fall into one of four quadrants: NW, NE, SW, and SE. The north–south dividing line is Flagler Street, and the east–west dividing line is Miami Avenue. Numbering starts where these axes cross, with the numbers of streets and the numbers of actual addresses getting higher the farther away they are from that intersection. Avenues run north–south and streets east–west. Some municipalities and neighborhoods, including Miami Beach, Coral Gables, Coconut Grove, and Key Biscayne, have their own street naming and numbering systems, so a map is a good idea. In South Beach all north–south roads are named; the main drags are Ocean Drive, Collins and Washington avenues, and Alton Road. The east–west streets are numbered; 1st Street is at the beach's southernmost point, and numbers get progressively higher as you head north.

AIR TRAVEL TO & FROM MIAMI

BOOKING

When you book, look for nonstop flights and remember that "direct" flights stop at least once. Try to avoid connecting flights, which require a change of plane. Two airlines may operate a connecting flight jointly, so ask whether your airline operates every segment of the trip; you may find that the carrier you prefer flies you only part of the way. To find more booking tips and to check prices and make online flight reservations, log on to www.fodors.com.

Consider, too, whether other major airports in the area might be more convenient or less expensive to your final destination. For example, many travelers choose to fly into Fort Lauderdale International Airport for its generally cheaper fares.

CARRIERS

🛪 Major Airlines **AirTran** ☎ 800/825-8538. **America West** ☎ 800/235-9292. **American** ☎ 800/433-7300. **American Transair** ☎ 800/225-2995. **Continental** ☎ 800/525-0280. **Delta** ☎ 800/221-1212. **Midway** ☎ 800/446-4392. **Northwest** ☎ 800/225-2525. **Southwest** ☎ 800/435-9792. **Spirit Air** ☎ 800/772-7117. **United** ☎ 800/241-6522. **US Airways** ☎ 800/428-4322.

🛪 Foreign Carriers **ACES** ☎ 800/846-2237. **Aeroflot** ☎ 888/340-6400. **Aerolineas Argentina** ☎ 800/333-0276. **Aeromexico** ☎ 800/237-6639. **Aeropostal** ☎ 888/912-8466. **Air Aruba** ☎ 800/882-7822. **Air Canada** ☎ 888/247-2262. **Air France** ☎ 800/237-2747. **Air Jamaica** ☎ 800/523-5585. **Alitalia** ☎ 800/223-5730. **Avensa** ☎ 800/428-3672. **Avianca** ☎ 800/284-2622. **Aviateca** ☎ 800/535-8780. **Bahamasair** ☎ 800/222-4262. **British Airways** ☎ 800/247-9297. **BWIA** ☎ 800/538-2942. **Cayman Airways** ☎ 800/422-9626. **Copa** ☎ 800/359-2672. **El Al** ☎ 800/223-6700. **Lacsa** ☎ 800/225-2272. **Lan Chile** ☎ 800/735-5526. **Lan Peru** ☎ 800/735-5590. **LOT Polish Airlines** ☎ 800/223-0593. **LTU** ☎ 800/888-0200. **Lufthansa** ☎ 800/645-3880. **Martinair Holland** ☎ 800/627-8462. **Mexicana** ☎ 800/531-7921. **Nica** ☎ 800/831-6422. **Northwest/KLM** ☎ 800/225-2525. **Qantas** ☎ 800/227-4500. **Surinam** ☎ 800/327-6864. **Swiss International Air Lines** ☎ 877/359-7947. **Taca** ☎ 800/535-8780. **Transbrasil** ☎ 800/872-3153. **Varig** ☎ 800/468-2744. **VASP** ☎ 800/732-8277. **Virgin Atlantic** ☎ 800/862-8621.

🛪 Regional Airlines **American Eagle** ☎ 800/433-7300. **Comair** ☎ 800/221-1212. **Delta Express** ☎ 800/325-5205. **Gulfstream International** ☎ 800/992-8532. **Jet Blue** ☎ 800/538-2583 to Fort Lauderdale. **US Air Express** ☎ 800/428-4322.

🛪 Seaplane **Chalk's Ocean Airways** ☎ 800/424-2557, ⊕ www.flychalks.com offers daily service from Watson Island in Miami and Ft. Lauderdale International Airport to Bimini and Paradise Island.

CHECK-IN & BOARDING

Always **find out your carrier's check-in policy.** Plan to arrive at the airport about two hours before your scheduled departure time for domestic flights and 2½ to 3 hours before international flights. You may need to arrive earlier if you're flying from one of the busier airports or during peak air-traffic times. To avoid delays at airport-security checkpoints, try not to wear any metal. Jewelry, belt and other buckles, steel-toe shoes, barrettes, and underwire bras are among the items that can set off detectors.

Assuming that not everyone with a ticket will show up, airlines routinely overbook planes. When everyone does, airlines ask for volunteers to give up their seats. In return, these volunteers usually get a several-hundred-dollar flight voucher, which can be used toward the purchase of another ticket, and are rebooked on the next flight out. If there are not enough volunteers, the airline must choose who will be denied boarding. The first to get bumped are passengers who checked in late and those flying on discounted tickets, so get to the gate and check in as early as possible, especially during peak periods.

Always **bring a government-issued photo I.D.** to the airport; even when it's not required, a passport is best.

CUTTING COSTS

The least expensive airfares to Greater Miami are priced for round-trip travel and must usually be purchased in advance. Airlines generally allow you to change your return date for a fee; most low-fare tickets, however, are nonrefundable. It's smart to call a number of airlines and check the Internet; when you are quoted a good price, book it on the spot—the same fare may not be available the next day, or even the next hour. Always check different routings and look into using alternate airports. Also, price off-peak flights, which may be significantly less expensive than others. Travel agents, especially low-fare specialists (⇨ Discounts & Deals), are helpful.

Consolidators are another good source. They buy tickets for scheduled flights at reduced rates from the airlines, then sell them at prices that beat the best fare available directly from the airlines. (Many also offer reduced car-rental and hotel rates.) Sometimes you can even get your money back if you need to return the ticket. Carefully read the fine print detailing penalties for changes and cancellations, purchase the ticket with a credit card, and confirm your consolidator reservation with the airline.

🔃 Consolidators **AirlineConsolidator.com** ☎ 888/468-5385 ⊕ www.airlineconsolidator.com; for international tickets. **Best Fares** ☎ 800/880-1234 or 800/576-8255 ⊕ www.bestfares.com; $59.90 annual membership. **Cheap Tickets** ☎ 800/377-1000 or 800/652-4327 ⊕ www.cheaptickets.com. **Expedia** ☎ 800/397-3342 or 404/728-8787 ⊕ www.expedia.com. **Hotwire** ☎ 866/468-9473 or 920/330-9418 ⊕ www.hotwire.com. **Now Voyager Travel** ⊠ 45 W. 21st St., Suite 5A, New York, NY 10010 ☎ 212/459-1616 🖷 212/243-2711 ⊕ www.nowvoyagertravel.com. **Onetravel.com** ⊕ www.onetravel.com. **Orbitz** ☎ 888/656-4546 ⊕ www.orbitz.com. **Priceline.com** ⊕ www.priceline.com. **Travelocity** ☎ 888/709-5983, 877/282-2925 in Canada, 0870/876-3876 in the U.K. ⊕ www.travelocity.com.

ENJOYING THE FLIGHT

State your seat preference when purchasing your ticket, and then repeat it when you confirm and when you check in. For more legroom you can request one of the few emergency-aisle seats at check-in if you're capable of moving obstacles comparable in weight to an airplane exit door (usually between 35 pounds and 60 pounds)—a Federal Aviation Administration requirement of passengers in these seats. Seats behind a bulkhead also offer more legroom, but they don't have underseat storage. Don't sit in the row in front of the emergency aisle or in front of a bulkhead, where seats may not recline.

Ask the airline whether a snack or meal is served on the flight. If you have dietary concerns, request special meals when booking. These can be vegetarian, low-cholesterol, or kosher, for example. It's a good idea to pack some healthful snacks and a small (plastic) bottle of water in your carry-on bag. On long flights try to maintain a normal routine to help fight jet lag. At night get some sleep. By day eat

light meals, drink water (not alcohol), and **move around the cabin** to stretch your legs. For additional jet-lag tips consult *Fodor's FYI: Travel Fit & Healthy* (available at bookstores everywhere).

Smoking policies vary from carrier to carrier. Many airlines prohibit smoking on all of their flights; others allow smoking only on certain routes or certain departures. Ask your carrier about its policy.

FLYING TIMES

Approximate flying times to Miami are 3 hours from Chicago, 5 hours from Los Angeles, 6 hours from London, 3 hours 20 minutes from Montreal, 2 hours 50 minutes from New York, and 3 hours 5 minutes from Toronto.

HOW TO COMPLAIN

If your baggage goes astray or your flight goes awry, complain right away. Most carriers require that you **file a claim immediately.** The Aviation Consumer Protection Division of the Department of Transportation publishes *Fly-Rights,* which discusses airlines and consumer issues and is available online. You can also find articles and information on mytravelrights.com, the Web site of the nonprofit Consumer Travel Rights Center.

🔃 Airline Complaints **Aviation Consumer Protection Division** ⊠ U.S. Department of Transportation, Office of Aviation Enforcement and Proceedings, C-75, Room 4107, 400 7th St. SW, Washington, DC 20590 ☎ 202/366-2220 ⊕ airconsumer.ost.dot.gov. **Federal Aviation Administration Consumer Hotline** ⊠ for inquiries: FAA, 800 Independence Ave. SW, Washington, DC 20591 ☎ 800/322-7873 ⊕ www.faa.gov.

RECONFIRMING

Check the status of your flight before you leave for the airport. You can do this on your carrier's Web site, by linking to a flight-status checker (many Web booking services offer these), or by calling your carrier or travel agent.

AIRPORTS & TRANSFERS

Miami International Airport (MIA), 7 mi west of downtown Miami, is the only airport in Greater Miami that provides scheduled service. If you're destined for the north side of Miami-Dade County, though, consider flying into Fort Lauderdale International Airport. It is less crowded and more user-friendly, and you may also find greatly reduced fares on airlines that don't serve MIA. More than 1,400 daily flights make MIA the ninth-busiest passenger airport in the world. Approximately 34 million visitors pass through annually, more than half of them international travelers. Altogether, more than 100 airlines serve nearly 150 cities and five continents with nonstop or one-stop service from here, more than any other airport in the western hemisphere.

The airport is undergoing a $5.4 billion expansion program that is expected to be finished within the next six to eight years. If local politics don't muddy the waters, ambitious plans will provide a much-needed boost to retail facilities, and expanded gate and public areas are expected to reduce congestion. For the time being, gridlock in and out of the airport—especially during holidays and peak periods—is the rule and not the exception. The airport has already added additional parking garages with easy-to-follow color designations. Long-term parking is $4 per hour for the first and second hour, $2 for the third hour, and a maximum of $10 per 24-hour period. Short-term parking is $2.50 per half hour, with a maximum of $25 per day.

Getting around MIA is easy if you envision a horseshoe or U-shape terminal. Eight concourses extend out from the terminal; Concourse A is on the right or north side, E is in the center, and H is on the left or south side (a map of the airport is available on the MIA Web site, ⊕ www.miami-airport.com). If you're headed from one concourse to another, **take the Moving Walkway** on the skywalk (third) level; it links all eight concourses and the parking garages. Skycaps are available for hire throughout the airport, but on busy days be prepared to wait. Within Customs, portage is free only from baggage claim to the inspection line. A better bet: **grab a luggage cart**—they're free within Customs and $2 elsewhere.

A Tourist Information Center, open 6:30 AM–10:30 PM, is on Level 2, Concourse E; free brochures here tell you everything you'd want to know about the airport. Services for travelers include multilingual information and paging phones, a full-service bank and post office on Level 4 of Concourse B, myriad ATMs and currency exchange booths (the booth at Concourse E operates 24 hours a day), two 24-hour drugstores (although only the Concourse F location dispenses prescription drugs, 10–5 weekdays), a barbershop and hairstyling salon, and countless food and retail outlets. MIA has 14 duty-free shops that carry liquor, perfume, electronics, and various designer goods; international airline tickets and passports are required to enter. Lighted airport directories are located on columns throughout Level 2 of the terminal building and beside the elevators on Level 3.

International flights arrive at Concourses A, B, D, E, and F, as well as at the International Satellite Terminal located ¼ mi west of the main terminal. International passengers can be met outside U.S. Customs exits on the lower level of Concourse E or on the third level of Concourse B.

Also available on-site is the 260-sound-proof-room **Miami International Airport Hotel** (⊠ Concourse E, upper level ☎ 305/871–4100, ⊕ www.miahotel.com). If you have a layover (or an ambitious hour or two), you can use its health club, which has a pool, jogging track, and sundeck.

🛈 Airport Information Miami International Airport ☎ 305/876-7000 ⊕ www.miami-airport.com. Fort Lauderdale–Hollywood International Airport ☎ 954/359-1200 ⊕ www.fll.net.

AIRPORT TRANSFERS

Shuttle and limousine service are available outside baggage claim areas on Level 1. Taxis can be found on both the arrival (1) and departure (2) levels; **look for a uniformed county dispatcher** to hail a cab for you. On the mainland (i.e., west of Biscayne Bay) cabs cost $1.70 for the first mi and $.20 for each additional 1/11 of a mile thereafter (plus a $1 surcharge for trips originating at MIA or the Port of Miami);

the fare from the airport to downtown Miami averages $15–$19, and the Port is a flat fare of $18.

Flat-rate fares are set for five zones along the barrier island generally referred to as Miami Beach. The long, thin stretch of beachfront actually encompasses not only Miami Beach proper but Indian Creek Village, Surfside, Bay Harbor Islands, Bal Harbour, Sunny Isles, Golden Beach, and adjacent unincorporated areas. The fare zones comprise five east–west bands bound on the east by the Atlantic Ocean and on the west by the mainland. Flat-rate fares run $27 (South Beach)–$45 (North Dade, Sunny Isles) per trip, not passenger; they include tolls and the airport surcharge, but no gratuity.

For taxi service to destinations in the immediate vicinity of the airport, **ask the dispatcher to call an ARTS (Airport Region Taxi Service) cab** for you. These blue cars offer a short-haul flat fare in two zones. An inner-zone ride costs $8 the outer-zone fare is $11. The area of service runs north to 36th Street, west to the Palmetto Expressway (77th Avenue), south to Northwest 7th Street, and east to Douglas Road (37th Avenue). Maps are posted in cab windows on both sides.

Limo service is available through prior arrangement only, but SuperShuttle vans transport passengers on demand between MIA and local hotels, the Port of Miami, the Greyhound terminal, and even individual residences on a 24-hour basis. Shuttles are available throughout the lower level of the terminal outside baggage claim areas. Service extends from Palm Beach to Monroe County (including the Lower Keys). It's best to **make reservations 24 hours in advance for the return,** although the firm will try to arrange pickups within Miami-Dade County on as little as four hours' notice. Per-person rates average $9–$19; additional members of a party pay a lower rate for many destinations, and children under three ride free with their parents. There's a pet transport fee of $5 for a cat and $8 for a dog under 50 pounds in kennels.

FlightLink by Greyhound offers three departures daily connecting the airport with a number of local Greyhound terminals, including its Bayside (downtown) terminal (700 Biscayne Blvd.). Greyhound's Miami West terminal (4111 N.W. 27th St.) is adjacent to the airport.

Airport to airport transportation—between Miami and Fort Lauderdale international airports—may also be necessary. The proximity of the two airports (and sometimes cheaper airfares to one of them) makes this a handy option for travelers to South Florida. SuperShuttle runs from airport to airport for a flat rate of $23. **Tri-County Airport Express** (☎ 954/525–4000, 954/561–8888, or 800/244–8252 ⊕ www. floridalimo.com.) is a car service that leaves from Fort Lauderdale International Airport. It's best to call in advance to find out rates for shared car service from Fort Lauderdale to Miami Beach. Non-shared car service will run $60–$80, depending on how far south along Miami Beach you need to go.

Public transportation may not be the most user-friendly option, but it's definitely cheaper. For long hauls as far north as Palm Beach County, TriRail is the best bet and offers free shuttle service to and from MIA. Metrobus service is also available with routes connecting to both Metrorail and TriRail. Both are on Level 1, across Airport Drive from Concourse E. From the airport you can take Bus 7 to downtown, Bus 37 south to Coral Gables and South Miami or north to Hialeah, Bus J east to Miami Beach, and Bus 42 to Coconut Grove. For South Beach, take Bus J to 41st Street in Miami Beach and transfer to a southbound Bus H, which goes all the way to the South Point Drive. Some routes change after 7:00 PM and on weekends—although an Airport Owl line, running hourly from 11:50 PM to 5:40 AM, makes a loop to South Beach and back. If sticking to a budget is your priority, the bus is the best deal at around $1.25. **Grab a bus schedule at the airport tourist information center** or visit the Miami-Dade Transit Web site before you go for the latest schedule—and be prepared to wait.

🚕 Taxis & Shuttles **FlightLink by Greyhound** ☎ 888/BUS–N–FLYMiami-Dade Transit, **Metrobus**

☎ 305/770-3131 ⊕ www.co.miami-dade.fl.us/ transit. **SuperShuttle** ☎ 305/871-2000 from MIA, 954/764-1700 from Fort Lauderdale, 800/874-8885 elsewhere ⊕ www.supershuttle.com. **TriRail** ☎ 800/874-7245 ⊕ www.tri-rail.com.

BIKE TRAVEL

Great weather and flat terrain make Miami great for cycling, but as a general method of transportation it shouldn't be your first choice, given traffic and limited bike paths. You can opt for Miami-Dade Transit's "Bike and Ride" program, which lets permitted cyclists take single-seat two-wheelers on Metrorail and select bus routes. Bicycles are allowed on Metrorail weekdays before 6:30 AM, from 9 to 4, and after 6 PM, and anytime on weekends and major holidays. You can also store your bicycle in lockers at most Metrorail stations; leases are available for 3, 6, or 12 months.

BOAT & FERRY TRAVEL

If you enter the United States in a private vessel along the Atlantic Coast south of Sebastian Inlet, you must **call the U.S. Customs Service.** Customs clears most boats of less than 5 tons by phone, but you may be directed to a marina for inspection.

In Greater Miami all boats with motors, regardless of size, must be properly registered. Always obey "No Wake" signs; slow zones are strictly monitored and many serve to protect Florida's endangered manatees. **Watch for personal watercraft**: they're everywhere and their drivers don't always practice safe boating. For boating emergencies or environmental concerns, call the Florida Marine Patrol or the U.S. Coast Guard.

FARES & SCHEDULES

🚢 Boat & Ferry Information **Florida Marine Patrol** ☎ 800/342-5367. **U.S. Coast Guard** ☎ 305/535-4368 in Greater Miami, 800/432-1216 elsewhere. **U.S. Customs Service** ☎ 800/432-1216 for small-vessel arrival near Miami, 305/536-5263 for Port of Miami office.

BUSINESS HOURS

Most Greater Miami businesses are open weekdays 9–5; banks usually close sometime between 4 and 5, although larger

branches have drive-through windows that are open until 6 and for a few hours Saturday mornings. ATMs are everywhere for quick money, deposits, even cash advances 24 hours a day.

MUSEUMS & SIGHTS

Operating hours for sights and museums vary, but most are open daily, rain or shine. It's always best to check, though, since some have seasonal hours. For the most part, parks and beaches operate sunrise to sunset.

PHARMACIES

For late-night pharmacies, *see* Health.

RESTAURANTS & CLUBS

Miamians dine and party late. Restaurants in high-traffic areas stay open until at least midnight and there are a few 24-hour spots. Reservations are always a good idea, since some places take a break on Monday or may close for lunch—there are even a few seasonal restaurants. No one goes to a club before 11 PM and on South Beach many stay open 'til 5 AM.

SHOPS

Most stores are open daily 10–6, but those in malls close as late as 9 PM Monday–Saturday. Shops in complexes with movie theaters, restaurants, and other attractions, and those in South Beach, generally stay open until 11. Some of the larger grocery chains operate a limited number of 24-hour stores, but most close at 9 or 10.

BUS TRAVEL

Most motor coaches that stop in the Miami area are chartered tour buses. Regularly scheduled, interstate Greyhound buses stop at five terminals in Greater Miami.

RESERVATIONS

🚌 Bus Information **Greyhound** ☎ 800/231-2222 ⊕ www.greyhound.com.
🚌 Bus Terminal Information **Homestead** ⊠ 5 N. E. 3rd Rd. ☎ 305/247-2040. **Miami Bayside-Downtown** ⊠ 700 Biscayne Blvd. ☎ 305/374-6160. **Miami South** ⊠ 20505 S. Dixie Hwy. ☎ 305/296-9072. **Miami West–Airport** ⊠ 4111 N. W. 27th St. ☎ 305/871-1810. **North Miami** ⊠ 16560 N.E. 6th Ave. ☎ 305/688-8645.

Metrobus stops are marked with blue-and-green signs with a bus logo and route information. If you want to get around by bus or rapid transit, **call Miami-Dade Transit for exact bus routes.** It's staffed with people who can give you specific information and route schedules. If you call from your hometown, they can also mail you a map of Miami-Dade showing all the bus routes and their numbers.

The frequency of service varies widely from route to route, depending on the demand, so call in advance to **obtain specific bus schedules.** Buses on the most popular routes run every 10 to 15 minutes. The fare is $1.25 (exact change only); 60¢ for seniors (65 and older) and students. Transfers cost 25¢ and 10¢, respectively. Some express routes carry surcharges of $1.50.

⑦ Bus Information Miami-Dade Transit, **Metrobus**
☎ 305/770-3131 ⊕ www.co.miami-dade.fl.us/transit.

CAMERAS & PHOTOGRAPHY

The *Kodak Guide to Shooting Great Travel Pictures* (available at bookstores everywhere) is loaded with tips.
⑦ Photo Help Kodak Information Center ☎ 800/242-2424 ⊕ www.kodak.com.

EQUIPMENT PRECAUTIONS

Don't pack film or equipment in checked luggage, where it is much more susceptible to damage. X-ray machines used to view checked luggage are extremely powerful and therefore are likely to ruin your film. Try to ask for hand inspection of film, which becomes clouded after repeated exposure to airport X-ray machines, and keep videotapes and computer disks away from metal detectors. Always keep film, tape, and computer disks out of the sun. Carry an extra supply of batteries, and be prepared to turn on your camera, camcorder, or laptop to prove to airport security personnel that the device is real.

CAR RENTAL

If your vacation is South Beach–based, you may prefer not to rent a car because parking is difficult and taxis are ubiquitous here. If you want to take side trips or explore Greater Miami, consider renting a car for the day. **If you're not staying in South Beach, rent a car.** If your day trip is last-minute, ask your hotel concierge about arranging for a car rental; otherwise **book in advance for cheaper rental rates.**

Florida is a bazaar of car-rental companies, with more discounts and fine print than any other state. Rates in Greater Miami average $25 a day and $150 a week for an economy car with air-conditioning, automatic transmission, and unlimited mileage. For a convertible—one of South Florida's great winter pleasures—add 15%–20%. Bear in mind that rates fluctuate tremendously depending on demand and season, and you'll find the best deal on a weekly or weekend rental. Rental cars are more expensive—and harder to find—during peak holidays.

Avis, Budget, Dollar, Hertz, National, and Royal all have counters on the lower level of MIA, although no one has actual cars on the premises. Just about everybody offers free shuttles to nearby lots though, as is evidenced by the gridlock of minivans and buses in and out of the airport. Simply **flag a courtesy shuttle outside baggage claim** for your preferred company. You can also price local companies for even lower rates. Either way, check on availability, whether service is 24 hours, and hidden costs. Prices are usually best during off-peak periods.

Miami's TOP (Tourist Oriented Police) officers heavily patrol the airport triangle where most car-rental lots are located. Despite this and the absence of tags and stickers identifying a car as a rental, to avoid being targeted as a tourist **make sure you know where you're going before you set off.** Local legislation requires that all rental companies provide area maps. You can also rent cellular phones and many of the larger companies offer computerized navigation systems.

⑦ Major Agencies **Alamo** ☎ 800/327-9633
⊕ www.alamo.com. **Avis** ☎ 800/331-1212, 800/879-2847 or 800/272-5871 in Canada, 0870/606-0100 in the U.K., 02/9353-9000 in Australia, 09/526-2847 in New Zealand ⊕ www.avis.com. **Budget** ☎ 800/527-0700, 0870/156-5656 in the U.K.

⊕ www.budget.com. **Dollar** ☎ 800/800-4000, 0800/085-4578 in the U.K. ⊕ www.dollar.com. **Hertz** ☎ 800/654-3131, 800/263-0600 in Canada, 0870/844-8844 in the U.K., 02/9669-2444 in Australia, 09/256-8690 in New Zealand ⊕ www.hertz.com. **National Car Rental** ☎ 800/227-7368, 0870/600-6666 in the U.K. ⊕ www.nationalcar.com.

CUTTING COSTS

For a good deal, book through a travel agent who will shop around. Also, price local car-rental companies—whose prices may be lower still, although their service and maintenance may not be as good as those of major rental agencies—and research rates on the Internet. Consolidators that specialize in air travel can offer good rates on cars as well (⇨ Air Travel). Remember to ask about required deposits, cancellation penalties, and drop-off charges if you're planning to pick up the car in one city and leave it in another. If you're traveling during a holiday period, also make sure that a confirmed reservation guarantees you a car.

🚩 Local Agencies **Alba Rent A Car** ☎ 305/870-9778. **Excellence Luxury Car Rental** ☎ 305/526-0000, 888/526-0055 in U.S. only. **Specialty Auto Rentals** ☎ 888/871-2770.

INSURANCE

When driving a rented car you are generally responsible for any damage to or loss of the vehicle. You also may be liable for any property damage or personal injury that you may cause while driving. Before you rent, see what coverage you already have under the terms of your personal auto-insurance policy and credit cards.

For about $9 to $25 a day, rental companies sell protection, known as a collision- or loss-damage waiver (CDW or LDW), that eliminates your liability for damage to the car; it's always optional and should never be automatically added to your bill. In most states you don't need a CDW if you have personal auto insurance or other liability insurance. However, **make sure you have enough coverage to pay for the car.** If you do not have auto insurance or an umbrella policy that covers damage to third parties, purchasing liability insurance and a CDW or LDW is highly recommended.

REQUIREMENTS & RESTRICTIONS

In Florida you must be 21 to rent a car, and rates may be higher if you're under 25. Child seats are compulsory for children under five.

SURCHARGES

Before you pick up a car in one city and leave it in another, ask about drop-off charges or one-way service fees, which can be substantial. Also inquire about early-return policies; some rental agencies charge extra if you return the car before the time specified in your contract, while others give you a refund for the days not used. To avoid a hefty refueling fee, fill the tank just before you turn in the car, but be aware that gas stations near the rental outlet may overcharge. It's almost never a deal to buy the tank of gas that's in the car when you rent it; the understanding is that you'll return it empty, but some fuel usually remains. Surcharges may apply if you're under 25 or if you take the car outside the area approved by the rental agency. You'll pay extra for child seats (about $8 a day) and usually for additional drivers (up to $25 a day, depending on location).

CAR TRAVEL

I–95 is the major expressway connecting South Florida with points north; State Road 836 is the major east–west expressway and connects to Florida's Turnpike, State Road 826, and I–95. Seven causeways link Miami and Miami Beach, I–195 and I–395 offering the most convenient routes; the Rickenbacker Causeway extends to Key Biscayne from I–95 and U.S. 1. **Remember U.S. 1 (a.k.a. Dixie Highway)**—you'll hear it often in directions. It starts in Key West, hugs South Florida's coastline, and heads north straight through to Maine.

Greater Miami traffic is among the nation's worst, so definitely **avoid driving during the rush hours of 7–9 AM and 5–7 PM.**

Road construction is constant; **pay attention to the brightly lit, roadside Smart Signs that warn drivers of work zones and street closings.** During rainy weather be especially cautious of flooding in South Beach and Key Biscayne. The Web site www.dot.state.fl.us lists roadwork updates for Florida's interstates.

Courtesy may not be the first priority of Miami drivers, who may suddenly change lanes or stop to drop off passengers when they shouldn't. **Watch out for short-tempered drivers** who may shout, gesticulate, honk, or even approach the car of an offending driver.

Even when your driving is beyond censure, you should **be especially careful in rental cars.** Despite the absence of identifying marks and the stepped-up presence of TOP (Tourist Oriented Police) patrols, cars piled with luggage or driven by hesitant drivers are prime targets for thieves. Keep car doors locked, and only ask questions at toll booths, gas stations, and other evidently safe locations. Don't stop if your car is bumped from behind, you see a disabled vehicle, or even if you get a flat tire. Drive to the nearest gas station or well-lighted locale and telephone the police from there. It's a good idea to **bring or rent a cellular phone,** as well.

EMERGENCY SERVICES

If you're in a rental, your obvious choice is to call the rental company whose number should be with your rental papers in the glove compartment.

🚗 **AAA** ☎ 800/222-4357; **Aventura** ✉ 20801 Biscayne Blvd., Suite 101 ☎ 305/682-2100; **Kendall** ✉ 7074 S.W. 117th Ave., Snapper Creek Plaza ☎ 305/270-6450; **South Miami** ✉ 6101 Sunset Dr. ☎ 305/661-6131.

GASOLINE

Gas stations are usually open late or 24 hours and are self-serve; most accept credit or debit cards directly at the pump. Gasoline costs a few cents more per gallon here than in the rest of Florida (with the exception of the Keys). Gasoline cost about $1.75 a gallon at press time.

PARKING

Many parking garages fill up at peak times. This is particularly true in Miami Beach and Coconut Grove, where streetside parking is impossible and spaces in municipal lots cost a fortune. Thankfully, these neighborhoods are the most pedestrian-friendly in Greater Miami. On Miami Beach valet parking is offered at most dining and entertainment venues (although it can cost as much as $20 on a busy weekend night). "Cabbing" it in South Beach is easy and inexpensive, but if you have to drive, call the **City of Miami Beach's Parking Hotline** (☎ 305/673-PARK) for garages convenient to where you're going. **Don't be tempted to park in a tow-away zone,** as the fees are high and you'll be surprised at how quickly the tow trucks arrive. If your car is towed, contact the municipality for details on how to retrieve your vehicle.

ROAD CONDITIONS

During Florida's frequent summer lightning storms, power to street lights may temporarily go out; stop as you would at a four-way stop sign and proceed with caution. **Make sure your lights are on when it's raining** so other drivers can see you, and watch for flooding.

RULES OF THE ROAD

Drive to the right and pass on the left. Keep change handy, since tolls are frequent and can range from 50¢ to as much as $1.50. Right turns are permitted at red lights (after a complete stop), unless otherwise indicated. At four-way stop signs it's first-come, first-go; when in doubt, yield to the right. Speed limits are 55 mph on state highways, 30 mph within city limits and residential areas, and 55–70 mph on interstates and Florida's Turnpike. Be alert for signs announcing exceptions and school zones (15 mph).

All front-seat passengers are required to wear seat belts, and children under five must be fastened securely in child safety seats or boosters; children under 12 are required to ride in the rear seat. Florida's Alcohol–Controlled Substance DUI Law is one of the toughest in the United States. A blood alcohol level of .08 or higher can have serious repercussions even for the first-time offender.

Cell phone use while driving is discouraged, although it's currently still legal.

CHILDREN IN MIAMI

While Miami and Miami Beach's reputation as a chic urban metropolis may be incongruous with traveling with children, fear not. Though somewhat weak in the attractions department, Greater Miami's ideal climate puts much of the attraction on the child-friendly outdoors. The tried-and-true beach experience is the most obvious choice; kids can't get enough of the water, and Miami has more than 15 mi of beach. Expansive kid-friendly resorts with "water playgrounds," public pools, and lush, tropical parks give you even more options for tiring little ones. Miami also has a year-round calendar of special events and outdoor festivals, many of which are geared toward children or have special kid-friendly activities and areas.

Key to an enjoyable family vacation (underscore stress-free) is ensuring something for everyone—so do your homework before arriving. Call ahead and ask the visitors bureau to send you a copy of its "Fun & Sun Kids' Guide to Greater Miami and the Beaches." The best bet is *South Florida Parenting Magazine* (distributed free throughout the tri-county area) for ideas on what to see and do in any specific month; check for event round-ups, as well as special offers at area restaurants. Places that are especially appealing to children are indicated by a rubber-duckie icon (🦆) in the margins of this guide.

Fodor's Around Miami with Kids (available in bookstores everywhere) can help you plan your days together.

Don't forget sunscreen. In winter, when it doesn't feel as warm, your kids (and you) might be burning and you won't even know it. Also, depending on where you're exploring, in summer you'll want to **bring along insect repellent and drinking water.** If you are renting a car, don't forget to arrange for a car seat when you reserve. For general advice about traveling with children, consult *Fodor's FYI: Travel with Your Baby* (available in bookstores everywhere).

BABY-SITTING

If you need a baby-sitter, check with your hotel concierge or front desk. Many hotels offer baby-sitting or can refer you to a reputable service. If you use the Yellow Pages, **be sure to double-check references.**

CONCIERGES

Concierges, found in many hotels, can help you with theater tickets and dinner reservations: a good one with connections may be able to get you seats for a hot show or prime-time dinner reservations at the restaurant of the moment. You can also turn to your hotel's concierge for help with travel arrangements, sightseeing plans, services ranging from aromatherapy to zipper repair, and emergencies. **Always tip** a concierge who has been of assistance (⇨ Tipping).

CONSUMER PROTECTION

Whether you're shopping for gifts or purchasing travel services, **pay with a major credit card** whenever possible, so you can cancel payment or get reimbursed if there's a problem (and you can provide documentation). If you're doing business with a particular company for the first time, contact your local Better Business Bureau and the attorney general's offices in your state and (for U.S. businesses) the company's home state as well. Have any complaints been filed? Finally, if you're buying a package or tour, always consider travel insurance that includes default coverage (⇨ Insurance).

🗂 BBBs **Council of Better Business Bureaus** ✉ 4200 Wilson Blvd., Suite 800, Arlington, VA 22203 ☎ 703/276-0100 🖷 703/525-8277 ⊕ www.bbb.org.

CRUISE TRAVEL

The Dante B. Fascell Port of Miami, in downtown Miami near Bayside Marketplace and the MacArthur Causeway, justifiably bills itself as the cruise capital of the world. Home to 18 ships and the largest year-round cruise fleet in the world, the port accommodates more than 3 million passengers a year. It has 12 air-conditioned terminals, duty-free shopping, and limousine service. Taxicabs are at all terminals and Avis is at the port, although other rental companies offer shuttle service to off-site locations. Parking is $10 per day, and short-term parking is a flat rate of $4. From here, two-, three-, four-, five-, and seven-day cruises depart for the Bahamas, Belize, and Eastern and Western Caribbean, with longer sailings to the Far East, Europe, and South America.

To learn how to plan, choose, and book a cruise-ship voyage, consult *Fodor's FYI:*

Plan & Enjoy Your Cruise (available in bookstores everywhere).

🚢 Cruise Lines **Carnival Cruise Lines** ☎ 800/327-9501. **Celebrity Cruises** ☎ 800/437-3111. **Norwegian Cruise Lines** ☎ 800/327-7030. **Royal Caribbean International** ☎ 800/255-4373.

🚢 Cruise Terminal Information **Dante B. Fascell Port of Miami** ✉ 1015 North American Way ☎ 305/371-7678 ⊕ www.co.miami-dade.fl.us/portofmiami.

CUSTOMS & DUTIES

IN AUSTRALIA

Australian residents who are 18 or older may bring home A$400 worth of souvenirs and gifts (including jewelry), 250 cigarettes or 250 grams of cigars or other tobacco products, and 1,125 milliliters of alcohol (including wine, beer, and spirits). Residents under 18 may bring back A$200 worth of goods. Members of the same family traveling together may pool their allowances. Prohibited items include meat products. Seeds, plants, and fruits need to be declared upon arrival.

🛂 **Australian Customs Service** ✆ Regional Director, Box 8, Sydney, NSW 2001 ☎ 02/9213-2000 or 1300/363263, 02/9364-7222 or 1800/020-504 quarantine-inquiry line ☎ 02/9213-4043 ⊕ www.customs.gov.au.

IN CANADA

Canadian residents who have been out of Canada for at least seven days may bring in C$750 worth of goods duty-free. If you've been away fewer than seven days but more than 48 hours, the duty-free allowance drops to C$200. If your trip lasts 24 to 48 hours, the allowance is C$50. You may not pool allowances with family members. Goods claimed under the C$750 exemption may follow you by mail; those claimed under the lesser exemptions must accompany you. Alcohol and tobacco products may be included in the seven-day and 48-hour exemptions but not in the 24-hour exemption. If you meet the age requirements of the province or territory through which you reenter Canada, you may bring in, duty-free, 1.5 liters of wine *or* 1.14 liters (40 imperial ounces) of liquor *or* 24 12-ounce cans or bottles of beer or ale. Also, if you meet the local age requirement for tobacco products, you may bring

in, duty-free, 200 cigarettes and 50 cigars. Check ahead of time with the Canada Customs and Revenue Agency or the Department of Agriculture for policies regarding meat products, seeds, plants, and fruits.

You may send an unlimited number of gifts (only one gift per recipient, however) worth up to C$60 each duty-free to Canada. Label the package UNSOLICITED GIFT—VALUE UNDER $60. Alcohol and tobacco are excluded.

🛂 **Canada Customs and Revenue Agency** ✉ 2265 St. Laurent Blvd., Ottawa, Ontario K1G 4K3 ☎ 800/461-9999 in Canada, 204/983-3500, 506/636-5064 ⊕ www.ccra.gc.ca.

IN NEW ZEALAND

All homeward-bound residents may bring back NZ$700 worth of souvenirs and gifts; passengers may not pool their allowances, and children can claim only the concession on goods intended for their own use. For those 17 or older, the duty-free allowance also includes 4.5 liters of wine or beer; one 1,125-milliliter bottle of spirits; and either 200 cigarettes, 250 grams of tobacco, 50 cigars, *or* a combination of the three up to 250 grams. Meat products, seeds, plants, and fruits must be declared upon arrival to the Agricultural Services Department.

🛂 **New Zealand Customs** ✉ Head office: The Customhouse, 17-21 Whitmore St., Box 2218, Wellington ☎ 09/300-5399 or 0800/428-786 ⊕ www.customs.govt.nz.

IN THE U.K.

From countries outside the European Union, including the U.S., you may bring home, duty-free, 200 cigarettes, 100 cigarillos, 50 cigars, 100 cigarillos, or 250 grams of tobacco; 1 liter of spirits or 2 liters of fortified or sparkling wine or liqueurs; 2 liters of still table wine; 60 milliliters of perfume; 250 milliliters of toilet water; plus £145 worth of other goods, including gifts and souvenirs. Prohibited items include meat products, seeds, plants, fruits, and dairy products.

🛂 **HM Customs and Excise** ✉ Portcullis House, 21 Cowbridge Rd. E, Cardiff CF11 9SS ☎ 0845/010-9000 or 0208/929-0152 advice service, 0208/929-6731 or 0208/910-3602 complaints ⊕ www.hmce.gov.uk.

DISABILITIES & ACCESSIBILITY

At Miami International Airport, TDD services are readily accessible throughout the terminal and disabled parking is available in the Dolphin and Flamingo garages on the third level, close to the Moving Walkway. Most rest rooms can accommodate wheelchairs, but an already commenced $10 million rehab will ensure that all meet ADA requirements. Many of the larger rental-car companies offer hand controls, but 24-hour notice or more may be required. Florida recognizes disabled parking permits from other states and Canada but not those of other countries. You can get a 90-day permit for $15 from the **Miami-Dade County Tax Collector's** office; make sure to bring your disabled permit and passport. They don't take credit cards, but you can pay with traveler's checks.

On TriRail (⇨ Metrorail and Commuter Trains), all trains and stations are accessible to persons with disabilities; Miami-Dade also offers lift-equipped buses on more than 50 routes, including one from the airport. Miami Beach has a tourism hot line with information on accessibility, sign-language interpreters, rental cars, and area recreational activities for the disabled. Several parks have accessible tennis courts and water sports, and the beaches at 10th Street and Ocean Drive and at 72nd Street and Collins Avenue have ramps and surf chairs. Miami Beach's boardwalk is accessible at South Pointe Park, 5th Street, and 46th Street.

🏢 Local Resources **ADA** ☎ 305/375-3566. **City of Miami Beach** ☎ 305/673-6427, 305/673-7575 TDD. **City of Miami Department of Parks and Recreation** ☎ 305/461-7201 or 305/461-7201. **Miami-Dade Parks & Recreation Leisure Access Services** ☎ 305/755-7848 Voice/TDD. **Miami-Dade Tax Collector** ✉ 140 W. Flagler St., Miami ☎ 305/375-5678. For information on public transportation, call the **Miami-Dade Transit Agency Special Transportation Service** ☎ 305/263-5400, weekdays 8-5. **Randle Eastern Ambulance Service Inc.** ☎ 305/718-6400 operates at all hours. **Wheelchair Getaways** ☎ 561/748-8414 in Florida, 800/637-7577 in the U.S. and Canada rents vans equipped with lifts.

Deaf Services Bureau ✉ 1250 N.W. 7th St., Suite 207, Miami 33125 ☎ 305/560-2866 TDD, 305/668-4407 voice provides sign-language interpreter referrals. TDD service for the hearing-impaired is available when dialing 911 for fire, police, medical, and rescue emergencies. For **operator and directory assistance,** ☎ 800/688-4486 is TDD only. The operators at **Florida Relay Service** ☎ 800/955-8771 TDD, 800/955-8770 voice can translate TDD messages into speech for nonusers, and vice-versa. No charges apply to local calls.

The **Miami Lighthouse for the Blind** ☎ 305/856-2288 serves as a clearinghouse for information to assist the visually impaired.

LODGING

Despite the Americans with Disabilities Act, the definition of accessibility seems to differ from hotel to hotel. Some properties may be accessible by ADA standards for people with mobility problems but not for people with hearing or vision impairments, for example.

If you have mobility problems, ask for the lowest floor on which accessible services are offered. If you have a hearing impairment, check whether the hotel has devices to alert you visually to the ring of the telephone, a knock at the door, and a fire/emergency alarm. Some hotels provide these devices without charge. Discuss your needs with hotel personnel if this equipment isn't available, so that a staff member can personally alert you in the event of an emergency.

If you're bringing a guide dog, get authorization ahead of time and write down the name of the person with whom you spoke.

RESERVATIONS

When discussing accessibility with an operator or reservations agent, ask hard questions. Are there any stairs, inside *or* out? Are there grab bars next to the toilet *and* in the shower/tub? How wide is the doorway to the room? To the bathroom? For the most extensive facilities meeting the latest legal specifications, opt for newer accommodations. If you reserve through a toll-free number, consider also calling the hotel's local number to confirm the information from the central reservations office. Get confirmation in writing when you can.

TRANSPORTATION

Complaints Aviation Consumer Protection Division (⇨ Air Travel) for airline-related problems. **Departmental Office of Civil Rights** ✉ for general inquiries, U.S. Department of Transportation, S-30, 400 7th St. SW, Room 10215, Washington, DC 20590 ☎ 202/366-4648 📠 202/366-9371 ⊕ www.dot. gov/ost/docr/index.htm. **Disability Rights Section** ✉ NYAV, U.S. Department of Justice, Civil Rights Division, 950 Pennsylvania Ave. NW, Washington, DC 20530 ☎ ADA information line 202/514-0301, 800/ 514-0301, 202/514-0383 TTY, 800/514-0383 TTY ⊕ www.ada.gov. **U.S. Department of Transportation Hotline** ☎ for disability-related air-travel problems, 800/778-4838 or 800/455-9880 TTY.

TRAVEL AGENCIES

In the United States, the Americans with Disabilities Act requires that travel firms serve the needs of all travelers. Some agencies specialize in working with people with disabilities.

Travelers with Mobility Problems Access Adventures/B. Roberts Travel ✉ 206 Chestnut Ridge Rd., Scottsville, NY 14624 ☎ 585/889-9096 ⊕ www.brobertstravel.com ✎ dltravel@prodigy. net, run by a former physical-rehabilitation counselor. **Accessible Vans of America** ✉ 9 Spielman Rd., Fairfield, NJ 07004 ☎ 877/282-8267, 888/282-8267, 973/808-9709 reservations 📠 973/808-9713 ⊕ www.accessiblevans.com. **CareVacations** ✉ No. 5, 5110-50 Ave., Leduc, Alberta, Canada, T9E 6V4 ☎ 780/986-6404 or 877/478-7827 📠 780/986-8332 ⊕ www.carevacations.com, for group tours and cruise vacations. **Flying Wheels Travel** ✉ 143 W. Bridge St., Box 382, Owatonna, MN 55060 ☎ 507/451-5005 📠 507/451-1685 ⊕ www. flyingwheelstravel.com.

DISCOUNTS & DEALS

Be a smart shopper and compare all your options before making decisions. A plane ticket bought with a promotional coupon from travel clubs, coupon books, and direct-mail offers or purchased on the Internet may not be cheaper than the least expensive fare from a discount ticket agency. And always keep in mind that what you get is just as important as what you save.

DISCOUNT RESERVATIONS

To save money, look into discount reservations services with Web sites and toll-free numbers, which use their buying power to get a better price on hotels, airline tickets (⇨ Air Travel), even car rentals. When booking a room, always **call the hotel's local toll-free number** (if one is available) rather than the central reservations number—you'll often get a better price. Always ask about special packages or corporate rates.

Airline Tickets Air 4 Less ☎ 800/AIR4LESS; low-fare specialist.

Hotel Rooms Accommodations Express ☎ 800/444-7666 or 800/277-1064 ⊕ www.acex. net. **Central Reservation Service** (CRS) ☎ 800/ 555-7555 or 800/548-3311 ⊕ www.crshotels.com. **Hotels.com** ☎ 800/246-8357 ⊕ www.hotels.com. **Quikbook** ☎ 800/789-9887 ⊕ www.quikbook.com. **Steigenberger Reservation Service** ☎ 800/223-5652 ⊕ www.srs-worldhotels.com. **Turbotrip.com** ☎ 800/473-7829 ⊕ www.turbotrip.com.

PACKAGE DEALS

Don't confuse packages and guided tours. When you buy a package you travel on your own, just as though you had planned the trip yourself. Fly/drive packages, which combine airfare and car rental, are often a good deal. In cities, ask the local visitor's bureau about hotel and local transportation packages that include tickets to major museum exhibits or other special events.

ECOTOURISM

Southern Florida encompasses two major nature preserves; naturalists the world over flock to Biscayne and Everglades national parks. When you visit these and other parks, follow the basic rule of environmental responsibility: take nothing but pictures, leave nothing but footprints. **Be careful around the fragile dunes and reefs and don't touch the underwater coral.** Don't pick the sea grass. Damage to the environment may also incur a stiff fine. For details about these parks, consult *Fodor's South Florida* (available in bookstores everywhere).

E-MAIL SERVICE

Save the cost of phone calls and avoid the delays of postal service by using e-mail. If you're sans laptop and modem, get a free e-mail account from any of the larger service providers or try www.hotmail.com.

You can log on free at the local library, or try Kafka's Kafe in South Beach. A used bookstore, newsstand, and cyber café, it's very Europeanlike. High-speed access for five minutes is $1, for one hour $9, rates drop after 7 PM. If you're in one of the larger hotels, you can use their business center to send and receive e-mail.

📠 E-mail Service **Kafka's Cybernet Kafe** ✉ 1464 Washington Ave., Miami Beach ☎ 305/673-9669.

EMERGENCIES

📠 Doctors & Dentists **Miami-Dade County Medical Association** ☎ 305/324-8717 is open weekdays 9-5 for medical referrals. **East Coast District Dental Society** ☎ 305/667-3647 is open weekdays 9-4:30 for dental referrals. After hours, stay on the line and a recording will direct you to a dentist. **Dental Referral Service** ☎ 800/577-7322 is open weekdays 8-8 for dental referrals. **Visitors Medical Hotline** ☎ 305/674-2273 is a 24-hour medical referral service provided by Mt. Sinai Medical Center and the visitors bureau.

📠 Emergency Services Dial **911** for police, ambulance, or fire rescue. You can dial free from pay phones. For 24-hour **Poison Control**, call 800/222-1222.

📠 Hospitals **Aventura Hospital** ✉ 20900 Biscayne Blvd., Aventura ☎ 305/682-7000. **Baptist Hospital of Miami** ✉ 8900 N. Kendall Dr., Miami ☎ 786/596-1960, 786/596-6556 emergency, 786/596-6557 physician referral. **Jackson Memorial Medical Center** ✉ 1611 N.W. 12th Ave., near Dolphin Expressway, Miami ☎ 305/585-1111, 305/585-6901 emergency, 305/547-5757 physician referral. **Mercy Hospital** ✉ 3663 S. Miami Ave., Coconut Grove ☎ 305/854-4400, 305/285-2171 emergency, 305/285-2929 physician referral. **Miami Children's Hospital** ✉ 3100 S.W. 62nd Ave., Miami ☎ 305/666-6511 press 6 for emergencies. **Mt. Sinai Medical Center** ✉ 4300 Alton Rd., I-195 off Julia Tuttle Causeway, Miami Beach ☎ 305/674-2121, 305/674-2200 emergency, 305/674-2273 physician referral. **Parkway Medical Center East** ✉ 160 N.W. 170th St., North Miami Beach ☎ 305/651-1100, 888/836-3848 physician referral. **South Miami Hospital** ✉ 6200 S.W. 73rd St., South Miami ☎ 305/661-4611, 305/662-8181 emergency, 305/596-6557 physician referral. **South Shore Hospital & Medical Center** ✉ 630 Alton Rd., Miami Beach ☎ 305/672-2100 Ext. 3201 for emergencies.

📠 Hotlines **Abuse Registry** ☎ 800/962-2873, 800/453-5145 TTY. **Domestic Violence Hotline**

☎ 800/500-1119. **Drug Helpline** ☎ 800/662-4357. **Mental Health/Suicide Intervention** ☎ 305/358-4357. **Missing Children Information Clearing House** ☎ 888/356-4774. **Rape Treatment Center Hotline** ☎ 305/585-7273.

📠 24-Hour Pharmacies **Eckerd Drug** ✉ 9031 S.W. 107th Ave., Miami ☎ 305/274-6776. **Walgreens** ✉ 4895 E. Palm Ave., Hialeah ☎ 305/231-7454 ✉ 2750 W. 68th St., Hialeah ☎ 305/828-0268 ✉ 12295 Biscayne Blvd., North Miami ☎ 305/893-6860 ✉ 5731 Bird Rd., Miami ☎ 305/666-0757 ✉ 1845 Alton Rd., South Beach, Miami Beach ☎ 305/531-8868 ✉ 3007 Aventura Blvd., Aventura ☎ 305/936-2483 ✉ 791 N.E. 167th St., North Miami Beach ☎ 305/652-7332.

GAY & LESBIAN TRAVEL

Greater Miami in general and South Beach in particular are especially gay- and lesbian-friendly. Many of the shops post rainbow flags, and some hotels cater specifically to a gay clientele. Gay beaches include Ocean Drive at 12th Street in South Beach and Haulover Park's northernmost beach (enter at 159th Street and Collins Avenue). The largest concentration of gay nightspots is in the Art Deco District. South Beach tends to embrace everyone, though, and most clubs are decidedly gay-friendly. In March, the Dade Human Rights Foundation hosts the five-day Winter Party (🌐 www.winterparty.com), and the Colony Theater on Lincoln Road is home to the 10-day Gay & Lesbian Film Festival. By far the best-known gay event is Thanksgiving week's White Party (🌐 www.whitepartyweek.com) with more than 10,000 gay men and women gathering for county-wide festivities.

Pick up a copy of one of the many free publications distributed at clubs and retail establishments. For nightlife, good bets are the free weeklies, *New Times* and *Street Miami,* and the club rag *Hotspots. Express Gay News* (🌐 www.expressgaynews.com) and *The Weekly News* (🌐 www.theweeklynews.org) offer actual news, even running AP wire stories. The *Miami Herald* runs a regular column, "Outlooks," detailing gay and lesbian life in South Florida, and offers a direct link to information on gay-friendly hotels, restaurants, clubs, and other community resources from its homepage. The Greater Miami Convention & Visitors Bureau and the Miami-Dade Gay & Lesbian Chamber of Commerce provide tourist information for gay and lesbian visitors.

For details about the gay and lesbian scene, consult *Fodor's Gay Guide to the USA* (available in bookstores everywhere).

Local Information Miami-Dade Gay & Lesbian Chamber of Commerce, ✉ 4500 Biscayne Blvd., Miami ☎ 305/534-3336 ⊕ www.gogaymiami.com.

Gay- & Lesbian-Friendly Travel Agencies Different Roads Travel ✉ 8383 Wilshire Blvd., Suite 520, Beverly Hills, CA 90211 ☎ 323/651-5557 or 800/429-8747 (Ext. 14 for both) 📠 323/651-5454 ✉ lgernert@tzell.com. **Kennedy Travel** ✉ 130 W. 42nd St., Suite 401, New York, NY 10036 ☎ 212/840-8659, 800/237-7433 📠 212/730-2269 ⊕ www.kennedytravel.com. **Now, Voyager** ✉ 4406 18th St., San Francisco, CA 94114 ☎ 415/626-1169 or 800/255-6951 📠 415/626-8626 ⊕ www.nowvoyager.com. **Skylink Travel and Tour/Flying Dutchmen Travel** ✉ 1455 N. Dutton Ave., Suite A, Santa Rosa, CA 95401 ☎ 707/546-9888 or 800/225-5759 📠 707/636-0951; serving lesbian travelers.

GUIDEBOOKS

Plan well and you won't be sorry. Guidebooks are excellent tools—and you can take them with you. You may want to check out pocket-size, color-photo-illustrated *Citypack Miami,* with a supersize city map, available at on-line retailers and bookstores everywhere.

HEALTH

If you're unaccustomed to strong, subtropical sun, you run the risk of a severe sunburn or dehydration if you do not take adequate precautions. Try to hit the beach or the streets before 10 AM or after 3 PM. If you must be out at midday, **limit strenuous exercise, drink plenty of liquids, and wear a hat.** Even on overcast or cool days you are vulnerable to burning, so use a sunscreen with an SPF of at least 15, and have children wear waterproof SPF 30 or better.

Although in past years isolated incidents of mosquito-transferred encephalitis were reported in central and north Florida (and immediate precautions taken), mosquitoes and sand flies (no-see-ums) aren't so much

a health issue as a nuisance. In the wet late spring and summer months a good insect repellent is a priority. For kids, make sure to use a product that does not contain DEET, which can be toxic to some children.

DIVERS' ALERT
Do not fly within 24 hours of scuba diving.

HOLIDAYS

Major national holidays are New Year's Day (Jan. 1); Martin Luther King Day (3rd Mon. in Jan.); Presidents' Day (3rd Mon. in Feb.); Memorial Day (last Mon. in May); Independence Day (July 4); Labor Day (1st Mon. in Sept.); Columbus Day (2nd Mon. in Oct.); Thanksgiving Day (4th Thurs. in Nov.); Christmas Eve and Christmas Day (Dec. 24 and 25); and New Year's Eve (Dec. 31).

INSURANCE

The most useful travel-insurance plan is a comprehensive policy that includes coverage for trip cancellation and interruption, default, trip delay, and medical expenses (with a waiver for preexisting conditions).

Without insurance you'll lose all or most of your money if you cancel your trip, regardless of the reason. Default insurance covers you if your tour operator, airline, or cruise line goes out of business—the chances of which have been increasing. Trip-delay covers expenses that arise because of bad weather or mechanical delays. Study the fine print when comparing policies.

U.K. residents can buy a travel-insurance policy valid for most vacations taken during the year in which it's purchased (but check preexisting-condition coverage).

Always **buy travel policies directly from the insurance company**; if you buy them from a cruise line, airline, or tour operator that goes out of business you probably won't be covered for the agency or operator's default, a major risk. Before making any purchase, review your existing health and home-owner's policies to find what they cover away from home.

Travel Insurers In the U.S.: **Access America** ✉ 2805 N. Parham Rd., Richmond, VA 23294 ☎ 800/284-8300 📠 804/673-1491 or 800/346-9265 ⊕ www.accessamerica.com. **Travel Guard International** ✉ 1145 Clark St., Stevens Point, WI

54481 ☎ 715/345-0505 or 800/826-1300 🖷 800/955-8785 ⊕ www.travelguard.com.

FOR INTERNATIONAL TRAVELERS

For information on customs restrictions, *see* Customs & Duties.

CAR RENTAL

When picking up a rental car, non-U.S. residents need a reservation voucher for any prepaid reservations that were made in the traveler's home country, a passport, a driver's license, and a travel policy that covers each driver.

CAR TRAVEL

Gas stations are plentiful. Most stay open late (24 hours along large highways and in big cities), except in rural areas, where Sunday hours are limited and where you may drive long stretches without a refueling opportunity. Highways are well paved. Interstate highways—limited-access, multi-lane highways whose numbers are prefixed by "I–"—are the fastest routes. Interstates with three-digit numbers encircle urban areas, which may have other limited-access expressways, freeways, and parkways as well. Tolls may be levied on limited-access highways. So-called U.S. highways and state highways are not necessarily limited-access but may have several lanes.

Along larger highways, roadside stops with rest rooms, fast-food restaurants, and sundries stores are well spaced. State police and tow trucks patrol major highways and lend assistance. If your car breaks down on an interstate, pull onto the shoulder and wait for help, or have your passengers wait while you walk to an emergency phone (available in most states). If you carry a cell phone, dial *55, noting your location on the small green roadside mileage markers.

Driving in the United States is on the right. Do obey speed limits posted along roads and highways. Watch for lower limits in small towns and on back roads. Florida does require front-seat passengers to wear seat belts. On weekdays between 6 and 10 AM and again between 4 and 7 PM expect heavy traffic. To encourage carpooling, some freeways have special lanes for so-called high-occupancy vehicles (HOV)—cars carrying more than one passenger.

Bookstores, gas stations, convenience stores, and rest stops sell maps (about $3) and multiregion road atlases (about $10).

CONSULATES & EMBASSIES

🗗 Australia **Australian Consulate** ✉ 2525 S.W. 3rd Ave., Miami ☎ 305/858-7633

🗗 Canada **Consulate of Canada** ✉ First Union Financial Center, Suite 1600, 200 S. Biscayne Blvd., Miami ☎ 305/579-1600

🗗 United Kingdom **British Consulate** ✉ Brickell Bay Office Tower, 1001 S. Bayshore Dr., Suite 2110, Miami ☎ 305/374-1522

CURRENCY

The dollar is the basic unit of U.S. currency. It has 100 cents. Coins are the copper penny (1¢); the silvery nickel (5¢), dime (10¢), quarter (25¢), and half-dollar (50¢); and the golden $1 coin, replacing a now-rare silver dollar. Bills are denominated $1, $5, $10, $20, $50, and $100, all mostly green and identical in size; designs and background tints vary. In addition, you may come across a $2 bill, but the chances are slim. The exchange rate at this writing is US$1.44 per British pound, US$0.63 per Canadian dollar, US$0.51 per Australian dollar, and US$0.42 per New Zealand dollar.

ELECTRICITY

The U.S. standard is AC, 110 volts/60 cycles. Plugs have two flat pins set parallel to each other.

EMERGENCIES

For police, fire, or ambulance, **dial 911** (0 in rural areas).

INSURANCE

Britons and Australians need extra medical coverage when traveling overseas.

🗗 Insurance Information In the U.K.: **Association of British Insurers** ✉ 51 Gresham St., London EC2V 7HQ ☎ 020/7600-3333 🖷 020/7696-8999 ⊕ www.abi.org.uk. In Australia: **Insurance Council of Australia** ✉ Insurance Enquiries and Complaints, Level 12, Box 561, Collins St. W, Melbourne, VIC 8007 ☎ 1300/780808 or 03/9629-4109 🖷 03/9621-2060 ⊕ www.iecltd.com.au. In Canada: **RBC Insurance**

✉ 6880 Financial Dr., Mississauga, Ontario L5N 7Y5 ☎ 800/668-4342 or 905/816-2400 🖷 905/813-4704 ⊕ www.rbcinsurance.com. In New Zealand: **Insurance Council of New Zealand** ✉ Level 7, 111-115 Customhouse Quay, Box 474, Wellington ☎ 04/472-5230 🖷 04/473-3011 ⊕ www.icnz.org.nz.

MAIL & SHIPPING

You can buy stamps and aerograms and send letters and parcels in post offices. Stamp-dispensing machines can occasionally be found in airports, bus and train stations, office buildings, drugstores, and the like. You can also deposit mail in the stout, dark blue, steel bins at strategic locations everywhere and in the mail chutes of large buildings; pickup schedules are posted. You can deposit packages at public collection boxes as long as the parcels are affixed with proper postage and weigh less than one pound. Packages weighing one or more pounds must be taken to a post office or handed to a postal carrier.

For mail sent within the United States you need a 37¢ stamp for first-class letters weighing up to 1 ounce (23¢ for each additional ounce) and 23¢ for postcards. You pay 80¢ for 1-ounce airmail letters and 70¢ for airmail postcards to most other countries; to Canada and Mexico you need a 60¢ stamp for a 1-ounce letter and 50¢ for a postcard. An aerogram—a single sheet of lightweight blue paper that folds into its own envelope, stamped for overseas airmail—costs 70¢.

To receive mail on the road, have it sent c/o General Delivery at your destination's main post office (use the correct five-digit ZIP code). You must pick up mail in person within 30 days and show a driver's license or passport.

PASSPORTS & VISAS

When traveling internationally, carry your passport even if you don't need one (it's always the best form of I.D.) and **make two photocopies of the data page** (one for someone at home and another for you, carried separately from your passport). If you lose your passport, promptly call the nearest embassy or consulate and the local police.

Visitor visas aren't necessary for Canadian or European Union citizens, or for citizens of Australia who are staying fewer than 90 days.

🔀 Australian Citizens **Passports Australia** ☎ 131-232 ⊕ www.passports.gov.au. **United States Consulate General** ✉ MLC Centre, Level 59, 19-29 Martin Pl., Sydney, NSW 2000 ☎ 02/9373-9200, 1902/941-641 fee-based visa-inquiry line ⊕ usembassy-australia.state.gov/sydney.

🔀 Canadian Citizens **Passport Office** ✉ to mail in applications: 200 Promenade du Portage, Hull, Québec J8X 4B7 ☎ 819/994-3500, 800/567-6868, 866/255-7655 TTY ⊕ www.ppt.gc.ca.

🔀 New Zealand Citizens **New Zealand Passports Office** ✉ For applications and information, Level 3, Boulcott House, 47 Boulcott St., Wellington ☎ 0800/22-5050 or 04/474-8100 ⊕ www.passports.govt.nz. **Embassy of the United States** ✉ 29 Fitzherbert Terr., Thorndon, Wellington ☎ 04/462-6000 ⊕ usembassy.org.nz. **U.S. Consulate General** ✉ Citibank Bldg., 3rd floor, 23 Customs St. E, Auckland ☎ 09/303-2724 ⊕ usembassy.org.nz.

🔀 U.K. Citizens **U.K. Passport Service** ☎ 0870/521-0410 ⊕ www.passport.gov.uk. **American Consulate General** ✉ Danesfort House, 223 Stranmillis Rd., Belfast, Northern Ireland BT9 5GR ☎ 028/9032-8239 🖷 028/9024-8482 ⊕ usembassy.org.uk. **American Embassy** ✉ for visa and immigration information or to submit a visa application via mail (enclose a SASE), Consular Information Unit, 24 Grosvenor Sq., London W1 1AE ☎ 09055/444-546 for visa information (per-minute charges), 0207/499-9000 main switchboard ⊕ usembassy.org.uk.

TELEPHONES

All U.S. telephone numbers consist of a three-digit area code and a seven-digit local number. Within many local calling areas you dial only the seven-digit number. Within some area codes you must dial "1" first for calls outside the local area. To call between area-code regions, dial "1" then all 10 digits; the same goes for calls to numbers prefixed by "800," "888," "866," and "877"—all toll free. For calls to numbers preceded by "900" you must pay—usually dearly.

For Miami telephone information, *see* Telephones, *below.*

For international calls, dial "011" followed by the country code and the local number. For help, dial "0" and ask for an overseas operator. The country code is 61 for Australia, 64 for New Zealand, 44 for the United Kingdom. Calling Canada is the same as calling within the United States. Most local phone books list country codes and U.S. area codes. The country code for the United States is 1.

For operator assistance, dial "0." To obtain someone's phone number, call directory assistance at 555–1212 or occasionally 411 (free at many public phones). To have the person you're calling foot the bill, phone collect; dial "0" instead of "1" before the 10-digit number.

At pay phones, instructions often are posted. Usually you insert coins in a slot (usually 25¢–50¢ for local calls) and wait for a steady tone before dialing. When you call long-distance, the operator tells you how much to insert; prepaid phone cards, widely available in various denominations, are easier. Call the number on the back, punch in the card's personal identification number when prompted, then dial your number.

LANGUAGE

If you know Spanish you'll be well received in Greater Miami and better prepared to mix among both locals and international visitors. While the city's not officially considered bilingual, it may as well be.

LIMOUSINES

Miami is a city of expensive cars and limos, so arranging for limousine service is not a problem. Expect at least $60 per hour with a three-hour minimum; airport service is about $60 and prior arrangements are necessary. Unfortunately, some companies are frequently in and out of business; if you rely on the Yellow Pages, look for a company that has a street address, not just a phone number. One of the oldest companies in town, Vintage Rolls-Royce Limousines, chauffeurs clients around in Rolls-Royces dating from the 1940s.

🚗 Limousine Services **Carey South Florida Limousine** ☎ 305/893-9850 or 800/824-4820. **Sterling Limousine** ☎ 305/567-9200 or 888/239-9200. **Vintage Rolls-Royce Limousines** ☎ 305/662-5763 or 800/888-7657.

MEDIA

Greater Miami is a media hub, offering access to information from around the world and in many languages. For international and foreign language papers, check out one of the larger hotels or book store chains, or try the popular News Café in Coconut Grove or South Beach. The main Coral Gables branch of Books & Books, Inc. (265 Aragon Ave., ⊕ www. booksandbooks.com) is a terrific independent bookstore that's worth a trip for magazines and books.

NEWSPAPERS & MAGAZINES

Greater Miami's major newspaper is the *Miami Herald.* Your best bets for weekend happenings are the free alternative weekly *New Times* or *Street,* a free weekly with entertainment news, local art and film reviews, events, and nightlife. For Spanish-language news, turn to *El Nuevo Herald.* Regional editions of the *Wall Street Journal* and the *New York Times* can be found just about everywhere—including vending machines—and many of Europe and Latin America's major dailies and fashion glossies are available at newsstands.

RADIO & TELEVISION

Greater Miami is served by all the major cable networks. Major broadcast television stations include WAMI (Telefutur, Spanish–international), WBFS (UPN), WBZL (WB), WFOR (CBS), WLTV (Univision, Spanish–international), WPBT (PBS), WPLG (ABC), WSCV (Telemundo, Spanish–international), WSVN (Fox), and WTVJ (NBC).

Radio stations in Greater Miami include WDNA/88.9 (jazz), WEDR/99.1 (urban), WHYI/100.7 (Top 40), WIOD/610AM (news), WKIS/99.9 (country), WLRN 91.3 (National Public Radio), WQAM/560AM (sports), WZTA/94.9 (hard rock), and WBGG/105.9 (classic rock). Near the airport, you can find basic tourist information, broadcast successively in English, French, German, Portuguese, and Spanish, on the low-wattage WAEM/102.3.

METRORAIL & COMMUTER TRAINS

Elevated Metrorail trains run from downtown Miami north to Hialeah and south along U.S. 1 to Dadeland. The system operates daily 5 AM–midnight. Trains run every six minutes during peak hours, every 15 minutes during weekday mid-hours, and every 30 minutes after 8 PM and on weekends. The fare is $1.25; 25¢ transfers to Metromover or Metrobus must be purchased at the station where you originally board the system. Parking at Metrorail stations costs $2.

Metromover resembles an airport shuttle and runs on two loops around downtown Miami, linking major hotels, office buildings, and shopping areas. The system spans 4½ mi, including the 1½-mi Omni Loop, with six stations to the north, and the 1-mi Brickell Loop, with six stations to the south. Service runs daily, every 90 seconds during rush hour and every three minutes off-peak, 6 AM–midnight along the inner loop and 6 AM–10:30 PM on the Omni and Brickell loops. The fare is 25¢; transfers to Metrorail are $1.

Tri-Rail, South Florida's commuter train system, offers daily service connecting Miami-Dade with Broward and Palm Beach counties via Metrorail (transfer at the TriRail–Metrorail Station at the Hialeah station, at 79th Street and East 11th Avenue). They also offer shuttle service to and from MIA from their airport station at 3797 N.W. 21st Street. Tri-Rail stops at 18 stations along a 71-mi route. Fares are established by zones, with prices ranging from $3.50 to $9.25 for a round-trip ticket.
🚆 **Metrorail** and **Metromover** ☎ 305/770–3131 ⊕ www.co.miami-dade.fl.us/transit. **TriRail** ☎ 800/874–7245.

MONEY MATTERS

Plastic is everywhere in Greater Miami and debit and credit cards are readily accepted. If not, there's sure to be an ATM nearby offering almost full-service bank services, including cash advances and money transfers. You can use a tried-and-true traveler's check at most restaurants, hotels, and stores as well, it's just not as convenient. Larger banks, especially in downtown Miami or South Beach, offer currency exchange.

Although Greater Miami is a relatively expensive destination, a smart shopper can find bargains in just about every category, from a $1 quick bite at a walk-up window in Little Havana to significantly lower room rates at hotels a few blocks off the beach. You can expect to spend an average of about $6 for breakfast, $12 for lunch, and $30 for dinner, while daily hotel rates average $136. Greens fees at public golf courses are $14–$20, but fees can approach $250 at the toniest private courses. Adult admission to area attractions typically costs $12–$14, but remember that the outdoors is a major attraction in itself, and many of Greater Miami's outdoor events and festivals are free.

Prices throughout this guide are given for adults. Substantially reduced fees are almost always available for children, students, and senior citizens. For information on taxes, *see* Taxes.

ATMS

ATMs may cost you as much as $2.50 per transaction, so **use your own bank's ATM** if possible. Be wary at night and go to a safe, well-lighted location (machines at Publix Groceries throughout Miami and Miami Beach are free and usually well-trafficked).

CREDIT CARDS

Throughout this guide, the following abbreviations are used: **AE**, American Express; **D**, Discover; **DC**, Diners Club; **MC**, MasterCard; and **V**, Visa.
🚆 Reporting Lost Cards **American Express** ☎ 800/441–0519. **Discover** ☎ 800/347–2683. **Diners Club** ☎ 800/234–6377. **MasterCard** ☎ 800/622–7747. **Visa** ☎ 800/ 847–2911.

MOTORCYCLE RENTAL

You'll notice that motorcycles, Vespas, and scooters are a popular mode of transportation. In Miami you can rent all of the above, including a Harley (at American Road Collection) or a Honda bike, with daily rentals starting at $109. Even with unlimited mileage, motorcycles still cost more than a car, but then that's not the point.

Expect to pay for insurance and a security deposit. Florida law doesn't require a helmet, but it's worth the additional charge. You must be 21 with a credit card, valid driver's license, and motorcycle endorsement.

Vespas and scooters are available at Deco Scooter Rentals from about $40 a day. Ask for hotel pick-up service.

Motorcycle Rental Contacts American Road Collection ⊠ 1416 18th St., Miami Beach ☏ 305/673-8113. **Cruise America** ⊠ 5801 N.W. 151st St., Miami ☏ 800/327-7799 or 305/828-1198 ⊕ www.cruiseamerica.com. **Deco Scooter Rentals** ⊠ 215 6th St., Miami Beach ☏ 305/538-0202.

NATIONAL PARKS

Look into discount passes to save money on park entrance fees. For $50, the National Parks Pass admits you (and any passengers in your private vehicle) to all national parks, monuments, and recreation areas, as well as other sites run by the National Park Service, for a year. (In parks that charge per person, the pass admits you, your spouse and children, and your parents, when you arrive together.) Camping and parking are extra. The $15 Golden Eagle Pass, a hologram you affix to your National Parks Pass, functions as an upgrade, granting entry to all sites run by the NPS, the U.S. Fish and Wildlife Service, the U.S. Forest Service, and the Bureau of Land Management. The upgrade, which expires with the parks pass, is sold by most national-park, Fish-and-Wildlife, and BLM fee stations. A major percentage of the proceeds from pass sales funds National Parks projects.

Both the Golden Age Passport ($10), for U.S. citizens or permanent residents who are 62 and older, and the Golden Access Passport (free), for persons with disabilities, entitle holders (and any passengers in their private vehicles) to lifetime free entry to all national parks, plus 50% off fees for the use of many park facilities and services. (The discount doesn't always apply to companions.) To obtain them, you must show proof of age and of U.S. citizenship or permanent residency—such as a U.S. passport, driver's license, or birth certificate—and, if requesting Golden Access, proof of disability. The Golden Age and Golden Access passes are available only at

NPS-run sites that charge an entrance fee. The National Parks Pass is also available by mail and via the Internet.

National Park Foundation ⊠ 11 Dupont Circle NW, 6th floor, Washington, DC 20036 ☏ 202/238-4200 ⊕ www.nationalparks.org. **National Park Service** ⊠ National Park Service/Department of Interior, 1849 C St. NW, Washington, DC 20240 ☏ 202/208-6843 ⊕ www.nps.gov. **National Parks Conservation Association** ⊠ 1300 19th St. NW, Suite 300, Washington, DC 20036 ☏ 202/223-6722 ⊕ www.npca.org.

Passes by Mail & Online National Park Foundation ⊕ www.nationalparks.org. **National Parks Pass** National Park Foundation ⬠ Box 34108, Washington, DC 20043 ☏ 888/467-2757 ⊕ www.nationalparks.org; include a check or money order payable to the National Park Service, plus $3.95 for shipping and handling (allow 8 to 13 business days from date of receipt for pass delivery), or call for passes.

PACKING

You can generally swim year-round in Greater Miami, so **pack a bathing suit.** If it's winter at home, don't fret. You can easily pick one up in the many South Beach shops. Although they're not cheap. **Bring a sun hat and sunscreen**; the sun can be fierce, even in winter when it might be chilly or overcast. Be prepared for sudden summer storms with a fold-up umbrella that fits easily into your luggage.

For the most part, daytime dress is casual—especially in flip-flop and sarong-wearing South Beach. In the evenings, although most restaurants won't require jacket or tie there is opportunity to spiff up. Think trendy as opposed to dressy in South Beach—the term du jour is *casual chic.* In winter months a sweater and a jacket are recommended; in the summer air-conditioners are on overdrive so you might need a light sweater. Finally, comfortable walking shoes are a good idea for the many outdoor activities.

In your carry-on luggage pack an extra pair of eyeglasses or contact lenses and enough of any medication you take to last a few days longer than the entire trip. You may also ask your doctor to write a spare prescription using the drug's generic name, as brand names may vary from country to country. In luggage to be checked, **never pack prescription drugs, valuables, or undeveloped film.** And don't forget to carry with you the addresses of offices that handle refunds of lost traveler's checks. Check *Fodor's How to Pack* (available at online retailers and bookstores everywhere) for more tips.

To avoid customs and security delays, carry medications in their original packaging. Don't pack any sharp objects in your carry-on luggage, including knives of any size or material, scissors, nail clippers, and corkscrews, or anything else that might arouse suspicion.

To avoid having your checked luggage chosen for hand inspection, don't cram bags full. The U.S. Transportation Security Administration suggests packing shoes on top and placing personal items you don't want touched in clear plastic bags.

CHECKING LUGGAGE

You're allowed to carry aboard one bag and one personal article, such as a purse or a laptop computer. Make sure what you carry on fits under your seat or in the overhead bin. Get to the gate early, so you can board as soon as possible, before the overhead bins fill up.

Baggage allowances vary by carrier, destination, and ticket class. On international flights, you're usually allowed to check two bags weighing up to 70 pounds (32 kilograms) each, although a few airlines allow checked bags of up to 88 pounds (40 kilograms) in first class. Some international carriers don't allow more than 66 pounds (30 kilograms) per bag in business class and 44 pounds (20 kilograms) in economy. On domestic flights, the limit is usually 50 to 70 pounds (23 to 32 kilograms) per bag. In general, carry-on bags shouldn't exceed 40 pounds (18 kilograms). Most airlines won't accept bags that weigh more than 100 pounds (45 kilograms) on domestic or international flights. Expect to pay a fee for baggage that exceeds weight limits. Check baggage restrictions with your carrier before you pack.

Airline liability for baggage is limited to $2,500 per person on flights within the United States. On international flights it amounts to $9.07 per pound or $20 per kilogram for checked baggage (roughly $640 per 70-pound bag), with a maximum of $634.90 per piece, and $400 per passenger for unchecked baggage. You can buy additional coverage at check-in for about $10 per $1,000 of coverage, but it often excludes a rather extensive list of items, shown on your airline ticket.

Before departure, itemize your bags' contents and their worth, and label the bags with your name, address, and phone number. (If you use your home address, cover it so potential thieves can't see it readily.) Include a label inside each bag and **pack a copy of your itinerary.** At check-in, make sure each bag is correctly tagged with the destination airport's three-letter code. Because some checked bags will be opened for hand inspection, the U.S. Transportation Security Administration recommends that you leave luggage unlocked or use the plastic locks offered at check-in. TSA screeners place an inspection notice inside searched bags, which are re-sealed with a special lock.

If your bag has been searched and contents are missing or damaged, file a claim with the TSA Consumer Response Center as soon as possible. If your bags arrive damaged or fail to arrive at all, file a written report with the airline before leaving the airport.

🗗 Complaints **U.S. Transportation Security Administration Contact Center** ☎ 866/289–9673 ⊕ www.tsa.gov.

REST ROOMS

Free public facilities are not widely available in Greater Miami, but most municipal buildings have free rest rooms that are open to the public during business hours. Along Miami Beach, rest rooms are free and open 'til 5; Miami-Dade County park facilities close at sundown. Rest rooms at gas, bus, and rail stations are an option but may not be the cleanest choices. While not, strictly speaking, open to the public, rest rooms in lobbies of large hotels are often accessible; if there's an attendant, tip 25¢–50¢. Or order some refreshments from a restaurant and use theirs.

SAFETY

Greater Miami is as safe for visitors as any American city its size, but it's always a good idea to exercise extra caution when you're on vacation. Unfamiliarity with a location combined with carrying more money than usual can increase your safety risks. Instead, **know where you're going,** and be especially wary when driving in strange neighborhoods and leaving the airport. With the exception of heavily trafficked areas in Miami Beach and Coconut Grove, it's also best not to walk alone at night. You can ask your concierge or front desk staff which areas to avoid. Don't assume that valuables are safe in your hotel room; **use in-room safes** or the hotel's safe-deposit boxes. Carry your money like you do at home: in small amounts. And **don't carry a waist pack**—it separates you from the locals. Try to use ATMs only during the day or in brightly lighted, well-traveled locales. If you're shopping, don't leave purchases in the car.

BEACH SAFETY

Before swimming **make sure there's no undertow.** Rip currents, caused when the tide rushes out through a narrow break in the water, can overpower even the strongest swimmer. If you do get caught in one, resist the urge to swim straight back to shore—you'll tire before you make it. Instead, stay calm. Swim parallel to the shore line until you are outside the current's pull, then work your way in to shore.

While at the beach, **steer clear of anything that looks like a blue bubble in the sand or water.** These are either jellyfish or Portuguese man-of-wars, and stings from their tentacles can cause a painful allergic reaction. Beaches with lifeguards usually post signs warning bathers. Don't forget lots of sunscreen and drinking water. Overexposure and dehydration are oft-treated medical emergencies in South Florida. While not too serious, they can quickly dampen vacation spirits.

SENIOR-CITIZEN TRAVEL

Businesses in Miami and Miami Beach offer many discounts to seniors and AARP members. Restaurant discounts (Florida is famous for early-bird specials) may be limited to certain menus, days, or hours, so call ahead to check. Nearly all hotels offer some sort of discount, as do many movie theaters and attractions. All Miami-Dade transit routes (via bus or rail) are discounted for seniors 65-plus.

To qualify for age-related discounts, mention your senior-citizen status up front when booking hotel reservations (not when checking out) and before you're seated in restaurants (not when paying the bill). Be sure to have identification on hand. When renting a car, ask about promotional car-rental discounts, which can be cheaper than senior-citizen rates.

F Educational Programs Elderhostel ⌧ 11 Ave. de Lafayette, Boston, MA 02111-1746 ☎ 877/426-8056, 978/323-4141 international callers, 877/426-2167 TTY ☎ 877/426-2166 ⊕ www.elderhostel.org. Interhostel ⌧ University of New Hampshire, 6 Garrison Ave., Durham, NH 03824 ☎ 603/862-1147 or 800/733-9753 ☎ 603/862-1113 ⊕ www.learn.unh.edu.

SIGHTSEEING TOURS

BICYCLE TOURS

A two-hour bike tour of the Art Deco District leaves from the **Miami Beach Bicycle Center** (⌧ 601 5th St., South Beach, Miami Beach ☎ 305/674–0150) at 10:30 AM on the third Sunday of each month. This tour costs $20 with a rental bike and $10 with your own bike; make sure to call ahead, as the schedule can be erratic.

BOAT TOURS

Island Queen, Island Lady, and *Pink Lady* (⌧ 401 Biscayne Blvd., Miami ☎ 305/ 379–5119) are 150-passenger double-decker tour boats docked at Bayside Marketplace. They offer daily 90-minute narrated tours of the Port of Miami and Millionaires' Row, at a cost of $15 per person, $7 under 12.

For something a little more private and luxe, **RA Charters** (☎ 305/854–7341 or 305/989–3959 ⊕ www.racharters.com) sails out of the Dinner Key Marina in Coconut Grove. Full- and half-day charters include snorkeling and even sailing lessons, with extended trips to the Florida Keys and Bahamas. For a romantic night, have Captain Masoud pack some gourmet fare and sail sunset to moonlight while you enjoy

Biscayne Bay's spectacular skyline view of Miami. Call for prices and details.

HELICOPTER TOURS

For a bird's-eye view, try **Biscayne Helicopters** (☎ 305/252–3883). They're out of Tamiami Airport and $400 buys you a half hour for up to four passengers with flyovers of Miami International Airport, downtown Miami, South Beach, Key Biscayne, and the Biscayne Bay skyline.

RICKSHAW TOURS

Coconut Grove Rickshaw operates two-person rickshaws along Main Highway in Coconut Grove's Village Center, nightly 8 PM–2 AM. You'll find them parked streetside throughout the neighborhood or in front of the major entertainment complexes. Prices start at $5 per person for a 10-minute ride through Coconut Grove or $10 per person for a 20-minute lovers' moonlight ride to Biscayne Bay.

SPECIAL-INTEREST TOURS

Everglades Safari Park (⊠ 26700 S.W. 8th St., 9 mi west of Krome Ave., Miami ☎ 305/226–6923 ⊕ www.evsafaripark. com) is actually an attraction featuring a jungle trail and an alligator show and farm, but the highlight is the airboat tour of the Everglades. Open daily, rain or shine (unless there's lightning), adults are $15, children 5–11 $5, and under 5 free. Leave an hour plus for this one, more if you want to spend time on the jungle trail.

Style Ventures (⊠ 1109 Ponce de León Blvd., Coral Gables ☎ 305/444–8428 or 800/332–6386 ⊕ www.travelwithstyle. com) offers a variety of customized tours. Primarily a group tour operator with tour packages to other regions of Florida as well, it gives private tours costing a little more ($29–$170 per person depending on number of participants and itinerary), but are well worth it. Choose either city, Everglades, deep-sea fishing, gallery, nightlife, and shopping tours, or plan your own with the professional staff. Accessible vehicles and trained guides are provided for travelers with special needs.

Tropical Tours (☎ 305/248–4181) provides an overview of southern Miami-Dade County's 80,000 acres of

agriculture. Highlights include visits to an orchid nursery, tropical fruit grove, and u-pick-em field, which in winter offers plentiful bounty. Cost is $15 adults, $7.50 children under 15; tours are available on request and depart from the **Robert Is Here Fruit Stand** (⊠ 192nd Ave. and 344th St., Homestead)

WALKING TOURS

The **Art Deco District Tour** (⊠ 1001 Ocean Dr., South Beach, Miami Beach ☎ 305/531–3484 ⊕ www.mdpl.org) operated by the Miami Design Preservation League is a 90-minute guided walking tour that departs from the league's welcome center at the Oceanfront Auditorium. It costs $15 (tax-deductible) and starts at 10:30 AM Saturday and 6:30 PM Thursday. Private group tours can be arranged with advance notice. You can go at your own pace with the league's self-guided $10 audio tour, which takes roughly an hour and a half and is available in English, Spanish, French, and German.

Professor Paul George (⊠ 1345 S.W. 14th St., Miami ☎ 305/858–6021), a history professor at Miami Dade College and past president of the Florida Historical Society, leads a variety of walking and boat tours, as well as tours via Metrorail and Metromover. Pick from tours covering downtown, the Miami River, or neighborhoods such as Little Havana and Coconut Grove. George starts Saturdays at 10 and Sundays at 11 at various locations, depending on the tour; the tours generally last about 2½ hours. Call for each weekend's schedule and for additional tours by appointment. Tours start at $15 per person and prices vary by tour and group size.

STUDENTS IN MIAMI

Although spring break does not assume the proportions in Miami and Miami Beach that it does elsewhere in Florida, Greater Miami is a popular destination for students, so discounts are ubiquitous. To qualify, make sure you mention your student status up front when booking hotel reservations—don't wait until checking out. Restaurants may restrict student discounts to certain menus, days, or hours. Miami-Dade public transportation offers student fares and some movie theaters, museums, and attractions also feature discounts. The biggest plus for students are discounts at area gyms, which can otherwise be expensive, and college nights at bars (try spots near area colleges and universities).

🔢 **I.D.s & Services** **STA Travel** ✉ 10 Downing St., New York, NY 10014 ☎ 212/627-3111, 800/777-0112 24-hr service center 🖷 212/627-3387 ⊕ www.sta. com. **Travel Cuts** ✉ 187 College St., Toronto, Ontario M5T 1P7, Canada ☎ 800/592-2887 in the U.S., 416/979-2406 or 866/246-9762 in Canada 🖷 416/979-8167 ⊕ www.travelcuts.com.

TAXES

SALES TAX

Greater Miami's sales tax is currently 6.5%, but tourist taxes can raise the total to as much as 12.5% on accommodations and 8.5% on meals. It's all a bit complicated, since the tax may change depending on which municipality you're in and what you're buying. Ask about additional costs up front if they're not posted.

TAXIS

Except in South Beach, it's difficult to hail a cab on the street; in most cases you'll need to call a cab company or have a hotel doorman hail one for you. Fares run $3 for the first mile and $2 every mile thereafter; flat-rate fares are also available from the airport to a variety of zones. Fares are set by the board of county commissioners, so if you have a question or complaint, call the **Metro-Dade Passenger Transportation Regulatory Service** (☎ 305/375–2460), informally known as the Hack Bureau. There's no additional charge for up to five passengers or for luggage. Many cabs now accept credit cards; inquire when you call or before you get in the car.

Recent taxi-regulating legislation, hospitality training, and increased competition should rein in most surly drivers. But Greater Miami still has cabbies who are rude and in some cases even dishonest, taking advantage of visitors who don't know the area, so **try to be familiar with your route and destination.**

🔢 Taxi Companies **Central Taxicab Service** ☎ 305/532-5555. **Diamond Cab Company** ☎ 305/545-5555. **Flamingo Taxi** ☎ 305/759-8100. **Metro Taxi** ☎ 305/

888-8888. **Society Cab Company** ☎ 305/757-5523. **Super Yellow Cab Company** ☎ 305/888-7777. **Tropical Taxicab Company** ☎ 305/945-1025. **Yellow Cab Company** ☎ 305/633-0503.

TELEPHONES

Area codes in Greater Miami are 305 and 786. All local calls must start with one of these area codes. In other words, local calls are 10-numbers long.

Calls from public telephone booths cost 35¢. Cell-phone rental is available through some car rental agencies and many of the larger resort and convention hotels.

To reach an operator, dial 0. To reach directory assistance anywhere within the United States, dial 411.

TIME

Miami is in the Eastern U.S. time zone and adopts Daylight Savings Time between April and October (clocks are set one hour ahead). For Miami time and temperature, call ☎ 305/324–8811.

TIPPING

The customary tip for a doorman who calls for a taxi or a valet who brings your car around is $1. Bellhops are usually given $2 per bag in luxury hotels, $1 per bag elsewhere. Hotel maids should be tipped at least $2 per day of your stay. For concierge service, tips depend on the request: $3–$5 for basic dinner or tour reservations and perhaps $10 for above-and-beyond service, like getting you on the guest list of a popular club or having your laptop repaired. Taxi drivers should receive 15%–20% of the fare and skycaps $1 per bag.

If you're sitting at the bar, bartenders should get 50¢–$1 per drink. Maitre d's and wine stewards should be rewarded for special efforts.

Tip waiters 15%–20% of your bill before tax. **Check your bill before tipping** though, since many restaurants here do you the favor of adding the gratuity. Restaurants in Miami-Dade must now provide customers with written notice of their tipping policy and post an anti-discrimination statement in English, Spanish, and Creole—in other words, if they choose to charge an automatic 15%, they'd better post it.

TOURS & PACKAGES

Because everything is prearranged on a prepackaged tour or independent vacation, you spend less time planning—and often get it all at a good price.

BOOKING WITH AN AGENT

Travel agents are excellent resources. But it's a good idea to collect brochures from several agencies, as some agents' suggestions may be influenced by relationships with tour and package firms that reward them for volume sales. If you have a special interest, find an agent with expertise in that area; the American Society of Travel Agents (ASTA; ⇨ Travel Agencies) has a database of specialists worldwide. You can log on to the group's Web site to find an ASTA travel agent in your neighborhood.

Make sure your travel agent knows the accommodations and other services of the place being recommended. Ask about the hotel's location, room size, beds, and whether it has a pool, room service, or programs for children, if you care about these. Has your agent been there in person or sent others whom you can contact?

Do some homework on your own, too: local tourism boards can provide information about lesser-known and small-niche operators, some of which may sell only direct.

BUYER BEWARE

Each year consumers are stranded or lose their money when tour operators—even large ones with excellent reputations—go out of business. So check out the operator. Ask several travel agents about its reputation, and try to **book with a company that has a consumer-protection program.** (Look for information in the company's brochure.) In the United States, members of the United States Tour Operators Association are required to set aside funds ($1 million) to help eligible customers cover payments and travel arrangements in the event that the company defaults. It's also a good idea to choose a company that participates in the American Society of Travel Agents' Tour Operator Program; ASTA will act as mediator in any disputes between you and your tour operator.

Remember that the more your package or tour includes, the better you can predict the ultimate cost of your vacation. Make sure you know exactly what is covered, and beware of hidden costs. Are taxes, tips, and transfers included? Entertainment and excursions? These can add up.

🚩 Tour-Operator Recommendations **American Society of Travel Agents** (⇨ Travel Agencies). **National Tour Association** (NTA) ✉ 546 E. Main St., Lexington, KY 40508 ☎ 859/226-4444 or 800/682-8886 🖷 859/226-4404 ⊕ www.ntaonline.com. **United States Tour Operators Association** (USTOA) ✉ 275 Madison Ave., Suite 2014, New York, NY 10016 ☎ 212/599-6599 🖷 212/599-6744 ⊕ www.ustoa.com.

TRAIN TRAVEL

Amtrak provides service from 500 destinations to the Greater Miami area, including three trains daily from New York City. The trains make several stops along the way; north–south service stops in the major Florida cities of Jacksonville, Orlando, Tampa, West Palm Beach, and Fort Lauderdale. For extended trips, or if you want to visit other areas in Florida, come via Auto Train from Lorton, Virginia, just outside of Washington, D.C., to Sanford, Florida, just outside of Orlando. From there it's less than a four-hour drive to Miami. Note: you must be traveling with an automobile to purchase a ticket on the Auto Train.

FARES & SCHEDULES

The Auto Train runs daily with one departure at 4 PM (however, car boarding ends one hour earlier). Fares vary depending on class of service and time of year, but expect to pay between $269 and $346 for a basic sleeper seat and car passage each way.

🚩 Train Information **Amtrak** ✉ 8303 N.W. 37th Ave., Miami ☎ 800/872-7245, ⊕ www.amtrak.com.

TRANSPORTATION AROUND MIAMI

Greater Miami's public transportation system leaves much to be desired. Waits at bus stops can be lengthy, and locals complain that trains don't get you where you need to go—at least conveniently. The network consists of more than 600 Metrobuses on 70 routes, the 21-mi Metrorail elevated rapid-transit system, and the Metromover, an elevated light-rail system serving downtown Miami and vicinity. Free maps, schedules, information on special transportation services for the disabled, and a "First-Time Rider's Kit" are available from the Miami-Dade Transit Agency; reduced-fare tokens, sold 10 for $10, are available at all Metrorail stations (regular fare is $1.25; transfers are an additional 25¢. Miami Beach also has an inexpensive trolley system, Electrowave, that traverses the major shopping areas and key sites.

Transit Information Miami-Dade Transit Agency ☎ 305/770-3131 weekdays 6 AM-10 PM and weekends 9 AM-5 PM ⊕ www.co.miami-dade.fl.us/mdta.

TRAVEL AGENCIES

A good travel agent puts your needs first. Look for an agency that has been in business at least five years, emphasizes customer service, and has someone on staff who specializes in your destination. In addition, **make sure the agency belongs to a professional trade organization.** The American Society of Travel Agents (ASTA)—the largest and most influential in the field with more than 20,000 members in some 140 countries—maintains and enforces a strict code of ethics and will step in to help mediate any agent-client disputes involving ASTA members if necessary. ASTA (whose motto is "Without a travel agent, you're on your own") also maintains a Web site that includes a directory of agents. (If a travel agency is also acting as your tour operator, *see* Buyer Beware *in* Tours & Packages.)

Local Agent Referrals American Society of Travel Agents (ASTA) ✉ 1101 King St., Suite 200, Alexandria, VA 22314 ☎ 703/739-2782 or 800/965-2782 24-hr hotline ⎙ 703/684-8319 ⊕ www.astanet.com. **Association of British Travel Agents** ✉ 68-71 Newman St., London W1T 3AH ☎ 020/7637-2444 ⎙ 020/7637-0713 ⊕ www.abta.com. **Association of Canadian Travel Agencies** ✉ 130 Albert St., Suite 1705, Ottawa, Ontario K1P 5G4 ☎ 613/237-3657 ⎙ 613/237-7052 ⊕ www.acta.ca. **Australian Federation of Travel Agents** ✉ Level 3, 309 Pitt St., Sydney, NSW 2000 ☎ 02/9264-3299 or 1300/363-416 ⎙ 02/9264-1085 ⊕ www.afta.com. au. **Travel Agents' Association of New Zealand** ✉ Level 5, Tourism and Travel House, 79 Boulcott

St., Box 1888, Wellington 6001 ☎ 04/499-0104 ⎙ 04/499-0786 ⊕ www.taanz.org.nz.

TROLLEY TRAVEL

In Miami Beach, electric trolleys run every few minutes up and down Washington Avenue with turnabouts at Lincoln Road Mall and South Pointe Park. A newer route runs from 16th Street to 23rd Street on Collins Avenue, then along Washington Avenue to the convention center, the botanical gardens, and the Holocaust Memorial. Rides are 25¢, and trolleys operate Monday–Saturday 8 AM–1 AM and Sundays and holidays 10 AM–1 AM.

Electrowave ☎ 305/535-9160 or 305/843-9283.

VISITOR INFORMATION

Tourist Information Florida Tourism Industry Marketing Corporation (FLA USA–Visit Florida) ☎ 888/7FLA-USA automated, ⊕ www.flausa.com. **Miami Metro Area Convention & Visitors Bureaus Greater Miami Convention & Visitors Bureau** ✉ 701 Brickell Ave., Suite 2700, Miami 33131 ☎ 305/539-3000 main number, 800/283-2707, 305/539-3063 visitor services in the U.S ⎙ elsewhere, dial the country's toll-free AT&T access code followed by ☎ 800/240-4282, 0800-013-0011 in the U.K., 800/881-011 in Australia, 800/225-5277 in Canada. **Sunny Isles Beach Resort Association Visitor Information Center** ✉ 17100 Collins Avenue, Suite 208, Sunny Isles Beach 33160 ☎ 305/947-5826. **Surfside Tourist Board** ✉ 9301 Collins Ave., Surfside, 33154 ☎ 305/864-0722 or 800/327-4557 ⎙ 305/993-5128.

Miami Metro Area Visitor Centers Bayside Marketplace ✉ 401 Biscayne Blvd., Miami 33132 ☎ 305/539-8070. **Sears** ✉ 3655 S.W. 22nd St., Coral Gables ☎ 305/460-3477 ✉ 1625 N.W. 107th Ave., Miami International Mall, Miami ☎ 305/470-7863 ✉ 1625 W. 49th St., Westland Mall, Hialeah ☎ 305/364-3827.

Miami Metro Area Chambers of Commerce Coconut Grove Chamber of Commerce ✉ 2820 McFarlane Rd., Coconut Grove Miami, 33133 ☎ 305/444-7270 ⎙ 305/444-2498. **Coral Gables Chamber of Commerce** ✉ 50 Aragon Ave., Coral Gables 33134 ☎ 305/446-1657 ⎙ 305/446-9900, ⊕ www.gableschamber.org. **Florida Gold Coast Chamber of Commerce** ✉ 1100 Kane Concourse, Suite 210, Bay Harbor Islands, 33154 ☎ 305/866-6020 ⎙ 305/866-0635 serves the beach communities of Bal Harbour, Bay Harbor Islands, Golden Beach, North Bay

Village, Sunny Isles Beach, and Surfside. **Greater Homestead-Florida City Chamber of Commerce** ✉ 43 N. Krome Ave., Homestead 33030 ☎ 305/247-2332 or 888/FLCITY1, ⊕ www.chamberinaction.com. **Greater Miami Chamber of Commerce** ✉ 1601 Biscayne Blvd., Miami 33132 ☎ 305/350-7700 🖶 305/374-6902. **Greater North Miami Chamber of Commerce** ✉ 13100 W. Dixie Hwy., North Miami 33181 ☎ 305/891-7811 🖶 305/893-8522. **Greater South Dade-South Miami-Kendall Chamber of Commerce** ✉ 6410 S.W. 80th St., South Miami 33143-4602 ☎ 305/661-1621 🖶 305/666-0508 ⊕ www.chambersouth.com. **Key Biscayne Chamber of Commerce** ✉ Key Biscayne Bank Bldg., 87 W. McIntyre St., Key Biscayne 33149 ☎ 305/361-5207 🖶 305/361-9411, ⊕ www.keybiscaynechamber.org. **Miami Beach Chamber of Commerce** ✉ 1920 Meridian Ave., Miami Beach 33139 ☎ 305/672-1270 🖶 305/538-4336, ⊕ www.miamibeachchamber.com.

🗐 **Government Advisories Consular Affairs Bureau of Canada** ☎ 800/267-6788 or 613/944-6788 ⊕ www.voyage.gc.ca. **U.K. Foreign and Commonwealth Office** ✉ Travel Advice Unit, Consular Division, Old Admiralty Building, London SW1A 2PA ☎ 0870/606-0290 or 020/7008-1500 ⊕ www.fco.gov.uk/travel. **Australian Department of Foreign Affairs and Trade** ☎ 300/139-281 travel advice, 02/6261-1299 Consular Travel Advice Faxback Service ⊕ www.dfat.gov.au. **New Zealand Ministry of For-** eign Affairs and Trade ☎ 04/439-8000 ⊕ www.mft.govt.nz.

WEB SITES

Do check out the World Wide Web when planning your trip. You'll find everything from weather forecasts to virtual tours of famous cities. Be sure to visit Fodors.com (⊕ www.fodors.com), a complete travel-planning site. You can research prices and book plane tickets, hotel rooms, rental cars, vacation packages, and more. In addition, you can post your pressing questions in the Travel Talk section. Other planning tools include a currency converter and weather reports, and there are loads of links to travel resources.

For general visitor information, try the visitor bureau's www.miamiandbeaches.com. The *Miami Herald*'s entertainment section, at www.herald.com, includes recent restaurant reviews and ratings, as well as links to other sites of interest to vacationers. So does the alternative weekly *Miami New Times*: www.miaminewtimes.com. There's a slew of local on-line guides, but good places to start are www.miami.com, www.miamicitysearch.com, and www.southbeach-usa.com.

EXPLORING MIAMI & MIAMI BEACH

1

2 <

Updated by
Patty
Shillington

THINK OF MIAMI AS A TEENAGER: a young beauty with growing pains, cocky yet confused, quick to embrace the latest fads, exasperating yet lovable. It may help you understand how best to tackle this imperfect paradise.

As cities go, Miami and Miami Beach really are young. Just a little more than 100 years ago, Miami was mosquito-infested swampland, with an Indian trading post on the Miami River. Then hotel builder Henry Flagler brought his railroad to the outpost known as Fort Dallas. Other visionaries—Carl Fisher, Julia Tuttle, William Brickell, and John Sewell, among others—set out to tame the unruly wilderness. Hotels were erected, bridges were built, the port was dredged, electricity arrived. The narrow strip of mangrove coast was transformed into Miami Beach. And the tourists started to come.

Greater Miami is many destinations in one. At its best it offers an unparalleled multicultural experience: melodic Latin and Caribbean tongues, international cuisines and cultural events, and an unmistakable joie de vivre—all against a frankly beautiful beach backdrop. In Little Havana the air is tantalizing with the perfume of strong Cuban coffee. In Coconut Grove, Caribbean steel drums ring out during the Miami/Bahamas Goombay Festival. Anytime in colorful Miami Beach restless crowds wait for entry to the hottest new clubs.

Many visitors don't know that Miami and Miami Beach are really separate cities. Miami, on the mainland, is South Florida's commercial hub. Miami Beach, on 17 islands in Biscayne Bay, is sometimes considered America's Riviera, luring refugees from winter with its warm sunshine; sandy beaches; graceful, shady palms; and tireless nightlife. The natives know well that there's more to Greater Miami than the bustle of South Beach and its Art Deco District. In addition to well-known places such as Coconut Grove and Bayside, the less reported spots, like the Museum of Contemporary Art in North Miami; the burgeoning Design District in Miami; and the mangrove swamps of Matheson Hammock Park, in Coral Gables, are great insider destinations.

Don't mistake the great Miami outdoors for the beach. Hang up your beach towel long enough to check out Fairchild Tropical Garden, a serene oasis of lush palms, flowering vines, and tranquil overlooks. Take a canoe ride on the Oleta River and you'll be surrounded by unspoiled tropical hammocks and mangrove forests. On Key Biscayne, grassy dunes and fertile wetlands seem a world away from the urban hubbub. Whatever you do, savor the moment. Miami may grow up one of these days, and when it does, it won't be quite the same.

Getting Your Bearings

Miami-Dade County sprawls over 2,000 square mi along the southeastern tip of Florida. Unless you don't intend to leave your hotel or your immediate neighborhood, you'll need a car to see the sights. Public transportation exists, but it does not easily reach many places you'll want to visit. Rent a convertible if you can—there's nothing quite like putting on some shades and feeling the wind in your hair as you drive across one of the causeways that link Miami to Miami Beach and Key Biscayne.

Downtown has become the lively hub of the mainland city, now more accessible thanks to the Metromover rail extension. Park at one of the outlying Metrorail stations and take the train in, connecting to the Metromover if need be. In South Beach you absolutely don't need a car. Park it and use the inexpensive Electrowave shuttle—or your feet—to get around. In Coconut Grove metered street parking is hard to come by. Try parking at CocoWalk, Streets of Mayfair, or the garage at Mary Street and Oak Avenue, and stroll the neighborhood.

Finding your way around Greater Miami is easy if you know how the street numbering system works. Miami is laid out on a grid with four quadrants—northeast, northwest, southeast, and southwest—centered at Miami Avenue and Flagler Street. Miami Avenue separates east from west, and Flagler Street separates north from south. Avenues and courts run north–south; streets, terraces, and ways run east–west. Roads run diagonally, northwest–southeast. In Miami Beach, numbered streets run east–west, with the numbers increasing as you go north. South Beach runs up to Dade Boulevard, Mid-Beach from there to 63rd Street, and North Beach from 63rd to the northern boundary of the city. The numbering on north–south thoroughfares gives you a pretty accurate idea of the nearest cross street: 500 Ocean Drive is at 5th Street, 7100 Collins Avenue is at 71st Street, 17800 Ocean Boulevard is at 178th Street, and so forth. So far, so good.

Confusion arises because Coral Gables and Hialeah do not generally follow the same system. Even some longtime Coral Gables residents don't know the names of their streets. And along the curve of Biscayne Bay the symmetrical grid shifts 45 degrees. It's best to buy a detailed map, stick to the major roads, and ask directions early and often. However, make sure you're in a safe neighborhood or public place when you seek guidance; cabbies and cops are good resources.

NORTH MIAMI-DADE

If you want to catch a glimpse of what Florida looked like to visitors in the 1950s and 1960s, drive north along the stretch of A1A from the Sunny Isles Causeway at Northwest 163rd Street. But hurry. The most precious resource of northeast Miami-Dade County—its land—is being tapped by developers, and the tacky souvenir malls and beachfront motels of old are quickly being supplanted by luxury condos. A bevy of colorful neighborhood restaurants reveals this area's diverse ethnic makeup. North Miami Beach is home to dozens of Asian eateries, and tiny restaurants in North Miami serve up savory East Indian and Jamaican specialties such as oxtail, curried goat, and jerk chicken. This buzz of activity, however, is offset by a number of remarkably unspoiled nature enclaves.

Numbers in the text correspond to numbers in the margin and on the Northern Greater Miami map.

A Good Tour

Start your tour at the south end of **Haulover Beach Park** ❶ ▶. From here you'll have one of the area's few unimpeded beachfront views. Head north on A1A into Sunny Isles Beach, often referred to simply as Sunny Isles, where uncrowded beaches attract groups of Latin American and European visitors. As you cruise through Sunny Isles, keep an eye out for classic tourist landmarks, such as the Newport Fishing Pier, at 170th Street, where you can rent fishing gear, buy bait, and cast in, plus mom-and-pop souvenir stores and swimwear shops. Catch a fleeting glimpse of the corny '50s architectural details, such as the sphinxes at the Suez Oceanfront Resort, at 18215 Collins Avenue, and the nomads and camel statues at the Sahara Beach Club Ocean Condos, 18335 Collins Avenue. It's only a matter of time before these motels are torn down to make way for luxury condos. Continue north to the tiny, wealthy town of **Golden Beach** ➋, at whose end (at County Line Road) you should turn around and return south to the William Lehman Causeway. Follow the causeway west, passing the sleek condos of Aventura. Once you've had an eyeful of Aventura's upscale diversions—consisting primarily of shopping (the Aventura Mall is one of South Florida's largest) and spas—head south on Biscayne Boulevard. To the west you'll see **Greynolds Park** ➌, spreading out south of Route 856. A little farther on you'll pass the **Ancient Spanish Monastery** ➍, an example of Romanesque architecture from 12th-century Spain. Continue south to the Sunny Isles Causeway, at 163rd Street. On the east side of the boulevard, toward the water, is the **Oleta River State Park** ➎. Here you can spy endangered West Indian manatees and waterbirds in the lagoon surrounding a mangrove island. The last stop on your tour can be the **Museum of Contemporary Art (MOCA)** ➏, a dramatic warehouselike space that houses a cutting-edge collection.

TIMING   A driving tour of the area requires about 45 minutes. Add to this any time you plan to spend in parks, shops, at the MOCA, or at the beach.

What to See

➍ **Ancient Spanish Monastery.** Tucked away in a peaceful hammock only a few blocks from a busy commercial district, this medieval structure is one of the oldest buildings in the western hemisphere. Originally constructed in Segovia, Spain, in the 1100s, the monastery was occupied by Cistercian monks for nearly 700 years before it was converted into a granary and stable. In 1925 William Randolph Hearst purchased the cloisters and outbuildings and had them dismantled, planning to reconstruct them on his San Simeon, California, estate. Twenty-six years and some financial troubles later, the 11,000 crates holding the stones were sold at auction, and the buildings were reassembled here. An opportunity to admire the Romanesque architecture is the main reason to come here. ⊠ *16711 W. Dixie Hwy., at N.E. 167th St., North Miami Beach* ☎ *305/945–1461* ⊕ *www.spanishmonastery.com* ⊠ *$4.50* ⊙ *Weekdays 10–4, Sun. 1–5.*

Arch Creek Park and Museum. Site of a unique natural stone bridge used by ancient Native American tribes, this park has 8 acres of tropical hardwood hammock, a museum–nature center, a wildlife sanctuary, and naturalist-guided tours. ⊠ *1855 N.E. 135 St., North Miami* ☎ *305/944–6111* ⊕ *www.miamidade.gov/parks/Parks/arch_creek.htm* ⊠ *Free* ⊙ *Daily sunrise–sunset.*

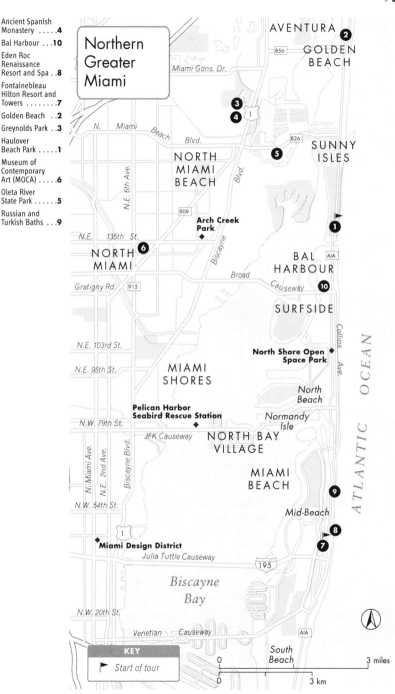

Northern
Greater
Miami

❷ Golden Beach. You won't actually be able to visit the sand in this 2-mi-long enclave of private oceanfront homes—the beaches are for residents only. But as you drive through town you'll appreciate the beautifully landscaped properties, a welcome sight after miles of high-rise condos. ⊠ *A1A between N.E. 195th St. and County Line Rd., Golden Beach.*

❸ Greynolds Park. Tranquil Greynolds Park has bike and nature trails and a place where you can rent paddleboats. A rookery provides roosting and nesting areas for wading birds. In the mangrove wetland you may spot cattle egrets, anhingas, white ibis, green herons, or double-crested cormorants. There are also guided bird walks and owl prowls. ⊠ *17530 W. Dixie Hwy., at N.E. 175th St., North Miami Beach* ☎ *305/945–3425* ⊕ *www.miamidade.gov/parks/Parks/greynolds.htm* ☒ *Weekdays free, weekends parking $4* ⊙ *Daily sunrise–sunset.*

★ ☺ ⚑ ❶ Haulover Beach Park. Far from the action of South Beach, Haulover preserves the Miami of the late '60s. You can fire up the barbecue grills, get in on a pickup volleyball game, rent kayaks, or bike on one of the trails. There are also showers and a concession stand. Sand on the eroded beach hasn't been replaced, and the narrow strand is perfect for beachgoers who don't relish a trek across hot sand to get to the water. Kite flying is popular here, and there are kite shops to get you started. An underground path leads to the Haulover Park Marina, home to the largest charter/drift-fishing fleet in South Florida. A clearly marked clothing-optional section at the north end of the beach draws 5,000–7,000 birthday-suited beachgoers on any given Sunday. ⊠ *10800 Collins Ave., north of Bal Harbour, North Miami-Dade, Miami Beach* ☎ *305/947–3525* ⊕ *www.miamidade.gov/parks/Parks/haulover_park.htm* ☒ *$4 per vehicle* ⊙ *Daily sunrise–sunset.*

need a break? Since 1954 **Wolfie Cohen's Rascal House** (⊠ 17190 Collins Ave., at 172nd St., Sunny Isles ☎ 305/947–4581) is one of Florida's best delis. It opens early and closes as late as 2 AM on weekends. Grab a booth or order takeout for the beach. And don't miss the breakfasts. As soon as you sit down you're greeted with baskets of breads, rolls, and danishes—and you can load them in a doggie bag when you leave.

❻ Museum of Contemporary Art (MOCA). Inaugurated in 1996 in a Charles Gwathmey–designed facility, this museum seeks to keep abreast of the latest trends in all artistic mediums. The permanent collection numbers more than 350 works, and exhibitions place an emphasis on promising new artists. The last Friday of the month (7–10) brings Jazz at MOCA. ⊠ *770 N.E. 125th St., between N.E. 7th Ct. and 8th Ave., North Miami* ☎ *305/893–6211* ⊕ *www.mocanomi.org* ☒ *$5 Wed.–Sun., donations welcome Tues. and for Jazz at MOCA* ⊙ *Tues.–Sat. 11–5, Sun. noon–5.*

❺ Oleta River State Park. The largest urban park in Florida, Oleta has nearly 1,000 acres of lush greenery, which provide a welcome respite from urban clutter. In this tranquil wilderness are bald eagles, dolphins, ospreys, and manatees, who stay the winter. Outdoor adventurers can fish, bike, or rent canoes or kayaks. The 30-foot hill is a virtual mountain in flat Florida, and mountain bikers will find 10 mi of trails for beginners

Fodor's Choice
★

and intermediates, a dual slalom course, and various bridges. ⊠ *3400 N.E. 163rd St., between Biscayne Blvd. and Collins Ave., North Miami Beach* ☎ *305/919–1846* ⊕ *www.floridastateparks.org/oletariver* 🎫 *$1 per person on foot or bike; $5 per vehicle* ⊙ *Daily 8–sunset.*

MID-BEACH TO BAL HARBOUR

The Miami Beach of picture postcards—glamorous sprawling hotels and showgirls with feathered headdresses—doesn't only survive here, it thrives. Multimillion-dollar renovations in recent years to such landmark 1950s hotels as the Fontainebleau and Eden Roc have revived their glitzy splendor, not subdued it. And amid the high-rise hotels and condominium communities that characterize the area are some delightfully uncrowded beaches.

Numbers in the text correspond to numbers in the margin and on the Northern Greater Miami map.

A Good Tour

Take Arthur Godfrey Road (41st Street) east to Collins Avenue, and head north. Previous visitors will immediately notice a stunning change to the landscape. In 2002 Robert Haas's landmark six-story trompe-l'oeil mural on the side of the **Fontainebleau Hilton Resort and Towers** ❼ ► was torn down to make way for a condominium/hotel. As you round the corner, the front of the massive curved Fontainebleau will come into view, followed by the **Eden Roc Renaissance Resort and Spa** ❽, both of which recapture the glamour of the 1950s and '60s.

As you continue driving north on Collins, the condo canyon begins—high-rise after nondescript high-rise. If you're looking for some low-key self-indulgence, stop at the Castle Beach Club, at 54th Street, for a soak in the **Russian and Turkish Baths** ❾. At 74th Street check out the mosaic wall and band shell, used by the community for dances and skating. To the east is the North Shore, a section of waterfront preferred by families and those who like things quiet; metered parking is plentiful, and there's a pleasant old shopping street to meander along. Continuing north, you'll come upon the family-friendly North Shore Open Space Park, a pristine strip of sand dunes and sea grapes with a boardwalk. Between 88th and 96th streets you'll pass through the peaceful French Canadian enclave of Surfside, with its quiet beaches, family-operated motels, and time-warp hotels. Then it's on to ritzy **Bal Harbour** ❿, home to world-class shops and elegant condos.

TIMING   Allow about 30 minutes for this drive, plus additional time to relax on the beach, explore hotels, or shop at Bal Harbour.

What to See

★ ❿ **Bal Harbour.** Best known for its elegant shopping mall, this manicured village is the smallest and one of the wealthiest municipalities in Miami-Dade County. Bal Harbour, a planned community, was incorporated in 1946 after having served as a United States Air Force training facility during World War II. The barracks are long gone, and today along the date palm–lined stretch of Collins Avenue are luxury condos, the Sheraton Bal Harbour Beach Resort, and the restored Sea View and Beach House hotels. At the posh Bal Harbour Shops, white-helmeted guards stand at the door. ⊠ *Collins Ave., between 96th and 103rd Sts., Bal Harbour* ⊕ *www.balharbourshops.com.*

8 **Eden Roc Renaissance Resort and Spa.** This immense Morris Lapidus creation has been returned to the flamboyant splendor of its heyday. (Note the dramatic sunken lobby and golden fleur-de-lis motifs throughout the majestic lobby.) The Eden Roc drew top entertainers in the 1960s—Frank Sinatra, Dean Martin, and Sammy Davis, Jr., all took the stage here. Today the hotel is well known for its sybaritic attraction, the Spa of Eden, and its popular beachside bar. ⊠ *4525 Collins Ave., between 45th and 46th Sts., Mid-Beach, Miami Beach* ☎ *305/531–0000* ⊕ *www.edenrocresort.com.*

▶ **7** **Fontainebleau Hilton Resort and Towers.** Whether or not garish opulence is your cup of tea, this Morris Lapidus–built 1950s extravaganza is worth a look. As you enter the vast lobby you can easily imagine a parade of guests in evening wear gliding down the grand staircase, illuminated by the awe-inspiring chandeliers and reflected in the many mirrored columns. Outside, amid tropical foliage, the lagoon pool and waterfall, complete with a bar hidden inside, cover a half acre. Latin-accented floor shows with scantily clad performers and a 10-piece orchestra live on at the Club Tropigala. ⊠ *4441 Collins Ave., between 44th and 45th Sts., Mid-Beach, Miami Beach* ☎ *305/538–2000* ⊕ *www.fontainebleau.hilton.com.*

| off the beaten path | **PELICAN HARBOR SEABIRD RESCUE STATION- –** Walk among pelicans and other seabirds who are being nursed back to health after encounters with fish hooks, commercial nets, and other man-made dangers. Feeding time is 4:15. ⊠ *1275 N.E. 79th St. Causeway (JFK Causeway), in Pelican Harbor Marina, North Bay Village* ☎ *305/751–9840* ⊕ *www.pelicanharbor.bizland.com* ⊠ *Free* ⊙ *Daily sunrise–sunset.* |

9 **Russian and Turkish Baths.** Pamper yourself without all the trappings of a designer spa. These baths, at the Castle Beach Club, include a saltwater whirlpool, tiled Russian sauna, redwood Finnish sauna, and a Turkish *hamam*—a wet eucalyptus steam room. Towels are provided, and you can sweat all day for one price or buy extra services such as an oak leaf *platza* (massage), mud rubs, salt scrubs, or regular massages. ⊠ *5445 Collins Ave., at 54th St., Mid-Beach, Miami Beach* ☎ *305/867–8313* ⊠ *$22* ⊙ *Daily noon–midnight.*

| need a break? | A hotel filled with 1950s cars? But of course. At **Dezerland Hotel** (⊠ 8701 Collins Ave., at 87th St., North Beach, Miami Beach ☎ 305/865–6661), vintage Caddies and T-Birds decorate the lobby. In the buffet-style restaurant you can dine in booths fashioned from the backseats of vintage cars. As gimmicks go, this one will make you smile. |

WHAT'S FREE WHEN

If you want to see Greater Miami on the cheap, you'll be pleasantly surprised to find a number of free attractions as well as other sights that are free on certain days of the week. Arch Creek Park and Museum, where you can take naturalist-guided tours and inspect a natural stone bridge used by ancient Native Americans, is always free. So is the Pelican Harbor Seabird Rescue Station, where injured birds are nursed back to health. The Miami Beach Botanical Garden is a free urban oasis, while across the street is the stunning outdoor Holocaust Memorial, for which donations are welcome but not required. Weekdays are free at Greynolds Park, with bike and nature trails, guided bird walks, and paddleboats for rent. Housed in a former synagogue, the Jewish Museum of Florida is free on Saturdays. Don't miss the art deco chandeliers and impressive stained-glass windows. Among art museums, Miami Dade College's

Centre and Frances Wolfson Art galleries and the Rubell Family Collection of contemporary art are free all the time, and admission to the Museum of Contemporary Art is by donation on Tuesdays and the last Friday night of the month (in conjunction with Jazz at MOCA). On Sundays you can visit for free the Little Havana home where young Elián González lived during his short and controversial stay in the United States. Free tours of Coral Gables' Biltmore Hotel are offered on Sunday afternoons. And then, of course, Miami is filled with parks, neighborhoods of architectural interest, and swank to funky shopping districts that you can explore for free (well, perhaps not completely free).

SOUTH BEACH

The hub of South Beach (no self-respecting local calls it SoBe) is the 1-square-mi Art Deco District, fronted on the east by Ocean Drive and on the west by Alton Road. In recent years the story of South Beach has become a big part of the story of Miami. Back in the early 1980s the neighborhood's vintage hotels were badly run down, catering mostly to retirees on fixed incomes. Some were abandoned, and some served as crack houses. The Morris Lapidus–designed Lincoln Road pedestrian mall, known as the 5th Avenue of the South during its heyday in the 1950s, languished. The entire area had a decidedly depressed feel. But a group of visionaries led by the late Barbara Baer Capitman, a spirited New York transplant, saw this group of buildings as architecturally significant and worth protecting from mindless urban renewal. Even then, the buildings of South Beach composed a peerless collection of art deco architecture dating from the 1920s to the 1950s.

Capitman was well into her sixties when she stepped in front of bulldozers ready to tear down the Senator, an art deco hotel. The Senator fell, but thanks to preservationists 40 others were saved. As the movement picked up, investors started restoring the interiors and repainting the exteriors of classic South Beach buildings. The area is now distinguished as the nation's first 20th-century district to be listed on the National Register of Historic Places, with 800 significant buildings making the roll.

As the restoration proceeded, South Beach's vibrant pastel palette (a sign of artistic liberty—originally, the deco hotels were primarily white) was made famous by the classic 1980s television show *Miami Vice*. Talented chefs and restaurateurs saw the potential of the increasingly attractive, hotel-intensive neighborhood. A $16 million face-lift revived Lincoln Road Mall. Fashion photographers, music video producers, and movie directors took note of the emerging location and began shooting here. Ocean Drive emerged as an emblem of hip style. As South Beach gained exposure, celebrities such as singer Gloria Estefan, the late designer Gianni Versace, and recording mogul Chris Blackwell bought a piece of the action.

Life along Ocean Drive unfolds 24 hours a day. Beautiful people pose in hotel lounges and sidewalk cafés, tanned cyclists zoom past palm trees, and visitors flock to see the action. If Ocean Drive is the heartbeat of South Beach, then Lincoln Road has become its soul. Its quirky blend of cultural venues, artists' galleries, boutiques, restaurants, and cafés has recently fallen victim to high rents, and a large movie and retail complex at the Alton Road end of the mall may detract from its flavor but adds to the entertainment offerings. But Lincoln Road still has character. Café crowds spill onto the sidewalks, weekend markets draw all kinds of visitors and their dogs, and thanks to a few late-night lounges the scene is just as present and alive at night.

You'll notice right away that several things are plentiful in South Beach. Besides the plethora of surgically enhanced bodies and cell phones, there are a lot of cars for a small area, and plenty of attentive meter maids. On-street parking is scarce, tickets are given freely when meters expire, and towing charges are high. Check your meter to see when you must pay to park; times vary by district. No quarters? Try the municipal lot west of the convention center; the 17th Street Garage between Pennsylvania and Meridian; the 16th Street Garage between Collins and Washington; or the 7th Street Garage at Washington and Collins. Better yet, take advantage of the Electrowave shuttle—it only costs a quarter and runs until the wee hours of the morning.

Numbers in the text correspond to numbers in the margin and on the South Beach map.

A Good Walk

Start this walk early (8 AM) if you want to watch the awakening city without distraction. At this hour you're also likely to see a fashion photo shoot in progress, since photographers like early morning light. On the other hand, a walk later in the day puts you in the thick of South Beach's action. That action has made the stretch of Ocean Drive from 1st to 23rd streets—primarily the 10-block stretch from 5th to 15th streets—the most talked-about beachfront in America.

If you're really up for a good walk, start your day at the up-and-comingest part of South Beach: SoFi, so called because it's *South of Fifth* Street. Here **South Pointe Park** ➊ ► lies at the southern tip of the Beach. Walk north on Ocean Drive to get to **Browns Hotel** ➋, Miami Beach's oldest, and a very un-deco, hotel. Walking two blocks west (Washington Avenue) and two blocks north brings you to the **Jewish Museum of Florida** ➌. From here return to Ocean Drive and head north, or, if you don't have the legs for it, begin your South Beach walking tour north of Fifth, where you're likely to see plenty of models and others who do have the legs for it.

A bevy of art deco jewels hugs the drive here, while across the street lies palm-fringed **Lummus Park** ➍. Cross to the west side of Ocean Drive, where there are many sidewalk cafés; find one that's open and have a bite. Then walk north, taking note of the Park Central Hotel (No. 640), built in 1937 by deco architect Henry Hohauser. If you're in the vicinity of 10th Street after 10 AM, recross Ocean Drive to the beach side and visit the **Art Deco District Welcome Center** ➎, in the 1950s-era Oceanfront Auditorium. Rent a tape or hire a guide for an Art Deco District tour.

Look back across Ocean Drive and take a peek at the wonderful flying-saucer architecture of the Clevelander, at No. 1020. On the next block you'll see the late Gianni Versace's Spanish-Mediterranean **Casa Casuarina** ➏, formerly known as the Amsterdam Palace. Graceful fluted columns stand guard at the Leslie (No. 1244) and the empty 1941 Carlyle (No. 1250); to their north is the much-photographed **Cardozo** ➐.

Walk two blocks west (away from the ocean) on 13th Street to Washington Avenue, and step inside the 1937 Depression moderne Miami Beach Post Office, designed by Howard Cheney, to see the rotunda and the Works Project Administration–era mural. Turn left on Washington and walk 2½ blocks south to the **Wolfsonian–Florida International University** ➑, where design and art used as propaganda from 1885 to 1945 are the focus. Along the way, you'll notice the mix of chic restaurants, club-kid and alternative shops, delicatessens, and nightclubs that have spiced up a once derelict neighborhood.

Return north on Washington past 14th Street, and turn left on **Espanola Way** ➒, a narrow street of Mediterranean-revival buildings, eclectic shops, and a weekend market. Continue west to Meridian Avenue and turn right. Three blocks north of Espanola Way is the redesigned **Lincoln Road Mall** ➓, part of must-see South Beach. Look beyond the lively parade of pedestrians and you'll find architectural gems.

The next main street north of Lincoln Road is 17th Street, and to the east is the Miami Beach Convention Center, where Muhammad Ali (then known as Cassius Clay) defeated Sonny Liston for the world heavyweight boxing championship in 1964. It was also the site of the highly charged 1968 Republican National Convention and both the Republican and Democratic National Conventions in 1972. Walk behind the massive building to the corner of Meridian Avenue and 19th Street to see the chilling **Holocaust Memorial** ⑪, a monumental record honoring the 6 million Jewish victims of the Nazi Holocaust. Just east is the compact

South Beach

MIAMI BEACH

Prairie Ave.

Royal Palm Ave.

Sheridan Ave.

Indian Creek Dr.

28th St.

Sunset Isles

Alton Rd.

Meridian Ave.

Prairie Ave.

Governor Hotel

23rd St.

22nd St.

21st St.

Adams Tyler Hotel

Plymouth

13

20th St.

Park Ave.

Liberty Ave.

Dade Blvd.

11

12

Convention Center Dr.

Miami Beach Convention Center

19th St.

James Ave.

A1A

West Ave.

18th St.

17th St.

Colony Theater

ArtCenter/ South Florida

Lincoln Theatre

Delano Hotel

National Hotel

Bay Rd.

16th St.

Lincoln Road Millennium Bldg.

Lincoln Rd. Mall

10

420 Lincoln Rd.

15th St.

Espanola Way

9

Miami Beach Community Church

14th Pl.

14th St.

13th St.

12th St.

Flamingo Park

Miami Beach Post Office

Washington Ave.

Drexel Ave.

7

Carlyle

11th St.

6

Leslie

Meridian Ave.

Euclid Ave.

Pennsylvania Ave.

8

Collins Ave.

Lummus Park

10th St.

5

Clevelander

Biscayne Bay

West Ave.

Alton Rd.

Lenox Ave.

Michigan Ave.

Jefferson Ave.

9th St.

8th St.

4

7th St.

Atlantic Ocean

6th St.

Park Central Hotel

41

5th St.

4th St.

Ocean Dr.

3rd St.

3

Miami Beach Marina

2nd St.

1st St.

2

Biscayne St.

KEY

▶ Start of walk

South Pointe Park

1

0   1/2 mile

0   500m

Miami Beach Botanical Garden ⓰, home to a Japanese garden and other tropical displays.

As you head along Park Avenue, take note of some off-the-beaten-path architectural jewels: the Adams Tyler Hotel at 2030 Park, with rooftop ornamentation—inspired by the 1939 World's Fair—pointing toward space; the Streamline-style Plymouth at 336 21st Street, its distinctive sculpted facade concealing an elevator shaft; and the 1939 Governor Hotel at 435 21st Street, rich in such details as a shiny stainless-steel marquee, glass etched with wildlife figures, and a terrazzo floor. Continue east through Collins Park and its enormous baobab trees to the **Bass Museum of Art** ⓭, a stark 1930 Streamline building that once housed Miami Beach's first library. Then walk across the street and peek inside the windows of the Miami City Ballet's home, where dancers may be practicing their arabesques. Return to Ocean Drive in time to pull up a chair at an outdoor café, order an espresso, and settle down for some people-watching, South Beach's most popular pastime. Or grab some late rays at the beach, which has unofficial gay, mixed, and family zones. You can go back to Lummus Park to play volleyball or to skate, or head north to the boardwalk for a stroll (skating and bicycling are not allowed).

TIMING   To see only the art deco buildings on Ocean Drive, allow one hour. Depending on your interests, schedule at least five hours for the whole tour, and include a drink or meal at a café and browsing time in the shops on Ocean Drive, along Espanola Way, and at Lincoln Road Mall.

Start your walking tour as early in the day as possible. In winter the street becomes increasingly crowded as the day wears on, and in summer, afternoon heat and humidity can be unbearable, wilting even the hardiest soul. Finishing by midafternoon also enables you to hit the beach and cool your heels in the warm sand.

What to See

❺ **Art Deco District Welcome Center.** Run by the Miami Design Preservation League, the center provides information about the buildings in the district. A gift shop sells 1930s–1950s art deco memorabilia, posters, and books on Miami's history. Several tours—covering Lincoln Road, Espanola Way, North Beach, the entire Art Deco District, among others—start here. You can rent audiotapes for a self-guided tour, join one of the regular Saturday- and Wednesday-morning and Thursday-evening walking tours, or take a bicycle tour. All of the options provide detailed histories of the art deco hotels. Don't miss the special boat tours during Art Deco Weekend, in early January. A second location, behind the Miami Beach Community Church, has art deco merchandise and furniture. ⊠ *1001 Ocean Dr., at Barbara Capitman Way (10th St.), South Beach* ☎ *305/531–3484* ⊡ *Tours $15* ☉ *Sun.–Thurs. 10–10, Fri. and Sat. 10 AM–midnight* ⊠ *520 Lincoln Rd., South Beach* ☎ *305/672-2014.*

⓭ **Bass Museum of Art.** The Bass, in historic Collins Park, is part of the new Miami Beach Cultural Park, which includes the Miami City Ballet's Arquitectonica-designed facility and the Miami Beach Regional Library. The original building, constructed of keystone, has unique Maya-inspired carvings. The new expansion designed by Japanese architect Arata Isozaki houses another wing, a café, and an outdoor sculpture garden. Special exhibitions join a diverse collection of European art. Works on permanent display include *The Holy Family,* a painting by Peter Paul Rubens; *The Tournament,* one of several 16th-century Flemish tapestries; and works by Albrecht Dürer and Henri de Toulouse-Lautrec. Special exhibits often cost a little extra. ⊠ *2121 Park Ave., at 21st St., South Beach* ☎ *305/673–7530* ⊕ *www.bassmuseum.org* ☜ *$6* ⊗ *Tues.–Wed. and Fri.–Sat. 10–5, Thurs. 10–9, Sun. 11–5.*

need a break? If your feet are giving out, head to the **Delano Hotel** (⊠ 1685 Collins Ave., at 17th St., South Beach ☎ 305/672–2000) for a drink. This surrealistic place lives up to its hype, with a soaring lobby-bar-restaurant area that epitomizes South Beach style. Or, for a more historically accurate ambiance, have a martini in the bar of the **National Hotel** (⊠ 1677 Collins Ave., south of 17th St., South Beach ☎ 305/532–2311); then take a peek at the pool.

② **Browns Hotel.** It's a familiar refrain. An old South Beach hotel, previously "modernized," has been meticulously restored to its original appearance. The difference for Miami Beach's oldest hotel, built in 1915, is that it has been un-deco-ed, undoing a 1935 face-lift that covered up its original Wild West appearance. The original clapboard exterior has been revealed. The Dade County pine floors are beautiful and intact. This landmark building is another illustration that SoFi is now where the restoration action is. ⊠ *112 Ocean Dr., at 1st St., South Beach* ☎ *305/674–7977.*

❼ **Cardozo.** This 1939 Hohauser-designed Streamline Moderne classic, owned by Gloria Estefan, was one of the first art deco hotels to be revived, and it is now one of the most photographed hotels on the beach. It's beautifully restored inside and out, with wrought-iron furniture and hardwood floors. Look for the eyebrows over the windows. ⊠ *1300 Ocean Dr., at 13th St., South Beach* ☎ *305/535–6500.*

❻ **Casa Casuarina.** In the early 1980s, before South Beach turned fabulous, the late Italian designer Gianni Versace purchased this Spanish Mediterranean-style residence built before the arrival of art deco. Today the ornate three-story palazzo includes a guest house and a copper-dome rooftop observatory and pool. In 1997 Versace was tragically shot and killed in front of his home. The spot where he fell has turned into a morbid tourist attraction where hundreds of people have their picture taken every day. ⊠ *1114 Ocean Dr., at 11th St., South Beach* ☎ *no phone.*

★ **❾** **Espanola Way.** There's a decidedly Bohemian feel to this street lined with Mediterranean-revival buildings constructed in 1925. Al Capone's gambling syndicate ran its operations upstairs at what is now the Clay Hotel, a youth hostel. At a nightclub located here in the 1930s, future bandleader Desi Arnaz strapped on a conga drum and started beating out a rumba rhythm. Visit this quaint avenue on a weekend afternoon, when merchants and craftspeople set up shop to sell everything from handcrafted bongo drums to fresh flowers. Between Washington and Drexel avenues the road has been narrowed to a single lane, and Miami Beach's trademark pink sidewalks have been widened to accommodate sidewalk cafés and shops selling imaginative clothing, jewelry, and art. ⊠ *Espanola Way, between 14th and 15th Sts. from Washington to Jefferson Aves., South Beach.*

need a break? Take a respite from the crowds and the heat at the **Front Porch Café** (⊠ 1418 Ocean Dr., between 14th and 15th Sts., South Beach ☎ 305/531–8300), where you can have a salad or a sandwich. If you're hungry but don't have time to stop, pick up a bite at **Le Sandwicherie** (⊠ 229 14th St., between Collins and Washington Aves., South Beach ☎ 305/532–8934).

⓫ Holocaust Memorial. A bronze sculpture depicts refugees clinging to a giant bronze arm that reaches out of the ground and 42 feet into the air. Enter the surrounding courtyard to see a memorial wall and hear the music that seems to give voice to the 6 million Jews who died at the hands of the Nazis. It's easy to understand why Kenneth Triester's dramatic memorial is in Miami Beach: the city's community of Holocaust survivors was once the second largest in the country. ⊠ *1933–1945 Meridian Ave., at Dade Blvd., South Beach* ☎ *305/538–1663* ⊕ *www. holocaustmmb.org* ⊡ *Donations welcome* ☉ *Daily 9–9.*

❸ Jewish Museum of Florida. Listed on the National Register of Historic Places, this former synagogue, built in 1936, contains art deco chandeliers, 80 impressive stained-glass windows, and a permanent exhibit, *MOSAIC: Jewish Life in Florida,* which depicts more than 235 years of the Florida Jewish experience. The museum also hosts changing exhibits and events and has a museum store. ⊠ *301 Washington Ave., at 3rd St., South Beach* ☎ *305/672–5044* ⊕ *www.jewishmuseum.com* ⊡ *$5, Sat. free* ☉ *Tues.–Sun. 10–5.*

Ⓒ ❿ Lincoln Road Mall. A playful 1990s redesign spruced up this open-air pedestrian mall, adding a grove of 20 towering date palms, five linear pools, and colorful broken-tile mosaics to the futuristic 1950s vision of Fontainebleau designer Morris Lapidus. Some of the shops are owner-operated boutiques with a delightful variety of clothing, furnishings, garden supplies, and decorative design. Others are the typical chain stores of American malls. Remnants of tired old Lincoln Road—beauty-supply and discount electronics stores on the Collins end of the strip—somehow fit nicely into the mix. The new Lincoln Road is fun, lively, and friendly for people old, young, gay, and straight—and their dogs. Folks skate, scoot, bike, or jog here. The best times to hit the road are during Sunday morning farmers' markets and on weekend evenings, when cafés bustle, art galleries open shows, street performers make the sidewalk their stage, and stores stay open late.

Fodor's Choice
★

Two of the landmarks worth checking out at the eastern end of Lincoln Road are the massive 1940s keystone building at 420 Lincoln Road, which has a 1945 Leo Birchanky mural in the lobby, and the 1921 mission-style Miami Beach Community Church, at Drexel Avenue. The Lincoln Theatre (No. 541–545), at Pennsylvania Avenue, is a classical four-story art deco gem with friezes. The New World Symphony, a national advanced-training orchestra led by Michael Tilson Thomas, rehearses and performs here, and concerts are often broadcast via loudspeakers, to the delight of visitors. Just west, a fabulous Cadillac dealership sign was discovered underneath the facade of the Lincoln Road Millennium Building, on the south side of the mall. At Euclid Avenue there's a monument to Lapidus, who in his 90s watched the renaissance of his whimsical creation.

Farther west, toward Biscayne Bay, the street is lined with chic food markets, cafés, and boutiques. Here you'll find the ArtCenter/South Florida (No. 924), between Jefferson and Michigan avenues, home to one of the first arts groups to help resurrect the area. At Lenox Avenue, a black-and-white art deco movie house with a Mediterranean barrel-tile roof is now the Colony Theater (No. 1040), where live theater and experimental films are presented. ⊠ *Lincoln Rd., between Collins Ave. and Alton Rd., South Beach.*

need a break?   Lincoln Road is a great place to cool down with an icy treat while touring South Beach. Try the homemade ice cream and sorbets—including Indian mango, key lime, and litchi—from the **Frieze Ice Cream Factory** (⊠ 1626 Michigan Ave., South Beach ☎ 305/538–2028). Or try an authentic Italian gelato at the sleek glass-and-stainless-steel **Gelateria Parmalat** (⊠ 670 Lincoln Rd., between Euclid and Pennsylvania Aves., South Beach ☎ 786/276–9475). If you visit on a Sunday, stop at one of the many juice vendors, who will whip up made-to-order smoothies from mangos, oranges, and other fresh local fruits.

🕲 ❹ **Lummus Park.** Its goofy, colorful lifeguard stands are fitting symbols for this popular beach. Once part of a turn-of-the-20th-century plantation owned by brothers John and James Lummus, this palm-shaded oasis on the beach side of Ocean Drive attracts families to its children's play area. Senior citizens predominate early in the day; then younger folk take over with volleyball, in-line skating along the wide and winding sidewalk, and a lot of posing. In the center of it all, a natural venue has emerged for outdoor concerts that have included such big-name performers as Luciano Pavarotti, Cab Calloway, and Lionel Hampton. ⊠ *East of Ocean Dr. between 5th and 15th Sts., South Beach.*

🕲 ⑫ **Miami Beach Botanical Garden.** Like the rest of Miami, this botanical garden is a work in progress. The community is working to restore the site, which was founded in the 1960s but neglected for decades. Already this 5-acre patch of tropical foliage sandwiched between the huge Miami Beach Convention Center and the Holocaust Memorial has become both a tranquil oasis just blocks from frenetic South Beach and a venue for cultural events. There's also a Japanese garden and gift shop. ⊠ *2000 Convention Center Dr., South Beach* ☎ *305/673–7256* ⊕ *www.miamibeachbotanicalgarden.org* ⊠ *Free* ⊙ *Tues.–Sun. 9–5.*

off the beaten path

MIAMI CHILDREN'S MUSEUM—This new Architectonica-designed museum, both imaginative and geometric in appearance, opened in the summer of 2003 directly across the MacArthur Causeway from Parrot Jungle Island. Twelve galleries house hundreds of interactive, bilingual exhibits. Children can scan plastic groceries in the supermarket, play doctor and patient in the emergency room, learn about mapmaking and cruise ships, and combine colors, rhythms, and math in the world-music studio. ⊠ *980 MacArthur Causeway, Watson Island, Miami* ☎ *305/373–5437* ⊕ *www. miamichildrensmuseum.org* ⊠ *$8* ☉ *Daily 10–6.*

PALM, STAR, AND HIBISCUS ISLANDS—Off the MacArthur Causeway, these private islands offer luxurious shelter to affluent residents and low-key celebrities. One of their most notorious residents, Al Capone, lived on Palm Island in the 1920s; local-girl-made-good Gloria Estefan lives here now. You can drive through and ogle the houses.

PARROT JUNGLE ISLAND—South Florida's original tourist attraction—it opened in 1936 in South Miami—closed in 2002 but reopened in 2003 on an island between Miami and Miami Beach. The park is home to more than 1,100 exotic birds, a few orangutans and snakes, a squadron of flamingos, and a rare albino alligator, plus amazing orchids and other flowering plants. Kids enjoy the hands-on (make that wings-on) experience of having parrots perch on their shoulders. The Japanese garden that once stood on the Parrot Jungle site is being reconstructed adjacent to the attraction. ⊠ *1111 Parrot Jungle Trail, off MacArthur Causeway (I–395), Watson Island, Miami* ☎ *305/258–6453* ⊕ *www.parrotjungle.com* ⊠ *$25.63, parking $6* ☉ *Daily 10–6, last admission 4:30.*

▶ ❶ **South Pointe Park.** The southernmost tip of Miami Beach is a great place to enjoy the ocean. From the 50-yard Sunshine Pier, which adjoins the 1-mi-long jetty at the mouth of Government Cut, you can fish or just relax while watching huge ships pass. Facilities include two observation towers, rest rooms, and volleyball courts. No bait or tackle is available in the park. ⊠ *1 Washington Ave., at Biscayne St., South Beach.*

★ ❽ **Wolfsonian–Florida International University.** An elegantly renovated 1927 storage facility is now both a research center and home to the 70,000-plus-item collection of modern design and "propaganda arts" amassed by Miami native Mitchell ("Micky") Wolfson Jr., a world traveler and connoisseur. Broad themes of the 19th and 20th centuries—nationalism, political persuasion, industrialization—are addressed in permanent and traveling shows. Included in the museum's eclectic holdings, which represent art deco, art moderne, art nouveau, Arts and Crafts, and other aesthetic movements, are 8,000 matchbooks collected by Egypt's King Farouk. ⊠ *1001 Washington Ave., at 10th St., South Beach* ☎*305/531–1001* ⊕*www.wolfsonian.fiu.edu* ⊠*$5* ☉ *Mon.–Tues. and Fri.–Sat. 11–6; Thurs. 11–9; Sun. noon–5.*

DOWNTOWN MIAMI

Downtown Miami dazzles from a distance. Its complex skyline of stark marble monoliths, gaudily illuminated glass towers, a futuristic arena, and sleek steel structures suggests a thoroughly modern metropolis. Rapid-transit trains zoom across a neon-hue bridge arcing high over the Miami River before disappearing into a cluster of high-rises. Enormous white cruise ships hover in the background at the Port of Miami, and jets steadily descend on their approach to Miami International Airport. The city looks equipped for the 21st century.

Yet zoom in on Flagler Street, Downtown's epicenter, and it resembles nothing so much as an international marketplace. Music blares from storefront radios, food vendors tout their wares, garish shops lure passersby with discounted sneakers and cameras and electronics, while throngs of people, speaking everything but English, go about their business.

By day downtown Miami's streets are clogged with Latin American shoppers loading up on bargains. Yet downtown Miami is not always high on the list of places to visit. Because of traffic congestion and expensive parking, locals tend to avoid the area (except in November, when the Miami Book Fair International draws an astonishing half-million attendees). Other than catching a Miami Heat game at the Downtown arena or bringing out-of-towners to the touristy Bayside Marketplace, residents don't much venture into Downtown.

And that's a pity, because it's an area that deserves exploring. There are architectural landmarks, such as the Gusman Center and the sturdy Flagler Palm Cottage. Bayfront Park is a beautiful patch of green and a great place to contemplate the bay, where sea breezes seem to soften the city's hard edges and bathe the surroundings in a dreamy mist. And the neighborhood is home to the Historical Museum of Southern Florida, the Miami Art Museum, and other sophisticated attractions.

Thanks to the Metromover, which runs inner and outer loops through Downtown and to nearby neighborhoods to the south and north, this is an excellent tour to take by rail. Attractions are conveniently located within about two blocks of the nearest station. If you're coming from north or east of Downtown, leave your car near a Metromover stop and take the Omni Loop downtown. If you're coming from south or west of Downtown, park your car at a Metrorail station and take a leg of the 21-mi elevated commuter system downtown.

Numbers in the text correspond to numbers in the margin and on the Downtown Miami map.

A Good Tour

Make your way to the Metrorail/Metromover Government Center Station, board the southbound Brickell Avenue Loop, and get off at the Financial District stop. From the station, turn left, and head toward **Brickell Avenue** ❶ ▶, where sleek high-rises, international banks, and a handful of restaurants have replaced the mansions of yesteryear. Cross Brickell at Southeast 8th Street to look at the First Presbyterian Church, a 1949

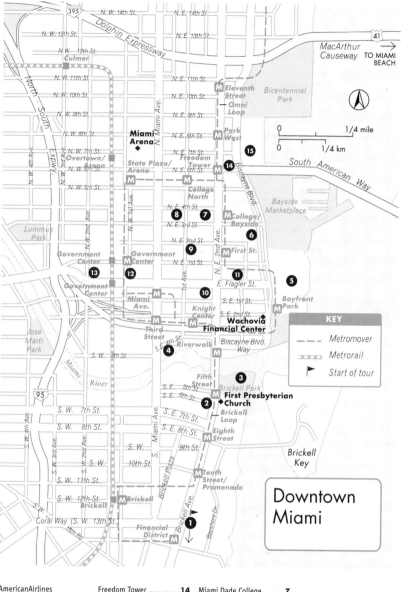

Downtown Miami

KEY

- – – – Metromover
- ▪▪▪▪ Metrorail
- ▶ Start of tour

keystone structure with a distinctive verdigris roof. As you head north on Brickell toward Downtown, you'll arrive at **Brickell Village ❷**. This burgeoning neighborhood of low-rise condos and shops near Fifth Street Station has some rather popular restaurants, particularly for the evening.

As you walk across the Miami River via the Brickell Avenue Bridge, notice the bridge's bronze plaques of native wildlife and its dramatic statue of a Tequesta Indian, one of Miami's original inhabitants, his arrow poised toward the sun. From the bridge, check out the parcel of riverfront land on the right, the site of the **Miami Circle ❸**. A multimillion-dollar development was halted here when archaeologists discovered a circular stone formation and other ancient artifacts. After crossing the bridge, go left to the Hyatt Regency Miami, adjacent to the James L. Knight Convention Center. Walk down Southeast 4th Street to an old yellow-frame house, **Flagler Palm Cottage ❹**, a 19th-century anachronism in this modern neighborhood. From the adjoining Bijan's Fort Dallas Restaurant and Raw Bar you can look out over the Miami River, a hub of Native American commerce hundreds of years ago (and, more recently, drug running).

From here you can reboard the Metromover at Riverwalk Station to ride past the following sights, or you can remain on foot to head back to Brickell (which becomes Southeast 2nd Avenue) and walk up to Southeast 2nd Street. You'll instantly notice the proliferation of Brazilian flags in the storefronts. This lively part of Downtown draws crowds of South American shoppers. Turn right at Southeast 2nd Street and continue for two blocks, passing the towering 55-story Wachovia Financial Center (formerly the First Union Financial Center), the second-tallest building in Florida; royal palms grace its 1-acre Palm Court plaza. Proceed until you reach Biscayne Boulevard at the southwest corner of **Bayfront Park ❺**. Across the street is the Hotel Inter-Continental Miami, a 34-story marble monolith with *The Spindle,* a huge sculpture by Henry Moore, in the lobby. Rising up in the corner of the park is the white *Challenger* Memorial, commemorating the space shuttle that exploded in 1986.

Continue north on Biscayne on foot, past **Plaza Bolivar ❻**, a tribute by Cuban immigrants to their adopted country. You'll reach the JFK Torch of Friendship, a plaza adorned with plaques representing all the South and Central American countries except Cuba, and Bayside Marketplace, the popular entertainment, dining, and retail complex. If you reboarded Metromover, get off at the College/Bayside Station to visit Bayside and to continue the next part of the tour on foot. From Bayside, cross Biscayne and walk up Northeast 3rd Street to Northeast 2nd Avenue, where you'll come upon **Miami Dade College ❼**, home of two worthy art galleries. One block farther west stands the **U.S. Courthouse ❽**, notable for the epic Depression-era mural inside, which depicts Floridian progress.

Turn south on Northeast 1st Avenue and walk one block to Northeast 2nd Street. On the corner stands the 1922 **Historic Gesu Church ❾**, one of South Florida's oldest. Return to Northeast 2nd Avenue; then turn right. Before you is the architectural clutter that characterizes downtown Miami: a cacophony of gaudy outlet shops, homely storefronts, and the occasional gem of a building. One of those is the 1938 art moderne Alfred I. DuPont Building, between Northeast 1st Street and Flagler, notable for its distinctive facade and ornate marble floors; another, the 1927 Italian Renaissance Ingraham Building, at 25 Southeast 2nd Avenue, has frescoed ceilings in the lobby. Across the street at 174 East Flagler, the landmark **Gusman Center for the Performing Arts** ⑩ is a stunning movie palace that now serves as a concert hall. If you feel like doing some shopping in a Latin American setting, **Galeria International Mall** ⑪ is a block away.

Now head west on Flagler Street, downtown Miami's commercial spine. As you pass through a cluster of busy electronics, sporting goods, and shoe stores, you'll be in one of the first areas of Miami to be carved out of the pine woods and palmetto scrub when Henry Flagler's railroad arrived in 1896. You'll see the 1936 Streamline moderne building housing Burdines department store. (On the back of the building is a huge mural of whales painted by the artist Wyland. It's visible from the outer loop of the Metromover route.) After one more block on Flagler, the **Dade County Courthouse** ⑫ comes into view; it still bears its old name even though the county is now called Miami-Dade. If you're here between October and March, look for the flock of urban vultures (literally) that circle above the ziggurat roof. After crossing 1st Avenue you'll arrive at the **Miami-Dade Cultural Center** ⑬, home of the Miami Art Museum, the Historical Museum of Southern Florida, and the Miami-Dade Public Library.

From the adjacent Metrorail–Metromover Government Center Station, you can reboard the Metromover's Downtown Inner Loop and get a bird's-eye view of the downtown area. As you pass the State Plaza–Arena Station, look two blocks north to see the pink Miami Arena, a venue for concerts and community events. Ride the Omni Loop to get a close-up look at the **Freedom Tower** ⑭, where the track heads north. To get an even closer view of the tower, once a processing center for Cuban refugees, walk north from College North Station to Northeast 6th Street, then two blocks east to Biscayne. The Omni Loop continues north over the MacArthur Causeway past the Miami Herald Building, past the site of the Performing Arts Center scheduled to open in early 2006, and on to Omni Center, which houses a hotel and defunct mall. Stay on the train for the return trip and a beautiful view of the **AmericanAirlines Arena** ⑮, the architecturally progressive venue that replaced the Miami Arena as home of the Miami Heat.

TIMING   To walk and ride to the various points of interest, allow three hours. If you want to spend additional time eating and shopping at Bayside, allow at least five hours. To include museum visits, allow seven hours.

What to See

⑮ **AmericanAirlines Arena.** This 20,000-seat arena, built by the noted Miami-based firm Arquitectonica, hosts the NBA Miami Heat, concerts, and other events. Part of the bayfront renewal, the sleek, futuristic arena has shops and restaurants, including Gloria and Emilio Estefan's pineapple-topped Bongos Cuban Café. ⊠ *601 Biscayne Blvd., between N.E. 6th and 8th Sts., Downtown* ☎ *786/777–1000* ⊕ *www.aaarena.com.*

❺ Bayfront Park. An oasis among the skyscrapers, this park extends east from busy, palm-lined Biscayne Boulevard to the bay. A landfill in the 1920s, it became the site of a World War II memorial in 1943, which was revised in 1980 to include the names of later war victims. Japanese sculptor Isamu Noguchi redesigned the park in 1989 to include two am-phitheaters, a memorial to the *Challenger* space shuttle astronauts, and a fountain honoring the late Florida congressman Claude Pepper and his wife. At the park's north end, the Friendship Torch, dedicated in 1964, honors John F. Kennedy and includes plaques representing Peru, Bolivia, Venezuela, Ecuador, Colombia, and Panama—and an empty space where Cuba should be. ⊠ *Biscayne Blvd. between S.E. 2nd and N.E. 3rd Sts., Downtown.*

▶ **❶ Brickell Avenue.** A canyon rimmed by tall buildings, Brickell (rhymes with fickle) has the densest concentration of international banking offices in the United States. From the end of the Metromover line you can look south to where several architecturally interesting condominiums rise be-tween Brickell Avenue and Biscayne Bay. Arquitectonica designed three of these buildings: the Palace (1541 Brickell Ave.), the Imperial (1627 Brickell Ave.), and the Atlantis (2025 Brickell Ave.). In 2003 the mon-umental Four Seasons Hotel and Tower, a 70-story skyscraper, opened at 1435 Brickell Avenue, replacing Downtown's Wachovia Financial Cen-ter (55 stories) as Florida's tallest building. Israeli artist Yacov Agam painted the rainbow exterior of Villa Regina (1581 Brickell Ave.). ⊠ *Brickell Ave. between 15th Rd. and Biscayne Blvd. Way, Downtown.*

❷ Brickell Village. You can spend a delightful evening outdoors in Brick-ell Village, a neighborhood rarely discovered by visitors. After check-ing out the shops and condos by day, return at sunset for drinks at the **Big Fish** (⊠ 55 S.W. Miami Avenue Rd., at S.E. 5th St. ☏ 305/373–1770), a riverfront restaurant decorated with metal fish scales that's hard to find but worth the effort. From here you can see Downtown's dazzling skyline, the neon art that adorns the span of the Metrorail bridge, and the nonstop activity along the Miami River. You can get homemade gelato or tiramisu at **Perricone's Marketplace and Café** (⊠ 15 S.E. 10th St. ☏ 305/374–9449). The venerable blues and rock bar (est. 1912) **Tobacco Road** (⊠ 626 S. Miami Ave. ☏ 305/374–1198) is a great stop for live music. And there's no hurry to leave, as they close at 5 AM. Just north at the Miami River is the **Brickell Avenue Bridge.** More of an outdoor art piece than a mere bridge, it's decorated with a bronze sculp-ture of a Tequesta Indian, a collage of native wildlife, and a series of smaller bronze plaques of area fauna on both sides of the bridge, works of Manuel Carbonell (1995). ⊠ *Brickell Ave. between S.E. 5th St. and Biscayne Blvd. Way, Downtown.*

⓬ Dade County Courthouse. Built in 1928, this was once the tallest build-ing south of Washington, D.C. It may not be as romantic as Califor-nia's San Juan Capistrano, where swallows return every year, but turkey vultures roost here each winter. Just look overhead, and you'll see them soaring in graceful circles over Downtown. ⊠ *73 W. Flagler St., at N. Miami Ave., Downtown* ☏ *305/349–7000.*

❹ Flagler Palm Cottage. Now somewhat wedged between huge modern structures, this modest but cheerful-looking 1897 house built of local pine was once scheduled for demolition. Fortunately, it was moved from its previous Downtown location to this site for preservation and is now the only building of its type and age in downtown Miami. Though not open to visitors, it has an exterior worth seeing as an interesting example of late-19th-century Miami architecture. ⊠ *66 S.E. 4th St., between S. Miami Ave. and S.E. 1st St., Downtown.*

⓮ Freedom Tower. In the 1960s this imposing Spanish baroque structure was the Cuban Refugee Center, processing more than 500,000 Cubans who entered the United States after fleeing Fidel Castro's regime. Built in 1925 for the *Miami Daily News,* it was inspired by the Giralda, an 800-year-old bell tower in Seville, Spain. Preservationists were pleased to see the tower's exterior restored in 1988. ⊠ *600 Biscayne Blvd., at N.E. 6th St., Downtown* ☎ *no phone.*

⓫ Galeria International Mall. If you have any doubt that you're in a bustling international city, step inside this indoor mall. Packed with visitors from South America, Europe, and beyond, the food court brims with authentic ethnic fast food: grilled meats from Brazil, *masala dosa* (Southern Indian rice and split-pea pancakes filled with spicy potatoes), *empanadas* from Latin America, fruit shakes from Cuba, and subs from the United States. ⊠ *243 E. Flagler St., east of N.E. 2nd Ave., Downtown* ☎ *305/371–4536.*

★ **⓾ Gusman Center for the Performing Arts.** Rudy Vallee, Martha Raye, Elvis Presley, and Jackie Gleason all performed in this former movie palace, now restored as a concert hall with a fabulous marquee. Resembling a Moorish courtyard inside, with twinkling "stars" in the "sky," it hosts the annual Miami International Film Festival and other cultural events. ⊠ *174 E. Flagler St., at N.E. 2nd Ave., Downtown* ☎ *305/374–2444* ⊕ *www.gusmancenter.org.*

❾ Historic Gesu Church. The oldest Miami church to remain on its original site, this 1922 building was designed in the Venetian style, with Spanish influences. Salient architectural features are the three-story portico, stained-glass windows by Franz Mayer, and a rose window. There are 25 masses weekly in both English and Spanish. ⊠ *118 N.E. 2nd St., at N.E. 1st Ave., Downtown* ☎ *305/379–1424* ⊙ *Daily 8–5.*

off the
beaten
path

LITTLE HAITI – Once known as Lemon City for the fragrant fruit grown here by early settlers, Little Haiti is now a colorful Caribbean community with brightly painted buildings, Creole-language signs, and attractive storefront murals. This is not a wealthy community but one in which refugees from the western hemisphere's poorest country seek their share of the American dream. By day Little Haiti is a reasonably safe neighborhood to explore, but there is little here at night.

The heart of Little Haiti is on North Miami Avenue, from 54th to 59th streets. The **Caribbean Marketplace** (⊠ 5927 N.E. 2nd Ave., Little Haiti), patterned after the Iron Market in Port-au-Prince, is now shuttered. Throughout Little Haiti, tiny *botanicas* (a spiritual

CloseUp

UNCOVERING A CITY'S ANCIENT HISTORY

P RESENT-DAY MIAMIANS *have always been aware of the Native American roots planted here long before the arrival of Spanish explorers—after all, the city's name is believed to be the word for "sweet water" in an indeterminate Native American tongue. But there is little visible evidence of the activities of its first people, the Tequesta. It wasn't until 1998, with the discovery of a unique archaeological find—a mysterious 38-foot ring of stone dubbed the Miami Circle— that the community decided its prehistoric past just might be worth preserving.*

At a routine dig at the mouth of the Miami River, the site of a new condo project, archaeologists discovered a series of basins cut into limestone bedrock in a perfect circular pattern when viewed from above. The circle contained postholes, a carving that resembled an eye, and other artifacts, including charcoal samples carbon-dated to AD *100. The circle's east–west axis suggests that it may have been an astronomical tool to signal the summer and winter solstice or a Tequesta temple or council house.*

The state and county acquired the site and are planning how best to preserve this fascinating relic for future generations, who may discover the Miami Circle's yet-unknown purpose.

kind of drug store) sell candles and potions, a reminder that voodoo is a real and living faith in the neighborhood. But there are also countless storefront *églises* (Christian churches). Several small, inexpensive restaurants serve specialties such as pigeon peas and rice, oxtail, and goat stew.

❸ **Miami Circle.** When a construction project got under way here in 1998, workers uncovered a 38-foot-diameter stone formation and other mysterious relics. After heated pleas from archaeologists, preservationists, and Native Americans, the county decided to acquire the land and preserve the site. The area is covered and protected while plans for preservation are worked out, but you can get a view from the bridge. ⊠ *East of the Brickell Ave. Bridge at Miami River, Downtown* ⊕ *www.nps.gov/ bisc/miamicircle.htm.*

❼ **Miami Dade College.** The campus houses two galleries: the third-floor **Centre Gallery** mounts photography, painting, and sculpture exhibitions, and the fifth-floor **Frances Wolfson Art Gallery** presents smaller photo exhibits. ⊠ *300 N.E. 2nd Ave., between N.E. 3rd and 4th Sts., Downtown* ☎ *305/237–3278* ⊕ *www.mdc.edu* ☎ *Free* ☉ *Mon.–Wed. and Fri. 10–4, Thurs. noon–6.*

★ ☾ ⓭ **Miami-Dade Cultural Center.** Containing three cultural resources, this fortresslike 3-acre complex is a Downtown focal point. The **Miami Art Museum** (☎ 305/375–3000 ⊕ www.miamiartmuseum.org) presents major touring exhibitions of work by international artists, focusing on art since 1945. Open Tuesday–Friday 10–5 (until 9 the third Thursday of the month) and weekends noon–5, the museum charges $5 admission ($6 including the historical museum). At the **Historical Museum of Southern Florida** (☎ 305/375–1492 ⊕ www.historical-museum.org) you'll be treated to pure South Floridiana, with exhibits celebrating Miami's multicultural heritage and history, including an old Miami streetcar, cigar labels, and a railroad exhibit, plus a display on prehistoric Miami. Admission is $5 ($6 including the art museum)—and hours are Monday–Wednesday and Friday–Saturday 10–5, Thursday 10–9, and Sunday noon–5. The **Miami-Dade Public Library** (☎ 305/375–2665)—open Monday–Wednesday and Friday–Saturday 9–6, Thursday 9–9, plus Sunday 1–5 October–May—contains nearly 4 million holdings and a Florida Department that includes rare books, documents, and photographs recording Miami history. It also has art exhibits in the auditorium and in the second-floor lobby. ⊠ *101 W. Flagler St., between N.W. 1st and 2nd Aves., Downtown* ☎ *305/375–2665.*

> **off the beaten path**
>
> **MIAMI DESIGN DISTRICT –** Just north of downtown Miami, the Design District consists of 1 square mi of furniture showrooms, eclectic accessories boutiques, art studios, and interior design firms that are open to the public. Some design showrooms, like **Holly Hunt** (⊠ 3833 N.E. 2nd Ave., Design District ☎ 305/571–2012), combine furniture with art and photography exhibits, thereby merging the discrete worlds of decor and visual art. Murals on either side of the Buick Building mark the entrance to the neighborhood, which also has its own arts-oriented high school. Grab a bite to eat at the lush **Piccadilly Garden Restaurant and Lounge** (⊠ 35 N.E. 40th St., Design District ☎ 305/573–8221). ⊠ *N.E. 36th St. to N.E. 42nd St. between N.E. 2nd Ave. and N. Miami Ave., Design District* ☾ *Weekdays 10–5; some stores by appointment.*

❻ **Plaza Bolivar.** Flags of South and Central American countries fly, and there's a statue of Ponce de León and a plaque inscribed with A CUBAN SALUTE TO THE BICENTENNIAL. According to the inscription, the plaque was presented by THE CUBANS WHO LEFT BEHIND FAMILY, FRIENDS AND ALL OUR POSSESSIONS IN SEARCH OF FREEDOM AND OPPORTUNITY, AND ONLY IN AMERICA, THE LAND OF ENDLESS OPPORTUNITY, HAVE WE FOUND THE RIGHTS THAT WE LOST IN OUR HOMELAND. ⊠ *Biscayne Blvd., between N.E. 2nd and 3rd Sts., Downtown.*

> **off the beaten path**
>
> **RUBELL FAMILY COLLECTION –** A must-see for contemporary-art lovers, the private collection of Mera and Don Rubell includes work by artists from the 1970s to the present, including Jeff Koons, Cindy Sherman, Damien Hirst, Keith Haring, and Ansel M. Keifer. It's housed in a 40,000-square-foot former Drug Enforcement Agency confiscation center. Exhibitions are rotated, and there are public

programs November–May. ⊠ *95 N.W. 29th St., between N. Miami Ave. and N.W. 1st Ave., near Design District, Downtown* ☎ *305/ 573–6090* 💲 *Free* ⊙ *Wed.–Sun. 10–6 or by appointment.*

❽ U.S. Courthouse. Built of keystone in 1931, the neoclassical courthouse originally housed Miami's main post office as well (the post office moved out in the 1980s). In what was once the second-floor central court-room is *Law Guides Florida Progress,* a huge Depression-era mural by Denman Fink. Surrounding the central figure of a robed judge are several images that define the Florida of the 1930s: fish vendors, palm trees, beaches, and a Pan Am airplane winging off to Latin America. No cameras or tape recorders are allowed in the building. ⊠ *300 N.E. 1st Ave., between N.E. 3rd and 4th Sts., Downtown* ☎ *305/523–5075* ⊙ *Weekdays 8:30–5.*

LITTLE HAVANA

First settled en masse by Cubans in the early 1960s, following that country's Communist revolution, Little Havana holds a potent brew of Latin cultures from throughout the Americas. This is a predominantly working-class area of recently arrived immigrants and elderly residents on fixed incomes, for as each exile generation prospers, it moves west. But the neighborhood is still the core of Miami's Hispanic community and a magnet for Anglos looking to immerse themselves in Latin culture. Little Havana, especially East Little Havana, brims with immigrant optimism, and new arrivals are welcomed every day. Spanish is the language that predominates, but don't be surprised if the cadence is less Cuban and more Salvadoran or Nicaraguan.

Abutting the Miami River and downtown Miami to the east, Northwest 7th Street to the north, and Coral Way to the south, Little Havana treats its western boundary on Southwest 27th Avenue as its point of entry. The main commercial zone is bounded by Northwest 1st Street, Southwest 9th Street, Ronald Reagan Avenue (Southwest 12th Avenue), and Teddy Roosevelt Boulevard (Southwest 17th Avenue). Calle Ocho (Southwest 8th Street) is the axis of the neighborhood.

Little Havana sprawls over a number of old Miami neighborhoods first settled in the early 20th century, following Miami's incorporation in 1896. Suburbs sprang up west of the Miami River and south of Flagler Street's commerce. Riverside—as Little Havana was then known—quickly became home to well-heeled southern families, who were followed in the 1930s by the county's growing Jewish population. A predominantly Jewish community throughout the '40s and '50s, Little Havana was then home to jazz clubs that marqueed Nat King Cole and Count Basie as well as kosher butcher shops that eventually gave way to Cuban meat markets. Present-day residents live in streets lined with a mix of humble little houses, well-preserved coral-rock bungalows vernacular to the turn of the last century, and time-worn tenements.

The area began to redefine itself in the '50s, when Cubans opposed to Fulgencio Batista's dictatorship began trickling in, but it was Fidel Cas-

Cuban
Memorial
Boulevard 1

Domino Park ...5

El Aguila
Vidente 2

El Credito
Cigar Factory ...3

La Casa
de los Trucos ...4

Little Havana

KEY

▶ Start of walk

tro's takeover of Cuba in 1959 and the later Freedom Flights of the '60s and early '70s that indelibly altered the local landscape. Members of Cuba's middle class fled their homeland, bringing very little with them except an entrepreneurial spirit. They quickly filled the fading neighborhood's relatively cheap housing, as family and friends joined them. Soon, boarded-up stores reopened with the familiar merchant names of prerevolutionary Cuba, restaurants started dishing up Latin comfort food, and a bustling economy emerged.

In 1980 more change came to Little Havana when upward of 125,000 Cuban refugees flooded into South Florida during the exodus from the Port of Mariel. Many were poor and uneducated, and more than 10,000 came directly from Cuba's prisons and mental institutions. A run-down way station for Latin Americans headed toward bigger and better things, the area is Miami's version of Ellis Island, a jumping-off point for each new wave of immigrants. Indeed, Little Havana is now a misnomer. The influx of Cubans has been somewhat limited by U.S. immigration policy, but the *balseros* (rafters) still trickle in illegally. Now most of the new arrivals are Central and South American refugees fleeing difficult economies and oppressive governments. As the political epicenter for the Latin American community, whatever the country, Little Havana's main drags—Flagler Street and Calle Ocho—are often sites of protests, demonstrations, and flag-waving, horn-honking, traffic-stopping marches. They frequently make international headlines, as in the case of Elián González, the Cuban youngster who, in 1999, arrived in South Florida via an inner tube, his mother having perished on the way.

In the neighborhood, corner bodegas seem derived from another place and time, and their regulars gather to share neighborhood gossip and political opinions. Elaborate, costly statues of saints stand in tiny, overgrown yards in front of dingy houses. Street vendors sell plastic bags filled with ripe tomatoes, peeled oranges, fat limes. Cuban cafeterias share the street with Nicaraguan bakeries and Central American taquerías.

Some of the restaurants host traditional flamenco performances and Sevillaña *tablaos* (dances performed on a wood-plank stage, using castanets), and some clubs feature recently arrived Cuban acts. Intimate neighborhood theaters host top-notch productions ranging from Spanish classics to contemporary satire. Throughout the year a variety of festivals commemorate Miami's Hispanic heritage, and residents from no fewer than five countries celebrate their homeland's independence days in Little Havana. If you're in Miami in March—and don't mind huge crowds—plan on attending the granddaddy of them all, the Calle Ocho Street Party. The 23-block extravaganza is part of Carnaval Miami and features top Latin entertainment. On the last Friday of every month Little Havana takes its culture to the streets for Cultural Fridays, between 7 and 10 PM on Eighth Street at 15th Avenue. Art expositions, music, and avant-garde street performances bring a young, hip crowd to the neighborhood.

Numbers in the text correspond to numbers in the margin and on the Little Havana map.

A Good Walk

An ideal place to discover the area's flavor, both literally and figuratively, is along Calle Ocho (Southwest 8th Street), at the eastern end of Tamiami Trail between Southwest 12th and 27th avenues. You'll need to drive in, but definitely park, since the only way to really experience the neighborhood is on foot; metered spots are readily available, and it's not too hard to find a free spot on a side street. Throughout your walk make sure to stop in the sundry retail establishments; perhaps buy a breezy guayabera shirt—always in vogue in white cotton. It's hard to miss the record stores, whose speakers flood the street with the sounds of salsa and *danzones* (danceable Cuban music). Browse through neighborhood bookstores for Spanish titles from Gabriel García Marquez to Zoe Valdes—you may even find some editions in English.

Start at **Cuban Memorial Boulevard ❶ ▶**, a section of Southwest 13th Avenue just south of Calle Ocho. Memorials to Cuban patriots line the boulevard, and the plaza here is the scene of frequent political rallies. On Mother's Day older women adorn a statue of the Virgin Mary with floral wreaths and join in song to honor her. Believers claim a miracle occurs here each midafternoon, when a beam of sunlight shoots through the foliage overhead directly onto the Christ child in the Virgin's arms. Religious faith of a different sort is evident near the kapok tree that towers over the boulevard: you may see an offering left by a Santero (practitioner of Santería) hoping to win the blessings of a saint.

On Calle Ocho to the east of the boulevard is **El Aguila Vidente** (The Seeing Eagle) ❷, one of many neighborhood *botánicas* that cater to Santeros. The shop welcomes the respectfully curious. A particularly worthwhile stop is next door at the **El Credito Cigar Factory** ❸. At this family-owned business, one of about a half-dozen cigar factories in the neighborhood, employees deftly hand-roll more than a million stogies each year. If you enjoy cigars, you'll be impressed by the ones they sell here.

On Calle Ocho, between Southwest 13th and 17th avenues, you'll find the Walkway of the Stars. The Latin version of its Hollywood namesake, the strip of sidewalk embedded with stars honors many of the world's top Hispanic celebrities, among them the late salsa queen Celia Cruz, crooner Julio Iglesias, and superstar Gloria Estefan. The Tower Theater is a center for cultural activities and headquarters of the Hispanic Film Festival, held each spring. Stop in at **La Casa de los Trucos ❹**, a magic store where the owners sometimes demonstrate their skills. Farther west on Calle Ocho is **Domino Park ❺**, at 15th Avenue. The game tables are always two deep with guayabera-clad men—it wasn't until the last decade that the park's male domino aficionados even allowed women into their domain.

TIMING   If a quick multicultural experience is your goal, set aside an hour or two to do this tour on foot. For real ethnic immersion, allow more time; eating is a must, as well as a peek at the area's residential streets lined with distinctive homes. Especially illuminating are Little Havana walking and bike tours led by Dr. Paul George (1345 S.W. 14th St., Miami, ☎ 305/858–6021), a history professor at Miami Dade College and past president of the Florida Historical Society.

What to See

▶ ❶ **Cuban Memorial Boulevard.** Two blocks in the heart of Little Havana are filled with monuments to Cuba's freedom fighters. Among the memorials are the *Eternal Torch of the Brigade 2506,* commemorating those who were killed in the failed Bay of Pigs invasion of 1961; a bust of 19th-century hero Antonio Maceo; and a bas-relief map of Cuba depicting each of its *municipios.* There's also a bronze statue in honor of Tony Izquierdo, who participated in the Bay of Pigs invasion, served in Nicaragua's Somozan forces, and interestingly enough was also on the CIA payroll. ⊠ *S.W. 13th Ave., south of S.W. 8th St., Little Havana.*

❺ **Domino Park.** Officially named Máximo Gomez Park, it's really known as a gathering place for Miami's domino players. Anti-Castro politics are as fierce as the clacking of domino tiles and as thick as the cigar smoke among the Cuban men who spend hours at the tables. Unwelcome in the past, women have started to make inroads into this macho setting. Although some of the male regulars seem less than friendly, others are happy to compete with any good player with a few dollars to stake. The colorful backdrop, a mural of world leaders, was painted by schoolchildren in honor of the Summit of the Americas held in Miami in 1994. A display outside the park's doors has photos of the city dating from the early 1900s. ⊠ *S.W. 8th St. and S.W. 15th Ave., Little Havana* ⊙ *Daily 9–6.*

❷ **El Aguila Vidente (The Seeing Eagle).** This store offers one-stop shopping for practitioners of Santería, an Afro-Cuban religion that incorporates some tenets of Catholicism. Santeros worship patron saints, both evil and good, by making offerings; the saints are said to bestow love, money, and even revenge. Some Santeros are uncomfortable with too many questions, so practice tact. ⊠ *1122 S.W. 8th St., between S.W. 11th and 12th Aves., Little Havana* ☎ *305/854–4086* ⊙ *Mon.–Sat. 11–7.*

❸ **El Credito Cigar Factory.** Through the giant storefront windows you can see cigars being rolled. Many of the workers at this family business dating back three generations learned their trade in prerevolutionary Cuba. Today the tobacco leaf they use comes primarily from the Dominican Republic and Mexico, and the wrappers from Connecticut, making theirs a truly multinational product. A walk-in humidor has more than 40 brands favored by customers such as Arnold Schwarzenegger, Bill Clinton, Robert De Niro, and Bill Cosby. ⊠ *1106 S.W. 8th St., near S.W. 11th Ave., Little Havana* ☎ *305/858–4162* ⊙ *Weekdays 8–6, Sat. 8–4.*

off the beaten path

ELIÁN GONZÁLEZ'S HOUSE – This humble two-bedroom home was where 6-year-old Elián stayed for nearly six months after surviving a raft journey from Cuba that killed his mother. From this same house he was removed by federal agents in a predawn raid that ultimately united him with his father, who took him home to Cuba. The Miami relatives have since moved, but they bought the property to turn it into a shrine and museum. ⊠ *2319 N.W. 2nd St., at N.W 23rd Ave., Little Havana* ☎ *no phone* ⊠ *Free* ⊙ *Sun. 10–6.*

❹ **La Casa de los Trucos.** This popular magic store first opened in Cuba in the 1930s. Its exiled owners reopened it here in the '70s, and when they're in, they perform magic acts for customers. ⊠ *1343 S.W. 8th St., Little Havana* ☎ *305/858–5029* ⊙ *Mon.–Sat. 10–6.*

need a break?

Sorry, there's no Starbucks in Little Havana—the locals probably wouldn't touch the stuff, anyway—but everywhere are walk-up windows peddling the quick energy of thimble-size *café cubano* for as little as 35¢. The locals call it *un cafecito* (literally, a small coffee), but be warned that it's high-octane and is sure to keep you going through this tour. In the mood for something refreshing? Try **Las Pinareños** (⊠ 1334 S.W. 8th St., Little Havana), a *frutería* (fruit stand), for fresh cold coconut juice served in a whole coconut, mango juice, or other *jugos* (juices).

COCONUT GROVE

Eclectic and intriguing, Miami's Coconut Grove has from the beginning stayed true to its nature—and to its natural surroundings. First inhabited in 1834, the oldest settlement in South Florida was formally established in 1873, a full two decades before Miami arrived on the scene. By then the village was already home to a multicultural collection of new residents: Bahamian blacks, white Key Westers (called "Conchs"), and New England intellectuals lured to the balmy sliver of a village on pristine Biscayne Bay. The community they built attracted artists, writers, and scientists who established winter homes here. By the end of World War I more people listed in *Who's Who* had addresses in Coconut Grove than in any other place in the United States. It might be considered the tropical equivalent of New York's Greenwich Village.

Just as it was then, Coconut Grove is still a haven for writers and artists. Confined within a relatively small area, the Miami neighborhood has never quite outgrown its image as a small village, even though it covers 3 square mi. And the Grove has changed over the decades. In the 1960s it went through a hippie period, the 1970s brought out a laid-back funkiness, and it withstood an invasion of new-wave teenyboppers in the 1980s. Things seem to have balanced out, and today the tone is upscale, urban, and fun.

During the day it's business as usual in Coconut Grove, much as in any other Miami neighborhood. But in the evening, especially on weekends, it seems as if someone flips a switch and the streets come alive. Locals and tourists jam into small boutiques, sidewalk cafés, and stores lodged in two massive retail-entertainment complexes. For blocks in every direction, students, honeymooning couples, families, and prosperous retirees flow in and out of a mix of galleries, restaurants, bars, bookstores, comedy clubs, and theaters. With this weekly influx of traffic, parking can pose a problem. There's a new well-lighted city garage at 3315 Rice Street, or look for police to direct you to parking lots where you'll pay $5–$10 for an evening's slot. If you're staying in the Grove, leave the car behind, and your night will get off to an easier start.

Although nighttime is the right time to see Coconut Grove, don't neglect the area's daytime pleasures. Take a casual drive through neighborhoods, where you'll see in the diverse architecture the varied origins of the Grove's pioneers. Posh estates mingle with rustic cottages, modest frame homes, and stark modern dwellings, often on the same block. If you're into horticulture, you'll be impressed by the Garden of Eden–like foliage that seems to grow everywhere without care. In truth, residents are determined to keep up the Grove's village-in-a-jungle look, so they lavish attention on exotic plantings even as they battle to protect any remaining native vegetation. These and other efforts demonstrate just how thoroughly Coconut Grove has remained true to its roots.

Numbers in the text correspond to numbers in the margin and on the Southern Greater Miami map.

A Good Tour

From downtown Miami take Brickell Avenue south. Follow the signs to Vizcaya and Coconut Grove, and you'll reach South Miami Avenue. This street turns into South Bayshore Drive a few miles down. Continue south and watch on your left for the entrance to the don't-miss **Vizcaya Museum and Gardens** ⑲ ☞, an estate with an Italian Renaissance–style villa. Spend some time in the building and on the grounds; then head less than 100 yards farther down the road. On your right is the **Miami Museum of Science and Space Transit Planetarium** ⑳, a hands-on museum with animated displays for all ages.

As you leave the museum and head toward the village center of Coconut Grove, South Bayshore switches from four lanes to two and back again. Before you hit the village, you may wish to stop at David T. Kennedy Park, which has 28 waterfront acres of Australian pine, lush lawns, and walking and jogging paths. If you're interested in the history of air travel, take a quick detour down Pan American Boulevard to see the 1930s art deco former Pan American Airways terminal, which has been horribly "renovated" inside to become **Miami City Hall** ㉑. You'll also see the Coconut Grove Convention Center, where antiques, boat, and home shows are held, and Dinner Key Marina, where seabirds soar and sailboats ride at anchor. As South Bayshore curves to the right, you'll see placid Pea-

Southern
Greater
Miami

cock Park in front of you, a bayfront oasis with boardwalks, and across the street on your right, a 1921 oolitic limestone building called the House-keepers Club, listed on the National Register of Historic Places.

South Bayshore heads directly into McFarlane Road, which takes a sharp right into the center of the action. Forsake the earthly for a moment and turn left on Main Highway, driving less than a half mile to Devon Road and the coral-rock **Plymouth Congregational Church** ㉒.

Return to Main Highway and to the historic village of Coconut Grove. As you reenter the village center, note on your left the Coconut Grove Playhouse. On your right, beyond the benches and shelter, is the entrance to the **Barnacle Historic State Park** ㉓, a residence built by Commodore Ralph Munroe in 1891. The house and grounds offer a glimpse into Miami's early Anglo years. After getting your fill of history, relax and spend the evening mingling with Coconut Grove's artists and intellectuals. Shop along Grand Avenue and Mary Street, and be sure to check out **CocoWalk** ㉔ and the **Streets of Mayfair** ㉕, two collections of stores and restaurants.

TIMING Plan on devoting from six to eight hours to enjoy Vizcaya, other bayfront sights, and the village's shops, restaurants, and nightlife.

What to See

㉓ **Barnacle Historic State Park.** A pristine bayfront manse sandwiched between cramped luxury developments, Barnacle is Miami's oldest house still standing on its original foundation. To get here, you'll hike along an old buggy trail through a tropical hardwood hammock and landscaped lawn leading to Biscayne Bay. Built in 1891 by Florida's first snowbird—New Yorker Commodore Ralph Munroe—the large home, built of timber Munroe salvaged from wrecked ships, has many original furnishings, a broad sloping roof, and deeply recessed verandas that channel sea breezes into the house. If your timing is right, you may catch one of the monthly Moonlight Concerts, and the old-fashioned picnic on the Fourth of July is popular. ⊠ *3485 Main Hwy., Coconut Grove* ☎ *305/448–9445* ⊕*www.floridastateparks.org/thebarnacle* ⊠*$1, concerts $5* ⊙ *Fri.–Mon. 9–4; tours 10, 11:30, 1, and 2:30, but call ahead; concerts evenings near the full moon, 6–9, call for dates.*

㉔ **CocoWalk.** This indoor-outdoor mall has three floors of nearly 40 name-brand (Victoria's Secret, Gap, Banana Republic, etc.) and independent shops that stay open almost as late as its popular restaurants and clubs. Kiosks with beads, incense, herbs, and other small items are scattered around the ground level; street entertainers hold court on weekends; and the movie theaters and nightspots are upstairs. If you're ready for an evening of touristy people-watching, this is the place. ⊠ *3015 Grand Ave., Coconut Grove* ☎ *305/444–0777* ⊕ *www.cocowalk.com* ⊙ *Sun.–Thurs. 11–10, Fri.–Sat. 11 AM–midnight.*

Kampong. With nearly 10 acres of exquisite, flamboyant flowering trees and fruits, this former home and garden of horticulturist Dr. David Fairchild is one of five gardens administered by the Hawaii-based National Tropical Botanical Garden. ⊠ *4013 Douglas Rd., Coconut Grove*

☎ *305/442–7169* ⊕ *www.ntbg.org/kampong.html* ⊡ *$10* ⊙ *Tours by appointment, second Sat. Sept.–Apr.*

㉑ Miami City Hall. Built in 1934 as the terminal for the Pan American Airways seaplane base at Dinner Key, the building retains its nautical-style art deco trim. Sadly, the interior is generic government, but a 1938 Pan Am menu on display (with filet mignon, *petit pois au beurre*, and Jenny Lind pudding) lets you know Miami officials appreciate from whence they came. ⊠ *3500 Pan American Dr., Coconut Grove* ☎ *305/250–5400* ⊙ *Weekdays 8–5.*

㉚ ㉒ Miami Museum of Science and Space Transit Planetarium. This museum is chock-full of hands-on sound, gravity, and electricity displays for children and adults alike. A wildlife center houses native Florida snakes, turtles, tortoises, and birds of prey. Outstanding traveling exhibits appear throughout the year, and virtual reality, life-science demonstrations, and Internet technology are on hand every day. The museum's association with the Smithsonian Institution means top-notch exhibitions and, within the next several years, the creation of the waterfront Science Center of the Americas, which will feature the latest technology; interactive exhibits on such topics as dinosaurs, ecosystems, and the ancient Americas; large-screen theaters; and research and education facilities. If you're here the first Friday of the month, stick around for a laser-light rock-and-roll show, presented in the planetarium at 9. ⊠ *3280 S. Miami Ave., Coconut Grove* ☎ *305/646–4200* ⊕ *www.miamisci.org* ⊡ *Museum, planetarium, and wildlife center $10; laser show $7* ⊙ *Daily 10–6.*

> **need a break?** Coconut Grove is packed with places to eat, from humble to grand. One congenial waterfront choice is **Monty's Stone Crab–Seafood House** (⊠ 2550 S. Bayshore Dr., Coconut Grove ☎ 305/858–1431), for fresh seafood or delectable stone crab claws.

㉒ Plymouth Congregational Church. Opened in 1917, this coral-rock church is built in the mission style. The front door, made of hand-carved walnut and oak with wrought-iron fittings, came from an early 17th-century monastery in the Pyrénées. Also on the 11-acre grounds are the first schoolhouse in Miami-Dade County (one room), which was moved to this property, and the site of the original Coconut Grove waterworks and electric works. ⊠ *3400 Devon Rd., Coconut Grove* ☎ *305/444–6521* ⊙ *Weekdays 9–4:30, Sun. service 10 AM.*

㉕ Streets of Mayfair. Home to the Limited, Borders, and many other shops and restaurants, this mall is best known for its entertainment venues, including a comedy club and the Iguana Cantina, a nightclub. On Saturday there's a farmers' market with fresh produce, flowers, baked goods, and handicrafts. ⊠ *2911 Grand Ave., Coconut Grove* ☎ *305/448–1700* ⊕ *www.streetsofmayfair.com* ⊙ *Sun.–Thurs. 11–10, Fri.–Sat. 11–11.*

► **㉙ Vizcaya Museum and Gardens.** Of the 10,000 people living in Miami between 1912 and 1916, about 1,000 of them were gainfully employed by Chicago industrialist James Deering to build this Italian Renais-
FodorsChoice ★

CloseUp

WITH CHILDREN?

There's far more to do in Miami with children than go to the beach. At the top of kids' a-list (attraction list), Parrot Jungle Island offers free-flying entertainment and lots of hands-on stuff—you can hand-feed the birds, let parrots perch on your shoulders, and even stroke a tarantula. Across the MacArthur Causeway from Parrot Jungle is the new Miami Children's Museum, which offers a range of interactive exhibits for curious young ones. In addition to seeing the usual and unusual suspects at the Miami Seaquarium, families can now learn about and swim with dolphins, but you have to be at least 52" tall and willing to spend a fair amount of money for the privilege. The landmark Venetian Pool in Coral Gables is as much fun as it is historic. Aptly named, with secret caves and stone bridges, it has probably the most aesthetically pleasing wading pool you'll ever see (sorry, no children under 3 are allowed in the pool).

At Miami Metrozoo, one of the largest cageless zoos in the country, younger kids can be steered to PAWS (the children's petting zoo) and a great playground with age-appropriate areas. It's a pretty big place though, and shade is at a premium, so little ones might get tired. Not to worry; just hop on the monorail or try the tram tour. An airboat ride at the Everglades Alligator Farm is sure to please young and old alike. You'll zip and spin across the shallow grassy water, and the reptile shows are a big hit with children, too. And if kids get tired of all the animals and action, there's always the beach.

sance–style winter residence. Once comprising 180 acres, the grounds now occupy a 30-acre tract that includes a native hammock and more than 10 acres of formal gardens with fountains overlooking Biscayne Bay. The house, open to the public, contains 70 rooms, 34 of which are filled with paintings, sculpture, antique furniture, and other fine and decorative arts. The pieces date from the 15th through the 19th centuries and represent the Renaissance, baroque, rococo, and neoclassical movements. So unusual and impressive is Vizcaya that visitors have included many major heads of state. Guided tours are available. Moonlight tours, in particular, offer a unique look at the gardens; call for reservations. ⊠ *3251 S. Miami Ave., Coconut Grove* ☎ *305/250–9133* ⊕ *www.vizcayamuseum.com* ✉ *$12* ☉ *House and ticket booth daily 9:30–4:30, garden daily 9:30–5:30.*

CORAL GABLES

You can easily spot Coral Gables from the window of a Miami-bound jetliner—just look for the massive orange tower of the Biltmore Hotel rising from a lush green carpet of trees concealing the city's gracious homes. The canopy is as much a part of this planned city as its distinctive architecture, all attributed to the vision of George E. Merrick nearly 100 years ago.

The story of this city began in 1911, when Merrick inherited 1,600 acres of citrus and avocado groves from his father. Through judicious investment he nearly doubled the tract to 3,000 acres by 1921. Merrick dreamed of building an American Venice here, complete with canals and homes. Working from this vision, he began designing a city based on centuries-old prototypes from Mediterranean countries. Merrick embraced the Garden City theory of urban planning that was so popular in the 1920s and planned lush landscaping, magnificent neighborhood entrances, and broad boulevards named for Spanish explorers, cities, and provinces. Relying on the advice of his uncle, artist Denman Fink, Merrick hired architects trained abroad to create neighborhoods, or villages, with a single architectural or historical style, such as Florida pioneer, Chinese, French, Dutch South African, and Italian.

Unfortunately for Merrick, the devastating no-name hurricane of 1926, followed by the Great Depression, prevented him from fulfilling many of his plans. He died at 54, an employee of the post office. His city languished until after World War II, but then it grew rapidly. Today Coral Gables has a population of about 43,000. In its bustling downtown, more than 150 multinational companies maintain headquarters or regional offices, and the University of Miami campus in the southern part of the Gables brings a youthful vibrancy to the area—the median age of residents here is 38. A southern branch of the city extends down the shore of Biscayne Bay through neighborhoods threaded with canals. The gorgeous Fairchild Tropical Garden and beachfront Matheson Hammock Park dominate this part of the Gables.

Like much of Greater Miami, Coral Gables has realized the aesthetic and economic importance of historic preservation and has passed a Mediterranean design ordinance that rewards businesses for maintaining their buildings' original architectural style. Even the street signs are preserved for their historical value. These ground-level markers are hard to see in daylight, impossible to see at night, but such inconveniences can be tolerated, and not only to honor the memory of Merrick. The community of broad boulevards and Spanish-Mediterranean architecture is entirely justified in calling itself the City Beautiful.

Numbers in the text correspond to numbers in the margin and on the Southern Greater Miami map.

A Good Tour

Heading south from downtown Miami on Brickell Avenue, turn right onto Coral Way, a historic roadway characterized by an arch of banyan trees, and continue until you reach the grand entrance onto **Miracle Mile ❶ ▶**. Actually only a half-mile long, this stretch of Coral Way, from Douglas Road (Southwest 37th Avenue) to Le Jeune Road (Southwest 42nd Avenue) is the heart of downtown Coral Gables. Park your car and take time to explore the area on foot. Cafeterias stand cheek by jowl with top-notch bistros, and independent bookstores share customers with major book chains. There's a heavy concentration of bridal shops here, as well as ever-changing owner-operated boutiques that are a welcome change from typical mall fare.

At some point you'll want to get back on wheels. Head west on Coral Way past the plentiful shops, and you'll pass the 1930s **Actors' Playhouse at the Miracle Theatre** ❷ on your left. Cross Le Jeune Road and bear right to continue on Coral Way, catching an eyeful of the ornate 1928 Spanish Renaissance **Coral Gables City Hall** ❸ and the adjacent Merrick Park. Heading west, you will see the Granada Golf Course—the oldest operating course in Florida. Make a slight right onto South Greenway Drive to continue along the golf course, and notice the stands of banyan trees that separate the fairways. At the end of the golf course the road makes a horseshoe bend, but continue west and cross Alhambra Circle to loop around the restored Merrick-designed **Alhambra Water Tower** ❹, a city landmark dating from 1924. Return to Alhambra and follow it south to the next light, at Coral Way, where you can turn left and ogle beautifully maintained Spanish-style homes from the 1920s. Although there is only a small sign to announce it, at the corner of Coral Way and Toledo Street is the **Coral Gables Merrick House and Gardens** ❺, Merrick's boyhood home. After a stop there, take a right back onto Coral Way and turn left on Granada. Four blocks ahead is the **De Soto Plaza and Fountain** ❻, also Merrick-designed.

Head to 9 o'clock, three-quarters of the way around the roundabout surrounding the fountain, and turn right onto De Soto Boulevard. Coming into view on your right is the Merrick-designed **Venetian Pool** ❼, which Esther Williams made famous. After visiting the pool, double back on De Soto, crossing Granada at the fountain roundabout, and continue on DeSoto for a magnificent vista of the Biltmore Hotel, which, you guessed it, was designed by Merrick. Before you reach the hotel, you'll see the **Coral Gables Congregational Church** ❽ on your right, one of the first churches built in this planned community. At the **Biltmore Hotel** ❾ (parking to the right), enjoy the grounds and public areas. After you've visited the hotel, turn right on Anastasia Avenue, and proceed to the four-way stop at Granada. Turn right on Granada and follow its winding way south past Bird Road; you'll eventually reach Ponce de León Boulevard. Turn right and follow the boulevard until you reach the entrance to the main campus of the **University of Miami** ❿. Turn right at the first stoplight (Stanford Drive) to enter the campus, and park in the lot on your right, which is designated for visitors to the Lowe Art Museum, where you can view fine art.

Now take a drive through Merrick's internationally themed Gables neighborhoods, which he called villages. He planned these residential areas, some of which are very small, to contrast with the Mediterranean look of the rest of the city. From Lowe Art Museum, cross Ponce De León and follow Maynada Street south to Hardee Road. Turn left on Hardee; between Leonardo and Cellini streets is **French City Village** ⓫. Continuing east on Hardee, you'll pass **French Country Village** ⓬ between San Vincente and Maggiore streets. When you reach Le Jeune, turn right and drive five blocks south to Maya Avenue to see **Dutch South African Village** ⓭, which runs for two blocks to Riviera Drive. At Riviera, turn right and enjoy the sprawling, elegant homes on both sides of the street. At the corner of Castania Avenue, you will see the **Chinese Village** ⓮. Turn right at Castania and in two blocks turn left on Le Jeune and cross Dixie Highway. If you feel like a shopping break, you can stop at the Village of Merrick Park, a striking Mediterranean-style, indoor-outdoor mall that has some of the same world-class stores as Bal Harbour Shops. (You can also hop on one of the electric-hybrid trolleys in central Coral Gables to get here.) Otherwise, immediately after crossing Dixie Highway, take a soft left turn onto Blue Road, which wends its way west through Riviera Country Club to Santa Maria Street, where you'll turn right. As you head north through the golf course toward Bird you'll encounter **Southern Colonial Village** ⓯, also known as Florida Pioneer Village. When you reach Bird, take a right and proceed back to Le Jeune. Turn left on Le Jeune and drive four blocks north to Viscaya Avenue. If you turn right here, you'll shortly reach **French Normandy Village** ⓰.

Returning to Le Jeune, you can head north, back to Miracle Mile, or south, to scenic Old Cutler Road. Old Cutler Road curves down through the uplands of southern Florida's coastal ridge toward the 83-acre **Fairchild Tropical Garden** ⓱. After admiring the tropical flora, backtrack a quarter mile north on Old Cutler Road to the entrance of the lovely **Matheson Hammock Park** ⓲ and its beach.

TIMING To see all the sights described here, you'll need two full days. Strolling Miracle Mile should take a bit more than an hour unless you plan to shop (don't forget the side streets); in that case, allow four hours. Save time—perhaps an hour or two—for a refreshing dip at the Venetian Pool, and plan to spend at least an hour getting acquainted with the Biltmore, longer if you'd like to order a drink and linger poolside or enjoy the elaborate Sunday brunch. Allow an hour to visit the Lowe Art Museum and another hour for the drive through the villages. You'll need a minimum of two hours to do Fairchild Tropical Garden justice, and if you want to spend time at the beach, Matheson Hammock Park will require at least another two hours.

What to See

☺ ❷ **Actors' Playhouse at the Miracle Theatre.** This renovated 1940s-era movie house now stages theatrical productions, most of which are good family fare—shows like *Man of La Mancha, Pajama Game,* and *West Side Story*—presented by pros. Musical theater for younger audiences is offered in the 300-seat Children's Balcony Theatre. ✉ *280 Miracle Mile, near Salzedo St., Coral Gables* ☎ *305/444–9293* ⊕ *www.actorsplayhouse.org.*

> **need a break?** For a burger and a beer, stop by **JohnMartin's** Irish pub (✉ 253 Miracle Mile, at Ponce de León Blvd., Coral Gables ☎ 305/445–3777). The popular spot also offers updated Irish dishes and live Irish and folk music on many evenings.

❹ **Alhambra Water Tower.** Finished in 1924, this city landmark (which used to store water) has a decorative Moorish-style exterior. After more than 50 years of disuse and neglect, the lighthouselike tower was completely restored in 1993, with a copper-rib dome and playful multicolor frescoes. It remains empty and unused. ⊠ *Alhambra Circle, Greenway Ct., and Ferdinand St., Coral Gables.*

★ ➒ **Biltmore Hotel.** Bouncing back stunningly from dark days as an army hospital, this hotel has become the jewel of Coral Gables—a dazzling architectural gem with a colorful past. First opened in 1926, it was a hotspot for the rich and glamorous of the Jazz Age until it was converted to an Army–Air Force regional hospital in 1942. The Veterans Administration continued to operate the hospital after World War II, until 1968. Then the Biltmore lay vacant for nearly 20 years before it underwent extensive renovations and reopened as a luxury hotel in 1987. Its 16-story tower, like the Freedom Tower in downtown Miami, is a replica of Seville's Giralda Tower. The magnificent pool, the largest hotel pool in the continental United States, is steeped in history—Johnny Weissmuller of Tarzan fame was a lifeguard there, and in the 1930s grand aquatic galas featuring alligator wrestling, synchronized swimming, and bathing beauties drew thousands. More recently it was President Clinton's preferred place to stay and golf. To the west is the Biltmore Country Club, a richly ornamented Beaux Arts–style structure with a superb colonnade and courtyard; it was reincorporated into the hotel in 1989. On Sunday free tours are offered at 1:30, 2:30, and 3:30. ⊠ *1200 Anastasia Ave., near De Soto Blvd., Coral Gables* ☎ *305/445–1926* ⊕ *www.biltmorehotel.com.*

➊➍ **Chinese Village.** These eight homes, intended to resemble a traditional Chinese residential compound, are easily the most exotic of Merrick's creations, since his Persian and Tangiers villages never got past the drawing board. Their designer, Henry Killam Murphy, was an expert in Chinese architecture; he also designed several universities in China. Among the borrowed architectural elements that set these homes apart are the latticework on balconies, the blue-tile eaves and roofs, and the window grills. Notice the bamboolike ornamentation on the concrete-and-stucco wall that defines the block. ⊠ *5100 blocks of Riviera Dr. and Maggiore St. between Sansovino and Castania Aves., Coral Gables.*

➌ **Coral Gables City Hall.** This 1928 building has a three-tier tower topped with a clock and a 500-pound bell. A mural by Denman Fink (George Merrick's uncle and artistic adviser during the planning of Coral Gables) inside the dome ceiling on the second floor depicts the four seasons. Although not as well known as Maxfield Parrish, Fink clearly shares his contemporary's utopian vision. Far more attractive (at least on the outside) than many modern city halls, this municipal building also displays paintings, photos, and advertisements touting 1920s Coral Gables. The Junior Orange Bowl parade starts here in late December every year, and a farmers' market runs on Saturday 8 AM–1 PM, mid-January through the end of March. ⊠ *405 Biltmore Way, at Hernando Ave., Coral Gables* ☎ *305/446–6800* ⊙ *Weekdays 8–5.*

➑ **Coral Gables Congregational Church.** With George Merrick as a charter member (he donated the land on which it stands), this parish was organized in 1923. Rumor has it Merrick built this small church, the first in the Gables, in honor of his father, a Congregational minister. The original interiors are still in magnificent condition, and a popular jazz series is held here. ⊠ *3010 De Soto Blvd., at Anastasia Ave., Coral Gables* ☎ *305/448–7421* ⊕ *www.coralgablescongregational.org* ⊗ *Weekdays 8:30–7, Sun. services at 9:15 and 11* AM.

❺ Coral Gables Merrick House and Gardens. In 1976 the city of Coral Gables acquired George Merrick's boyhood home. Restored to its 1920s appearance, it contains Merrick family furnishings and artwork. The breezy veranda and oolitic limestone construction—also called coral rock—are architectural details you'll see repeated on many of the grand homes along Coral Way. At this writing, the house was closed to the public for another renovation but was expected to reopen by 2005. ⊠ *907 Coral Way, at Toledo St., Coral Gables* ☎ *305/460–5361* ⊡ *House $5, grounds free* ⊗ *House Wed. and Sun. 1–4; grounds daily 8–sunset. Also by appointment.*

❻ De Soto Plaza and Fountain. Water flows from the mouths of four faces sculpted on a classical column that stands on a pedestal in this Denman Fink–designed fountain from the early 1920s. The closed eyes of the face looking west symbolize the day's end. ⊠ *Intersection of Granada Blvd. and Sevilla Ave., Coral Gables.*

⓭ Dutch South African Village. Marion Syms Wyeth designed these five homes to recall Dutch South Africa; they're distinguished by their white-stucco walls, round windows, and ornamented facades. ⊠ *Le Jeune Rd. at Maya Ave., Coral Gables.*

off the beaten path

EVERGLADES ALLIGATOR FARM – Here's your chance to see gators, gators, gators—2,500 or so—and other wildlife, of course, such as blue herons, snowy egrets, and perhaps a rare roseate spoonbill. You can also take in alligator wrestling, reptile shows, and other animal exhibits as well as an airboat ride (they're not allowed inside Everglades National Park). This place is a little over 30 mi south of Miami, just south of the former pioneer town of Homestead. ⊠ *40351 S.W. 192 Ave., Florida City* ☎ *305/247–2628* ⊕ *www.everglades.com* ⊡ *$17 includes airboat tour* ⊗ *Daily 9–6.*

⓱ Fairchild Tropical Garden. FodorśChoice ★ With 83 acres of lakes, sunken gardens, a 560-foot vine pergola, orchids, bellflowers, coral trees, bougainvillea, rare palms, and flowering trees, Fairchild is the largest tropical botanical garden in the continental United States. The tram tour highlights the best of South Florida's flora; then set off exploring on your own. A 2-acre rain-forest exhibit showcases tropical rain-forest plants from around the world complete with a waterfall and stream. The conservatory, Windows to the Tropics, houses rare tropical plants, including the Titan Arum (*Amorphophallus titanum*), a fast-growing variety that attracted thousands of visitors when it bloomed in 1998. (It was only the sixth documented bloom in this country in the 20th century.) The Keys Coastal Habitat, created in a marsh and mangrove area in 1995 with assistance from the Tropical Audubon Society, provides food and shelter to resident and migratory birds. Check out the Montgomery Botanical Center, a research facility devoted to palms and cycads. Spicing up Fairchild's calendar are plant sales, moonlight strolls, symphony concerts, and genuinely special events year-round, such as the Ramble in November and the International Mango Festival the second weekend in July. The excellent bookstore–gift shop carries books on gardening and horticulture, and the Garden Café serves sandwiches and, seasonally, smoothies made from the garden's own crop of tropical fruits. ⊠ *10901 Old Cutler Rd., Coral Gables* ☎ *305/667–1651* ⊕ *www.fairchildgarden.org* 🎫 *$10* ⊙ *Daily 9:30–4:30.*

⓫ **French City Village.** The homes on the north side of this stretch of Hardee Road reflect the inspiration of formal 17th- and 18th-century French Empire design, and the walls surrounding the cluster feature pavilion-like entryways. ⊠ *1000 block of Hardee Rd. between Leonardo and Cellini Sts., Coral Gables.*

⓬ **French Country Village.** These 18 homes were designed by Frank Forster, Edgar Albright, and Philip Goodwin. The houses represent a range of styles predominant in 18th-century rural France. Among them you'll spot a châteaulike residence with a slate roof and cylindrical turret. ⊠ *500 block of Hardee Rd. between San Vincente and Maggiore Sts., Coral Gables.*

⓰ **French Normandy Village.** When designing these 11 homes, architects John and Coulton Skinner used half-timbering and shingled gable roofs to evoke 15th- and 16th-century provincial France. In the 1930s this village served as a men's dormitory for the University of Miami. ⊠ *Le Jeune Rd. at Viscaya Ave., Coral Gables.*

🐚 ⓲ **Matheson Hammock Park.** In the 1930s the Civilian Conservation Corps developed this 100-acre tract of upland and mangrove swamp on land donated by a local pioneer, Commodore J. W. Matheson. The park, one of Miami-Dade County's oldest and most scenic, has a bathing beach where the tide flushes a saltwater "atoll" pool through four gates. The marina has 243 slips, 71 dry-storage spaces, a bait-and-tackle shop, and a top-rated seafood restaurant built into a historic coral rock building. ⊠ *9610 Old Cutler Rd., Coral Gables* ☎ *305/665–5475* ⊕ *www. miamidade.gov/parks/Parks/matheson_beach.htm* 🎫 *Parking for beach and marina $4 per car, $10 per RV; limited free upland parking* ⊙ *Daily 6–sunset pool winter, daily 8:30–5; summer, weekends 8:30–6.*

off the
beaten
path

MIAMI METROZOO – Don't miss a visit to this top-notch zoo, the only subtropical zoo in the continental United States. Its 290 acres, 14 mi south of Miami, are home to more than 900 animals that roam on islands surrounded by moats. Take the monorail for a cool overview, then walk around to take a closer look at such attractions as the Tiger Temple, where white tigers roam; the African Plains exhibit, where giraffes, ostriches, and zebras graze in a simulated natural habitat; and the refreshing Asian River Life exhibit, with real komodo dragons. The newest addition is the Wings of Asia aviary, featuring about 300 exotic birds representing 70 species. The birds fly free within the jungle-like enclosure. There's also a petting zoo with a meerkat exhibit and interactive opportunities, such as those at Dr. Wilde's World and the Ecology Theater, where kids can touch

Florida animals like alligators and opossums. An educational and entertaining wildlife show is given three times daily. In addition to standard fare, the snack bar offers local favorites such as Cuban sandwiches, *arepas* (corn pancake sandwiches), and Cuban coffee—and cold beer. ⊠ *12400 Coral Reef Dr. (S.W. 152nd St.), Richmond Heights, Miami* ☎ *305/251–0400* ⊕ *www.co.miami-dade.fl.us/parks/Parks/metrozoo.htm* ⚏ *$12, 45-min tram tour $2* ☉ *Daily 9:30–5:30, last admission 4.*

★ ► ❶ **Miracle Mile.** Even with competition from some impressive malls, this half-mile stretch of retail stores continues to thrive because of its intriguing mixture of unique boutiques, bridal shops, art galleries, charming restaurants, and upscale nightlife venues. ⊠ *Coral Way between S.W. 37th and S.W. 42nd Aves., Coral Gables.*

off the beaten path

PINECREST GARDENS – This lush tropical park opened in 2003 on the 20-acre site of the original Parrot Jungle, which is now on an island near downtown Miami. Trails cut through coral rock, shaded by massive oaks and bald cypress, and showcasing the region's natural flora remain a draw. A new playground has been added, and a public library and café are planned. ⊠ *11000 Red Rd. (S.W. 57th Ave.), at S.W. 111th St., Pinecrest* ☎ *305/669–6942* ⊕ *www.pinecrest-fl.gov/gardens/* ⚏ *$5* ☉ *Daily 8–sunset.*

Pinewood Cemetery. Once the preserve of the Tequesta Indians 3,000–4,000 years ago, this hidden wooded site sits in the midst of affluent suburbia. Gravestones bear the names of pioneer families, and much of the native flora has identifying markers, making this a pleasant place to wander around. ⊠ *Sunset Dr. and Erwin Rd., Coral Gables.*

❶ **Southern Colonial Village.** Also known as Florida Pioneer Village (the name used by architects John and Coulton Skinner), this collection of five homes adapts Greek revival and Colonial revival styles. ⊠ *Santa Maria St. at Mendavia Ave., Coral Gables.*

off the beaten path

SOUTH MIAMI – Just southwest of the University of Miami is a picturesque city called South Miami, not to be confused with the even more southerly region known as South Miami-Dade. Stately old homes and towering trees line Sunset Drive—a one-horse-drawn carriage road until the early 1900s and now a city-designated Historic and Scenic Road to and through the town. (Sunset Drive is the western extension of Coral Gables' Sunset Road.) The town's distinctive commercial district of friendly shops and restaurants now includes a huge retail and entertainment complex, the Shops at Sunset Place. The mall's offerings—among which are Steven Spielberg's GameWorks, a Virgin Megastore, NikeTown, and an IMAX theater—are especially popular with teenagers but have added to the traffic woes of the community.

❿ **University of Miami.** With almost 15,000 full-time, part-time, and non-credit students, UM is the largest private research university in the

Southeast. These days it's headed by president Donna Shalala, the former Secretary of Health and Human Services under Clinton. Walk around campus and visit the **Lowe Art Museum,** which hosts traveling exhibitions and has a permanent collection of 8,000 works that include Renaissance, baroque, American, Latin American, and Native American arts and crafts. In 1999 the museum merged with the Cuban Museum of the Americas, bringing a rich collection of art and artifacts to the campus. Rain or shine, the **John C. Gifford Arboretum,** on the northwest corner of the campus at San Amaro and Robbia streets, is a perfect place to stroll through the palms and flowering trees. UM is also the site of the popular Beaux Arts Festival the third weekend in January. ⊠ *1301 Stanford Dr., near Ponce de León Blvd., Coral Gables* ☎ *305/ 284–3535 or 305/284–3536* ⊕ *www.miami.edu* ☞ *Museum $5* ⊗ *Museum Tues.–Wed. and Fri.–Sat. 10–5, Thurs. noon–7, Sun. noon–5.*

⟲ ❼ **Venetian Pool.** Sculpted from a rock quarry in 1923 and fed by artesian
Fodor'sChoice wells, this 825,000-gallon municipal pool remains quite popular due to
★ its themed architecture—a fantasized version of a waterfront Italian village—created by Denman Fink. The pool has earned a place on the National Register of Historic Places and showcases a nice collection of vintage photos depicting 1920s beauty pageants and swank soirées held long ago. Paul Whiteman played here, Johnny Weissmuller and Esther Williams swam here, and you should, too (but no kids under 3). A snack bar, lockers, and showers make this must-see user-friendly as well. ⊠ *2701 De Soto Blvd., at Toledo St., Coral Gables* ☎ *305/460–5356* ⊕ *www.venetianpool.com* ☞ *Apr.–Oct. $9, Nov.–Mar. $6; free parking across De Soto Blvd.* ⊗ *June–Aug., weekdays 11–7:30, weekends 10–4:30; Sept.–Oct. and Apr.–May, Tues.–Fri. 11–5:30, weekends 10–4:30; Nov.–Mar., Tues.–Fri. 10–4:30, weekends 10–4:30.*

KEY BISCAYNE & VIRGINIA KEY

Once upon a time, these barrier islands were an outpost for fishermen and sailors, pirates and salvagers, soldiers and settlers. The 95-foot Cape Florida Lighthouse stood tall during Seminole Indian battles and hurricanes. Coconut plantations covered two-thirds of Key Biscayne, and there were plans as far back as the 1800s to develop the picturesque island as a resort for the wealthy.

Fortunately, the state and county governments set much of the land aside for parks, and both keys are now home to top-ranked beaches and golf, tennis, softball, and picnicking facilities. The long and winding bike paths that run through the islands are favorites for in-line skaters and cyclists. Incorporated in 1991, the village of Key Biscayne is a hospitable community of about 9,000 that enjoys hosting friendly community events such as a popular Fourth of July parade; Virginia Key remains undeveloped at the moment, making these two playground islands especially family-friendly.

Numbers in the text correspond to numbers in the margin and on the Southern Greater Miami map.

A Good Tour

Day or night, there are few drives prettier than the one to Key Biscayne and Virginia Key. And if you're in a convertible on a balmy day—well, this kind of drive is what South Florida living is all about. You can also make this tour on in-line skates or bicycle.

From I–95 take the Key Biscayne exit to the Rickenbacker Causeway (a $1 toll covers your round-trip). If you plan to skate or bike, just park anywhere along the causeway after the toll booth and take off. The beaches on either side of the causeway are popular for water sports, with sailboards, sailboats, and Jet Skis available for rental. Officially known as the William Powell Bridge, the causeway bridge rises 75 feet, providing a spectacular if fleeting view of the cruise ships at the Port of Miami, to the north. You can also see the high-rises looming at the tip of South Beach to the northeast, the bright blue Atlantic straight ahead, and sailboat-dotted Biscayne Bay to the south. South of Powell Bridge you'll see anglers fishing off the **Old Rickenbacker Causeway Bridge** ㉖ ▶ among the hungry seabirds.

After the causeway turns southeast on Virginia Key, you can spy the gold geodesic dome of the **Miami Seaquarium** ㉗, a longtime sightseeing attraction, and the University of Miami Rosenstiel School of Marine and Atmospheric Science. Visit the undersea world of South Florida and beyond; then cross the Bear Cut Bridge (popular for fishing) onto lush Key Biscayne. Past the marina on your right, winding Crandon Boulevard takes you to **Crandon Park** ㉘, whose Tennis Center is the site of the NASDAQ-100 Open each March. The park is also home to one of South Florida's best-loved beaches.

As you approach the village of Key Biscayne, take note of the iguana-crossing signs warning motorists of the many green reptiles that scamper about the area. Follow Crandon through Key Biscayne's downtown, where shops and a village green mainly serve local residents. As you drive through town you'll see luxurious beachfront condos and smaller buildings on your left and single-family houses on your right. Peek down some of the side streets—especially those along waterways—and you can spot spectacular bayfront mansions. Crandon turns into Grapetree Drive as you enter **Bill Baggs Cape Florida State Park** ㉙, a 410-acre park with great beaches, two excellent cafés, picnic areas, and at its southern tip the brick Cape Florida Lighthouse and light keeper's cottage.

After you've taken the sun, or perhaps a bicycle ride, in the park, backtrack on Crandon to the causeway. On your way to the mainland, there's a panoramic view of downtown Miami as you cross the bridge.

TIMING Set aside the better part of a day for this tour, saving a few late-afternoon hours for Crandon Park and the Cape Florida Lighthouse.

What to See

Fodor'sChoice ㉙ **Bill Baggs Cape Florida State Park.** Thanks to great beaches, sunsets, and a lighthouse, this park at Key Biscayne's southern tip is worth the drive. It has boardwalks, 18 picnic shelters, and two cafés that serve light lunches. A stroll or ride along walking and bicycle paths provides wonderful views of Miami's dramatic skyline. From the southern end of the park you can see a handful of houses rising over the bay on wooden stilts, the remnants of Stiltsville, built in the 1940s and now dying a natural death. Bill Baggs has bicycle and skate rentals, a playground, fishing piers, kayak rentals, and, on request, guided tours of the cultural complex and the **Cape Florida Lighthouse,** South Florida's oldest structure. The lighthouse was erected in 1845 to replace an earlier one destroyed in an 1836 Seminole attack, in which the keeper's helper was killed. Plantings around the lighthouse and keeper's cottage recall the island's past. The restored cottage and cookhouse offer free tours at 10 AM and 1 PM Thurs.–Mon. Be there a half hour beforehand. ⊠ *1200 S. Crandon Blvd., Key Biscayne* ☎ *305/361–5811 or 305/361–8779* ⊕ *www. floridastateparks.org/capeflorida* ⊡ *$5 per vehicle with up to 8 people; $1 per person on foot, bike, bus, or motorcycle* ☉ *Daily 8–sunset.*

🕐 ㉘ **Crandon Park.** This laid-back park in northern Key Biscayne is popular with families, and many educated beach enthusiasts rate the 3½-mi beach here among the top 10 beaches in North America. The sand is soft, there are no riptides, there's a great view of the Atlantic, and parking is both inexpensive and plentiful. Because it's a weekend favorite of locals, you'll get a good taste of multicultural Miami flavor: salsa and hip-hop, jerk chicken and barbecue ribs. The **Crandon Family Amusement Center** (☎ 305/361–0099) at Crandon Park was once the site of a zoo. Now it has a restored carousel (it's $1 for three rides), splash pool, outdoor roller rink, and playground. There are even swans, waterfowl, and hundreds of huge iguanas running loose. A jungle hayride, available from 10 AM to 1 PM on Saturdays, includes a narrated tour where you can hear the tales of Tequesta Indians and pirates that once inhabited this lush barrier island. At the north end of the beach is the free **Marjory Stoneman Douglas Biscayne Nature Center** (☎ 305/361–6767). Here you can explore seagrass beds on a tour with a naturalist; see red, black, and white mangroves; and hike along the beach and hammock in the Bear Cut Preserve. Nature center hours vary, so call ahead. ⊠ *4000 Crandon Blvd., Key Biscayne* ☎ *305/361–5421* ⊕ *www.co.miami-dade.fl.us/parks/ crandon.htm* ⊡ *Free, parking $4* ☉ *Daily 8–dusk.*

🕐 ㉗ **Miami Seaquarium.** This classic but aging visitor attraction stages shows with sea lions, dolphins, and Lolita the killer whale. The Crocodile Flats exhibit has 26 Nile crocodiles. You can visit a shark pool, a tropical reef aquarium, and West Indian manatees. Discovery Bay, an endangered mangrove habitat, is home to indigenous Florida fish and rays, alligators, herons, egrets, and ibis. The big draw now is W.A.D.E., the park's Water and Dolphin Exploration Program. A two-hour session offers one-on-one interaction with the dolphins, but it's expensive—$140 to touch, kiss, and swim with them, but the price does include park admission, towel, and snacks. (Call for reservations.) The Seaquarium is awaiting approval for an expansion and was cited for electrical and other code violations in 2003; in the meantime, the only sure thing that's being added is a halfway house and hospital for the huge, gentle manatees who too often fall victim to boat propellers. ⊠ *4400 Rickenbacker Causeway, Virginia Key, Miami* ☎ *305/361–5705* ⊕ *www.miamiseaquarium.com* ⊡ *$25.63, parking $5* ☉ *Daily 9:30–5, last admission 4.*

need a break?

For some really gritty local flavor and color, seek out **Jimbo's** (⊠ off Rickenbacker Causeway at Arthur Lamb Jr. Rd., Virginia Key, Miami ☎ 305/361–7026), a hard-to-find but impossible-to-miss hangout. To get here, turn on Arthur Lamb Jr. Road just south of the MAST (Maritime and Science Technology) Academy. Tell the toll-booth attendant you're headed to Jimbo's, and you'll save the $3 charge assessed to beachgoers. Follow the road past the sewer plant until you see a cluster of ramshackle buildings. This is the place. Have a cold beer and wander around the joint. Domestic wildlife—roosters, chickens, and dogs—shares space with herons and pelicans, and you might spot a manatee in the lagoon. The atmospheric shacks, sometimes occupied by rowdy live bands, have been used for countless TV, movie, video, and still-photo shoots. The lagoon in back was a location for the television series *Flipper*. Relax, watch the crusty characters playing boccie, and you'll feel delightfully removed from civilization.

▶ ㉖ **Old Rickenbacker Causeway Bridge.** Here you can watch boat traffic pass through the channel, pelicans and other seabirds soar and dive, and dolphins cavort in the bay. Park at the bridge entrance, about a mile from the tollgate, and walk past anglers tending their lines to the gap where the center draw span across the Intracoastal Waterway was removed. On the right, on cool, clear winter evenings, the water sparkles with dots of light from hundreds of shrimp boats. ⊠ *Rickenbacker Causeway south of Powell Bridge, east of Coconut Grove, Miami.*

need a break?

If you're none too eager to return to the mainland, stop at the **Rusty Pelican** (⊠ 3201 Rickenbacker Causeway, Virginia Key, Miami ☎ 305/361–3818), one of the few eateries in the area. Kick back, ignore the so-so seafood menu, order a cold beer or a frozen margarita, and admire the splendid view of the Miami skyline.

WHERE TO EAT

2

Updated by
Viviana
Carballo

MIAMI AND MIAMI BEACH'S RESTAURANT SCENE is much like the cities themselves, a quirky mix of exotic adventure and upscale glamour. You can sample dishes from all over the globe and pay just a few dollars, or you can have the meal of a lifetime and spend accordingly. Indeed, deep-pocketed diners can easily empty their wallets here. In the process you can enjoy the work of the celebrity chefs who have pioneered New World cuisine, a loose fusion of Latin American, Asian, and Caribbean flavors using fresh, local ingredients.

The most famous, and best, of Miami's high-end restaurants is Norman's, which has a truly dazzling New World menu. It is run by Norman Van Aken, who has now opened Mundo, an informal café offering tapas and half portions inspired by Spanish cuisine. Allen Susser, at Chef Allen's in Aventura, is also among the best chefs in the area. His style combines international influences and the finest of contemporary cuisine. Robbin Haas has perfected a sassy, contemporary take on Latin American food at Chispa, especially tapas and *cazuelitas* (small plates). And Douglas Rodriguez, another member, along with Van Aken and Susser, of the original "Mango Gang" (the first proponents of what came to be called fusion cuisine), has opened OLA, another informal restaurant where drinks, tapas, and half portions rule.

As locally renowned as Van Aken is nationally, Jonathan Eismann maintains his Lincoln Road eatery, Pacific Time, a pan-Asian take on New World cuisine. Nemo, a trendy near-oceanside spot, puts a global spin on a seafood-oriented menu, and in South Miami, Two Chefs provides fine dining to the suburbs.

Miami's Latin American influence is a fact of dining life that no food-loving resident would want to change. You can sample Brazilian *rodizio* (barbecue) at Porcão, downtown; taste Nicaraguan at Guayacan, in Little Havana; try Venezuelan at Caballo Viejo, in Westchester; dip into Colombian at Patacón's several outlets; or peruse Chilean at Sabores Chilenos, in Sweetwater. Given the hundreds of Cuban cafés and bodegas around Miami, it's almost impossible not to experience Cuban cuisine. Head to the glamorous but inexpensive Versailles, on Calle Ocho, home of South Florida's strongest shot of Cuban coffee, or lunch at Havana Harry's, in Coral Gables, for some excellent and reasonably priced home cooking.

Miami's most unusual import, though, comes from Vietnam. Amid the bodegas of Little Havana, Hy-Vong, a frustratingly slow but deliciously rewarding hole-in-the-wall, serves up chicken in pastry with watercress sauce and dolphin sautéed with mangos and green peppercorns. In the Gables, Miss Saigon Bistro delivers authentic Vietnamese fare in more sophisticated surroundings, complemented by live orchids.

North of Downtown

American

¢–$$$ ✕ **Soyka.** This eponymously named eatery is the fourth in restaurateur Mark Soyka's (News and Van Dyke cafés) empire. Slightly more upscale than the others, it serves marinated skirt steak, calves' liver with caramelized onions, and sesame-seared salmon for dinner. Most proponents appreciate the day menu more, with omelets, burgers, salads, pizza, and sandwiches. Love the food or merely tolerate it, no one can deny this urban eatery is a great space, with lots of chrome and cement, good martinis, and comforting desserts. ☒ *5556 N.E. 4th Ct., Morningside, Miami* ☎ *305/759–3117* 🖃 *AE, D, DC, MC, V.*

Contemporary

$$$–$$$$ ✕ **Chef Allen's.** At the 25-foot-wide picture window you can watch
Fodor'sChoice Allen Susser, a member of the original, self-designated "Mango Gang,"
★ create contemporary American masterpieces from a global menu that changes nightly. After a salad of baby greens and warm mushrooms or a rock-shrimp hash with roasted corn, consider swordfish with conch-citrus couscous, macadamia nuts, and lemon, or grilled lamb chops with eggplant timbale and a three-nut salsa. It's hard to resist the dessert soufflé; order it when you order your appetizer to eliminate a mouthwatering wait at the end of your meal. ☒ *19088 N.E. 29th Ave., Aventura* ☎ *305/935–2900* 🖃 *AE, DC, MC, V.*

$$$–$$$$ ✕ **OLA.** Standing for Of Latin America, OLA is a serious reference to Latin Americaís foods and flavors. Returning to Miami (he was formerly at Yuca) after years in Manhattan, chef Douglas Rodriguez is in top form. His signature ceviches, inspired by his trips to South America, are featured at a ceviche bar with a handsome waterfall backdrop. Empanadas of all sorts, *arepitas* (cornmeal cakes) topped with caviar, plantain-crusted mahimahi, beef tenderloin *churrasco* with a chunky crab salad *chimichurri* (a sauce of oil, vinegar, and herbs), and crackling crispy Cuban pork with oregano-lime mojo are only a few of Rodriguez's innovative dishes. ☒ *5061 Biscayne Blvd., Morningside, Miami* ☎ *305/758–9195* 🖃 *AE, DC, MC, V* ⊗ *No lunch.*

$–$$$ ✕ **Hanna's Gourmet Diner.** Meals are served in a long, silvery structure riveted across the street from the Florida East Coast Railway tracks, although this amusingly eclectic, mainly French-influenced diner won't remind you a bit of the fare on Amtrak. Hannah's is the place to head when you have a hankering for sautéed calves' liver—or grilled snapper; rack of lamb; rare tuna; a big, juicy New York strip; or chicken *chasseur* (wine and mushroom sauce). Helpful hint: the fruit tart, one of Miami's best desserts, is in heavy demand on busy nights, so order your slice when you choose your main course. ☒ *13951 Biscayne Blvd., North Miami Beach* ☎ *305/947–2255* 🖃 *AE, MC, V.*

★ ¢–$$ ✕ **Biscayne Wine Merchants.** True to its name, this casually elegant establishment lines its walls with wine racks; untrue to it, it's no longer in its original spot on Biscayne Boulevard. That's only relevant if you get lost, though. The specials change often—not the location—but look for Brie in phyllo with kumquat jalapeño glaze, Portobello mushrooms in red wine sauce, steak with bordelaise sauce, classic bouillabaisse, and cassoulet with lamb shank, sausage, and duck. As for the wine, you're sure to quaff a good vintage—and at a more reasonable price than you're probably accustomed to. ☒ *738 N.E. 125th St., North Miami* ☎ *305/899–1997* 🖃 *AE, D, MC, V.*

¢–$ ✕ **Food Café.** Among the art galleries, furniture showrooms, and photography studios of the Design District, just north of Downtown,

Miami and Miami Beach's dining options are as diverse as their populations. Foodies will find lots of notable chefs, gorgeously appointed restaurants, and plenty of Miami-inspired culinary flair. The restaurants we list are the cream of the crop in each price category.

A note of caution: raw oysters have been identified as a problem for people with chronic illnesses of the liver, stomach, or blood, and for people with immune disorders. Since 1993 all Florida restaurants serving raw oysters are required to post a notice in plain view of all patrons warning of the risks associated with consuming them. A good rule of thumb is to order raw oysters only during months with names containing the letter "R."

Dining Times
Dining out is an essential part of Miami nightlife, and many restaurants don't even expect customers until late in the evening. Others cater to neighborhood folk and close just when places like South Beach start to heat up. No matter which type of restaurant you choose, you should double-check its status before you set out for the evening.

Dress
Jackets and ties are rarely required, even at the fancier restaurants. In their place a dress category called "casual chic" has emerged. It loosely translates to "black and expensive" (whether a T-shirt or a little dress). Shorts are appropriate in many places at lunchtime and at casual spots for dinner. Don't be embarrassed to call ahead and ask what to wear.

Even in warmer months it's a good idea to bring a light sweater or jacket. The hotter it gets outdoors, the more air-conditioners are worked.

Reservations
It's a fact of Miami life that a lot of people want to eat at the best restaurants, so at many of the hot spots reservations are imperative to avoid a long wait (and they're generally a good idea). We only mention when they're essential or not accepted. Try to reserve as far ahead as possible, at least a few days in advance. If you make a reservation from home, reconfirm as soon as you arrive, and if you change your mind or your plans, cancel your reservation—it's only courteous. Tables can be hard to come by if you want to dine between 8 and 10, and some places don't really get rolling until even later.

Tipping
When you get your check, you'll be reminded once again of Miami's international flavor: for the convenience of the city's many European and Latin American visitors, who are accustomed to the practice, a 15%–18% gratuity is included on most restaurant tabs. You can reduce or supplement that amount depending on your opinion of the service.

Wine, Beer & Spirits
The legal drinking age in Florida is 21; be prepared to show a photo ID if you're under 30. Some nightclubs where food is also served permit entrance to persons under 21. Each municipality has its own laws governing the sale of alcohol, but most prohibit sales before 1 PM on Sun-

day. It's illegal to walk with an open container of alcohol, and while driving, liquor must be unopened and in the trunk.

Prices The price of eating in Miami continues to rise. Typical entrée prices in the upper-echelon restaurants hover near the $30 mark, and even in more casual spots a $20 dish is typical. At lunch you can have a representative meal at a given restaurant, sometimes at half the cost of dinner. Another strategy is to order two or three appetizers and skip the entrée. Starters are usually more creative, and by ordering a selection you get a good idea of the chef's oeuvre. Some restaurants offer early-bird specials to diners who order before 6 PM, and in off-season discounts are ubiquitous—check local papers for coupons and special offerings. Dollar for dollar, the best values are still to be found in the city's ethnic restaurants. Sometimes you may have to sacrifice atmosphere, but the savings and the experience are usually worth it.

WHAT IT COSTS				
$$$$	**$$$**	**$$**	**$**	**¢**
AT DINNER	over $30	$20–$30	$15–$20	$10–$15	under $10

Prices are per person, for a main course at dinner.

Venezuelan native Lorena Garcia, owner and chef of this charming neighborhood restaurant, offers an eclectic menu that runs the gamut from *café con leche* to seared sashimi tuna. A popular place with locals, Food Café serves three meals a day that might include *cafecitos* (small, Cuban coffees), pastries, risottos, churrascos, and chicken paillard (flattened breast) as well as beer and wine. ⊠ *130 N.E. 40th St., Design District* ☎ *305/573–0444* ▭ *MC, V.*

Italian
¢–$ ✕ **Andiamo.** Miami did not used to be renowned for its pizza, but this storefront pizzeria connected to a car wash has residents raving about brick ovens and high-quality gourmet toppings like roasted eggplant, broccoli rabe, kalamata olives, and truffle oil. Order one of the specialty pizzas—like the divine Genovese, with potatoes, pancetta, caramelized onions, rosemary, and Gorgonzola cheese—or make up your own. Paninis and salads are pretty much the only alternatives here, but when the main item is so absorbing, nobody really minds. ⊠ *5600 Biscayne Blvd., Morningside, Miami* ☎ *305/762–5751* ▭ *AE, D, MC, V.*

Korean
¢–$$$ ✕ **Kyung Ju.** Serving the spiciest of Asian cuisines—Korean—this unstylish but wonderfully tasty spot has terrific tofu in a searing sauce of sesame, soy, ginger, and dried chilies; spicy seasoned beef and vegetable soup with ginger and garlic; and seasoned, boiled black codfish casserole. Mongolian barbecue is a grill-your-own house specialty, and everyone gets a free festival of vegetable garnishes: kimchi (pickled cabbage), spinach with sesame seeds, mustard greens, and pickled bean sprouts. The atmosphere

is limited to a TV, but the food is excitement enough. ⊠ *400 N.E. 163rd St., North Miami Beach* ☎ *305/947–3838* ▭ *AE, DC, MC, V.*

Mexican

¢–$$ ✕ **Paquito's.** A Mexican place to please both the gourmand and the glutton, Paquito's enlivens an otherwise massive, impersonal strip-mall hacienda with bright, colorful decor and ultrafriendly staff. All the standards—enchiladas, burritos, tortilla chips—are masterfully prepared. More ambitious cuisine includes tortilla soup with cheese *and* sour cream; a zesty mole *verde* with chicken, pork, or beef; turkey meatballs in *chipotle* (chile) sauce; and dolphinfish (mahimahi) with tomato, capers, and green olives. *Sopaipillas* (fried bits of dough with cinnamon and brown sugar) provide a sweet finish. ⊠ *16265 Biscayne Blvd., North Miami Beach* ☎ *305/947–5027* ▭ *AE, DC, MC, V.*

Peruvian

¢–$ ✕ **Las Delicias del Mar Peruano.** If ever there was a mom-and-pop place, this is it. Especially if Mom and Pop are Peruvian. This salute to the coastal cuisine of western Peru snaps with wonderfully fresh food and surprising flavors. Start with *papa a la huancaina,* a traditional boiled-potato appetizer whose creamy white cheese sauce is enlivened with chilies. Move from land to sea with shrimp creole, a creamy revelation with a pink sauce that's a silky delight, or try *cau cau de los mariscos,* a seafood stew that startles with its combination of mint and potato. The vast menu has plenty of landlubber eats, too. ⊠ *2937 Biscayne Blvd., Edgewater, Miami* ☎ *305/571–1888* ▭ *AE, MC, V.*

Steak

$$$–$$$$ ✕ **Shula's Steak House.** Prime rib, fish, and steaks displayed on a cart along with live, 3-pound lobsters are almost an afterthought to the *objets de sport* in this shrine for the NFL-obsessed. Dine in a manly wood-lined setting with a fireplace, surrounded by memorabilia of retired coach Don Shula's perfect 1972 season with the Miami Dolphins. Polish off the 48-ounce porterhouse steak and achieve a sort of immortality—your name on a plaque and an autographed picture of Shula to take home. Also for fans, there's Shula's Steak 2, a sports-celebrity hangout in the resort's hotel section, as well as a branch at the Alexander Hotel in Miami Beach. ⊠ *7601 N.W. 154th St., Miami Lakes* ☎ *305/820–8102* ▭ *AE, DC, MC, V.*

Mid-Beach & North

Colombian

¢–$ ✕ **Patacón.** If you haven't familiarized yourself with Colombian cuisine, let this minimally decorated minichain initiate you. And a delicious intro it can be, too—crisp *empanaditas,* stuffed with ground meat and potato, are elevated by green chili sauce. Don't fill up, though. Main-dish soups, especially the *sancocho,* a stew including hen, tripe, oxtail, and corn on the cob—basically, whatever the cook has on hand—comfort the hungry soul. And so does the signature dish, *patacón pisao,* a huge, flattened fried plantain on which you can spread such condiments as shrimp, chicken, shredded meat, beans, and guacamole. ⊠ *18230 Collins Ave., Sunny Isles* ☎ *305/931–3001* ▭ *AE, DC, MC, V.*

Contemporary

$–$$$ ✕ **Crystal Café.** As cozy as Grandma's dining room, this "new Continental" restaurant takes the classics and lightens 'em up. Beef Stroganoff and chicken *paprikash* are two of the updated stars; osso buco literally falls off the bone. More contemporary choices include chicken Kiev stuffed with goat cheese and topped with a tricolor salad, and pan-seared duck breast with raspberry sauce. Macedonian chef-proprietor Klime Kovaceski, winner of multiple Golden Spoon awards, takes pride in serving more food than you can possibly manage, including home-baked rhubarb pie. ⊠ *726 41st St., Mid-Beach, Miami Beach* ☎ *305/673–8266* ▭ *AE, D, DC, MC, V* ⊙ *Closed Mon. No lunch.*

Continental

$$$–$$$$ ✕ **The Forge.** Legendary for its opulence, this restaurant has been wowing patrons in its present form for over 30 years. The Forge is a steak house, but a steak house the likes of which you haven't seen before. Antiques, gilt-framed paintings, a chandelier from the Paris Opera House, and Tiffany stained-glass windows from New York's Trinity Church are the fitting background for some of Miami's best steaks. The tried-and-true menu also includes prime rib, lobster thermidor, chocolate soufflé, and Mediterranean side dishes. For its walk-in humidor alone, the over-the-top Forge is worth visiting. ⊠ *432 Arthur Godfrey Rd., Mid-Beach, Miami Beach* ☎ *305/538–8533* ⚇ *Reservations essential* ▭ *AE, DC, MC, V* ⊙ *No lunch.*

Delicatessens

¢–$ ✕ **Arnie and Richie's.** Take a deep whiff when you walk in, and you'll know what you're in for: onion rolls, smoked whitefish salad, half-sour pickles, herring in sour-cream sauce, chopped liver, corned beef, pastrami. Deli doesn't get more delicious than in this family-run operation that's casual to the extreme. Most customers are regulars and seat themselves at tables that have baskets of plastic knives and forks; if you request a menu, it's a clear sign you're a newcomer. Service can be brusque, but it sure is quick. ⊠ *525 41st St., Mid-Beach, Miami Beach* ☎ *305/531–7691* ▭ *AE, MC, V.*

Italian

$$$$ ✕ **Timo.** Located 5 mi north of South Beach, Timo (Italian for thyme)
Fodor'sChoice is worth the trip. The handsome bistro, co-owned by chef Tim Andri-
★ ola, has dark-wood walls, Chicago brick, and a dominating stone-encased wood-burning stove. Banquettes around the dining room's periphery and a large flower arrangement at its center add to the quietly elegant feel. Andriola has an affinity for robust Mediterranean flavors: sweetbreads with bacon, honey, and aged balsamic; artisanal pizzas; and homemade pastas. Wood-roasted chicken and Parmesan dumplings in a truffled broth are not to be missed. Every bite of every dish attests to the care given. ⊠ *17624 Collins Ave., Sunny Isles* ☎ *305/936–1008* ▭ *AE, DC, MC, V.*

$–$$$ ✕ **Oggi Café.** It opened simply as a storefront pasta factory, and local patrons hungry for Italian started to wander in. That's all it took to become a staple in the community, and the place has since been expanded twice. Along with handmade pastas, grilled beef, poultry, and fresh fish

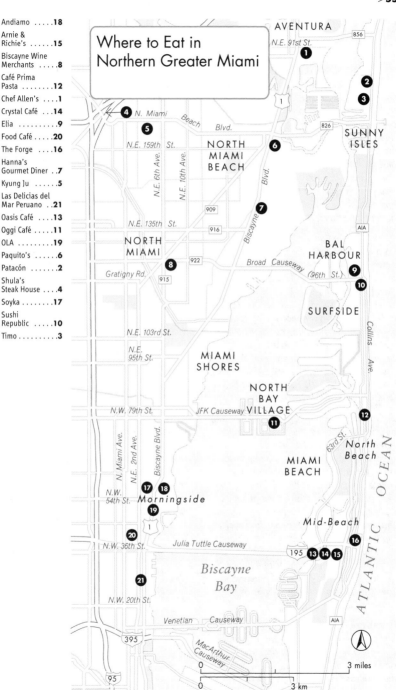

Where to Eat in
Northern Greater Miami

WITH CHILDREN?

MIAMI'S LEGACY OF ELDERLY RESIDENTS and more recent history of nightlife aficionados has left folks with children in a peculiar place. Many retired citizens resent noise or intrusions of any kind in their habitual places of culinary worship, and even the funkier restaurants simply don't want—or know what to do with— real kids as opposed to club kids. Hardly any restaurants have children's menus, let alone high chairs. What's a family to do?

1. Look for tile floors. Consider any restaurant that has a tile floor fair game, simply because it's easy to sweep up debris and wipe up spills. Eateries like **David's Cafe II** (✉ 1654 Meridian Ave., South Beach, Miami Beach ☎ 305/672–8707), a modern art deco dining room serving Cuban fare, may not look as if it's up to toddlers throwing handfuls of black beans. But the management is quick to assure you that any mess the babies make, the staff will clean. The superb food here is worth a little parental embarrassment.

2. Go Latin. This may be a generalization, but most Latinos, whether Cuban, South American, or Central American, love children—especially kids who like to eat. And even if the child is picky or cranky, the Latin culture demands that children be with their parents rather than be left at home. It's not unusual to see fairly young children sharing late-night black beans and suckling pig with their folks, even in the trendier spots such as **Larios on the Beach** (✉ 820 Ocean Dr., South Beach, Miami Beach ☎ 305/532–9577) Many Spanish and Latin restaurants also serve tapas or half portions that can be just right.

3. Ask about high chairs. If a restaurant has just one representative high chair, go. But reserve it for your offspring in advance. Even better are those eateries in the suburbs like **K. C. Kagney & Co.**

(✉ 11230 S.W. 137th Ave., Kendall, Miami ☎ 305/386–1555), a wacky diner with a fun menu and cute decor. Not only do you get a choice between high chairs and booster seats, the staff isn't at all mystified by little people.

4. Weather permitting, eat outside. You may be able to enjoy a more leisurely meal while children can play (a bit) without bothering other diners. And if your child should choose that moment to throw a temper tantrum, it's probably better in the open air. Sidewalk cafés in Coconut Grove, South Miami, and South Beach are ideal for kid-style munchies, and those on South Beach's Lincoln Road or Ocean Drive should provide plenty of distractions for little ones—in the forms of human foot traffic, pedigreed canines, and the occasional parrot or iguana.

5. Peer groups tell the story. If a restaurant has already seated someone else's child, it's safe to assume that management considers a child an appropriate member of a dining party. And don't go by the old adage that two's company, three's a crowd. Rather, the more the merrier. In other words, children can keep each other company. At best, if another child is misbehaving, you can revel in your own wee one's table manners. At worst, you can apply peer pressure: "Look how nicely that child is behaving, eating, sitting still."

6. Tip big. 'Nuff said.

— Jen Karetnick

dishes also rate raves. Breads, desserts, and salad dressings are all made on the premises, too, but don't worry if you can't get a seat—Oggi still supplies many of the finer area restaurants with its products, so chances are you'll run across them somewhere else. ☒ *1740 79th St. Causeway, North Bay Village* ☎ *305/866–1238* ☝ *Reservations essential* ☰ *AE, D, MC, V* ☺ *No lunch weekends.*

★ ¢–$$$ ✕ **Café Prima Pasta.** One of Miami's many signatures is this exemplary Argentine-Italian spot, which rules the emerging North Beach neighborhood. Service can be erratic, but you forget it all on delivery of fresh-made bread with a bowl of spiced olive oil. Tender carpaccio and plentiful antipasti are a delight to share, but the real treat here is the hand-rolled pasta, which can range from crab-stuffed ravioli to simple fettuccine with seafood. If overexposed tiramisu hasn't made an enemy of you yet, try this legendary one in order to add espresso notes to your unavoidable garlic breath. ☒ *414 71st St., North Beach, Miami Beach* ☎ *305/867–0106* ☰ *MC, V.*

Japanese

¢–$$ ✕ **Sushi Republic.** A long and narrow storefront with sponge-painted walls, this eatery prides itself on welcoming customers, so don't be surprised when the sushi chefs say, "Hi!" when you walk in. Nor should you expect anything but the freshest sashimi, which is elegantly presented and perfectly succulent. As far as cooked fare goes, the Republic is democratic—everything is even and consistent. *Shumai,* soft shrimp dumplings with *ponzu* (soy, rice vinegar, sake, seaweed, and dried bonito flakes) dipping sauce; whole fried soft-shell crab; and salmon teriyaki are particularly noteworthy. ☒ *9583 Harding Ave., Surfside* ☎ *305/867–8036* ☰ *AE, D, DC, MC, V* ☺ *Closed Mon. No lunch Sun.*

Mediterranean

★ $$$ ✕ **Elia.** A proponent of "small plates," Elia features "new Mediterranean" cuisine that uses ingredients from over 20 Mediterranean countries. Gutsy cooking and bold flavors maintain the authenticity of regional dishes with a modern twist. Though Elia is the perfect place to repair after a shop-till-you-drop adventure at Bal Harbour's high-end boutiques, the Tunisian lamb spareribs are worth a trip even if you are not in the neighborhood. ☒ *9700 Collins Ave., Bal Harbour* ☎ *305/ 866–2727* ☰ *AE, D, DC, MC, V.*

¢–$$ ✕ **Oasis Café.** No relation to the Oasis in South Beach, this coolly tiled Mediterranean restaurant with breezy decor puts an emphasis on health. The chefs stuff grape leaves, not arteries, making sure you don't keel over at the table. Natural-food enthusiasts feel right at home, thanks to such delicacies as eggplant salads, hummus, grilled sesame tofu, and sautéed garlic spinach for starters, and for entrées pan-seared turkey chop, roasted vegetable lasagna, grilled fresh fish on focaccia, or penne with turkey, tomato, saffron, and pine nuts. The homemade rum cake is a superb way to drink dessert. ☒ *976 41st St., Mid-Beach, Miami Beach* ☎ *305/674–7676* ☰ *AE, D, DC, MC, V.*

South Beach

American

$$–$$$ ✕ **Joe Allen.** Crave a good martini along with a terrific burger? Locals head to this hidden hangout in an exploding neighborhood of condos, town houses, and stores. The eclectic crowd includes kids and grandparents, and the menu has everything from pizzas to calves' liver to steaks. Start with an innovative salad, such as arugula with pear, prosciutto, and a Gorgonzola dressing, or roast-beef salad on greens with Parmesan. Home-style desserts include banana cream pie and ice-cream and cookie sandwiches. Comfortable and homey, this is the perfect place to go when you don't feel like going to a restaurant. ⊠ *1787 Purdy Ave., South Beach* ☎ *305/531–7007* ⊟ *MC, V.*

American/Casual

$–$$ ✕ **11th Street Diner.** Since serving its first plate of meat loaf in 1992, this diner has become a low-price, unpretentious hangout for locals. The best time to visit is weekend mornings, when the stragglers from the night before and early birds with their morning papers converge for conversation. At this busy, bustling eatery in a 1948 deco-style dining car, you can grab a corner booth and order a cherry cola, a blue plate special, or a milk shake and pretend you've traveled back in time. ⊠ *1055 Washington Ave., South Beach* ☎ *305/534–6373* ⊟ *AE, DC, MC, V.*

¢–$$ ✕ **Big Pink.** The decor in this innovative diner may remind you of a roller-
Fodor'sChoice skating rink—everything is pink Lucite, stainless steel, and campy (think
★ sports lockers as decorative touches). And the menu is a virtual book, complete with table of contents. But the food is solidly all-American, with dozens of tasty sandwiches, pizzas, turkey or beef burgers, and side dishes, each and every one composed with a gourmet flair. Customers comprise club kids and real kids, who alternate, depending on the time of day—Big Pink makes a great spot for brunch—but both like to color with the complimentary crayons. ⊠ *157 Collins Ave., South Beach* ☎ *305/532–4700* ⊟ *AE, MC, V.*

Cafés

¢–$$$ ✕ **News Café.** An Ocean Drive landmark, this 24-hour café attracts a crowd with snacks, light meals, drinks, and the people parade on the sidewalk out front. Most prefer sitting outside, where they can feel the salt breeze and gawk at the human scenery. Offering a little of this and a little of that—bagels, pâtés, chocolate fondue, sandwiches, and a terrific wine list—this joint has something for everyone. Although service can be indifferent to the point of laissez-faire, the café remains a scene. ⊠ *800 Ocean Dr., South Beach* ☎ *305/538–6397* ⚛ *Reservations not accepted* ⊟ *AE, DC, MC, V.*

¢–$$ ✕ **Van Dyke Café.** Just as its parent, News Café, draws the fashion crowd, this offshoot attracts the artsy crowd. Indeed, this place seems even livelier than its Ocean Drive counterpart, with pedestrians passing by on the Lincoln Road Mall and live jazz playing upstairs every evening—or, more to the point, every early morning. The kitchen serves dishes from mammoth omelets with home fries to soups and grilled dolphinfish sandwiches to basil-grilled lamb and pasta dishes, though it's

A FLASH IN THE PAN?

O NE OF MIAMI'S VIRTUES is also one of its greatest vices: the inability to remain static. While constant progress makes day-to-day life exciting for residents, this quick-change artist of a town can be frustrating for visitors who never know if a recommended restaurant will still be around or if a new place will be up and running smoothly when they get here. Indeed, many anticipated restaurants may still be in the planning stages or may have just opened but haven't stood the test of tourist season. However, several are worth mentioning and even exploring.

"It's getting happy in here" is one of Emeril Lagasse's stock phrases, and now he has brought his brand of happy to Miami Beach. You can expect a different gumbo each day and other New Orleans specialties at **Emeril's** (✉ 1601 Collins Ave., in the Loews Miami Beach, South Beach, Miami Beach ☎ 305/695–4550) This is Lagasse's ninth restaurant, so it stands to reason he has the winning formula down. With his name and personality sure to be a big draw, the restaurant is poised for success.

The much anticipated **Mundo** (✉ Village of Merrick Park, 320 San Lorenzo Ave., Coral Gables ☎ 305/442–6787) is Norman Van Aken's new New World café. Tapas and "small plates" dominate the menu, and a small market offering seasonal tropical fruits and vegetables shows off the local bounty. Set in a luxury mall in the center of Coral Gables, Mundo draws Van Aken's devoted fans as well as shoppers.

Ms. Yip's (✉ 1661 Meridian Ave., South Beach, Miami Beach ☎ 305/534–5488) is an interesting little gem. The restaurant specializes in authentic Cantonese food prepared by Hong Kong chefs the likes of

which have not been seen in Miami yet as well as dim sum. Ms. Yip's also houses a small market offering up to 40 homemade sauces, oils, and spices and ingredients packaged together for a particular dish.

Whether any of these restaurants will fulfill the promise of the advance press or last the season remains to be seen. But as always in Miami, the capricious culinary scene is, at the very least, an adventure.

best to stick to basics. There's an enticing list of drinks like Bellinis and Kir Royales. ⊠ *846 Lincoln Rd., South Beach* ☎ *305/534–3600* ⊟ *AE, DC, MC, V.*

Contemporary

$$$–$$$$ ✕ **Blue Door at the Delano.** In a hotel where style reigns supreme, this
Fodor'sChoice high-profile restaurant provides both glamour and tantalizing cuisine.
★ Acclaimed consulting chef Claude Troisgros combines the flavors of classic French cuisine with South American influences to create a seasonal menu that might include the Big Ravioli, filled with crab-and-scallop mousseline, or osso buco in Thai curry sauce with caramelized pineapple and bananas. Equally pleasing is dining with the crème de la crème of Miami (and New York and Paris) society. Don't recognize the apparent bigwig next to you? Just eavesdrop on his cell phone conversation, and you'll be filled in pronto. ⊠ *1685 Collins Ave., South Beach* ☎ *305/674–6400* ⌧ *Reservations essential* ⊟ *AE, D, DC, MC, V.*

$$$–$$$$ ✕ **Nemo.** The SoFi (South of Fifth Street) neighborhood may have emerged
Fodor'sChoice as a South Beach hot spot, but Nemo's location is not why this casually
★ comfortable restaurant receives raves. It's the menu, which often changes but always delivers, blending Caribbean, Asian, Mediterranean, and Middle Eastern influences and providing an explosion of cultures in each bite. Popular appetizers include garlic-cured salmon rolls with Tabiko caviar and wasabi mayo, and crispy prawns with spicy salsa *cruda.* Main courses might include wok-charred salmon or grilled Indian-spice pork chop. Hedy Goldsmith's funky pastries are exquisitely sinful. Bright colors and copper fixtures highlight the tree-shaded courtyard. ⊠ *100 Collins Ave., South Beach* ☎ *305/532–4550* ⊟ *AE, MC, V.*

★ **$$$–$$$$** ✕ **Talula.** Husband and wife Frank Randazzo and Andrea Curto have each collected numerous awards and fabulous press. At Talula they are cooking together for the first time while keeping their own styles: she, the cuisine she developed at Wish, joining Asian and tropical influences; he, from the Gaucho Room, grills with a Latin influence. Together they call their style "American creative." Barbecued quail with cascabel chili, steamed mussels in a saffron broth, grouper with lime and chili, and a tender and moist barbecued pork tenderloin stand out. The key lime pie alone is worth a visit. ⊠ *210 23rd St., South Beach* ☎ *305/672–0778* ⊟ *AE, MC, V.*

$$$–$$$$ ✕ **1220 at the Tides.** Ocean views, check. The model of the moment, double check. It's undeniably beautiful, done almost entirely in white—linens, candles, and original terrazzo floor—and seems out of place on increasingly tacky Ocean Drive. Designed by executive chef Roger Ruch, the progressive American fare is innovative without being overwhelming. Dishes such as the Island Princess, a conch tempura appetizer, and the citrus-glazed sea bass with plantain mash and banana catsup entrée acknowledge tropical influences, while more classic dishes such as the wood-roasted tenderloin of beef with truffle-honey demi-glace prove why this eatery is considered the last bastion of civilization on the Drive. ⊠ *The Tides hotel, 1220 Ocean Dr., South Beach* ☎ *305/604–5130* ⊟ *AE, D, MC, V.*

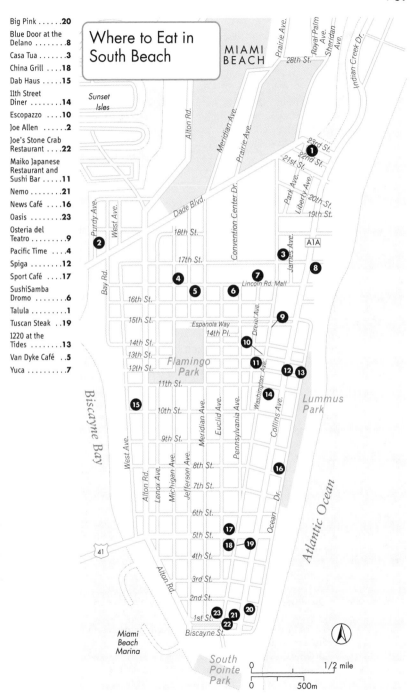

Big Pink **20**

Blue Door at the
Delano **8**

Casa Tua **3**

China Grill **18**

Dab Haus **15**

11th Street
Diner **14**

Escopazzo **10**

Joe Allen **2**

Joe's Stone Crab
Restaurant **22**

Maiko Japanese
Restaurant and
Sushi Bar **11**

Nemo **21**

News Café **16**

Oasis **23**

Osteria del
Teatro **9**

Pacific Time **4**

Spiga **12**

Sport Café **17**

SushiSamba
Dromo **6**

Talula **1**

Tuscan Steak . .**19**

1220 at the
Tides **13**

Van Dyke Café . .**5**

Yuca **7**

Where to Eat in South Beach

German

¢–$$ ✕ **Dab Haus.** Picture the inside of a U-boat, and you've got the idea: black walls, scarred-wood furniture, a haze of cigarette smoke that never dissipates, and art that can only be described as weird. But the food is the star at this German pub, almost totally removed from the South Beach hubbub. All the favorites are here, including a wonderfully spicy goulash, sauerbraten, schnitzels, homemade spaetzle, and sausages such as bratwurst and currywurst. Big draft beers—the servers recommend the thirst-quenching, cloudy *hefe weizen*—wash it all down; even the Nutella (chocolate and hazelnut spread) crepes that are hard to resist. ⊠ *1040 Alton Rd., South Beach* ☎ *305/534–9557* ⊟ *AE, D, DC, MC, V.*

Italian

★ $$$–$$$$ ✕ **Casa Tua.** To accommodate the demanding clientele of this exclusive boutique hotel as well as anyone willing to wait two weeks for a reservation, Casa Tua provides a charming restaurant. You can dine inside or alfresco under the trees. Either way, the idea is to make you feel as if you were at home in a Mediterranean beach house. The food is Italian—sophisticated yet simple dishes, such as truffle risotto and veal picatta, made with impeccable ingredients. The service is seamless and relaxed. And the elegant experience is a peaceful respite from Miami Beach's dizzing energy. ⊠ *1700 James Ave., South Beach,* ☎ *305/673–1010* ⚐ *Reservations essential* ⊟ *AE, MC, V.*

$$–$$$$ ✕ **Escopazzo.** A romantic storefront takes you away, like Calgon, from the din of bustling Washington Avenue. The northern Italian menu offers some of the area's best—and most expensive—Italian food. But innovative treatments of standard ingredients make it worth the outlay of cash. Sea bass gets "scales" of crusty potato, goat cheese and arugula are mixed into a risotto, and various soufflés feature vegetables and mixed seafood. Service can be slow as a speedboat in a manatee zone; pass the time by taking a tour of the 1,000-bottle wine cellar. ⊠ *1311 Washington Ave., South Beach* ☎ *305/674–9450* ⊟ *AE, DC, MC, V* ⊘ *No lunch.*

★ $$–$$$$ ✕ **Tuscan Steak.** Dark wood, mirrors, and green upholstery define this chic, masculine place, where big platters of meats and fish are served family style, assuming yours is a royal family. Tuscan can be busy as a subway stop, and still the staff is gracious and giving. The chefs take their cues from the Tuscan countryside, where pasta is rich with truffles and main plates are simply but deliciously grilled. Sip red wine with a house specialty: three-mushroom risotto with white truffle oil, gnocchi with Gorgonzola cream, Florentine T-bone with roasted garlic puree, or filet mignon with a Gorgonzola crust in a red wine sauce. Portions are enormous. Bring your friends and share, share, share. ⊠ *431 Washington Ave., South Beach* ☎ *305/534–2233* ⊟ *AE, DC, MC, V.*

★ $–$$$$ ✕ **Osteria del Teatro.** Thanks to word of mouth, this northern Italian restaurant is constantly full. Orchids grace the tables in the intimate gray-on-gray room with a low, laced-canvas ceiling, deco lamps, and the most refined clink and clatter along Washington Avenue. Regulars know not to order off the printed menu, however. A tremendous variety of daily specials offers the best options here. A representative appetizer is poached asparagus served over polenta triangles with a Gorgonzola sauce. Stuffed pastas, including spinach crepes overflowing with ricotta, can seem heavy but taste light; fish dishes yield a rosemary-marinated tuna or salmon in a pink peppercorn–citrus sauce. ⊠ *1443 Washington Ave., South Beach* ☎ *305/538–7850* ⚜ *Reservations essential* ▭ *AE, DC, MC, V* ⊗ *Closed Sun. No lunch.*

$–$$ ✕ **Spiga.** When you need a break from Miami's abundant exotic fare, savor the modestly priced Italian standards served with flair in this small, pretty place. Homemade is the hallmark here, where pastas and breads are fresh daily. Carpaccio *di salmone* (thinly sliced salmon with mixed greens) is a typical appetizer, and the *zuppa di pesce* (fish stew) is unparalleled. Entrées include ravioli *di vitello ai funghi shiitaki*, homemade ravioli stuffed with veal and sautéed with shiitake mushrooms. The cozy restaurant has become a neighborhood favorite, and customers sometimes bring in CDs for personalized enjoyment. ⊠ *1228 Collins Ave., South Beach* ☎ *305/534–0079* ▭ *AE, D, DC, MC, V.*

¢–$$ ✕ **Sport Café.** When World Cup time comes around, there's no question this place is run by true Italians, and you can't get a seat or hear anything much but go-o-o-o-o-o-o-al. The supercasual bistro is dominated by a giant TV inside and has many tables outside that afford a cityscape view. Pastas here are wonderfully good and even more wonderfully inexpensive. Lighter appetites appreciate the spry salad of white beans, tuna, and red onion; the light vegetable-puree soups; and bubbling thin-crust pizza. ⊠ *538 Washington Ave., South Beach* ☎ *305/674–9700* ▭ *MC, V.*

Japanese

$–$$$$ ✕ **SushiSamba Dromo.** This sibling to the New York City SushiSamba makes an eclectic pairing of Japanese cuisine with Brazilian. The results are fabulous if a bit mystifying: seared yellowfin tuna marinated in sugarcane juice, chicken teriyaki with Peruvian potato puree, shrimp and Latino vegetable tempura, and caramel rice pudding served in green tea-leaf cups. Loaded with customers, SushiSamba has a vibe that hurts the ears but warms the trendy heart. ⊠ *600 Lincoln Rd., South Beach* ☎ *305/673–5337* ⚜ *Reservations essential* ▭ *AE, MC, V.*

¢–$$ ✕ **Maiko Japanese Restaurant and Sushi Bar.** Ever-popular, ever-ready . . . it's not a battery, just a dependable place to order sushi standards, plus an amorous-sounding creation called the kissing roll—crab, avocado, and cucumber coated with the tiny flying-fish eggs. Models hang around for the steamed dumplings with *ponzu* sauce, while club kids line their bellies with flavorful teriyaki, sautéed eel, and soba noodle soups before drinking the night away. They also get a good jump on the evening with the sake, which Maiko presents in warm abundance. ⊠ *1255 Washington Ave., South Beach* ☎ *305/531–6369* ▭ *AE, DC, MC, V.*

Latin

$$$–$$$$ ✕ **Yuca.** Yuca, the potatolike staple of Cuban kitchens, also stands for the kind of Young Urban Cuban-American clientele the top-flight, indoor-outdoor eatery courts. The Nuevo Latino food rises to high standards: traditional corn tamales filled with conch and a spicy jalapeño-and-creole-cheese pesto; the namesake yuca stuffed with Mamacita's *picadillo* (spiced ground meat) and dressed in wild mushrooms on a bed of sautéed spinach; and plantain-coated dolphinfish with a tamarind tartar sauce. Desserts include classic Cuban rice pudding in an almond basket and coconut pudding in its shell. ☒ *501 Lincoln Rd., South Beach* ☎ *305/532–9822* ⊟ *AE, DC, MC, V.*

Mediterranean

$$$–$$$$ ✕ **Oasis.** Middle East via Miami Beach makes for an interesting combination. Part restaurant, part lounge, this restaurant has natural woods, Moroccan chairs, and lamplight that provides a comfortable glow. If the DJ is more lounge than you'd like, simply go for an early dinner. The menu offers all the expected standards: hummus, baba ghanoush, grape leaves, falafel, and skewers of beef, lamb, chicken, and shrimp, all carefully prepared and attractively served. For those who are a little less adventurous, pasta, fish, and filet mignon round out the menu. ☒ *840 1st St., South Beach* ☎ *305/673–2252* ⊟ *AE, MC, V.*

Pan-Asian

$$–$$$$ ✕ **Pacific Time.** Packed nearly every night, chef-proprietor Jonathan Eismann's superb eatery has a high blue ceiling, banquettes, plank floors, and an open kitchen. The brilliant American-Asian cuisine includes such entrées as cedar-roasted salmon, rosemary-roasted chicken, and dry-aged Colorado beef grilled with shiitake mushrooms. The cuttlefish appetizer and the Florida pompano entrée are masterpieces. Desserts include a fresh pear-pecan spring roll. ☒ *915 Lincoln Rd., South Beach* ☎ *305/534–5979* ⌔ *Reservations essential* ⊟ *AE, DC, MC, V.*

FodorsChoice

★

$–$$$$ ✕ **China Grill.** This crowded, noisy, ever-vaunted celebrity haunt turns out not Chinese food but rather "world cuisine," and in large portions meant for sharing. Crispy duck with scallion pancakes and caramelized black-vinegar sauce is a nice surprise, as is pork and beans with green apple and balsamic *mojo* (a garlicky Cuban marinade). Mechanical service delivers the acceptable broccoli rabe dumpling starter, the wild mushroom pasta entrée, or the flash-fried crispy spinach that shatters like a good martini glass thrown into a fireplace. Unless you're a frequent celebrity diner, don't expect your drinks to arrive before your food. ☒ *404 Washington Ave., South Beach* ☎ *305/534–2211* ⌔ *Reservations essential* ⊟ *AE, DC, MC, V* ⊘ *No lunch Sat.*

Seafood

¢–$$$$ ✕ **Joe's Stone Crab Restaurant.** This Miami phenomenon stubbornly refuses reservations despite phenomenal crowds. Prepare to wait up to an hour just to sign up for a table and another *three* hours to get one. The centerpiece of the ample à la carte menu is, of course, stone crab, with a piquant mustard sauce. Popular side orders include creamed garlic spinach, french-fried onions, fried green tomatoes, and hash browns. Desserts range from a famous key lime pie to apple pie with crumb-pecan topping. If you can't stand loitering hungrily while self-important patrons try to grease the maître d's palm, come for lunch, or get takeout and picnic on the beach. ☒ *11 Washington Ave., South Beach* ☎ *305/673–0365, 305/673–4611 for takeout, 800/780–2722 for overnight shipping* ⌔ *Reservations not accepted* ⊟ *AE, D, DC, MC, V* ⊘ *Closed May–Oct. 15. No lunch Sun. and Mon.*

Downtown Miami

American/Casual

¢–$ ✕ **Tobacco Road.** If you like your food the way you like your blues—gritty, honest, and unassuming—then this octogenarian joint will earn your respect. A musician wailing the blues also cooks jambalaya on-stage, although entertainment varies. And no one's weeping about the food. The Road-burger is a popular choice, as are the chili worthy of a fire hose and appetizers such as nachos and chicken wings. Don't let the rough-edged exterior deter you from finer dining. On Tuesday during the season, Tobacco Road offers a Maine lobster special, and fine single-malt Scotches are stocked behind the bar. ⊠ *626 S. Miami Ave., Downtown* ☎ *305/374–1198* ⊟ *AE, D, DC, MC, V.*

Chinese

$–$$ ✕ **Tony Chan's Water Club.** On the outstanding menu of more than 200 appetizers and entrées are minced quail tossed with bamboo shoots and mushrooms wrapped in lettuce leaves. Indulge in a seafood spectacular of shrimp, conch, scallops, fish cakes, and crabmeat tossed with broccoli in a bird's nest, or go for pork chops sprinkled with green pepper in a black bean–garlic sauce. A lighter favorite is steamed sea bass with ginger and garlic. Don't let the delicate flavors fool you—this restaurant is not just for the nosher but for the power-hungry power luncher who also wants a bay view. ⊠ *Doubletree Grand Hotel, 1717 N. Bayshore Dr., Downtown* ☎ *305/374–8888* ⊟ *AE, D, DC, MC, V* ⊘ *No lunch weekends.*

Contemporary

$$–$$$$ ✕ **Azul.** Azul has sumptuously conquered the devil in the details, from
Fodor'sChoice   chef Michelle Bernstein's exotically rendered French–Caribbean cui-
★   sine to the thoughtful service staff who graciously anticipate your broader dining needs. Does your sleeveless blouse leave you too cold to properly appreciate the poached eggs with lobster-knuckle hollandaise? Ask for one of the house pashminas, available in a variety of fashionable colors. Forgot your reading glasses and can't decipher the hanger steak with foie-gras sauce? Request a pair from the host. Want to see how the other half lives? Descend the interior staircase to Cafe Sambal, the all-day casual restaurant downstairs. ⊠ *Mandarin Oriental Hotel, 500 Brickell Key Dr., Brickell Key* ☎ *305/913–8288* ⌕ *Reservations essential* ⊟ *AE, MC, V* ⊘ *Closed Sun. No lunch Sat.*

$$–$$$ ✕ **Indigo.** The entire lobby here is one big open-wall eatery, where you can watch vacationers get ready to depart for the cruise ships—unless you're one of them—and sup on the globally influenced cuisine. The menu's a trifle too cutesy for serious gourmets, with categories like "salappzs and ladles" and "dare 2 share." Stone crab *croquetas* are a notable starter, and Moroccan *tagine* (stew) can be shared as an entrée. A great wine list and moderately priced brunches, lunch buffets, and happy-hour spreads suit the suits who work in nearby downtown. ⊠ *Hotel Inter-Continental, 100 Chopin Plaza, Downtown* ☎ *305/854–9550* ⊟ *AE, D, DC, MC, V.*

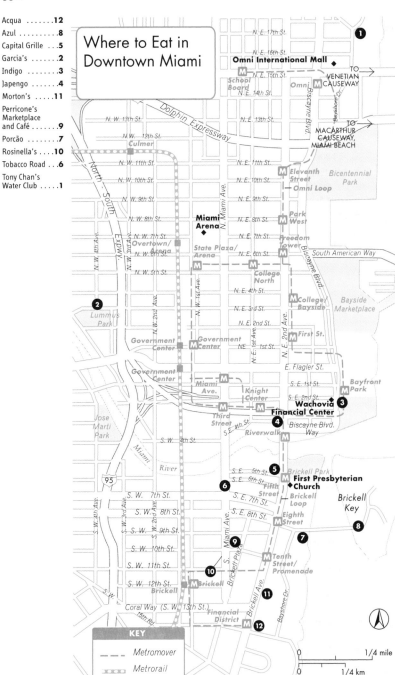

Where to Eat in Downtown Miami

KEY

--- Metromover

∎∎∎ Metrorail

0   1/4 mile

0   1/4 km

Italian

$$$–$$$$ ✕ **Acqua.** Off the main lobby on the seventh floor of the new Four Seasons Hotel, Acqua is, as expected from any Four Seasons property, elegant to a fault. Overlooking the pool terrace, the restaurant is divided in three distinct areas. The terrace, a more casual space, is sheltered by oversize umbrellas. The Galleria, at the entrance, is perfect for a drink or a snack, and the main restaurant area is designated for serious dining. The food is northern Italian, delicate, refined, and with an occasional touch of tropical ingredients. The wine list is impressive, and the risottos are spectacular. ✉ *Four Seasons Hotel, 1435 Brickell Ave., Downtown* ☎ *305/358–3535* ▱ *AE, MC, V.*

¢–$$ ✕ **Rosinella's.** Owner Tonino Doino and his mother, Rosinella, run this stylish pasta house with true Italian touches. A luscious appetizer of veal with creamy sauce of pureed tuna precedes beautiful grilled fish with greens and pastas with zesty sauces (especially the red-pepper-infused *arrabbiata*). Pureed vegetable soups are good and light, and thin-crust pizzas are delicious. If Rosinella has made gnocchi that day, ask for it with Gorgonzola sauce. A sister restaurant on Lincoln Road offers the same tasty fare in a busier atmosphere. ✉ *1040 S. Miami Ave., Downtown* ☎ *305/372–5756* ▱ *AE, DC, MC, V.*

¢–$ ✕ **Perricone's Marketplace and Café.** Brickell Avenue south of the Miami River is burgeoning with Italian restaurants, and this lunch place for local bigwigs is the biggest and most popular among them. It's housed partially outdoors and partially indoors in a 120-year-old Vermont barn. Recipes were handed down from grandmother to mother to daughter, and the cooking is simple and good. Buy your wine from the on-premises deli, and enjoy it (for a small corking fee) with homemade minestrone; a generous antipasto; linguine with a sauté of jumbo shrimp, fresh asparagus, and chopped tomatoes; or gnocchi with four cheeses. The homemade tiramisu and fruit tart are top-notch. ✉ *Brickell Village, 15 S.E. 10th St., Downtown* ☎ *305/374–9449* ▱ *AE, MC, V* ☉ *Closed Sun. No lunch Sat.*

Pan-Asian

$$$ ✕ **Japengo.** Hotel restaurants sure aren't the disappointments they used to be. This one, named for Marco Polo's handle for Japan, has an outstanding photographic mural of Hong Kong and a stunning quantity of hand-carved Lalique glass—not to mention top-rate sushi (if a rather traditional assortment). Pan-Asian dishes, including warm charsu duck on mixed baby greens with vegetable root chips and fresh plums, take Hawaii, China, Thailand, and even South America into account. Too exotic for your typical business traveler tastes? Don't worry—the place also supplies a grilled hamburger on focaccia. ✉ *Hyatt Regency, 400 S.E. 2nd Ave., Downtown* ☎ *305/679–3055* ▱ *AE, MC, V.*

Seafood

$–$$$ ✕ **Garcia's.** Pull up your rowboat for outdoor waterfront dining at this tiny seafood joint on the Miami River. The menu is simple and limited, but the fish sure is fresh. Grilled dolphinfish—on a sandwich or with various Cuban-style side dishes—is juicy and well-seasoned. Grouper chowder, the classic Cuban fish soup, excels here, and fried calamari benefits from a peppy cocktail sauce. The conch fritters are truly packed with conch, or you can enjoy fish, shrimp, and chicken on kabobs, the primary entrée option. This is a great place to bring children, and there's also a fish market inside. ⊠ *398 N.W. North River Dr., Downtown* ☎ *305/375–0765* ⊟ *MC, V.*

Steak

$$$$ ✕ **Porcão.** How now, Porcão—what's not to love? Not only does this Brazilian churrascaria serve outstanding *rodizio,* grilled meats sliced off skewers right at the table, a creative and enormous salad bar is included in the fixed $34 price. Pair pickled quail eggs with marinated chicken hearts, or veer toward the less exotic with thin-sliced prosciutto and bacon-wrapped chicken thighs. Satisfy the inner carnivore with lamb, filet mignon, and sirloin and the obvious sweet tooth with à la carte desserts such as flan in caramel sauce. Just don't weigh yourself afterward. ⊠ *801 S. Bayshore Dr., Downtown* ☎ *305/373–2777* ⊟ *AE, DC, MC, V.*

$$$–$$$$ ✕ **Morton's.** Morton's has the atmosphere of a private club, complete with dark mahogany paneling, spacious leather booths, subdued lighting, and crisp white tablecloths. Not bad for a chain (there's another in North Miami Beach). The open kitchen shows you how a real steak restaurant prepares double filet mignon, New York strip sirloin, and broiled Block Island swordfish steak. The unfussiest item here is also the best bargain—an umpteen-ounce sirloin burger with a side of hash browns, only available at lunch. ⊠ *1200 Brickell Ave., Downtown* ☎ *305/400–9990* ⊟ *AE, MC, V.*

★ **$$$** ✕ **Capital Grille.** Downtown's most elegant restaurant is a palace of protein. That is, the menu is traditional and oriented to beef, and the dining room handsome and filled mostly with men on a power lunch. Porterhouse, steak *au poivre,* various sirloins, and fillets, many of which hang in a locker in the center of the dining room to age, head the list. All is à la carte, even the baked potato. The cheesecake is tops. Still, service can be so relentlessly formal it's ridiculous—the waiters will walk miles to ensure that women get their menus first. ⊠ *444 Brickell Ave., Downtown* ☎ *305/374–4500* ⊟ *AE, D, DC, MC, V.*

Little Havana

Cuban

$–$$ ✕ **Versailles.** One of Miami's first Cuban restaurants and still its most ornate budget restaurant, Versailles dishes out heaping platters of traditional Cuban food amid mirrors, candelabras, and white tablecloths. The fun of Versailles is people-watching, though—that and the waitresses who call you *mi amor.* The coffee counter serves up the city's strongest cafecito, but if you can't handle it, ask for a *cortadito,* the same strong demitasse coffee but with steamed milk to soften the blow, and unless you like coffee syrup (Cuba equals sugar, after all), ask for it *sin azúcar* and add sugar to taste. ⊠ *3555 S.W. 8th St., between S.W. 35th and S. W. 36th Aves., Little Havana* ☎ *305/444–0240* ⊟ *AE, D, DC, MC, V.*

Italian

¢–$ ✕ **Tutto Pasta.** Some of the city's best Italian for the money comes out of this kitchen. Entrées rarely top $10, but they always please, especially

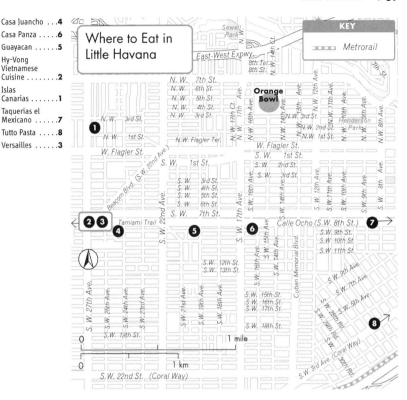

Where to Eat in
Little Havana

homemade pastas with red sauces. Start with delicious bruschetta, moz-
zarella with pignoli, prosciutto and sun-dried tomatoes, or a homemade
soup. Spaghetti with marinara, the cheapest entrée, might well be the
best because the sauce is that good. Pleasant service matches the casual
atmosphere. Fettuccine with chicken, mushrooms, and sun-dried tomatoes; homemade ravioli with spinach and ricotta; and a stew of snapper, seafood, and tomato sauce excel, as do house-baked desserts.
✉ *1751 S.W. 3rd Ave. at S.W. 18th Rd., Little Havana* ☎ *305/857–0709*
🖃 *MC, V.*

Latin

★ ¢–$$$ ✕ **Guayacan.** Offering counter service and a comfortable if simple din-
ing room, this family-run place serves all the traditional Nicaraguan foods
to a lot of traditional Nicaraguans: the signature grilled churrasco steak,
a sticky sweet *tres leches* (a dessert made with three different types of
milk), and rich, mellow Victoria beer. A simple half-chicken or a bone-
less strip steak served with three lusty, spicy sauces: pico de gallo,
chimichurri, and a basic hot sauce, sparks the palate. All come with *gallo
pinto* (red beans with rice and plenty of seasoning) and a good smat-
tering of local politics, culture, and around-town happenings. ✉ *1933
S.W. 8th St., Little Havana* ☎ *305/649–2015* 🖃 *AE, MC, V.*

FLORIDA FOODS

HEN THE LOCAL CHEFS claim they cook with indigenous items "right out of the backyard," they're telling the truth. South Florida's fortunate enough to have two annual growing seasons and plenty of warm, soothing ocean for tropically oriented fish and shellfish. In other words, Florida supplies fresh ingredients year-round, and it's not just about oranges and grapefruits anymore.

Take mangos, for instance. Lush and lovable, mangos show up on restaurant menus in salsas, coulis, smoothies, and of course, desserts. They have to—hundreds of varieties grow here, yielding thousands of pounds of fruit, and anyone with a mango tree knows they ripen almost faster than you can eat 'em.

The same goes for avocados, which are big and bright green and have a firm, fleshy texture. And size does count. Florida avocados, also called by the fanciful name "alligator pears," have about half the fat and twice the girth of California avocados. They make excellent guacamole, but they're even better sliced simply over field greens along with some hearts of palm, another South Florida specialty.

Key limes have gotten a lot of play in recent years, upstaging the orange. Though key limes—small, jaundiced-looking citrus fruit with as many seeds as Jim Carrey has teeth—can be bitter, cooks prize them for their acidic qualities and particularly enjoy using them in tart custard pastries called key lime pies.

The key lime pucker usually comes at the end of a meal, while fish native to Florida waters receive prime-time attention. The snapper family—including red, yellowtail, and hog varieties—is a mainstay on local menus. Although dolphinfish, also known as mahimahi, is a longtime favorite,

grouper has almost replaced it in popularity, since its mild but fleshy fillets adhere well to almost any recipe. The coastal waters off the Florida shoreline also yield some flavorful shrimp: look especially for Key West pinks, which are as pretty as a sunrise.

Stone crabs—a delicacy native to the region—ensure a predinner smile. You can enjoy these simply steamed claws, which are only in season from October through May, for several reasons: they're succulent and mild, with tender flesh; they're usually dressed with a creamy mustard dip; and while the crab sacrifices a claw, it isn't killed. In fact, stone crab anglers take one claw from the crab and throw it back into the water, where a new claw will generate over time. Now that's a good growing season.

— Jen Karetnick

¢–$ ✕ **Islas Canarias.** Since 1976 this has been a gathering place for Cuban poets, pop-music stars, and media personalities. Murals depict a Canary Islands street scene (owner Santiago Garcia's grandfather came from Tenerife). The low-priced menu, which includes breakfast, carries such Canary Islands dishes as baked lamb, ham hocks with boiled potatoes, and *tortilla española* (Spanish omelet with onions and chorizo), as well as Cuban standards like *palomilla* steak and fried kingfish. Don't miss the three superb varieties of homemade chips—potato, *malanga* (a tropical tuber), and plantain. ✉ *285 N.W. 27th Ave., Little Havana* ☎ *305/649–0440* ▭ *D, MC, V.*

Mexican

¢ ✕ **Taquerias el Mexicano.** Locals swear by the ultracheap, superspicy cooking at this restaurant and Mexican grocery. Browse for your favorite dried chilies, and contemplate a large menu loaded with typical favorites and a few surprises. The world's best hangover remedy might be *posole* (a rich stew with hominy and beef broth). Thick pork chops are bathed in a spicy green tomatillo sauce, and chicken fajitas bear no resemblance to the mall-chain version: they're spicy, juicy, and delightful. Swab everything with any of three homemade sauces, but be warned: the one designated "hot" will taste like a midday August sun. ✉ *521 S.W. 8th St., Little Havana* ☎ *305/858–1160* ▭ *MC, V.*

Spanish

$$–$$$$ ✕ **Casa Juancho.** This meeting place for the movers and shakers of the Cuban *exilio* community is also a haven for lovers of fine Spanish regional cuisine. Strolling balladeers serenade surrounded by brown brick, rough-hewn dark timbers, hanging smoked meats, and colorful Talavera platters. Try the hake prepared in a fish stock with garlic, onions, and Spanish white wine or the *carabineros a la plancha* (jumbo red shrimp with head and shell on, split and grilled). For dessert, *crema Catalana* is a rich pastry custard with a delectable crust of burnt caramel. The house features the largest list of reserved Spanish wines in the States. ✉ *2436 S.W. 8th St., Little Havana* ☎ *305/642–2452* ▭ *AE, D, DC, MC, V.*

$$ ✕ **Casa Panza.** At this moveable feast there is flamenco dancing and spontaneous singing. Tuesdays and Thursdays bring a candlelight sing-along in honor of the Virgin of the Dew. Friday there's a *paso doble* dance contest, and on Saturday all the Spanish dance schools have a standing invitation to show their moves in friendly rivalry. Every flamenco dancer and *cantaor* guitarist, Miami resident or visitor, comes to Casa Panza. And every day the large selection of tapas, traditional Spanish fare, the reasonably priced Spanish wine, and pitchers of sangria keep things moving, but the main attraction is the fun, organized, cheerful chaos. ✉ *1620 S.W. 8th St., Little Havana* ☎ *305/643–5343* ▭ *AE, MC, V.*

Vietnamese

★ ¢–$$ ✕ **Hy-Vong Vietnamese Cuisine.** Spring springs forth in spring rolls of ground pork, cellophane noodles, and black mushrooms wrapped in homemade rice paper. Folks'll mill about on the sidewalk for hours—come before 7 PM to avoid a wait—to sample the whole fish panfried with *nuoc man,* a garlic-lime fish sauce, not to mention the thinly sliced pork barbecued with sesame seeds, almonds, and peanuts. Beer-savvy proprietor Kathy Manning serves a half-dozen top brews (Double Grimbergen, Moretti, and Spaten, among them) to further inoculate the experience from the ordinary. Well, as ordinary as a Vietnamese restaurant on Calle Ocho can be. ⊠ *3458 S.W. 8th St., Little Havana* ☎ *305/446–3674* ⊟ *AE, D, MC, V* ☺ *Closed Mon. No lunch.*

Coconut Grove & Key Biscayne

Contemporary

★ **$$$** ✕ **Aria.** Choose your view: the 126-seat dining room near the exhibition kitchen or the alfresco area with views of landscaped gardens or breeze-brushed beaches. Then select your food, which may be even more difficult, given chef Jeff Vigila's artistry—items range from asparagus cappuccino with crab frittata and nutmeg foam to braised veal cheeks with langoustines, lentil ragout, and summer truffles. Aria is fortunate to have a master sommelier, whose palate is impeccable and whose wine list is impossible to resist. ⊠ *Ritz-Carlton, Key Biscayne, 455 Grand Bay Dr., Key Biscayne* ☎ *305/365–4500* ⌕ *Reservations essential* ⊟ *AE, D, DC, MC, V.*

French

$–$$ ✕ **Le Bouchon du Grove.** Waiters tend to lean on chairs while taking orders, and managers and owners freely mix with the clientele, making Le Bouchon perhaps the last remaining vestige of the Grove's bohemian days. The result is one big happy family, all enjoying traditional French pâtés, gratins, quiches, cassoulets, and steak frites. The super-charged atmosphere inside is equally matched by the throngs that tour the Grove outside the French doors. ⊠ *3430 Main Hwy., Coconut Grove, Miami* ☎ *305/448–6060* ⊟ *AE, MC, V.*

Indian

$–$$$ ✕ **Anokha.** "There is no doubt that all Indians love food," the menu says at Anokha, and there's also no doubt that all Miamians love *this* Indian food: shrimp cooked in pungent mustard sauce, fish soothed with an almond-cream curry, chicken wrapped in spinach and cilantro. The wait between starters—such as the Anokha roll, a combo of chicken and coriander enclosed in an egg-battered roti, and main courses such as the Kashmiri *rogan josh,* lamb in red curry sauce—can seem as long as a cab ride in Manhattan during rush hour. Don't fret—there's only one cook, and she's worth the delay. ⊠ *3195 Commodore Plaza, Coconut Grove, Miami* ☎ *786/552–1030* ⊟ *AE, MC, V* ☺ *Closed Mon.*

Italian

$–$$$$ ✕ **Bice.** This Milan-based worldwide chain, run by the Ruggeri family, took over the dining room in the sumptuous Wyndham Grand Bay Hotel, and despite doubts hurled by the skeptics actually improved upon it. A multihue wood floor and a huge mural backdrop are drop-dead decor highlights. Even more interesting is the Italian menu, with choices such as pumpkin ravioli in sage sauce, followed by Nebraska-raised filet mignon. ⊠ *Wyndham Grand Bay Hotel, 2669 S. Bayshore Dr., Coconut Grove, Miami* ☎ *305/860–0960* ⊟ *AE, DC, MC, V.*

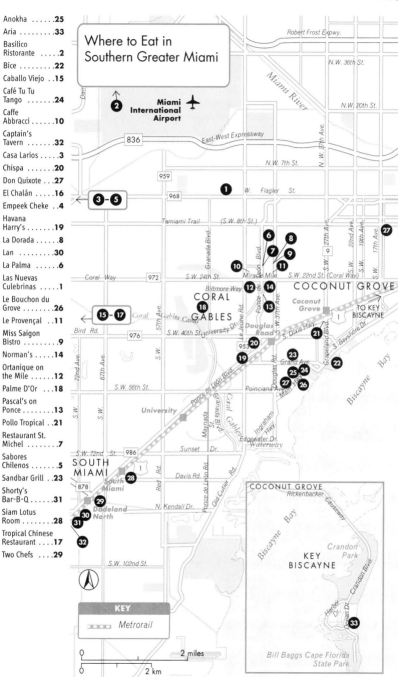

Where to Eat in
Southern Greater Miami

Latin

¢–$ ✕ **Café Tu Tu Tango.** An artistic concept follows from the rococo-modern arcades, where local artists set up their easels, through to the menu, which allows you to pick appetizers as if you were selecting paints from a palette of chips, dips, breads, and spreads. House specials include frittatas, crab cakes, *picadillo* empanadas (pastries stuffed with spicy ground beef and served with cilantro sour cream), and chicken and shrimp orzo paella, all to be enjoyed with some of the best sangria in the city. ✉ *CocoWalk, 3015 Grand Ave., Coconut Grove, Miami* ☎ *305/529–2222* ▤ *AE, MC, V.*

Mexican

¢–$ ✕ **Sandbar Grill.** The name doesn't invoke the Baja Peninsula quite the way it should, given the fish tacos, shrimp burritos, and *huevos rancheros* on the menu. No matter. After imbibing one of the 10 signature "hurricane" drinks, you won't care what the place is called, or even the fact that it's about as far from a sandbar as a real hurricane is from landfall in, say, January. ✉ *3064 Grand Ave., Coconut Grove, Miami* ☎ *305/444–5270* ▤ *AE, MC, V.*

Spanish

$$$–$$$$ ✕ **Don Quixote.** This elaborate, multiroom, multistory Spanish restaurant takes up a good city block, practically. The menu is proportionately grand: you need about as much time to read it as you do the eatery's namesake novel. Chances are you'll put down the menu halfway through, if only because you were tempted by too many tapas, including brandy-flamed Spanish sausage and marinated octopus on a bed of potatoes. If you can make it to main courses, you'll find veal chops braised with port and sautéed sea bass with asparagus and a hard-boiled egg among the blue ribbons. ✉ *3148 Commodore Plaza, Coconut Grove, Miami* ☎ *305/443–2774* ▤ *AE, D, MC, V.*

Coral Gables

Caribbean

$–$$$ ✕ **Ortanique on the Mile.** First, the place is gorgeous. Soft ochre walls and columns are hand painted with cascading ortaniques, a Jamaican hybrid orange, creating a warm, welcoming, and soothing atmosphere. Next, the food is vibrant in taste and color, as delicious as it is beautiful. Though there is no denying that the strong, full flavors are imbued with island breezes, chef/partner Cindy Hutson's personal cuisine goes beyond Caribbean refinements. The menu centers on fish, since Hutson has a special way with it, and the Caribbean bouillabaisse is not to be missed. ✉ *278 Miracle Mile, Coral Gables* ☎ *305/446–7710* ▤ *AE, MC, V.*

Contemporary

$$$–$$$$
Fodor'sChoice
★
✕ **Norman's.** Chef Norman Van Aken has created an international buzz by perfecting the art of New World cuisine—an imaginative combination rooted in Latin, North American, Caribbean, and Asian influences. Bold tastes are delivered in every dish, from a simple black-and-white-bean soup with sour cream, chorizo, and tortillas to a rum-and-pepper-

painted grouper on a mango–*habañero* chili sauce. The emphasis here is on service, and the ultragracious staff never seems harried, even when all seats are filled (usually every minute between opening and closing). ✉ *21 Almeria Ave., Coral Gables* ☎ *305/446–6767* ✍ *Reservations essential* ▭ *AE, DC, MC, V* ☺ *Closed Sun. No lunch.*

$$–$$$$ ✕ **Restaurant St. Michel.** Chef Stuart Bornstein's lace-curtained café with sidewalk tables would be at home across from a railroad station in Avignon or Bordeaux. The setting is utterly French, the little hotel it's in evokes the Mediterranean, and the cuisine is global. Lighter dishes include moist couscous chicken and pasta primavera. Among the heartier entrées are a plum-, soy-, and lemon-glazed fillet of salmon; sesame-coated loin of tuna; and local yellowtail snapper. ✉ *Hotel Place St. Michel, 162 Alcazar Ave., Coral Gables* ☎ *305/444–1666* ▭ *AE, DC, MC, V.*

Cuban

$–$$ ✕ **Havana Harry's.** When Cuban families want a home-cooked meal but
Fodor'sChoice don't want to cook it themselves, they come to this spacious, airy restau-
★ rant. In fact, you're likely to see whole families here, from babes in arms to grandmothers. The fare is traditional Cuban: the long thin steaks known as *bistec palomilla,* roast chicken with citrus marinade, and fried pork chunks; contemporary flourishes—mango sauce and guava-painted pork roast—are kept to a minimum. Most dishes come with white rice, black beans, and a choice of ripe or green plantains. The sweet ripe ones offer a good contrast to the savory dishes. This is excellent value. ✉ *4617 Le Jeune Rd., Coral Gables* ☎ *305/661–2622* ▭ *AE, MC, V.*

¢ ✕ **Pollo Tropical.** The best fast food in Miami includes delicious grilled chicken in many permutations, grilled shrimp, pork chunks, and fabulous sides. The chicken is marinated in a secret combination of spices and tropical juices and then grilled to a crisp, slightly overdone, but it's not only the *pollo* that's good at Pollo. Shrimp is sweet and tender, perfectly grilled, and served over yellow rice. Side dishes include black beans and white, boiled or fried, yuca; french fries; and even a Caesar salad. Key lime pie and tres leches served in small cups are very good. ✉ *2710 S. Dixie Hwy., Coral Gables* ☎ *305/448–9892* ▭ *MC, V.*

French

$$$$ ✕ **Palme D'Or.** An elegant room by any standards, the Biltmore's signature restaurant has been refurbished to maintain the architectural integrity of this landmark property. Space between tables, fine china and glassware, and impeccable service add to the feeling of luxury, and chef Philippe Ruiz executes modern French cooking to perfection. The menu is ample and allows you to construct your own tasting menu with half portions at reasonable prices. Categories range from foams and creams to grill and game, and several selections offer choices for both the traditionalist and the adventurous. ✉ *Biltmore Hotel, 1200 Anastasia Ave., Coral Gables* ☎ *305/445–1926* ✍ *Reservations essential* ▭ *AE, MC, V* ☺ *No lunch.*

$$$–$$$$ ✕ **Pascal's on Ponce.** Though not a native son, chef-proprietor Pascal Oudin
Fodor'sChoice has been cooking around Miami since the 1980s, when he opened Do-
★ minique's in the Alexander Hotel. His streamlined French cuisine disdains trends and discounts flash. Instead, you're supplied with substantive

delicacies such as sautéed sea bass wrapped in a crispy potato crust with braised leeks, veal rib eye *au jus,* and tenderloin of beef sautéed with snails and wild mushrooms. Service is proper, textures are perfect, and wines ideally complementary. The only dilemma is deciding between Oudin's *tarte tatin* (apple tart), Miami's only perfect soufflé, and a cheese course for dessert. ⊠ *2611 Ponce de León Blvd., Coral Gables* ☎ *305/444–2024* ⌔ *Reservations essential* ⊟ *AE, D, DC, MC, V* ☉ *No lunch weekends.*

$$$ ✕ **Le Provençal.** Like an old friend, this small, cozy restaurant is dependable and always welcoming. It consistently serves good, classic French food at very reasonable prices, service is personal and amiable, and colorful printed tablecloths and charming kitsch contribute to the inviting and cheery feel. Since the menu doesn't change very much, except for specials, you can always count on a terrific onion soup, a classic vichyssoise, and an excellent beef Bourguignon. ⊠ *382 Miracle Mile, Coral Gables* ☎ *305/448–8984* ⊟ *AE, MC, V.*

Italian

$$$ ✕ **La Palma.** Romantics read on: Italian restaurant La Palma is perhaps Miami's most love-inducing atmosphere. We're talking garden courtyards, white linens, candles, piano bar, impressionist art, even lounge singers—the sentimental works. Fortunately the food doesn't inspire weeping but rather laughing with joy, especially the osso buco and lobster risotto. While there's not much on the menu in the way of innovation, the warm, formal service and inviting decor make this a noteworthy recluse à deux. ⊠ *116 Alhambra Circle, Coral Gables* ☎ *305/445–8777* ⌔ *Reservations essential* ⊟ *AE, D, MC, V.*

$$–$$$ ✕ **Caffè Abbracci.** Long-running and much beloved, this Italian restaurant is more like a club than an eatery. Patrons tend to fare better when they're recognized, so go with a local or pretend you've been there before. Confidently order some cold and hot antipasti—including various carpaccios, porcini mushrooms, calamari, grilled goat cheese, shrimps, mussels—and a few festive entrées. Most pasta is made fresh, so consider sampling two or three, maybe with pesto sauce, Gorgonzola, and fresh tomatoes. ⊠ *318 Aragon Ave., Coral Gables* ☎ *305/441–0700* ⌔ *Reservations essential* ⊟ *AE, DC, MC, V* ☉ *No lunch weekends.*

Latin

$$–$$$$ ✕ **Chispa.** Meaning "spark" in Spanish, Chispa indeed sparkles. Chef Robbin Haas has taken command of the open kitchen, basing the menu on a melting pot of Latin flavors that reflects Miami's population. *Cazuelitas* let you have smaller portions as appetizers—from mussels with chipotle chili to Spanish cava fondue. Ceviches are assertively marinated, croquettes melt in your mouth, and skeptics can have flatbreads with various toppings (read: pizzas). Share plates and platters of grilled shrimp or suckling pig before guava cheesecake or churros with chocolate sauce. Exotic drinks are served at the 40-foot bar, and leather banquettes, Bahama shutters, and colorful Cuban tiles complete the hacienda feel. ⊠ *225 Altara Ave., Coral Gables* ☎ *305/648–2600* ⊟ *AE, MC, V.*

Fodor'sChoice
★

Spanish

$$$–$$$$ ✕ **La Dorada.** Named after the royal sea bream, the restaurant brings in fresh fish daily from the Bay of Biscay, rather than Biscayne Bay, setting the standard for fine Spanish cuisine in the city. Preparations are both classic and excellent: scallops sautéed with grapes, monkfish stuffed with shrimp, whole fish baked in rock salt. Not a lot of English is spoken here, thanks to an all-Spanish staff, so service can be a little off. But they do make an effort to please, catering to those whims that get across language barriers. ✉ *177 Giralda Ave., Coral Gables* ☎ *305/446–2002* ⊟ *AE, MC, V.*

¢–$$ ✕ **Las Nuevas Culebrinas.** At this Spanish *tapacería* (house of little plates), live each meal as if it were your last, though you may wait as long as some inmates do for an appeal. Tapas here are not small; some are entrée size: the succulent mix of garbanzos, ham, sausage, red peppers, and oil, or the Frisbee-size Spanish tortilla (omelet). Indulge in a tender fillet of crocodile, fresh fish, grilled pork, or the kicker, goat in Coca-Cola sauce. For dessert there's *crema Catalana,* caramelized at your table with a blowtorch. This is a good time to remind your kids not to touch. ✉ *4700 W. Flagler St., at N.W. 47th Ave., Coral Gables* ☎ *305/445–2337* ⊟ *AE, MC, V.*

Vietnamese

¢–$ ✕ **Miss Saigon Bistro.** The musical was the inspiration for this family-run restaurant, and yes, the soundtrack plays ad nauseam. But overall the effect is quaint rather than campy, and the dining room, decorated with orchids, is serene. The first act commences with delicate spring rolls, pork-stuffed crepes, or steamed mussels. Take intermission with tangy green papaya salad; then return to the second act for chicken with lemongrass or caramelized pork. Close down the show with grilled salmon with mango, and toast curtain calls with a bottle from the reasonably priced wine list. ✉ *146 Giralda Ave., Coral Gables* ☎ *305/446–8006* ⊟ *AE, DC, MC, V* ☺ *No lunch weekends.*

South & West Miami-Dade

Barbecue

¢–$$ ✕ **Shorty's Bar-B-Q.** Since 1951, when Shorty Allen opened his barbecue restaurant in a log cabin, it's been a local institution. Meals are served family style at long picnic tables, and cowboy hats hang on the walls along with animal horns, saddles, and mounted heads of boar and caribou. Longtime fans come for the barbecued pork ribs, chicken, and pork steak, all slow-cooked over hickory logs and drenched in Shorty's own warm, spicy sauce. If you've got room, try side orders of tangy baked beans, corn on the cob, and coleslaw. ✉ *9200 S. Dixie Hwy., South Miami* ☎ *305/670–7732* ⊟ *D, MC, V.*

Chilean

¢–$ ✕ **Sabores Chilenos.** Meaning Chilean flavors, this eatery serves exactly that: the authentic flavors of Chile's home cooking. The shoe-box locale is too modest to be properly called a restaurant. Display cases and shelves are filled with imported specialty products and homemade pastries. Small tables crowd the rest of the space. A board lists the day's specials, and the menu includes a variety of sandwiches. *Machas al Matico*, an elongated razor clam of pink flesh served in its own juices, is excellent, as is the traditional *pastel de choclo*, a sort of cornmeal lasagna. It's hard to find the entrance, at the corner of the mall near S.W. 108th Avenue and S.W. 2nd Street. ⊠ *10760 W. Flagler Plaza #6, Sweetwater* ☎ *305/554–4484* ▤ *MC, V.*

Chinese

¢–$$$ ⤬ **Tropical Chinese Restaurant.** This big, lacquer-free room feels as open and busy as a railway station, and the extensive menu is filled with tofu combinations, poultry, beef, pork, and tender seafood. You'll find unfamiliar items on the menu, too—early spring leaves of snow pea pods, for example, which are sublimely tender and flavorful. An exuberant dim sum lunch—brunch on the weekends—allows you to choose an assortment of small dishes from wheeled carts. In the open kitchen, 10 chefs prepare everything as if for dignitaries. ⊠ *7991 S.W. 40th St. (Bird Rd.), west of S.W. 79th Ave., Westchester, Miami* ☎ *305/262–7576 or 305/262–1552* ▤ *AE, DC, MC, V.*

Contemporary

$$–$$$$ ⤬ **Two Chefs.** Of the two Danish chefs—Jan Jorgensen and Soren Bredahl—who had cooked together for decades, Bredahl has gone back to Denmark. Their restaurant, decorated like a Williams-Sonoma catalog, still has an ever-changing menu, however. Scan for seared foie gras with gnocchi, an unusually textured combination that features reduced boysenberries. Unexpected concoctions are another untraditional tradition at Two Chefs—perhaps goat meat paired with lobster or an escargot potpie. ⊠ *8287 S. Dixie Hwy., South Miami* ☎ *305/663–2100* ▤ *AE, D, DC, MC, V* ⊙ *Closed Sun.*

Cuban

¢–$$$ ⤬ **Casa Larios.** Yes, South Florida has 1,000 Cuban restaurants, but this one stands out for its consistently excellent food. The chicken soup is golden yellow, pearly, salty—the perfect elixir. Look for specials like roast pork loin, roasted lamb, *caldo gallego* (white-bean soup with ham and greens), and the Argentine-inspired churrasco, a boneless strip steak with chimichurri. The restaurant spawned Larios on the Beach, on Ocean Drive, where Gloria Estefan and husband Emilio Estefan are partners, and who, if you're lucky, can sometimes be glimpsed. ⊠ *7705 W. Flagler St., near Mall of the Americas, West Miami-Dade Miami* ☎ *305/266–5494* ▤ *AE, MC, V.*

Italian

★ ¢–$ ⤬ **Basilico Ristorante.** The neighborhood just north of Miami International Airport has few interesting dining options, but this one is worth investigating. Run by an Argentine family, Basilico has a quiet dining room insulated from all the takeoffs and landings. Delicate, delightful food at a low price includes seafood with linguine, ravioli stuffed with lobster, a lusty dish of veal nestled in mashed potatoes, and homemade desserts. ⊠ *5879 N.W. 36th St., Virginia Gardens* ☎ *305/871–3585* ▤ *AE, DC, MC, V* ⊙ *Closed Sun. No lunch Sat.*

Native American

$$–$$$$ ✕ **Empeek Cheke.** Members of the Miccosukee Indian tribe spared no expense when they created this luxe steak house on the second floor of their art deco casino–hotel complex. "Everglades cuisine" figures highly here—check out alligator tail Provençal or panfried frogs' legs for a starter. Then move on to venison tenderloin, buffalo sirloin, or baked Florida grouper with lobster-shrimp sauce. Do read prices carefully—even less-exotic meats such as filet mignon can cost you, and the casino downstairs is limited to video slot machines, poker, and bingo, so don't expect a huge windfall to pay for your eats. ⊠ *Miccosukee Resort & Gaming, 500 S.W. 177th Ave., West Miami-Dade, Miami* ☎ *305/925–2559* ⊟ *AE, D, DC, MC, V* ☉ *No lunch.*

Peruvian

$ ✕ **El Chalán.** This modest family restaurant, in the same popular mini-mall as Tropical Chinese, doesn't pretend to be anything other than what it is. The friendly and efficient staff will describe unfamiliar dishes to help you choose among the Peruvian specialties, which come in portions large enough to share. To sample the cuisine, order the *piquéo Peruano,* comprising small portions of several dishes. But don't miss the *jaléa mixta,* a big mounded dish of breaded and deep-fried octopus, squid, fish, and shrimp, accompanied by fried yuca, red pickled onions, tartar sauce, and slices of lime. ⊠ *7971 S.W. 40th St. (Bird Rd.), west of S.W. 79th Ave., Westchester, Miami* ☎ *305/266–0212* ⊟ *MC, V.*

Pan-Asian

$–$$ ✕ **Lan.** Aside from rolls and summer-fresh sashimi, Lan, on the ground floor of an inaccessible megamall, supplies the connoisseur of all cuisines Asian with satays, pot stickers, braised ribs, and sake-steamed clams. The sushi bar's more interesting items include a "Thai Bomb"—lemongrass-chili-infused shrimp and calamari rolled in rice and sesame. Vegetarians get a nod, too, with "green plates," a grilled mushroom sampler or spinach seared with garlic and chilies. Innovative desserts include spring rolls or wontons stuffed with fruit and chocolate. It is all surprisingly good. ⊠ *Dadeland Station, 8332 S. Dixie Hwy., South Miami* ☎ *305/ 661–8141* ⊟ *AE, MC, V.*

Seafood

$–$$$ ✕ **Captain's Tavern.** The paneled walls may be hokey, but the interesting menu fortified with Caribbean and South American influences can take your mind off the surroundings. Beyond good versions of the typical fare—conch chowder and conch fritters—you'll find Portuguese fish stew, fish with various tropical fruits, a delightful black bean soup, and oysters in cream sauce with fresh rosemary, not to mention decadent desserts—all served in a beloved family fish house. ⊠ *9621 S. Dixie Hwy., South Miami* ☎ *305/666–5979* ⊟ *AE, MC, V.*

Thai

¢–$ ✕ **Siam Lotus Room.** This aqua-color example of motel architecture can almost blind the unsuspecting driver, but inside you'll find great eating—in fact, this is one of South Florida's best Thai restaurants. Jump at the chance to sample spicy jumping squid and savory, coconut-silky *tom kar* *pla,* a fish soup. The curries work on many levels, as they should: aroma, taste, and sensation. For dessert, the Thai doughnut complements thick, creamy Thai iced coffee. ☒ *6388 S. Dixie Hwy., South Miami* ☎ *305/666–8134* ⊟ *AE, MC, V.*

Venezuelan

$ ✕ **Caballo Viejo.** The strip mall on Bird Road and 79th Avenue has become the casual diner's restaurant row. This small, neat, and cheerful Venezuelan eatery has friendly, helpful service and a limited menu that nevertheless has something for everyone. *Arepitas* (small corn patties) are very good, as is the preposterous plantain sandwich with avocado, tomato, sliced chicken, and crumbled cheese. You can get Venezuelan newspapers or watch the Caracas version of *Star Search,* or a popular novela on Venevisión. Everyone gets into it, so don't ask to lower the volume; part of the global experience is the surround sound. ☒ *7921 S.W. 40th St. (Bird Rd.), west of S.W. 79th Ave., Westchester, Miami* ☎ *305/264–8772* ⊟ *MC, V.*

WHERE TO STAY

3

Updated by
Lisa Simundson **GREATER MIAMI HAS EXPERIENCED A VIRTUAL HOTEL RENAISSANCE** that has completely transformed the area's lodging landscape, thanks to a building boom in the late '90s. Not only have ultra-luxe brands opened their gilded doors for the first time in the Magic City, but dozens of properties—from the grandest oceanfront resort down to the smallest boutique hotel—have spruced up to meet them, pouring millions into upgrades and renovations. As the marketplace has become crowded with new entries, however, Miami's famously outrageous prices are holding steady or even dropping slightly—meaning a stay at even the most exclusive property is now within reason for many vacationers.

When deciding where to stay, take into account the different personalities of Miami's neighborhoods. If this is a stay-up-all-night, I'm-only-going-to-be-here-once vacation, reserve a room on South Beach's Ocean Drive and expect the party atmosphere to keep you up past your bedtime. If you're here for business, a hotel in Downtown or in Coral Gables will put you close to the business centers. If you'd prefer access to the ocean minus the frenzy of South Beach, the high- and low-rise properties of Mid-Beach, North Beach, Bal Harbour, and Sunny Isles are on the water and away from the hordes. If oceanfront isn't a priority—but close to the action is—rooms in funky Coconut Grove or the quieter streets of the Art Deco District might be your best bet.

North Miami-Dade

★ $$$$ 🏨 **Fairmont Turnberry Isle Resort & Club.** Finest of the grand resorts, especially with the addition of the Golf Learning Center, Turnberry is a tapestry of islands and waterways on 300 superbly landscaped acres by the bay. At the 1920s Addison Mizner–designed Country Club Hotel on the Intracoastal Waterway, oversize rooms are decorated in light woods and earth tones and have large curving terraces and hot tubs. The marina has moorings for 117 boats; there are two Robert Trent Jones golf courses and a free shuttle to the Aventura Mall. Perks for all ages include a private Ocean Club on the Atlantic and a Kids Club at Turnberry. ✉ *19999 W. Country Club Dr., Aventura 33180* ☎ *305/932–6200 or 800/327–7028* 🖷 *305/ 933–6560* ⊕ *www.turnberryisle.com* ⤷ *392 rooms, 41 suites* ⚒ *4 restaurants, in-room safes, minibars, cable TV, 2 18-hole golf courses, 11 tennis courts, 2 pools, health club, spa, steam room, beach, dock, windsurfing, boating, racquetball, 5 bars* ⊟ *AE, D, DC, MC, V.*

★ $$$$ 🏨 **Trump International Sonesta Beach Resort.** When Donald Trump came to town, it was clear the once-neglected north beach area of Sunny Isles was back. This 32-story oceanfront tower has panache without being snooty. Family-friendly recreation includes a grotto-style pool with waterfalls and rock formations; parents can watch their kids from the expansive pool deck, if they can tear their eyes away from superb ocean vistas. For convention goers, an oceanfront ballroom provides the same great views. Leisure time can be filled at the Aquanox Spa or shopping in Bal Harbour and Aventura. The American Classics car exhibit, on the beach, showcases 1950s convertibles and other vintage models. ✉ *18001 Collins Ave., Sunny Isles 33160* ☎ *305/692–5600 or 800/766–3782* 🖷 *305/692–5601* ⊕ *www.trumpsonesta.com* ⤷ *390 rooms* ⚒ *2 restau-*

The lodgings we list are the cream of the crop in each price category. We always list the facilities that are available—but we don't specify whether they cost extra. When pricing accommodations, always ask what's included and what costs extra. Remember that ocean view balconies and proximity to the beach significantly increase rates. All hotels listed have private bath unless otherwise noted.

Assume that hotels operate on the **European Plan** (EP, with no meals), unless we specify that they use the **Continental Plan** (CP, with a Continental breakfast).

3

Reservations
Although rooms are virtually always available in Miami, reservations are still essential if you have your heart set on a popular hotel during a busy time, such as the Christmas holidays or special events.

Tipping
After you settle into your room, the bellhops, valet parkers, concierges, and housekeepers, all of whom you should tip, will add to your expenses. With these added costs, plus parking fees of up to $16 per evening, you can easily spend 25% more than your room rate just to sleep in Miami.

Prices
There are hundreds of hotels, motels, resorts, and hostels to choose from, with prices ranging from $15 a night in a dormitory-style room to $2,000 a night or more in a penthouse suite.

Some hotels (especially on the mainland) have adopted steady year-round prices, but most adjust their rates to reflect seasonal demand. The peak occurs in winter, with a dip in summer and shoulder (spring and fall) seasons. Rate cards are a general guide, but always call before making a decision based on price; most hotels have a certain number of rooms offered at lower rates than those indicated on the rate card. You'll find great values between Easter and Memorial Day, which is actually a delightful time in Miami, and in September and October, the height of hurricane season.

WHAT IT COSTS				
$$$$	$$$	$$	$	¢
FOR 2 PEOPLE over $300	$200–$300	$150–$200	$100–$150	under $100

Prices are for two people in a standard double room in high season, excluding 12.5% city and resort taxes.

rants, microwaves, refrigerators, cable TV, 3 tennis courts, pool, spa, windsurfing, jet skiing, bar, lobby lounge, children's programs (ages 5–12), Internet, business services, meeting rooms ▤ *AE, D, DC, MC, V.*

$$–$$$$ 🖥 **Ocean Point Resort & Club.** Riding the crest of a new wave of upscale resorts in Sunny Isles, the all-suite Ocean Point fits right in with the amenities high-paying guests relish. There are Jacuzzi tubs with separate showers, in-room entertainment centers, a food market downstairs, and a traditional European spa on premises. Rooms are bright and spacious, the beach is relatively uncrowded, and the atmosphere is easy, not pompous—all in all, a viable alternative to the behemoths farther south. ⌂ *17375 Collins Ave., Sunny Isles 33160* ☎ *305/940–5422, 786/528–2500, or 866/623–2678* 🖷 *305/940–1658* ⊕ *www.oceanpointresort.com* ⇱ *40 rooms, 75 1-bedroom suites, 51 2-bedroom suites* ⚐ *Restaurant, in-room data ports, cable TV, kitchens or kitchenettes, pool, sauna, spa, beach, bar, laundry facilities, concierge, business services, meeting rooms, parking (fee)* ⊟ *AE, D, DC, MC, V.*

$–$$$ ⊡ **Marco Polo Ramada Plaza Beach Resort.** The Ramada's familiar name and appealing setting draw business travelers, families, and couples alike. This eclectic group can be seen around the heated pool, kiddie pool, and beachfront, or at the festive Tiki bar. The sports bar, shops, and art gallery make this resort somewhat of a small city. Of course, the hotel provides for rest, too: all rooms have two queen beds; most have full or partial ocean views; some have balconies; and a few have fully equipped kitchenettes. Clean and active (albeit miles from South Beach's action), it's worth checking into—especially for families. ⌂ *19201 Collins Ave., Sunny Isles, 33160* ☎ *305/932–2233 or 877/327–6363* 🖷 *305/935–5009* ⊕ *www.ramadaplazamiabeach.com* ⇱ *350 rooms, 20 suites* ⚐ *Restaurant, café, refrigerators, cable TV, 2 pools, gym, beach, concierge, meeting rooms* ⊟ *AE, D, DC, MC, V.*

$–$$$ ⊡ **Newport Beachside Resort.** Built before the latest luxury towers, Newport is still one of Sunny Isles' nicest hotels. This combination timeshare and hotel is a clean, safe place for families to enjoy outdoor activities, thanks to standard and wading pools, the beach, and a fishing pier—the only remaining hotel fishing pier in Miami. Inside, the lobby is large and bright, and so are the rooms—one- and two-bedroom suites, all with microwaves and mini-refrigerators. The locally famous Newport Pub, created by legendary Miami Beach restaurateur Wolfie Cohen, still serves sizzling good steaks. ⌂ *16701 Collins Ave., Sunny Isles, 33160* ☎ *305/949–1300 or 800/327–5476* 🖷 *305/947–5873* ⊕ *www.newportbeachsideresort.com* ⇱ *290 suites* ⚐ *4 restaurants, microwaves, refrigerators, cable TV, pool, gym, beach, bar, nightclub, shops, concierge, meeting rooms, some free parking* ⊟ *AE, D, DC, MC, V.*

$–$$ ⊡ **Don Shula's Hotel & Golf Club.** In a leafy community about 14 mi northwest of downtown Miami, the hotel is part of the Main Street shopping, dining, and entertainment complex, while the golf club (with par-72 championship and par-3 executive courses) is less than a mile away. A complimentary shuttle runs between the two properties, creating a 500-acre retreat for golfers and convention goers. When they're not teeing off, guests can work out in the hotel's 40,000-square-foot athletic club. Like steak? Don Shula's Steak House, at the club, serves hefty cuts of prime beef in an atmosphere that can best be described as "football elegant." ⌂ *6842 Main St., Miami Lakes 33014* ☎ *305/821–1150 or 800/247–4852* 🖷 *305/820–8071* ⊕ *www.donshulahotel.com* ⇱ *205 rooms, 17 suites (hotel); 89 rooms (club)* ⚐ *2 restaurants, cable TV, 2 golf courses, 9 tennis courts, 2 pools, fitness classes, gym, sauna, steam room, basketball, racquetball, volleyball, 2 bars, meeting rooms* ⊟ *AE, DC, MC, V.*

Alexander
Hotel **13**

Bay Harbor Inn . .**7**

Beach House
Bal Harbour **9**

Claridge
Hotel **17**

Comfort Inn
Oceanfront **10**

Days Inn North
Beach Hotel . . .**11**

Don Shula's Hotel
& Golf Club **1**

Eden Roc
Renaissance
Resort & Spa . .**15**

Fairmont
Turnberry Isle
Resort & Club . . .**2**

Fontainebleau
Hilton Resort
and Towers . . .**16**

Indian Creek
Hotel **19**

Marco Polo
Ramada Plaza
Beach Resort . . .**3**

Newport
Beachside
Resort **6**

Ocean Point
Resort & Club . . .**5**

Ocean Surf **12**

The Palms
South Beach . .**18**

Sheraton Bal
Harbour **8**

Traymore **20**

Trump
International
Sonesta Beach
Resort **4**

Wyndham
Miami Beach
Resort **14**

Where to Stay in
Northern
Greater Miami

Mid-Beach to Bal Harbour

$$$–$$$$ 🏨 **Alexander Hotel.** Amid the high-rises of the Mid-Beach district, this 16-story hotel exemplifies the elegance of Miami Beach. Immense suites are furnished with antiques and reproductions, each with a terrace that has ocean or bay views, a living and dining room, kitchen, and two baths. Thanks to Facemaker Salon & Spa Lounge and Shula's Steak House, you can pamper your body and appetite without leaving the property. Mandatory gratuities attached to everything from valet parking to bellhops to maid service to deliveries can add another $100 to your stay. ⊠ *5225 Collins Ave., Mid-Beach, Miami Beach 33140* ☎ *305/865–6500 or 800/327–6121* 🖷 *305/341–6554* ⊕ *www.alexanderhotel.com* ↪ *89 1-bedroom suites, 51 2-bedroom suites* ♨ *3 restaurants, cable TV, 2 pools, health club, hair salon, hot tubs, sauna, beach, windsurfing, boating, volleyball, baby-sitting, laundry service, concierge, meeting rooms* ☰ *AE, D, DC, MC, V.*

$$$–$$$$ 🏨 **Beach House Bal Harbour.** Staying here is the next best thing to having your own oceanfront home. Cookies at check-in, lollipops at turndown, and seashell collections are just a few of the homey touches in this 1956 building, one of three hotels on Miami Beach owned by the Rubell family, of Studio 54 fame (the Greenview and the Albion are the other two). Spacious rooms (with tiny bathrooms) are filled with Ralph Lauren furniture and Nantucket-style wainscoting. The low-key atmosphere extends outdoors to a screened-in porch and poolside spa. The Atlantic restaurant serves oh-so-comforting American cuisine. High-speed Internet access is property-wide, including the ocean's edge. ⊠ *9449 Collins Ave., Surfside 33154* ☎ *305/535–8600 or 877/782–3557* 🖷 *305/535–8601* ⊕ *www.rubellhotels.com* ↪ *170 rooms, 10 suites* ♨ *Restaurant, cable TV, pool, gym, spa, bar, concierge, business services* ☰ *AE, DC, MC, V.*

$$$–$$$$ 🏨 **Eden Roc Renaissance Resort & Spa.** This grand 1950s hotel designed by Morris Lapidus has the free-flowing lines of deco at its best. The public areas have a modern, elegant feel, especially the hip lobby bar with its low-slung, meandering couches. South Florida's only indoor rock-climbing wall is found at the popular 55,000-square-foot Spa of Eden, and the Aquatica Beach Bar and Grill, despite its casual moniker, satisfies the choosiest gourmand. Rooms blend a touch of the '50s with informal elegance. Larger-than-usual rooms boast roomy closets—a holdover from the days when northern snowbirds would stay for weeks or months at a time. ⊠ *4525 Collins Ave., Mid-Beach, Miami Beach 33140* ☎ *305/531–0000 or 800/327–8337* 🖷 *305/674–5555* ⊕ *www.edenrocresort.com* ↪ *349 rooms* ♨ *2 restaurants, cable TV, 2 pools, gym, spa, beach, basketball, racquetball, squash, sports bar, meeting rooms* ☰ *AE, MC, V.*

★ $$$–$$$$ 🏨 **Fontainebleau Hilton Resort and Towers.** This big, busy, and ornate grande dame completed a major renovation in 2003, while another project—Fontainebleau II, a hotel–condominium complex—is due in early 2005. Redesigned rooms are decked out in natural woods and rich tones, and the lobby has been restored to its Rat Pack–era glory, with grand deco flourishes everywhere. Guests enjoy free admission to *Club Tropigala,* one of the few hotel showrooms left on the beach. And for kids, Cookie's World is a water playground with a water slide and lazy river raft ride. ✉ *4441 Collins Ave., Mid-Beach, Miami Beach 33140* ☎ *305/538–2000 or 800/548–8886* 🖷 *305/673–5351* ⊕ *www.hilton.com* 📞 *920 rooms, 50 suites* ⌂ *3 restaurants, cable TV, 2 pools, gym, massage, beach, windsurfing, boating, jet skiing, parasailing, volleyball, 3 lounges, children's programs (ages 5–12), convention center* 🟰 *AE, D, DC, MC, V.*

★ **$$$–$$$$** 🏨 **The Palms South Beach.** Technically, South Beach is farther south, but this Mid-Beach standout feels SoBe thanks to its distinctive decor—including lush gardens with gazebo, fountains, walkways, and soaring palm trees (several with hammocks strung between them)—creating a welcome respite from beach excesses and the traffic roaring by on Collins. There are more large palms inside, in the Great Room lounge just off the lobby, and designer Patrick Kennedy used subtle, natural hues of ivory, green, and blue for the homey, well-lit rooms. ✉ *3025 Collins Ave., Mid-Beach, Miami Beach 33140* ☎ *305/534–0505 or 800/550–0505* 🖷 *305/534–0515* ⊕ *www.thepalmshotel.com* 📞 *220 rooms, 22 suites* ⌂ *Restaurant, room service, in-room data ports, in-room safes, minibars, cable TV, pool, beach, 2 bars, lobby lounge, concierge* 🟰 *AE, D, DC, MC, V.*

$$$–$$$$ 🏨 **Sheraton Bal Harbour.** Elegant without being pretentious, this Morris Lapidus–designed hotel is run by a staff that has service down to a science. The suites have marble bathrooms and Jacuzzis, and most rooms have full or partial views of the city, ocean, or Bal Harbour. The posh Bal Harbour shops are across the street. Other pluses include a lush oceanfront garden with waterfalls, a funky neon-laced bistro and bar, and 72,000 square feet of meeting space, all sitting on 10 acres of Atlantic coastline. Among the many family-friendly recreational options are a water entertainment complex and a kids' club. ✉ *9701 Collins Ave., Bal Harbour, Miami Beach 33154* ☎ *305/865–7511 or 800/999–9898* 🖷 *305/864–2601* ⊕ *www.sheratonbalharbourresort.com* 📞 *642 rooms, 52 suites* ⌂ *3 restaurants, cable TV, pool, wading pool, health club, hot tub, massage, beach, windsurfing, bar, baby-sitting, meeting rooms* 🟰 *AE, D, DC, MC, V.*

$$–$$$ 🏨 **Wyndham Miami Beach Resort.** Of the great Miami Beach hotels, this 18-story modern glass tower remains a standout, as does its polished staff offering exceptional service, from helping you find the best shopping to bringing you an icy drink on the beach. The bright rooms have a tropical blue color scheme and are filled with attentive details: mini-refrigerators, three layers of drapes (including blackout curtains), big closets, and bathrooms with high-end toiletries and a magnifying mirror. Two presidential suites were designed in consultation with the Secret Service, and a rooftop meeting room offers views of bay and ocean. ✉ *4833 Collins Ave., Mid-Beach, Miami Beach 33140* ☎ *305/532–3600 or 800/203–8368* 🖷 *305/534–7409* ⊕ *www.wyndham.com* 📞 *378 rooms, 46 suites* ⌂ *3 restaurants, cable TV, tennis court, pool, gym, massage, beach, bar, meeting rooms* 🟰 *AE, D, DC, MC, V.*

$–$$$ 🏨 **Bay Harbor Inn.** The inn's not on the ocean, but the tranquil Indian Creek flowing outside is sure to soothe. From your room's private porch, where you can sit with book or drink, you'll have a view of the village of Bal Harbour, a five-minute walk away. Rooms have queen-

and king-size beds, and baths are large. The Islands restaurant is very nice, but so is a walk over the bridge to Surfside for a wider selection of neighborhood bars and eateries. The hotel staff is composed largely of hotel students from Johnson & Wales University, so the service is enthusiastic but not flawlessly professional. ⊠ *9660 E. Bay Harbor Dr., Bal Harbour, 33154* ☎ *305/868–4141* ⊟ *305/867–9094* ⊕ *www. bayharborinn.com* ⤺ *22 rooms, 23 suites* ⚒ *Restaurant, cable TV, pool, bar, meeting rooms* ⊟ *AE, MC, V* ⊖ *CP.*

★ **$–$$$** ⊡ **Indian Creek Hotel.** This 1936 pueblo deco original may just be Miami's most charming and sincere lodge. Owner Marc Levin rescued the inn and filled its rooms with art deco furniture, much of it from the hotel basement. The garden rooms are minimalist in design, with dark-wood furniture and light green walls, in contrast to the creamy tones and plush furniture of the deco rooms. Suites have VCR–CD players and modem capabilities. The dining room has an eclectic and appetizing menu, which can also be enjoyed by the lush pool and garden. ⊠ *2727 Indian Creek Dr., Mid-Beach, Miami Beach 33140* ☎ *305/531– 2727 or 800/491–2772* ⊟ *305/531–5651* ⊕ *www.indiancreekhotelmb. com* ⤺ *55 rooms, 6 suites* ⚒ *Restaurant, refrigerators, cable TV, pool, meeting rooms* ⊟ *AE, D, DC, MC, V* ⊖ *CP.*

$–$$ ⊡ **Claridge Hotel.** This cool Mediterranean haven is the city's most impressive hotel renovation. The exterior has been restored to the canary-yellow glory of the 1928 original; inside, rich Venetian frescoed walls are hung with Peruvian oil paintings, while gleaming floors and majestic columns are crafted from volcanic stone. A Moroccan terrace overlooks the soaring inner atrium, which has a splash Jacuzzi at the far end. Rooms are a mix of Asian and European influences, with straw mats laid over wood floors, and ornate wood furniture. ⊠ *3500 Collins Ave., Mid-Beach, Miami Beach 33140* ☎ *305/604–8485 or 888/422– 9111* ⊟ *305/674–0881* ⊕ *www.claridgefl.com* ⤺ *42 rooms, 8 suites* ⚒ *Restaurant, in-room data ports, in-room safes, cable TV, hot tub, concierge, business services, parking (fee)* ⊟ *AE, D, DC, MC, V.*

¢–$ ⊡ **Comfort Inn Oceanfront.** For those comforted by the thought of a reliable brand, this is a good option. Not too far, but far enough from the action, the Atlantic is in the hotel's backyard, but so is a lovely pool area surrounded by palms. Rooms are decked in soft peach with blond woods and deep aqua carpeting; all have cable TV, but some also include wet bars, refrigerators, coffeemakers, and extra-spacious closets. Computer hook-ups in most rooms serve the business traveler who wants a quiet place to fire up the laptop, and an Internet café is five minutes away. ⊠ *6261 Collins Ave., North Beach, Miami Beach 33140* ☎ *305/868–1200 or 877/424–6423* ⊟ *305/868–3003* ⊕ *www. comfortinn.com* ⤺ *153 rooms* ⚒ *In-room data ports, cable TV, pool, exercise equipment, playground, laundry facilities, business services, meeting rooms, parking (fee)* ⊟ *AE, D, DC, MC, V* ⊖ *CP.*

¢–$ ⊡ **Days Inn North Beach Hotel.** Although the rooms and baths are small, the hotel itself is clean, and it's in a quiet, resurgent strip of Miami Beach. The natural attributes of South Beach—sun and sea—are here as well, with the big advantage of not having to fight for a parking spot or deal with creeping traffic. A good bet for families, this hotel has a game room, plus a bright breakfast room. ⊠ *7450 Ocean Terr., North Beach, Miami Beach 33141* ☎ *305/866–1631 or 888/825–6800* 🖷 *305/868–4617* ⊕ *www.daysinn.com* 📳 *92 rooms* ♢ *Restaurant, cable TV, pool, beach, bar, video game room, laundry facilities* ➡ *AE, D, DC, MC, V.*

★ ¢–$ 🏠 **Ocean Surf.** With a touch more privacy than other nearby hotels, this small, family-owned art deco hotel stands in a safe, quiet, beachfront neighborhood one block east of Collins Avenue. Modest in size and style, it's an affordable option if you want to get away from it all while scoring a free Continental breakfast. Rooms are generic hotel style, with doubles or queens; oceanfront rooms add a balcony overlooking the blue Atlantic. Wireless Internet access in the lobby extends to the front porch, should you care to surf the Web while watching the surf. ⊠ *7436 Ocean Terr., North Beach, Miami Beach 33141* ☎ *305/866–1648 or 800/555–0411* 🖷 *305/866–1649* ⊕ *www.oceansurf.com* 📳 *49 rooms* ♢ *Cable TV, beach* ➡ *AE, D, DC, MC, V* ⦙◯⦙ *CP.*

¢–$ 🏠 **Traymore.** Heading north on Collins from South Beach, the wall-to-wall hotels become wall-to-wall condos. Tucked between these is the Traymore, an economy hotel that mostly attracts Europeans. Like some other revived art deco hotels, this one has lost some of its character in the cleanup. Lodgings are basic, with functional furnishings and refrigerators in oceanfront rooms. Bottom line: if you're looking for an oceanfront hotel that won't break your budget, you found it. ⊠ *2445 Collins Ave., Mid-Beach, Miami Beach 33139* ☎ *305/534–7111 or 800/445–1512* 🖷 *305/538–2632* ⊕ *www.traymorehotel.com* 📳 *86 rooms, 2 suites* ♢ *Restaurant, cable TV, pool, beach, bar* ➡ *AE, D, DC, MC, V.*

South Beach

$$$$ 🏠 **Casa Grande.** With a luxe and spicy Eastern-tinged flavor that sets it apart from the typical icy-cool minimalism found on Ocean Drive, this Chris Blackwell all-suite has luxurious Balinese-inspired abodes done in teak and mahogany. Expect dhurrie rugs, Indonesian fabrics and artifacts, two-poster beds with ziggurat turns, full electric kitchens with good-quality utensils, and large baths—practically unheard of in the Art Deco District. Insulated windows keep the noise of Ocean Drive revelers at bay. Book well in advance for stays during peak periods. ⊠ *834 Ocean Dr., South Beach 33139* ☎ *305/672–7003 or 866/420–2272* 🖷 *305/673–3669* ⊕ *www.casagrandesuitehotel.com* 📳 *34 suites* ♢ *Café, in-room safes, kitchenettes, refrigerators, cable TV, in-room VCRs, beach, shops, laundry service, concierge, business services, travel services* ➡ *AE, D, DC, MC, V.*

$$$$ 🏠 **Delano Hotel.** Visitors to the Delano typically marvel at the lobby
Fodor'sChoice   hung with massive white, billowing drapes and yet try to act casual while
★   celebs like Jennifer Lopez, Beyonce Knowles, Will Smith, and Ashton Kutcher walk by. Fashion models and moguls gather beneath cabanas and pose by the pool, as heady aromas from the Blue Door and Robert De Niro's Ago restaurants waft by. Executive services are offered for business travelers, and all guests have the run of a rooftop bathhouse and solarium. Standard rooms average a roomy 400 square feet in size. ⊠ *1685 Collins Ave., South Beach 33139* ☎ *305/672–2000 or 800/555–5001* 🖷 *305/532–0099* ⊕ *www.ianschragerhotels.com* 📳 *184*

CloseUp

MIAMI'S ART DECO HOTELS

WITH APOLOGIES TO THE FLAMINGO, *Miami's most recognizable icons are the art deco hotels of South Beach. But why here? What did this city do to deserve some of the world's most beautiful and stylish buildings?*

The story begins in the 1920s, when Miami Beach established itself as America's Winter Playground. Long before Las Vegas got the idea, Miami Beach sprouted hostelries resembling Venetian palaces, Spanish villages, and French châteaux. To complement the social activities of the hotels, the city provided gambling, prostitution, and bootleg whiskey. Miami became a haven for out-of-town high rollers.

In the early 1930s, drawn south by the prospect of warm beaches and luxurious tropical surroundings, middle-class tourists fueled a second boom. More hotels had to be built, but it wouldn't do for Miami to open the same type of boring, staid hotels found across America. En masse, architects decided the motif of choice would be . . . art deco.

In truth, the design was art moderne. For purists, the term moderne was a bow to the Exposition Internationale des Arts Décoratifs et Industriels Modernes, held in Paris in 1925. Moderne offered a distinctive yet affordable design solution for the hotels, stores, clubs, and apartment buildings that would be built to accommodate the needs of a new breed of tourist.

An antidote to the gloom of the Great Depression, this look was cheerful and tidy. Along South Beach, Miami received an architectural makeover. Elaborating on the styles introduced in Paris, architects borrowed elements of American industrial design. The features of trains, ocean liners, and automobiles were stripped down to their streamlined essentials, inspiring new looks for the art deco hotels.

With a steel-and-concrete box as a foundation, architects dipped into this grab bag of styles to accessorize their hotels. Pylons, spheres, cylinders, and cubes thrust from facades and roofs. "Eyebrows," small ledges over windows, popped out to provide shade. Softening the boxy buildings' edges, designers added curved corners and wraparound windows. Sunlight, an abundant commodity in Miami Beach, was brought indoors by glass-block construction. Landscapers learned to create an illusion of coolness by planting palms and laying terrazzo floors.

A uniform style soon marked Miami's new hotels. A vertical central element raced past the roofline and into the sky to create a sense of motion. To add to the illusion that these immobile buildings were rapidly speeding objects, colorful bands known as racing stripes were painted around the corners. In keeping with the beachside setting, designers adorned hotels with nautical elements. Portholes appeared in sets of three on facades or within buildings. Images of seaweed, starfish, and rolling ocean waves were plastered, painted, or etched on walls. Some of the buildings looked as if they were ready to go to sea.

Art deco design translated the synchronized choreography of Busby Berkeley movie musicals into architecture. Ordinary travelers could now take a low-cost vacation in an oceanfront fantasy world of geometric shapes and amusing colors. All this was created not for millionaires but for regular folks, those who collected a weekly paycheck . . . who, for one brief, shining moment, could live a life of luxury.

— *Gary McKechnie*

rooms, 24 suites ♨ *Restaurant, cable TV, pool, health club, spa, beach, bar, lobby lounge, laundry service, concierge, business services* ▭ *AE, D, DC, MC, V.*

$$$$ ☷ **Fisher Island Club.** To reach ultraexclusive Fisher Island, you (and your car) will need to take a seven-minute ferry ride to the former estate of William K. Vanderbilt, a mansion forming the centerpiece of this resort. Recreation facilities include an 18-hole golf course and the challenging P. B. Dye–designed 9-hole golf course, the Spa Internazionale, and 18 lighted tennis courts—hard, grass, and clay. Rooms are diverse in form and decor. There are suites and villas, and the cottages that surround the mansion have hot tubs. ✉ *1 Fisher Island Dr., Fisher Island, Miami 33109* ☎ *305/535–6000 or 800/537–3708* 🖷 *305/535–6003* ⊕ *www. fisherisland-florida.com* ⇗ *20 suites, 7 villas, 3 cottages* ♨ *8 restaurants, cable TV, golf course, 18 tennis courts, 2 pools, spa, beach, concierge* ▭ *AE, DC, MC, V.*

$$$$ ☷ **Marlin Hotel.** Music-industry luminaries who come to record at the on-site South Beach Studios often stay at this miniboutique property, which has attracted the likes of Mick Jagger, U2, and Aerosmith. Every room is different, but hardwood floors, stainless-steel fixtures, and muted earth tones in all create a commonality. You'll stay connected with Web TV, dual-line cordless phones, and a dedicated e-mail address. Studio suites, with rattan sitting areas, are sizable; larger suites approximate villas. A rooftop deck invites sunbathing. ✉ *1200 Collins Ave., South Beach 33139* ☎ *305/604–5063 or 800/688–7678* 🖷 *305/672–2881* ⊕ *www. islandoutpost.com* ⇗ *11 suites* ♨ *In-room data ports, in-room safes, kitchenettes, cable TV, in-room VCRs, bar* ▭ *AE, D, DC, MC, V.*

$$$$ ☷ **Ritz-Carlton South Beach.** After $100 million in renovations to the former DiLido, a cherished art moderne, Melvin Grossman and Morris Lapidus–designed building, Miami's third Ritz-Carlton has all the amenities you'd expect (e.g., 24-hour "technology butler") while retaining the black terrazzo floors and the lobby's grand Lapidus staircase. A huge outdoor pool deck fronting the ocean is framed by the hotel's wings, which have been crafted to resemble the decks of an ocean liner. "State-rooms" feature the plush appointments of a luxury yacht. Speaking of yachts, Ritz guests can catch a Zodiac from the beach to a yacht anchored nearby for some offshore partying. ✉ *1 Lincoln Rd., South Beach 33139* ☎ *786/276–4000 or 800/241–3333* 🖷 *786/276–4100* ⊕ *www.ritzcarlton.com* ⇗ *375 rooms* ♨ *3 restaurants, room service, cable TV, pool, gym, spa, beach, concierge, business services, meeting rooms, parking (fee)* ▭ *AE, D, DC, MC, V.*

$$$$ ☷ **Setai.** Five-star fever continues with the fall 2004 opening of the Setai, a 40-story luxury residence tower that also includes an eight-story, 88-room boutique hotel. Ultra-luxe rooms range in size from 550 to 900 square feet and include high-speed Internet access and a host of other perks. "Exotic" doesn't begin to describe the striking furnishings. Resort amenities are equally lavish—three beachfront pools, private spa and fitness center, and teak-latticed cabanas tucked within a lush landscape of gardens and fountains. ✉ *101 20th St., South Beach 33139* ☎ *305/672–7900 or 877/ 997–3824* 🖷 *305/672–9922* ⊕ *www.setai.com* ⇗ *88 rooms* ♨ *Restaurant, 3 pools, health club, spa, concierge* ▭ *AE, D, DC, MC, V.*

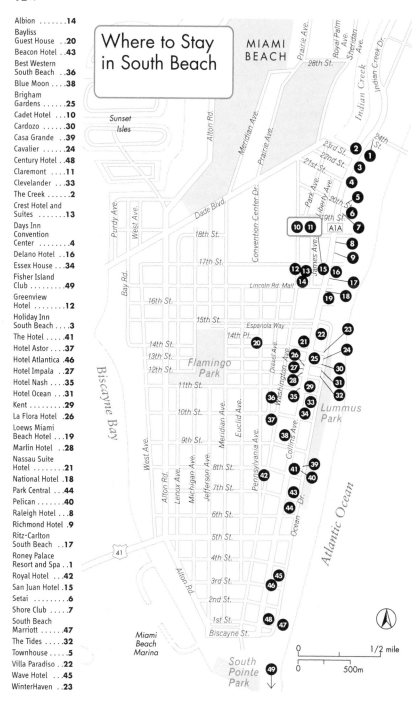

Where to Stay in South Beach

MIAMI BEACH

$$$$ ⊡ **Shore Club.** Exuding the glamour of Old Hollywood, this SoBe pied-à-terre is a hot spot for today's Tinseltown A-listers and visitors hoping to spy them. The sprawling property has room for private cabanas and a beach house on the sand and a series of gardens separated by courtyards and reflecting pools. Rooms are fairly large and serenely beautiful, with dashes of color among the blond-wood furniture and stainless-steel accents. Part of the upscale Nobu chain, the restaurant serves Japanese-Peruvian cuisine and draws healthy crowds. Other healthy crowds can be found at the rooftop Spa at the Shore Club. ⊠ *1901 Collins Ave., South Beach 33139* ☎ *305/695–3100 or 877/640–9500* ⓕ *305/695–3299* ⊕ *www.shoreclub.com* ⛵ *325 rooms* ♨ *3 restaurants, cable TV, 2 pools, health club, spa, beach, 2 bars, shop, meeting rooms* ☐ *AE, DC, MC, V.*

$$$$ ⊡ **The Tides.** Hotelier and music magnate Chris Blackwell has put a creative twist on what can often be a sterile Miami design motif (too much white!) by introducing hospitality-oriented elements into the chic surroundings. Some touches are small—telescopes in each room (they all have big windows facing the ocean) and a blackboard for messages to maids. Others are large—every room has a king-size bed, capacious closets, and generous baths, the result of turning 115 rooms into 45 suites. Pretty public spaces include a dining terrace at 1220, the gorgeous contemporary restaurant. The Olympic-size pool is the only one on Ocean Drive. ⊠ *1220 Ocean Dr., South Beach 33139* ☎ *305/604–5070 or 866/438–4337* ⓕ *305/604–5180* ⊕ *www.thetideshotel.com* ⛵ *45 suites* ♨ *Restaurant, in-room data ports, in-room safes, minibars, cable TV, pool, gym, beach, baby-sitting, dry cleaning, concierge, business services, meeting rooms, travel services* ☐ *AE, D, DC, MC, V.*

$$$–$$$$ ⊡ **The Hotel.** Despite its minimalist name, this boutique hotel has gotten maximum applause thanks to fashion designer Todd Oldham, who brought the colors of the sand and the sea indoors. Individually painted tiles, pale ash desks, and mosaic-pattern rugs delight the eyes; bejeweled bathrooms with tie-dyed robes, TVs with VCRs, and stereo systems are suitable distractions in the decidedly petite, yet soundproof, rooms. Add soft lighting and two-person bathtubs, and you have all the makings of a romantic retreat. The excellent restaurant Wish serves creative cuisine indoors or out. Best of all is the intimate rooftop pool with spectacular views of the sea. ⊠ *801 Collins Ave., South Beach 33139* ☎ *305/531–2222 or 877/843–4683* ⓕ *305/531–3222* ⊕ *www. thehotelofsouthbeach.com* ⛵ *48 rooms, 4 suites* ♨ *Restaurant, cable TV, pool, gym, bar, concierge, business services* ☐ *AE, D, DC, MC, V.*

$$$–$$$$

Fodor'sChoice

★ ⊡ **Loews Miami Beach Hotel.** Business meets pleasure in this enormous 18-story oceanfront resort, built from the ground up in 1998 and launching a demand for luxury properties that continues to this day. Not only did Loews manage to snag 99 feet of beach, it also took over the vacant St. Moritz next door and restored it to its original 1939 art deco magnificence. The entire complex combines boutique charm with updated opulence. How big is it? The Loews has 85,000 square feet of meeting space and an enormous ocean-view grand ballroom. Emeril Lagasse opened a restaurant here with a "bam" in 2003. ⊠ *1601 Collins Ave., South Beach 33139* ☎ *305/604–1601 or 800/235–6397* ⓕ *305/604–*

3999 ⊕ www.loewshotels.com ⤳ *733 rooms, 57 suites* ⚷ *4 restaurants, cable TV, pool, gym, beach, 2 lounges, children's programs (ages 4–12), meeting rooms* ⊟ *AE, D, DC, MC, V.*

$$$–$$$$ ⊞ **National Hotel.** The most spectacular feature of this resurrected 1939

Fodor'sChoice shorefront hotel is its palm-lined "infinity" pool—Miami Beach's longest,

★ at 205 feet. By day the pool is a picture-perfect backdrop for the film crews that often work here. Preserved pieces include the original chandelier in the hotel's ballroom and D'Lounge's oak bar and original club chairs. A major 2003 renovation gave rooms a new design scheme, combining the geometry of art deco with a soothing palate of colors and fabrics. Flat-screen TVs come with DVD and VCR. Step into the 1930s-style Martini Room bar and you'll be looking for Bogie. ⊠ *1677 Collins Ave., South Beach 33139* ☎ *305/532–2311 or 800/327–8370* ⧉ *305/534–1426* ⊕ *www.nationalhotel.com* ⤳ *143 rooms, 8 suites* ⚷ *Restaurant, in-room data ports, in-room safes, minibars, in-room VCRs, pool, gym, beach, bar, laundry service, concierge, meeting rooms, parking (fee), non-smoking floor* ⊟ *AE, DC, MC, V.*

$$$–$$$$ ⊞ **Raleigh Hotel.** Hidden behind a thick veil of greenery is one of the nicest oceanfront hotels in South Beach. Among the first Art Deco District hotels to be renovated, it has retained Victorian accents (hallway chandeliers and in-room oil paintings) to soften the 20th-century edges. A gorgeous fleur-de-lis pool is the focal point year-round, especially on December 31, when synchronized swimmers dive in at the stroke of midnight. Other pluses: spacious rooms and suites, the lobby coffee bar, a romantic restaurant (Tiger Oak Room), and the old-fashioned Martini Bar. ⊠ *1775 Collins Ave., South Beach 33139* ☎ *305/534–6300 or 800/848–1775* ⧉ *305/538–8140* ⊕ *www.raleighhotel.com* ⤳ *111 rooms, 18 suites* ⚷ *Restaurant, in-room data ports, in-room safes, refrigerators, cable TV, in-room VCRs, pool, gym, massage, beach, bar, laundry service, concierge, business services, meeting rooms, parking (fee)* ⊟ *AE, D, DC, MC, V.*

$$$–$$$$ ⊞ **South Beach Marriott.** Continuing the trend started by Loews, Marriott's move into South Beach was late and big, with nouveau art deco flourishes meant to conceal a pragmatic beach resort. The rooms are larger than most on the beach, with liberal splashes of very un-Marriott-like colors—echoing the sun and sand—that prove the mega-brand really is trying to fit in. A health club, quiet beach, and reliable service make this a safe bet for business types or families who want to experience South Beach while keeping the wildest partying at a distance. ⊠ *161 Ocean Dr., South Beach 33139* ☎ *305/536–7700 or 800/228–9290* ⧉ *305/536–9900* ⊕ *www.miamibeachmarriott.com* ⤳ *236 rooms, 9 suites* ⚷ *Restaurant, in-room data ports, cable TV, pool, health club, beach, 2 bars, laundry service, concierge, business services, meeting rooms, parking (fee)* ⊟ *AE, D, DC, MC, V.*

$$–$$$$ ⊞ **Blue Moon.** Former talk-show host and current media mogul Merv Griffin joined two hotels to create Blue Moon, for those who like the Ocean Drive scene but quickly tire of art deco. Designed to resemble a European estate rather than a 1930s box, the Blue Moon looks and feels nothing like other nearby boutique hotels, and service here tends to be more reliable. Rooms, though not huge, are airy and free of trendiness.

Griffin has since moved on, and the Blue Moon has joined the boutique Coral Collection chain, but it remains a quirky marriage of deco and Mediterranean styles. ⊠ *944 Collins Ave., South Beach 33139* ☎ *305/ 673–2262 or 800/724–1623* 🖷 *305/534–5399* ⊕ *www.bluemoonhotel. com* ⊷ *69 rooms, 6 suites* ♨ *Restaurant, in-room data ports, in-room safes, cable TV, pool, laundry service, meeting rooms, parking (fee)* ⊟ *AE, D, DC, MC, V.*

$$–$$$$ 📺 **Cardozo.** Perhaps it's because this hotel is owned by Gloria and Emilio Estefan that there's such lively and loud music in the lobby. But when you're through with the check-in tango, you can retreat to a quiet and comfortable room. Leopard-print blankets and other artifacts collected on Gloria's world tours, as well as large baths with mosaic-tile sinks and terra-cotta walls, distinguish this place from the pack. Whether you opt for room or suite, you'll have space to spread out. The views from oceanfront rooms are impressive (especially from Rooms 202 and 305), and all rooms have TV, VCR, and CD players. ⊠ *1300 Ocean Dr., South Beach 33139* ☎ *305/535–6500 or 800/782–6500* 🖷 *305/ 532–3563* ⊕ *www.cardozohotel.com* ⊷ *43 rooms, 4 suites* ♨ *Restaurant, in-room safes, minibars, cable TV, in-room VCRs, beach, bar, concierge, meeting room* ⊟ *AE, DC, MC, V.*

$$$ 📺 **Hotel Nash.** This boutique hotel dating from 1935 was awakened from a long art deco sleep when Miami designer Peter Page and manager Laura Sheridan—who came to Miami with Ian Schrager to open the Delano— created a South Beach rarity combining style and warmth. What is white elsewhere is sage green and blond wood here. Shield-shaped armoires conceal minibars, while tiled bathrooms with rain-forest shower heads are built for those who take grooming and primping seriously. (Framed floor-to-ceiling mirrors serve the same purpose.) Keep your eyes peeled for celebs who frequent Mark's, the restaurant run by James Beard Award–winning chef Mark Militello, downstairs. ⊠ *1120 Collins Ave., South Beach 33139* ☎ *305/674–7800 or 800/403–6274* 🖷 *305/538– 8288* ⊕ *www.hotelnash.com* ⊷ *52 rooms, 3 suites* ♨ *Restaurant, cable TV, minibars, 3 pools, concierge* ⊟ *AE, D, MC, V.*

$$$ 📺 **Richmond Hotel.** The entrance and lobby may not be as grand as those of the neighboring Delano, but the rooms here are among the most comfortable in South Beach, with chenille bedspreads, blond wood, plush sofas, and a soft 1930s floral design scheme. These are rooms that make you feel at home, though wireless Internet access keeps you in touch if you must. The grounds, with a large pool, half-moon hot tub, white-canvas cabanas, and an eye-catching curvy stream, have what your home is probably missing. The sidewalk slices through a wide lawn and past palm trees, creating an entryway to the Atlantic. ⊠ *1757 Collins Ave., South Beach 33139* ☎ *305/538–2331 or 800/327–3163* 🖷 *305/ 531–9021* ⊕ *www.richmondhotel.com* ⊷ *85 rooms, 6 suites* ♨ *Café, cable TV, pool, gym, hot tub, beach, laundry service, concierge, Internet* ⊟ *AE, D, DC, MC, V.*

$$–$$$ 📺 **Century Hotel.** Designed in 1939 by art deco master Henry Hohauser, the Century now garners an *InStyle* guest list. Like the Marriott across the street, it's a little south of the action, but that can be a good thing: the Century is a favorite of celebrities trying to keep a low profile. Next

door, the renowned Italian restaurant Joia casts a heavy shadow of cool aided by a steady influx of A-listers and local glitterati. The rooms have a certain spartan warmth and definitely feel stylish, if a little remote—but that's probably the point. ⊠ *140 Ocean Dr., South Beach 33139* ☎ *305/674–8855 or 888/982–3688* 🖷 *305/538–5733* ⊕ *www.centurysouthbeach.com* 🖙 *26 rooms* ⚲ *In-room data ports, in-room safes, cable TV, meeting rooms* ⊟ *AE, DC, MC, V* ⏐⊚⏐ *CP.*

$$–$$$ ⊡ **Essex House.** A favorite with Europeans, especially the British, Essex House moved into the upscale category over the past few years with a major renovation and such amenities as in-room spa services and a pool with Jacuzzi jets. The large suites, reached by crossing a tropical courtyard, are well worth the price: each has a wet bar, king-size bed, pull-out sofa, 100-square-foot bathroom, refrigerator, and hot tub. Rooms weigh in with comfy club chairs, elegant mahogany furniture, and marble tubs. ⊠ *1001 Collins Ave., South Beach 33139* ☎ *305/534–2700 or 800/553–7739* 🖷 *305/532–3827* ⊕ *www.essexhotel.com* 🖙 *61 rooms, 19 suites* ⚲ *In-room data ports, cable TV, pool, bar, dry cleaning, laundry service, meeting rooms, parking (fee)* ⊟*AE, D, MC, V* ⏐⊚⏐ *CP.*

★ $$–$$$ ⊡ **Hotel Astor.** Among the very best that South Beach has to offer, the Astor stands apart from the crowd by double-insulating walls against noise and offering such quiet luxuries as thick towels, down pillows, paddle fans, and a seductive pool. Rooms are built to recall deco ocean-liner staterooms, with faux-portholes, custom-milled French furniture, Roman shades, and sleek sound and video systems. A tasteful muted color scheme and the most comfortable king beds imaginable make for eminently restful nights, and excellent service eliminates any worries about practical matters. Metro Kitchen & Bar has created a dining buzz among the locals. ⊠ *956 Washington Ave., South Beach 33139* ☎ *305/531–8081 or 800/270–4981* 🖷 *305/531–3193* ⊕*www.hotelastor.com* 🖙 *40 rooms* ⚲ *Restaurant, room service, in-room data ports, in-room safes, minibars, pool, massage, bar, laundry service, concierge, Internet, business services, meeting room, parking (fee)* ⊟ *AE, DC, MC, V.*

$$–$$$ ⊡ **Hotel Ocean.** If the street signs didn't read Ocean Drive, you might suspect you were whiling away the day on the French Riviera. The tropical European feel is evident when you enter the shaded, bougainvillea-draped courtyard and see diners enjoying a complimentary breakfast in the hotel's brasserie. The two buildings connected by this courtyard contain a few surprises: soft beds; authentic 1930s collectibles and original art deco fireplaces; large foldout couches; clean, spacious baths; and sound-proof windows ensure that rooms (which average 425 square feet each) are comfortable and quiet. ⊠ *1230–38 Ocean Dr., South Beach 33139* ☎ *305/672–2579 or 800/783–1725* 🖷 *305/672–7665* ⊕ *www.hotelocean.com* 🖙 *14 rooms, 13 suites* ⚲ *Restaurant, in-room data ports, in-room safes, minibars, cable TV, in-room VCRs, bar, concierge* ⊟ *AE, D, DC, MC, V* ⏐⊚⏐ *CP.*

$$–$$$ ⊡ **La Flora Hotel.** Design elements like the 1929 terrazzo floors and the custom-made deco furniture transport you back to Miami Beach's glory days. The lobby bar even serves classic cocktails from the 1940s. Sip them while people-watching on Collins Avenue, or just rest here after a relaxing day at the beach, only a block away. Rooms are decorated in pastels slightly reminiscent of an Ikea catalog, and the roomy bathrooms are done in marble. The rate includes Continental breakfast, guests get discounts at a nearby gym, and room service has options from the nearby Japanese and Italian restaurants. ☒ *1238 Collins Ave., South Beach 33139* ☎ *305/531–3406 or 877/523–5672* 🖷 *305/538–0850* ⊕ *www.lafflorahotel.com* ⌁ *20 rooms, 8 suites* ⚘ *Cable TV, massage, concierge, business services, parking (fee)* ☰ *AE, D, DC, MC, V* ⦿ *CP.*

$$–$$$ ▣ **Nassau Suite Hotel.** For a boutique hotel one block from the beach, this airy retreat almost qualifies as a steal (by South Beach standards), especially with Continental breakfast included in the rate. The original 1937 floor plan of 50 rooms gave way to 22 spacious and smart-looking suites with king beds, fully equipped kitchens, hardwood floors, white wood blinds, and free high-speed Internet access. The Nassau is in the heart of the action yet quiet enough to give you the rest you need. Note: There's no bellhop and very limited parking. ☒ *1414 Collins Ave., South Beach 33139* ☎ *305/532–0043 or 866/859–4177* 🖷 *305/534–3133* ⊕ *www.nassausuite.com* ⌁ *22 suites* ⚘ *In-room data ports, kitchenettes, cable TV, concierge, business center.* ☰ *AE, D, DC, MC, V* ⦿ *CP.*

$$–$$$ ▣ **Pelican.** Dazzling, kitschy spaces with art deco–inspired frivolity characterize this offbeat hotel owned by the Diesel Jeans company. Individually designed rooms, with names like Me Tarzan, You Vain, are certainly clever, but all have tiny sleeping chambers in contrast to the triple-size bathrooms with outrageous industrial piping. Amenities like in-room CD players and bath products are certainly welcome, though. The hotel's celebrity guest list includes Yoko Ono, which figures, because room for room Pelican outweirds every place else in Miami. ☒ *826 Ocean Dr., South Beach 33139* ☎ *305/673–3373 or 800/773–5422* 🖷 *305/673–3255* ⊕ *www.pelicanhotel.com* ⌁ *25 rooms, 5 suites* ⚘ *Restaurant, café, in-room safes, refrigerators, cable TV, in-room VCRs, beach, bar, concierge, business services, parking (fee)* ☰ *AE, DC, MC, V.*

$$–$$$ ▣ **WinterHaven.** "Bright" and "airy" are not words usually associated with South Beach hotels, but this artfully restored classic is both. WinterHaven is a riot of color, from the garnet-and-aquamarine lobby lounge to the ginger-and-cream upholstery in guest rooms. Here, black-and-white photos of old South Beach hang over the custom-designed deco furniture. The two-story lobby and split-level mezzanine regularly host parties and fashion shoots, but if you take your complimentary breakfast up to the rooftop sundeck, you'll have a bird's-eye view of South Beach at dawn. ☒ *1400 Ocean Dr., South Beach 33139* ☎ *305/531–5571 or 800/395–2322* 🖷 *305/538–6387* ⊕ *www.winterhavenhotelsobe.com* ⌁ *71 rooms* ⚘ *In-room data ports, in-room safes, cable TV, bar, concierge, parking (fee)* ☰ *AE, D, DC, MC, V* ⦿ *CP.*

$–$$$ ▣ **Albion.** Avant-garde Boston architect Carlos Zapata updated this stylish 1939 nautical-deco building by Igor Polevitzky, and the place is full of his distinctive touches. The two-story lobby sweeps into a secluded courtyard and is framed by an indoor waterfall. A crowd of hip and friendly types makes up the clientele; they like to gather at the mezzanine-level pool, which has portholes that allow courtyard strollers an underwater view of the swimmers. As with other Rubell properties (the Beach House and the Greenview), guest rooms are minimalist in design, though filled with upscale touches. ⊠ *1650 James Ave., South Beach 33139* ☎ *305/913–1000 or 888/665–0008* 🖷 *305/674–0507* ⊕ *www. rubellhotels.com* ↘ *87 rooms, 9 suites* ♻ *Restaurant, in-room data ports, minibars, cable TV, pool, gym, bar, laundry service, concierge, meeting rooms* ⊟ *AE, D, DC, MC, V.*

$–$$$ 🏨 **Cavalier.** The Cavalier's 1936 facade is the very definition of art deco precision. Inside, standard rooms and suites exude a Caribbean warmth thanks to soft paint colors and wood accents. Rooms are loaded: entertainment centers that feature cable TV, VCRs, and CD players; queen-size beds; batik fabrics; deco-style furniture; and vintage black-and-white photos. Suites get an ocean view and king-size bed. And talk about location: you're right in the current of SoBe foot traffic and across the street from the great big Atlantic. ⊠ *1320 Ocean Dr., South Beach 33139* ☎ *305/604–5064 or 305/531–3555* 🖷 *305/531–5543* ⊕ *www. cavaliermiamibeach.com* ↘ *42 rooms, 3 suites* ♻ *In-room safes, minibars, cable TV, in-room VCRs, business services, travel services* ⊟ *AE, D, DC, MC, V.*

$–$$$ 🏨 **Holiday Inn South Beach.** The rates here are already a bargain for an oceanfront hotel on South Beach, but Holiday Inn's inclusive extras make the bang for your buck even better. Here's what's included in the rate: parking, beachside lounge chairs and umbrella, fitness center, lighted tennis courts, in-room safe, local calls, 800 access and incoming faxes, movie channels, and free dining for kids under 12. Plenty of on-site recreation—an oceanside pool, Jacuzzi, sand volleyball court, and water sports (fee)—gives this unpretentious choice a resort feel. Whenever you want to roam, Lincoln Road and Ocean Drive are steps away. ⊠ *2201 Collins Ave., South Beach 33139* ☎ *305/779–3200 or 800/435–1223* 🖷 *305/ 534–0966* ⊕*www.miamisouthbeachresort.com* ↘*355 rooms* ♻ *Restaurant, in-room data port, in-room safes, cable TV, pool, exercise equipment, bar, business services, free parking.*

$–$$$ 🏨 **Hotel Impala.** It's all very European here at the Impala, from the mineral water and orchids to the Mediterranean-style armoires, Italian fixtures, and triple-sheeted white-on-white modified Eastlake sleigh beds. Everything from wastebaskets to towels to toilet paper is of extraordinary quality. The building is a stunning tropical Mediterranean revival in the Art Deco District and is one block from the beach. Iron, mahogany, and stone on the inside are in sync with the sporty white-trim ocher exterior and quiet courtyard. Rooms are elegant, comfortable, and complete, each with a TV/VCR/stereo and a stock of CDs and videos. ⊠ *1228 Collins Ave., South Beach 33139* ☎*305/673–2021 or 800/646–7252* 🖷 *305/673–5984* ⊕ *www.hotelimpalamiamibeach.com* ↘ *14 rooms, 3 suites* ♻ *Restaurant, in-room data ports, cable TV, in-room VCRs, bar, laundry service, concierge* ⊟ *AE, D, DC, MC, V* ⦿ *CP.*

$–$$$ 🏨 **Park Central.** Across from the glorious beach, this seven-story 1937 classic, still a "blue jewel" with wraparound corner windows, knows just how to stay in the forefront of the art deco revival. Many fashionistas stay here, no doubt attracted by the soothing sculpture garden and compact pool, the setting of much parading about in swimming attire. Black-and-white photos of old beach scenes, hurricanes, and familiar faces attest to its longevity, and board games in the lobby add to its charm.

Rooms are decorated with Philippine mahogany furnishings—originals that have been restored. ✉ *640 Ocean Dr., South Beach 33139* ☏ *305/538–1611 or 800/727–5236* 🖷 *305/534–7520* ⊕ *www.theparkcentral. com* ➷ *115 rooms, 12 suites* ♿ *2 restaurants, in-room data ports, refrigerators, minibars, cable TV, pool, gym, bar, laundry service, concierge, Internet, meeting rooms* ▤ *AE, D, DC, MC, V.*

$–$$$ 🏨 **Royal Hotel.** *Austin Powers* meets *2001* in this avant-garde hotel that doesn't take itself too seriously. Each room only has two pieces of furniture: a "digital chaise lounge" and a bed, both molded white plastic contortions from designer Jordan Mozer. The bed has projecting wings for a phone and alarm clock and a headboard that arcs back like a car spoiler to double as a minibar. The chaise holds a TV–Web TV and keyboard for surfing the Net (high-speed, natch). Lest all this space-age technology make the room dull, a wild shag carpet and rainbow-paisley bathrobes remind you you're here to have fun—*Yeah, baby.* ✉ *758 Washington Ave., South Beach 33139* ☏ *305/673–9009 or 888/394–6835* 🖷 *305/673–9244* ⊕ *www.royalhotelsouthbeach.com* ➷ *38 rooms, 4 suites* ♿ *In-room safes, in-room data ports, cable TV, kitchenettes, microwaves, bicycles, lounge* ▤ *AE, D, DC, MC, V.*

$$ 🏨 **Roney Palace Resort and Spa.** The original Roney Plaza was a Miami Beach landmark and one of South Florida's first luxury resorts. Today it's the Roney Palace, making guests feel like royalty with possibly the largest rooms on the beach. All-suite choices include executive, one-bedroom, and two-bedroom suites, all casually furnished with blond-wood platform beds or other lightweight materials. The huge private beach, tropically landscaped pool, and water sports like parasailing and canoeing (extra) make it feel like a Caribbean resort. ✉ *2399 Collins Ave., South Beach 33139* ☏ *305/604–1000* 🖷 *305/538–7141* ⊕ *www.roney-palace. com* ➷ *510 suites* ♿ *3 restaurants, cable TV, pool, gym, spa, beach, 2 bars, concierge, meeting rooms, parking (fee)* ▤ *AE, D, DC, MC, V.*

$–$$ 🏨 **Beacon Hotel.** Terrazzo floors, whimsical furnishings, and an air of understated elegance reflect the hotel's original 1937 grand design. Art deco is in overdrive in this neighborhood, and the hotel is swept up in the energy of the district. A restaurant with sidewalk café allows you to check out passers-by. The beach is a stone's throw away. Inside, room size is moderate, and all have comfortable beds, fairly large closets, and an average-size bath. As at other hotels along this stretch, valet parking is a necessary evil since there's little room to park your car. ✉ *720 Ocean Dr., South Beach 33139* ☏ *305/674–8200 or 877/674–8200* 🖷 *305/674–8976* ⊕ *www.beacon-hotel.com* ➷ *79 rooms, 2 suites* ♿ *Restaurant, cable TV, gym, bar, laundry service, concierge, Internet, business services, meeting rooms, parking (fee)* ▤ *AE, D, DC, MC, V* ⊚ *CP.*

$–$$ 🏨 **Crest Hotel and Suites.** Poolside Adirondack chairs, a rooftop solarium, and relative solitude make this easygoing hotel a good place when the R&R you desire isn't rock-and-roll. The 1939 art deco hotel is not on a trendy street, but it's only steps from everything worth seeing. Streamlined furniture makes this look like a boutique hotel on the move. The simple rooms have a king- or two full-size beds, and suites include kitchenettes and microwaves. The whole place is clean as a whistle, maybe even cleaner. Two buildings are separated by a small coffee bar and an equally small pool. ⊠ *1670 James Ave., South Beach 33139* ☎ *305/531–0321 or 800/531–3880* 🖷 *305/531–8180* ⊕ *www.crestgrouphotels.com* 🖘 *43 rooms, 23 suites* ⌂ *Café, cable TV, pool, meeting rooms.* 🖃 *AE, DC, MC, V.*

$–$$ 🖳 **Days Inn Convention Center.** Nothing flashy and nothing trashy might be the motto. The lobby is bright and floral, with a fountain and gift shop. Rooms are standard hotel issue; deluxe rooms throw in impressive views of the ocean. If you're more concerned about your wallet than your image, this can be a good bet. Keep in mind that if you want something with character, you can find that elsewhere at these rates. Here you'll find the basic franchise dependables (including a pool)—and it's all literally seconds from the beach and the Miami Beach Convention Center. ⊠ *100 21st St., South Beach 33139* ☎ *305/538–6631 or 800/451–3345* 🖷 *305/674–0954* ⊕ *www.daysinnsouthbeach.com* 🖘 *172 rooms* ⌂ *Restaurant, in-room safes, some refrigerators, cable TV, pool, beach, bar, laundry service, parking (fee)* 🖃 *AE, D, DC, MC, V.*

$–$$ 🖳 **Townhouse.** You've probably seen images of its white rooms accented by a red-and-white beachball or the rooftop deck with waterbed chaise longues. Since its arrival on the scene, this boutique hotel designed by India Madhavi has been the site of many a fashion shoot and the destination of many a hipster. Rooms are simple and streamlined, white and welcoming, although they're not everybody's definition of cozy: You get a lozenge-shape lounging "pouf" rather than a couch. But such is the price of über-modernity—although this is actually the best budget buy for the style-hungry. Penthouse suites cost what standard rooms do elsewhere. ⊠ *150 20th St., east of Collins Ave., South Beach 33139* ☎ *305/534–3800 or 877/534–3800* 🖷 *305/534–3811* ⊕ *www.townhousehotel.com* 🖘 *69 rooms, 3 suites* ⌂ *Restaurant, cable TV, exercise equipment, lounge, laundry service* 🖃 *AE, D, MC, V* ⌘ *CP.*

$–$$ 🖳 **Wave Hotel.** Formerly the Lord Balfour Hotel, the Wave pulls off a difficult mix of kitsch and class that draws trendsetters. Bizarre modernist paintings and stainless-steel accents predominate in the lobby, which leads into a sedate little courtyard. Custom-made Italian furniture including platform beds and funky Murano glass chandeliers adorn guest rooms, which include the requisite CD-player stereo and data ports. Wave's in-room innovation is its (eponymously memorable) wave machine next to each bed—perfect for soothing jangled nerves after an encounter with Collins Avenue's wired nightclub scene. ⊠ *350 Ocean Dr., South Beach 33139* ☎ *305/673–0401 or 800/501–0401* 🖷 *305/531–9385* ⊕ *www.wavehotel.com* 🖘 *66 rooms* ⌂ *Restaurant, room service, in-room data ports, minibars, cable TV, bar* 🖃 *AE, D, DC, MC, V.*

$ 🖳 **Best Western South Beach.** It's all for one at this complex of five art deco hotels—the Kenmore, Taft, Bel-Aire, Coral House, and Davis—which offer budget-friendly rates including Continental breakfast. Each hotel is like a separate wing of the whole; yet each retains its own character. The Kenmore, for example, projects a no-nonsense 1930s utilitarian simplicity, while the Bel-Aire invites relaxation within a walled courtyard sheltering a winding sidewalk. The complex is within walking distance of the Miami Beach Convention Center and Lincoln Road

THE MEDIUM IS THE MASSAGE

BY COMBINING RESTFUL TREATMENTS, healthy (yet tasty) cuisine, and focused exercise programs, spas have positioned themselves as a mind, body, and soul retreat from the stresses of everyday life. In Miami, no self-respecting resort debuts without a lavish spa in place, and the competition to launch ever more exotic treatments and esoteric machinery has reached a fever pitch.

But be warned, not every spa is worthy of the name. The word is used very loosely, referring to anything from a three-level palace of relaxation to a spare room with a pair of massage tables. Among the big-dollar offerings, though, there is plenty of variety, depending on whether your preference is decadent pampering, unique treatments, a trendy clientele, or a good, old-fashioned sweat.

Best place to feel like a million bucks: The ultra-posh Fisher Island Club's Spa Internazionale has extremely personalized service and prices to match. you're after, this is the place. The very popular yoga classes include Yoga for Golf.

Best way to unwind after a meeting: The business-oriented JW Marriott and Mandarin Oriental push stress-reduction. JW Marriott's Spa 1111 specializes in European-style treatments, such as the one-hour Muscle Aching Massage and Hydrolifting Facial. The Spa at the Mandarin Oriental mixes Asian decor and techniques with a dash of Miami. The Detoxifying Sea of Senses combines skin brushing, body rubbing, and a close encounter with warmed algae.

Best adrenaline rush: The massive Eden Roc has all the typical spa offerings, plus a bewildering list of treatments, and oceanfront setting, and state-of-the-art fitness equipment. But what sets it apart is Mount Eden Roc, the only indoor rock climbing wall in South Florida.

Best way to bring up baby: The Pre-Natal Massage at the Eden Roc helps those in the second and third trimesters fight lower back pain and water retention. Newborns aren't neglected, either: the Infant Massage rubs baby the right way, then shows parents how to try it at home.

Best shot at rubbing shoulders with a star: Up on the roof at the celebrity-magnet Delano is the très-chic Agua spa. Early reservations are essential for the Milk and Honey body soak or the Manual Lift with Oxygen, which promises dramatic reshaping and firming of the face.

Best place to say "Om": The Spa at Doral added the East Coast's first Chopra Center for Well Being, founded by philosopher and New Age wellness guru Dr. Deepak Chopra, who emphasizes fitness of mind and spirit as a means to achieving physical health.

Best of the rest: The Spa at Shore Club is a serene rooftop affair, with a choice of indoor treatment rooms or outside terraces. The house specialty is Asian Ayurvedic scrubs and soaks. Ritz-Carlton has three hotels in Miami, each with its own spa: a 5,000-square-foot boutique spa at Coconut Grove, a 13,000-square-foot number in South Beach, and the big kahuna in Key Biscayne, whose signature treatment is the Fountain of Youth Ocean Balance, where you float free in the Atlantic.

New: Now a Fairmont, Turnberry Isle Resort & Club houses the Willow Stream luxury spa, where skin, body, and muscle therapies blend ancient ritual with modern science.

— Matt Windsor

Mall. The main lobby is inside the Kenmore. ✉ *1050 Washington Ave., South Beach 33139* ☎ *305/674–1930 or 888/343–1930* 📠 *305/534–6591* ⊕ *www.bestwestern.com* ⊐ *139 rooms, 18 suites* ⚲ *Cable TV, pool, Internet, business center* ☰ *AE, MC, V.* ⑂ *CP.*

$ ⊞ **Brigham Gardens.** You might be drawn to this small guest house one block from the beach by the chattering sound of Moluccan lorries or by the sight and scent of more than 80 species of plants and trees lining the walkways and patios. From the street it looks like a lush urban anomaly. Rooms—all with private baths—are homey and come equipped with refrigerators, microwaves, and coffeemakers (apartments have full kitchens) for budget-minded visitors intent on eating in. Stay seven days or longer, and you get a 10 percent discount. Pets are welcome, too. ✉ *1411 Collins Ave., South Beach 33139* ☎ *305/531–1331* 📠 *305/538–9898* ⊕ *www.brighamgardens.com* ⊐ *8 rooms, 12 suites* ⚲ *Fans, refrigerators, cable TV, meeting rooms* ☰ *AE, DC, MC, V.*

$ ⊞ **Cadet Hotel.** Clark Gable stayed in Room 225 when he came to Miami for Army Air Corps training in the 1940s. Although this Lincoln Road district hotel doesn't quite have the glamour to attract stars today, it's still a clean, friendly, and perfectly placed little hotel. For a pad that's a few minutes' walk from the Jackie Gleason Theater of the Performing Arts and the convention center and two blocks from the ocean, it's about half the cost of an Ocean Drive hotel. A 2002 room renovation brought bamboo floors, custom armoires, Egyptian linens, and upgraded bath amenities. Breakfast is on the house. ✉ *1701 James Ave., South Beach 33139* ☎ *305/672–6688 or 800/432–2338* 📠 *305/532–1676* ⊕ *www.cadethotel.com* ⊐ *42 rooms* ⚲ *In-room safes, minibars, cable TV, Internet, meeting rooms* ☰ *AE, D, DC, MC, V* ⑂ *CP.*

$ ⊞ **Hotel Atlantica.** Surrounded by the deco pastels and flourishes of its neighbors, the mock-country chalet facade of Hotel Atlantica is a pleasant change on the southern end of Collins Avenue. Owned by a Swiss couple (no surprise there), the hotel offers that level of personalized service you get when the owners are also checking you in. Rooms range in size from small singles to one-bedroom suites and are bright, clean, and attractive, with private baths, cable TV, and other staples, including voice mail. ✉ *321 Collins Ave., South Beach 33139* ☎ *305/532–7077 or 866/287–4801* 📠 *305/532–8767* ⊕ *www.hotelatlantica.com* ⊐ *24 rooms, 2 suites* ⚲ *Cable TV, in-room safe, refrigerators* ☰ *AE, D, DC, MC, V.*

$ ⊞ **Kent.** There are toys in the Day-Glo–colored lobby, beanbag chairs in the rooms, and chrome ceiling fans throughout at this fanciful SoBe hotel. But the highlight here is the third-floor Lucite Suite, where practically everything, from bed to desk to phones to tables, is made from translucent plastic, making it a great place to party (but a bad place to play hide-and-seek). Sure, the rooms are on the small side, and there isn't much of a view, but the atmosphere, proximity to the beach and clubs, the pumped-up staff, and great prices make the Kent hard to beat if you're in the mood for a good time. ✉ *1131 Collins Ave., South Beach 33139* ☎ *305/604–5068 or 866/826–5368* 📠 *305/531–0720* ⊕ *www. thekenthotel.com* ⊐ *53 rooms, 1 suite* ⚲ *In-room safes, refrigerators, cable TV, in-room VCRs, business services, meeting room, travel services* ☰ *AE, D, DC, MC, V.*

$ ⬛ **Villa Paradiso.** Peeking out from a sea of tropical foliage, quiet Villa Paradiso is a rather unassuming piece of deco architecture. But its charms are evident the minute you step into a secluded courtyard. Inside, the large rooms, which are more like apartments, have polished hardwood floors, French doors, and quirky wrought-iron furniture. Rooms are well suited for extended visits, with separate living and dining areas and access to laundry facilities. Free local calls and the prospect of enjoying conversation with fellow guests on the lush patio make this an affordable pleasure. ⊠ *1415 Collins Ave., South Beach 33139* ☎ *305/532–0616* 🖷 *305/673–5874* ⊕ *www.villaparadisohotel.com* ⟿ *17 studios* ⚬ *In-room data ports, kitchenettes, cable TV, laundry facilities* ⊟ *AE, DC, MC, V.*

¢–$$ ⬛ **Greenview Hotel.** This 1939 Henry Hohauser–designed art deco hotel was bought by the Rubell Family and renovated by Parisian designer Chahan Minassian (of Ralph Lauren's European Polo stores). The vibe is understated chic and seemingly straight out of a design magazine: wrought-iron scroll railings in the bi-level lobby and custom hand-crafted furnishings, mid-century modernist collectors' pieces, and pristine white upholstery in the simple rooms, which also have queen-size beds and large baths. The lack of on-premises amenities is tempered by the free access you have to those of the Albion, a block and a half away. ⊠ *1671 Washington Ave., South Beach 33139* ☎ *305/531–6588 or 887/782–3557* 🖷 *305/531–4580* ⊕ *www.rubellhotels.com* ⟿ *40 rooms, 2 suites* ⚬ *Cable TV, laundry service, concierge, Internet, business services* ⊟ *AE, DC, MC, V* ⧉ *CP.*

¢–$ ⬛ **Bayliss Guest House.** At the Bayliss, rooms are unexpectedly big and surprisingly inexpensive. Not only are the bedrooms large, so are the kitchen, the sitting room, and bath. Standard rooms minus kitchens are also available. An easy three blocks west of the ocean, the Bayliss is in a residential neighborhood that's comfortably close to—but far enough away from—the din of the Art Deco District. Can't do much better than this, if you don't mind carrying your own bags. There's very limited parking. ⊠ *500 14th St., South Beach 33139* ☎ *305/531–3488* 🖷 *305/531–4440* ⊕ *www.thebayliss.com* ⟿ *12 rooms, 7 suites* ⚬ *Refrigerators, cable TV, laundry facilities* ⊟ *AE, D, DC, MC, V.*

¢–$ ⬛ **Clevelander.** The first thing you'll notice about the Clevelander, if its reputation hasn't made it to your town, is the giant pool-bar complex, which attracts revelers for happy-hour drink specials and loud, live music every day of the week. Inside, a sports bar off the lobby is another of the hotel's five bars, while a sidewalk restaurant allows revelers to take a break from the party. Rooms have generous-sized baths and have been refreshed with new bedding and accents. Because of the partying, guests must be 21, and you won't get much sleep unless you choose a room away from the action. Thankfully, the staff seems to be having a blast. ⊠ *1020 Ocean Dr., South Beach 33139* ☎ *305/531–3485 or 800/815–6829* 🖷 *305/531–3953* ⊕ *www.clevelanderhotel.com* ⟿ *55 rooms* ⚬ *Restaurant, cable TV, pool, 5 bars* ⊟ *AE, DC, MC, V.*

¢ ⬛ **Claremont.** If your immediate surroundings are secondary to getting a room in South Beach, consider this place. Rooms are small, starkly simple, and offer the necessities—soft beds, private baths, and color TV—

WITH CHILDREN?

F YOU'RE TRULY EMPHASIZING a stress-free family vacation, then you don't want a sterile business hotel or a trendy hot spot. By nature, Miami's ocean resorts are usually family-friendly, although only a few offer organized children's programs. Short-term home or apartment rentals are an option and offer the benefit of added space and a kitchen (but then you have to cook).

A plus is that family vacations are usually in summer, when good hotel deals abound in South Florida. Most hotels in Greater Miami allow children under a certain age to stay in their parents' room at no extra charge, but a few may charge for them as extra adults; be sure to find out the cutoff age for children's discounts. Some hotels include breakfast for kids under 12 gratis, and a few offer summer promotions that include a second room free. Make sure to ask about family packages.

The resorts generally claim their children's programs are year-round, but double-check offerings for your vacation dates. Some hotels decrease program hours during slow periods or limit the number of participants. Also ask what charges there are, if any, and whether they accept children still in diapers. Kids' programs or not, make your stay more enjoyable by choosing accommodations with the right amenities. Rollaway beds and cribs, in-room microwaves, and refrigerators can make all the difference, but there may be added costs. If there's only a minibar in your room, note that it won't have much space to spare. If you have very young children, are the rooms childproofed? (Doubtful.) A few select hotels provide "kits" for this, but be prepared to bring your own.

Doral Golf Resort and Spa's Camp Doral ⊠ 4400 N.W. 87th Ave., Doral, Miami ☎ 305/592–2000 ⊕ www.doralresort.

com, ages 5–12, offers almost every activity under the sun, including tennis, golf, fishing, baseball, nature walks, and poolside bingo. No sun? No problem—an indoor playground is stocked with video games, toys, movies, and sports equipment. At **Fontainebleau Hilton Resort and Towers' Kid's Cove** ⊠ 4441 Collins Ave., Mid-Beach, Miami Beach ☎ 305/538–2000 ⊕ www.hilton.com, ages 5–12, cooking, movies, and arts and crafts are just some of the fun and games offered in this underwater-theme playroom. **Loews Miami Beach Hotel's SoBe Kid's Camp** ⊠ 1601 Collins Ave., South Beach, Miami Beach ☎ 305/604–1601 ⊕ www.loewshotels.com, ages 4–12, offers high-energy activities ranging from Krazy Kickball and sand sculpture contests to Ping-Pong challenges, pool games, and beach relays. Friday and Saturday night sessions include indoor games, crafts, dinner, and movies. As part of the **Sonesta Beach Resort's Just Us Kids** ⊠ 350 Ocean Dr., Key Biscayne 33149 ☎ 305/361–2021 or 800/766–3782 ⊕ www.sonesta.com, for kids and teens ages 5–17, specially trained counselors lead morning field trips, afternoon beach and pool games, and arts and crafts classes. It's free, except for meals and admission to attractions. The resort also has a Just Us Little Kids program for ages 3–4.

but the price is fair. Although you'll have to pay for parking, you can walk to the Lincoln Road Mall, Ocean Drive, and other South Beach attractions since they're only a few blocks away. On the downside, the rooms are slightly stuffy (bring some incense) and quite close to busy (and noisy) Collins Avenue. ✉ *1700 Collins Ave., South Beach 33139* ☎ *305/ 538–4661* 🖷 *305/538–9631* ⊕ *www.claremonthotelmiami.com* ⇲ *70 rooms* ♿ *Refrigerators, cable TV, parking (fee)* ☰ *AE, DC, MC, V.*

¢ 🖼 **The Creek.** A 1950s motor lodge that became a cheap, run-down youth hostel is now a still-cheap but spruced-up and arty abode for mostly young travelers looking for a comfy, friendly place to crash. They'll find it here in 18 "signature rooms," each designed by a different artist; no-frills standard rooms; cabana rooms that open onto the pool deck; and the mega-budget shared rooms ($17–$21 a night, depending on time of year). The Creek's social center is the large pool area, with outdoor grills, a patio bar, game room, and kitchen dispensing burgers, nachos, and other munchies. Note to the noise-intolerant—the music's loud until midnight. ✉ *2360 Collins Ave., South Beach 33139* ☎ *305/538–1951* 🖷*305/531–3217* ⊕*www.thecreeksouthbeach.com* ⇲ *60 private rooms, 25 dorm-style rooms* ♿ *Snack bar, cable TV with video games, pool, billiards, bar, lobby lounge, recreation room, Internet* ☰ *MC, V.*

¢ 🖼 **San Juan Hotel.** Simple and low frills, but what a location—right across
Fodor'sChoice the street from the Delano in the epicenter of the action on South Beach.
★ The cool lobby has clean art deco curves, and the friendly staff literally offer service with a smile. Brightly decorated rooms are basic but equipped with private baths, cable TVs, safes, and small fridges with microwaves or kitchenettes. If you're directing your feet to the cheaper side of the street, this is the place. ✉ *1680 Collins Ave., South Beach 33139* ☎ *305/538–7531 or 800/468–1688* 🖷 *305/532–5704* ⊕ *www. sanjuanhotelsouthbeach.com* ⇲ *80 rooms* ♿ *Refrigerators, microwaves, cable TV, pool* ☰ *AE, D, DC, MC, V.*

Downtown Miami

$$$$ 🖼 **Conrad Miami.** The downtown skyline continues to reach new heights of luxury with its latest steel-and-glass tower—a 36-story spire housing the Conrad, the country's first new-build, free-standing Conrad Hotel (a luxury offshoot of the Hilton brand). Part of a mixed-use development that includes office space and an up-market retail center, the hotel welcomes guests at a spectacular 25th-floor Sky Lobby overlooking Biscayne Bay, then pampers them with high-end amenities like flat-screen satellite TV, Bulgari toiletries, and Anichini linens. A health club and spa, extensive meeting space, pool terrace, and fine dining round out the activities. ✉ *1395 Brickell Ave., Downtown 33131* ☎ *305/ 503–6500 or 800/266–7237* 🖷 *305/533–7177* ⊕ *www.conradhotels. com* ⇲ *308 rooms, 105 suites* ♿ *Restaurant, cable TV, 2 tennis courts, pool, health club, spa, bar, lobby lounge, shops, baby-sitting, Internet, meeting rooms, parking (fee)* ☰ *AE, D, DC, MC, V.*

$$$$ 🖼 **Four Seasons Miami.** Pleasure before business? Perhaps. Stepping off
Fodor'sChoice busy Brickell Avenue, guests see a soothing water wall trickling down
★ from above. Inside, a cavernous lobby is barely big enough to hold the enormous sculptures—part of the hotel's $3.5 million collection show-

casing local artists. A 2-acre pool terrace on the 7th floor overlooks downtown Miami while making you forget you're in downtown Miami. Three pools include a foot-high wading pool with 24 "islands" from which cocktails are served. A shoe valet stands by with slippers and towels. Rooms are elegantly subdued, with nice touches like glass-enclosed showers, DVD/CD players, and window seats. ⊠ *1435 Brickell Ave., Downtown 33131* ☎ *305/358–3535 or 800/819–5053* ☒ *305/358–7758* ⊕ *www.fourseasons.com* ⮩ *182 rooms, 39 suites* △ *Restaurant, in-room safe, cable TV, 3 pools, health club, spa, 2 bars, children's programs (ages 4–12), Internet, business services, meeting rooms* ⊟ *AE, D, DC, MC, V.*

$$$$ ▦ **Mandarin Oriental Miami.** If you can afford to stay here, do. The lo-
Fodor'sChoice   cation, at the tip of Brickell Key in Biscayne Bay, is superb. Rooms fac-
★   ing west overlook the downtown skyline; to the east are Miami Beach and the blue Atlantic. There's also beauty in the details—sliding screens that close off baths, dark wood, crisp linens, room numbers hand-painted on rice paper at check-in. The Azul restaurant, with an eye-catching waterfall and private dining area at the end of a catwalk, serves Asian/Latin/Caribbean/French cuisine. The hotel has a 20,000-square-foot private beach and an indulgent on-site spa. ⊠ *500 Brickell Key Dr., Brickell Key 33131* ☎ *305/913–8288 or 866/888–6780* ☒ *305/913–8300* ⊕ *www.mandarinoriental.com* ⮩ *329 rooms* △ *2 restaurants, in-room data ports, in-room safes, cable TV, pool, spa, 2 bars, dry cleaning, laundry service, concierge, business services, meeting rooms, parking (fee)* ⊟ *AE, D, DC, MC, V.*

$$$ ▦ **Biscayne Bay Marriott.** The once-neglected northern end of downtown will see new life in 2006, when a $255 million performing arts center debuts, and this 31-story tourist-friendly waterfront property will be a stone's throw away. It's also convenient to Bayside Marketplace, the beaches, Coconut Grove, the Port of Miami, and AmericanAirlines Arena. Although the rooms are a bit impersonal, each has complimentary in-room coffee, satellite TV, and voice mail and data ports. For business travelers there are "Rooms That Work," with work stations, and an executive floor. Just for fun, jet skiing is available nearby, as is transportation to three area golf resorts. ⊠ *1633 N. Bayshore Dr., Downtown 33132* ☎ *305/374–3900 or 800/228–9290* ☒ *305/375–0597* ⊕ *www.marriott.com* ⮩ *599 rooms, 21 suites* △ *Restaurant, in-room data ports, in-room safes, minibars, cable TV, pool, health club, hair salon, bar, laundry services, concierge, business services, meeting rooms, parking (fee)* ⊟ *AE, D, DC, MC, V.*

$$$ ▦ **Hyatt Regency Miami.** If your vacation is based on boats, basketball, business, or bargains, you can't do much better than the Hyatt Regency, thanks to its adjacent convention facilities and prime location near the Brickell Avenue business district, Bayside Marketplace, AmericanAirlines Arena, the Port of Miami, and great downtown shopping. Distinctive public spaces are more colorful than businesslike, and guest rooms are a blend of avocado, beige, and blond. The James L. Knight International Center is accessible without stepping outside, as is the downtown Metromover and its Metrorail connection. Superb dining is available off the lobby at Japengo. ⊠ *400 S.E. 2nd Ave., Downtown 33131* ☎ *305/358–1234 or 800/233–1234* ☒ *305/358–0529* ⊕ *www.miami.hyatt.com*

↻ *562 rooms, 51 suites* ⚐ *2 restaurants, cable TV, pool, health club, lounge, laundry service, concierge, business services, parking (fee)* ☰ *AE, D, DC, MC, V.*

$$$ 🖼 **JW Marriott.** This grand downtown tower is a bona fide upscale property masquerading as a generic business hotel, with amenities and haute cuisine to prove it. If you're a finicky eater, consider creating your own menu in consultation with a top chef in the Trapiche Room restaurant. If you're stressed, a massage therapist at Spa 1111 can work out your kinks. Choose from a variety of massage techniques and body treatments; then feel the burn on the exercise machines. Depending on what you're here for, a 24-hour on-site business center or the 24-hour action on nearby South Beach will serve. ✉ *1109 Brickell Ave., Downtown 33131* ☎ *305/374–1224 or 800/228–9290* 🖷 *305/374–4211* ⊕ *www.marriott.com* ↻ *300 rooms, 22 suites* ⚐ *4 restaurants, in-room safes, cable TV, pool, health club, spa, bar, laundry service, concierge, business services, meeting rooms, parking (fee)* ☰ *AE, D, DC, MC, V.*

$$–$$$$ 🖼 **Hotel Inter-Continental Miami.** From the pool deck you don't see the ragtag street, only the clean view Miami likes best of itself: the Metromover, Brickell Avenue, the booming port, the beautiful bay, Bayside Marketplace, and Key Biscayne. The lobby's polished marble is softened by palms and oversize wicker. When you feel like working in, you'll enjoy the rooms' printer/fax/copy machines, data ports, voice mail, and ergonomically designed chairs. When you feel like working out, head to the fifth-floor fitness center. The large business hotel has 26 meeting and conference rooms (65,000 square feet), and Indigo restaurant draws an unpredictably trendy crowd. ✉ *100 Chopin Plaza, Downtown 33131* ☎ *305/577–1000 or 800/327–3005* 🖷 *305/577–0384* ⊕ *www.miami.interconti.com* ↻ *639 rooms, 33 suites* ⚐ *2 restaurants, cable TV, pool, health club, bar, laundry service, business services, meeting rooms, parking (fee)* ☰ *AE, D, DC, MC, V.*

$$–$$$ 🖼 **Doubletree Grand Hotel Biscayne Bay.** This elegant waterfront option is near many of Miami's headline attractions: the Port of Miami, beaches, Bayside Marketplace, AmericanAirlines Arena, and the new performing arts center (due 2006). Rooms are spacious, and most have a view of Biscayne Bay and the port. In-room amenities include voice mail, a coffeemaker, and other helpful items like blow-dryers. You can rent Jet Skis or take deep-sea fishing trips from a nearby marina. And while you're on the water, try Tony Chan's for a bite of its famous Peking duck and those gorgeous bay views. ✉ *1717 N. Bayshore Dr., Downtown 33132* ☎ *305/372–0313 or 800/222–8733* 🖷 *305/539–9228* ⊕ *www.doubletree.com* ↻ *152 rooms* ⚐ *Restaurant, in-room data ports, minibars, microwaves, cable TV, pool, health club, hot tub, bar, business services, meeting rooms* ☰ *AE, D, DC, MC, V.*

$$–$$$ 🖼 **Radisson Hotel Miami.** Steps away from the new performing arts center and next door to the Miami International University of Art and Design, the Radisson is smack in the middle of Miami's revitalized arts district. But whether you're artistically inclined, here for business, or just want to have fun, the Radisson's north downtown location is convenient to the beach, downtown shopping and entertainment, the Port of Miami, and Parrot Jungle Island, off the MacArthur Causeway. Con-

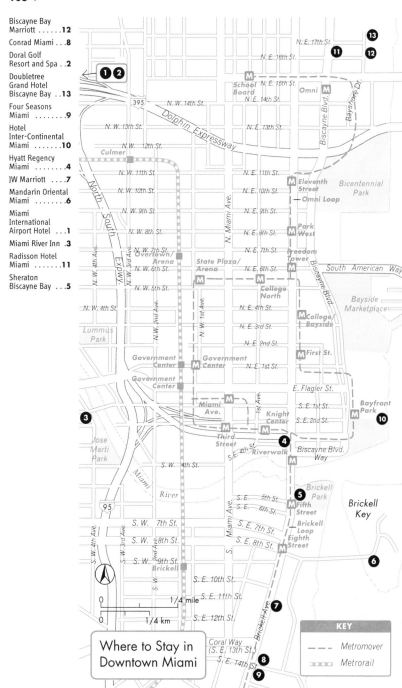

Where to Stay in
Downtown Miami

KEY

- - - Metromover

▫▫▫▫ Metrorail

temporary-style rooms have dramatic floor-to-ceiling windows, while the rooftop pool area offers a bird's-eye view of the city. ✉ *1601 Biscayne Blvd., Downtown 33132* ☎ *305/374–0000 or 800/333–3333* 🖷 *305/714–3811* ⊕ *www.radisson-miami.com* 🛏 *478 rooms, 50 suites* ♿ *2 restaurants, in-room data ports, cable TV, pool, gym, sauna, lobby lounge, baby-sitting, concierge, business services, meeting rooms* ▭ *AE, D, DC, MC, V.*

$$–$$$ 🏨 **Sheraton Biscayne Bay.** When you make the short drive through a grove of oak trees to the entrance, it's hard to believe that this waterfront hotel is on busy Brickell Avenue. As in most large hotels, the lobby is designed for business (as is the conference center) and has a bar, restaurant, and gift shop. But the back patio and green space take the corporate edge off. Rooms have all the extras you'd expect: iron/ironing boards, hair dryers, coffeemakers, servi-bars, voice mail, and high-speed Internet access. Thank management for providing self-parking (although valets are standing by). ✉ *495 Brickell Ave., Downtown 33131* ☎ *305/373–6000 or 800/284–2000* 🖷 *305/374–2279* ⊕ *www.sheraton.com* 🛏 *598 rooms, 14 suites* ♿ *Restaurant, cable TV, pool, health club, bar, concierge, meeting rooms, parking* ▭ *AE, D, DC, MC, V.*

¢–$$ 🏨 **Miami River Inn.** In five restored 1904 clapboard buildings, the only
Fodor'sChoice group of Miami houses left from that period, this inn dispenses the at-
★ tentive, personalized hospitality often lost in Miami Beach's gleaming deco towers. A glass of wine at check-in sets the welcoming tone. The working-class neighborhood is one of Miami's safest, even if it doesn't look it. Rooms (some with tub but no shower) are filled with antiques, and many have hardwood floors. All have TVs and phones. The most popular rooms overlook the river from the second and third floors. The heart of the city is a 10-minute stroll across the 1st Street Bridge. ✉ *118 S.W. South River Dr., Little Havana, 33130* ☎ *305/325–0045 or 800/ 468–3589* 🖷 *305/325–9227* ⊕ *www.miamiriverinn.com* 🛏 *40 rooms, 2 with shared bath* ♿ *Cable TV, pool, hot tub, laundry facilities, free parking.* ▭ *AE, D, DC, MC, V* ¶⊙¶ *CP.*

West Miami-Dade

★ $$$$ 🏨 **Doral Golf Resort and Spa.** With its five championship golf courses, including the Blue Monster—home of the annual PGA Ford Championship—this 650-acre resort is definitely golf central in Greater Miami. But there's more: the Arthur Ashe Tennis Center, with 11 courts; the lavish Spa at Doral, with its own luxury suites; two fitness centers; on-site shops and boutiques; a kids' camp and water park; five restaurants; and extensive meeting space. Add bright, airy rooms that showcase Florida inside and out, and you have a self-contained oasis of fun and relaxation just west of the airport. ✉ *4400 N.W. 87th Ave., Doral, Miami 33178* ☎ *305/592–2000 or 800/713–6725* 🖷 *305/591–4682* ⊕ *www.doralresort. com* 🛏 *696 rooms, 48 suites* ♿ *5 restaurants, cable TV, 5 18-hole golf courses, 11 tennis courts, pro shop, pool, exercise equipment, spa, fishing, basketball, volleyball, 3 bars, children's programs (ages 5–12), concierge, business services, meeting rooms* ▭ *AE, D, DC, MC, V.*

$$ 🏨 **Miami International Airport Hotel.** Airport hotels defeat the purpose of a vacation, but if you have an early flight or long layover you may need

LODGING ALTERNATIVES

Apartment Rentals

If you want a home base that's roomy enough for a family and comes with cooking facilities, consider a furnished rental. These can save you money, especially if you're traveling with a group. Home-exchange directories sometimes list rentals as well as exchanges. In Miami and Miami Beach, condominium and apartment rentals run the gamut from the very affordable (usually off the beach) to the ultra luxe. A number of local real-estate agencies handle short-term rentals; you can contact them through the chamber of commerce or the visitors bureau. **Hideaways International** ⊠ 767 Islington St., Portsmouth, NH 03801 ☎ 603/430–4433 or 800/843–4433 🖷 603/430–4444 ⊕ www.hideaways. com; membership $129. **Hometours International** 🖅 Box 11503, Knoxville, TN 37939 ☎ 865/690–8484 or 800/367–4668 ⊕ http://thor.he. net/~hometour. **Interhome** ⊠ 1990 N.E. 163rd St., Suite 110, North Miami Beach, FL 33162 ☎ 305/940–2299 or 800/ 882–6864 🖷 305/940–2911 ⊕ www. interhome.com. **Vacation Home Rentals Worldwide** ⊠ 235 Kensington Ave., Norwood, NJ 07648 ☎ 201/767–9393 or 800/633–3284 🖷 201/767–5510.

Bed-and-Breakfasts

Greater Miami does not have many traditional bed and breakfasts, but there are a few standouts tucked away off the beaten path. Florida Bed & Breakfast Inns is an association of small and historic lodging properties throughout the state. **Florida Bed & Breakfast Inns** 🖅 Box 6187, Palm Harbour, 34684 ☎ 800/ 524–1880 ⊕ www.florida-inns.com.

Home Exchanges

If you would like to exchange your home for someone else's, join a home-exchange organization, which will send you its

updated listings of available exchanges for a year and will include your own listing in at least one of them. It's up to you to make specific arrangements. **HomeLink International** 🖅 Box 47747, Tampa, FL 33647 ☎ 813/975–9825 or 800/638–3841 🖷 813/910–8144 ⊕ www.homelink.org; $106 per year. **Intervac U.S.** 🖅 Box 590504, San Francisco, CA 94159 ☎ 800/756–4663 🖷 415/435–7440 ⊕ www.intervacus. com; $50 yearly fee includes on-line access to listings, $99 per year pays for listing home in catalogue and on-line access.

Hostels

No matter what your age, you can save on lodging costs by staying at hostels. In some 5,000 locations in more than 70 countries around the world, Hostelling International (HI), the umbrella group for a number of national youth-hostel associations, offers single-sex, dorm-style beds and, at many hostels, rooms for couples and family accommodations. Membership in any HI national hostel association, open to travelers of all ages, allows you to stay in HI-affiliated hostels at member rates; one-year membership is about $25 for adults (C$26.75 in Canada, £13 in the U.K., $30 in Australia, and $30 in New Zealand); hostels run about $10–$30 per night. Members have priority if the hostel is full; they're also eligible for discounts around the world, even on rail and bus travel in some countries. **Hostelling International—American Youth Hostels** ⊠ 733 15th St. NW, Suite 840, Washington, DC 20005 ☎ 202/783–6161 🖷 202/783–6171 ⊕ www.hiayh. org. **Hostelling International—Canada** ⊠ 400–205 Catherine St., Ottawa, Ontario K2P 1C3, Canada ☎ 613/237–7884 🖷 613/237–7868 ⊕ www. hostellingintl.ca. **Youth Hostel Association of England and Wales** ⊠ Trevelyan House, 8

St. Stephen's Hill, St. Albans, Hertfordshire AL1 2DY, U.K. ☎ 0870/8708808 🖷 01727/844126 ⊕ www.yha.org.uk. **Australian Youth Hostel Association** ✉ 10 Mallett St., Camperdown, NSW 2050, Australia ☎ 02/9565-1699 🖷 02/9565-1325 ⊕ www.yha.com.au. **Youth Hostels Association of New Zealand** 🖃 Box 436, Christchurch, New Zealand ☎ 03/379-9970 🖷 03/365-4476 ⊕ www.yha.org.nz.

Hotels

Baymont Inns ☎ 800/428-3438 or 866/999-1111 ⊕ www.baymontinns.com. **Best Western** ☎ 800/528-1234 ⊕ www.bestwestern.com. **Choice** ☎ 800/424-6423 ⊕ www.choicehotels.com. **Clarion** ☎ 800/424-6423 ⊕ www.choicehotels.com. **Comfort Inn** ☎ 800/424-6423 ⊕ www.choicehotels.com. **Days Inn** ☎ 800/325-2525 ⊕ www.daysinn.com. **Doubletree Hotels** ☎ 800/222-8733 ⊕ www.doubletree.com. **Embassy Suites** ☎ 800/362-2779 ⊕ www.embassysuites.com. **Fairfield Inn** ☎ 800/228-2800 ⊕ www.marriott.com. **Four Seasons** ☎ 800/332-3442 ⊕ www.fourseasons.com. **Hilton** ☎ 800/445-8667 ⊕ www.hilton.com. **Holiday Inn** ☎ 800/465-4329 ⊕ www.ichotelsgroup.com. **Howard Johnson** ☎ 800/446-4656 ⊕ www.hojo.com. **Hyatt Hotels & Resorts** ☎ 800/233-1234 ⊕ www.hyatt.com. **Inter-Continental** ☎ 800/327-0200 ⊕ www.ichotelsgroup.com. **La Quinta** ☎ 800/531-5900 ⊕ www.lq.com. **Marriott** ☎ 800/228-9290 ⊕ www.marriott.com. **Omni** ☎ 800/843-6664 ⊕ www.omnihotels.com. **Quality Inn** ☎ 800/424-6423 ⊕ www.choicehotels.com. **Radisson** ☎ 800/333-3333 ⊕ www.radisson.com. **Ramada** ☎ 800/228-2828, 800/854-7854 international reservations ⊕ www.ramada.com or www.ramadahotels.com. **Renaissance**

Hotels & Resorts ☎ 800/468-3571 ⊕ www.renaissancehotels.com. **Ritz-Carlton** ☎ 800/241-3333 ⊕ www.ritzcarlton.com. **Sheraton** ☎ 800/325-3535 ⊕ www.starwood.com/sheraton. **Sleep Inn** ☎ 800/424-6423 ⊕ www.choicehotels.com. **Westin Hotels & Resorts** ☎ 800/228-3000 ⊕ www.starwood.com/westin. **Wyndham Hotels & Resorts** ☎ 800/822-4200 ⊕ www.wyndham.com.

RVs & Camping

There are more than 3,000 family camp sites in 45 Florida state parks. Under state policy, campers without reservations at Florida state parks are assured that 10% of each park's sites will be available for walk-ins on a first-come, first-served basis. Reservations in Florida state parks are made directly with the parks. For a free park guide, call ☎ 850/488-9872 or see ⊕ www.dep.state.fl.us/parks **Florida Association of RV Parks & Campgrounds** ✉ 1340 Vickers Dr., Tallahassee, FL 32303-3041 ☎ 850/562-7151 ⊕ www.floridacamping.com.

this option. The only hotel actually inside MIA lets you catch a few winks in soundproofed rooms while waiting for your chance to sit on the runway. A spa, rooftop pool, sauna and steam room, racquetball court, and restaurant help recharge the travel-weary batteries. Day and overnight rates are available. ⊠ *Miami International Airport, Concourse E, 2nd floor, West Miami-Dade, Miami 33159* ☎ *305/871–4100 or 800/327–1276* 🖷 *305/871–0800* ⊕ *www.miahotel.com* 🛏 *259 rooms, 3 suites* ⚖ *Restaurant, cable TV, pool, gym, sauna, spa, steam room, racquetball, bar, laundry service, concierge, meeting rooms* ▭ *AE, D, DC, MC, V.*

Coconut Grove

$$$$ 🏨 **Ritz-Carlton, Coconut Grove.** This grand addition to Miami's hotel landscape overlooks picturesque Biscayne Bay and the busy, tree-lined streets of Miami's bohemian-chic village, Coconut Grove. Rooms are appointed with marble baths, a choice of pillows, and private balconies. And there's a butler to solve every dilemma—technology butlers to resolve computer problems, travel butlers to meet your flight and guide you to the hotel, dog butlers to watch after Fido, and shopping and style guides to make sure you don't drop while you shop. A 5,000-square-foot spa is on hand to soothe away stress. ⊠ *3300 S.W. 27th Ave., Coconut Grove 33133* ☎ *305/644–4680 or 800/241–3333* 🖷 *305/644–4681* ⊕ *www.ritzcarlton.com* 🛏 *88 rooms, 27 suites* ⚖ *Restaurant, cable TV, pool, spa, concierge, business services, meeting rooms, parking (fee)* ▭ *AE, D, DC, MC, V.*

$$–$$$$ 🏨 **Wyndham Grand Bay.** Combining the classical elegance of Greece, a stepped facade that looks vaguely Aztec, a hint of the South, and a brush of the tropical, the Grand Bay is like no other hotel in South Florida. Guest rooms are filled with superb touches, including high-speed Internet connections, minibars, and in-room CD player/stereos. But what really sets the hotel apart are the atypically spacious terraces in every room—perfect for private dinners—with sweeping views of Biscayne Bay. Bice, a trendy Italian restaurant here, is extremely popular. ⊠ *2669 S. Bayshore Dr., Coconut Grove 33133* ☎ *305/858–9600 or 800/327–2788* 🖷 *305/859–2026* ⊕ *www.wyndham.com* 🛏 *130 rooms, 47 suites* ⚖ *Restaurant, minibars, cable TV, pool, health club, hair salon, sauna, bar, concierge, parking (fee)* ▭ *AE, DC, MC, V.*

$$$ 🏨 **Mayfair House.** The exclusive feel of Coconut Grove runs through this European-style luxury hotel and is mirrored in its Tiffany windows, polished mahogany and marble accents, imported ceramics and crystal, and impressive glass elevator. Individually furnished suites have terraces facing the street, screened by vegetation and wood latticework. Each room has a small Japanese hot tub on the balcony or a Roman tub inside, and 10 have antique pianos. A rooftop recreation area is peaceful, although the miniature lap pool is odd for such a large hotel. Head for the Mayfair Grill for hearty breakfast favorites, and Orchids for Floribbean seafood. ⊠ *Streets of Mayfair, 3000 Florida Ave., Coconut Grove 33133* ☎ *305/441–0000 or 800/433–4555* 🖷 *305/447–9173* ⊕ *www. mayfairhousehotel.com* 🛏 *179 suites* ⚖ *2 restaurants, snack bar, room service, cable TV, pool, hot tub, bar, laundry service, concierge, business services, parking (fee)* ▭ *AE, D, DC, MC, V.*

$–$$ **Doubletree Hotel at Coconut Grove.** Along Coconut Grove's hotel row, which faces some of the best waterfront in the country, the Doubletree is a short walk from popular Grove shops and restaurants and a quick drive from Miami's beaches and business districts. A complete renovation in 2003 gave the rooms a warmer, more contemporary feel; most offer terraces open to breezes from the bay and complimentary high-speed Internet access. ⊠ *2649 S. Bayshore Dr., Coconut Grove 33133* ☎ *305/858–2500 or 800/222–8733* 🖷 *305/858–9117* ⊕ *www. coconutgrove.doubletree.com* ⤴ *173 rooms, 19 suites* ♿ *Restaurant, in-room data ports, cable TV, pool, 2 bars, business services, meeting rooms, parking (fee)* ⊟ *AE, D, DC, MC, V.*

Key Biscayne

$$$$ **Ritz-Carlton, Key Biscayne.** One of three Ritz-Carltons in Miami, this
Fodor's Choice   14-story oceanfront tower includes rooms and one- and two-bedroom
★   suites. As with most Ritz-Carltons, first-class amenities are plentiful: an oceanfront spa with 21 treatment rooms, an 11-court tennis "garden" with tennis butler, a wellness center with yoga and tai chi, a private beach, and beachside water sports. In-room luxuries (robes, slippers, toiletries, scales) anticipate every need. They don't call the resort's signature restaurant Aria for nothing: a tenor is on hand to belt out birthday greetings and other requests. ⊠ *455 Grand Bay Dr., Key Biscayne 33149* ☎ *305/365–4500 or 800/241–3333* 🖷 *305/365–4505* ⊕ *www.ritzcarlton.com* ⤴ *452 rooms, 38 suites* ♿ *3 restaurants, in-room data ports, minibars, cable TV, 11 tennis courts, 2 pools, spa, beach, 2 lounges, concierge, business services, meeting rooms, parking (fee)* ⊟ *AE, D, DC, MC, V.*

★ $$$–$$$$ **Sonesta Beach Resort Key Biscayne.** Like Miami Beach, Key Biscayne boasts a strip of oceanfront resorts, though on a much smaller scale. This consistently good, family-friendly property rises like a Maya pyramid from the sand and offers acres of recreation, from ocean water sports like aqua biking and parasailing to a European spa, kids' programs, jewelry-making classes, and tennis and other court sports. Golf is nearby. Those who want to explore the secluded island of Key Biscayne can rent a Segway Human Transporter on site. ⊠ *350 Ocean Dr., Key Biscayne 33149* ☎ *305/361–2021 or 800/766–3782* 🖷 *305/365–2096* ⊕ *www. sonesta.com* ⤴ *284 rooms, 15 suites, 3 villas* ♿ *3 restaurants, snack bar, cable TV, 9 tennis courts, pool, exercise equipment, spa, beach, windsurfing, parasailing, bicycles, basketball, volleyball, 2 bars, children's programs (ages 5–17), meeting rooms* ⊟ *AE, D, DC, MC, V.*

Coral Gables

$$$–$$$$ **Biltmore Hotel.** Built in 1926, this landmark hotel has had several in-
Fodor's Choice   carnations over the years—including a stint as a hospital during World
★   War II—and has changed hands more than a few times. Through it all, this grandest of grande dames remains an opulent reminder of yesteryear, with its palatial lobby and grounds, enormous pool—said to be the largest hotel pool in the continental U.S.—and distinctive 315-foot tower, which rises above the canopy of trees shading Coral Gables. Fully up-

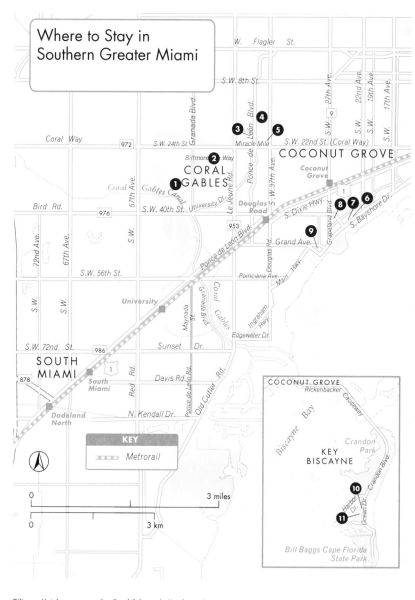

Where to Stay in Southern Greater Miami

dated, the Biltmore has on-site golf and tennis, a spa and fitness center, extensive meeting facilities, and the celebrated Palme d'Or restaurant. ⊠ *1200 Anastasia Ave., Coral Gables 33134* ☎ *305/445–1926 or 800/ 727–1926* 🖷 *305/913–3159* ⊕ *www.biltmorehotel.com* ➷ *244 rooms, 36 suites* ♧ *4 restaurants, cable TV, 18-hole golf course, 10 tennis courts, pool, health club, spa, 4 bars, meeting rooms, convention center* ⊟ *AE, D, DC, MC, V.*

$$$–$$$$ 🏨 **Hyatt Regency Coral Gables.** The exterior is overtly Spanish, courtesy of tile roofs and pink stucco. Inside, the lobby recalls a polished palace, with pillars and archways. Together they evoke the Alhambra, the 14th-century Moorish palace in southern Spain. As befits a business hotel, the staff is savvy and helpful, and rooms are designed to double as offices. Still, the mood is comfortable and residential. A business center and meeting facilities are tucked to the side so vacationers don't feel they're still in the corporate world. ⊠ *50 Alhambra Plaza, Coral Gables 33134* ☎ *305/441–1234 or 800/233–1234* 🖷 *305/ 441–0520* ⊕ *www.coralgables.hyatt.com* ➷ *192 rooms, 50 suites* ♧ *Restaurant, in-room data ports, cable TV, pool, health club, sauna, steam room, lobby lounge, business services, meeting rooms, parking (fee)* ⊟ *AE, D, DC, MC, V.*

★ $$–$$$ 🏨 **Omni Colonnade Hotel.** Built for business but beautiful enough to rival many luxury properties, the Omni has as its cornerstone the Rotunda, built in 1926 by Coral Gables pioneer George Merrick, who used it as a sales office. Today the entire hotel reflects the splendor of that era, thanks to a grand lobby and elegant rooms with executive desks, newspaper delivery, and 24-hour room service. A rooftop pool and sundeck, fully equipped health club, and a prime location at the hub of Coral Gables' shopping, dining, and entertainment district make this a good choice for business and leisure travelers alike. ⊠ *180 Aragon Ave., Coral Gables 33134* ☎ *305/441–2600 or 800/843–6664* 🖷 *305/ 445–3929* ⊕ *www.omnihotels.com* ➷ *140 rooms, 15 suites* ♧ *Restaurant, room service, in-room data ports, in-room fax, cable TV, pool, health club, business services, meeting rooms* ⊟ *AE, D, DC, MC, V.*

$$ 🏨 **David William Hotel.** Set on a picturesque boulevard just west of Coral Gables's busy shopping, dining, and entertainment district, the David William is a good fit for business or extended-stay travelers. Standard rooms include refrigerator, microwave, coffeemaker, and toaster oven, while one- and two-bedroom suites have full kitchens. Best of all, you can use the services and facilities at the nearby Biltmore, including the fitness center and spa, golf course, tennis courts, and pool. ⊠ *700 Biltmore Way, Coral Gables 33134* ☎ *305/445–7821 or 800/757–8073* 🖷 *305/913–1933* ⊕ *www.davidwilliamhotel.com* ➷ *70 rooms, 33 suites* ♧ *Restaurant, in-room data ports, cable TV, pool, health club, bar, laundry facilities, business services, meeting rooms* ⊟ *AE, D, DC, MC, V.*

$$ 🏨 **Hotel Place St. Michel.** Built in 1926, this historic and intimate inn is
Fodor'sChoice kept filled with the scent of fresh flowers, circulated by paddle fans. Art
★ nouveau chandeliers suspended from vaulted ceilings light the public areas. Each guest room has its own dimensions, personality, and antiques imported from England, Scotland, and France, although plusher beds would be a welcome improvement. Dinner at the superb Restaurant St.

Michel is a must, but there is also a more casual bar and dining area behind the lobby, better suited for quiet breakfasts or late-night aperitifs. The inn is within easy walking distance of Miracle Mile. ⊠ *162 Alcazar Ave., Coral Gables 33134* ☎ *305/444–1666 or 800/848–4683* 🖷 *305/529–0074* ⊕ *www.hotelplacestmichel.com* 🛏 *24 rooms, 3 suites* ⌂ *Restaurant, cable TV, bar, laundry service, parking (fee)* ▭ *AE, DC, MC, V* ⊚ *CP.*

NIGHTLIFE &
THE ARTS

4

NEW KIDS ON THE ROAD
The young musicians of the
New World Symphony ⇨*p.142*

REASON TO CHOOSE SHOES WISELY
Carpeted dance floor at crobar ⇨*p.129*

BEST LOUNGE PLANTS
The grass at Tantra and
the bamboo at Grass ⇨*pp.122 and 123*

OLDEST LIQUOR LICENSE
Tobacco Road ⇨*p.123*

FUÁCATA 'BOUT IT
Cuban/hip-hop fusion at Hoy Como Ayer ⇨*p.125*

Updated by
Carolyn
Keating

MIAMI'S PULSE POUNDS WITH NONSTOP NIGHTLIFE that reflects the area's potent cultural mix. On sultry, humid nights with the huge full moon rising out of the ocean and fragrant night-blooming jasmine intoxicating the senses, who can resist Cuban salsa, Jamaican reggae, and Dominican merengue, with some disco and hip-hop thrown in for good measure? When this place throws a party, hips shake, fingers snap, bodies touch. It's no wonder many clubs are still rocking at 5 AM.

The reputation of Miami and Miami Beach as playgrounds for the hip and famous is well deserved, making the nightlife here some of the best on the planet. But if you're in search of finer cultural fare, you face more of a challenge. The museums aren't as easy to find as the beaches. Theaters don't advertise as widely as nightclubs. And the art houses that show foreign films and independents are tucked away in the city's nooks and crannies. All that's starting to change, however; so you have your pick of entertainment here night and day. Whether you're interested in dancing 'til dawn to the hottest DJs or catching the newest work by Latin artists in exile, you'll want to head to a newsstand first.

FIND OUT WHAT'S GOING ON
The *Miami Herald* (⊕ www.herald.com) is a good source for information on what to do in town. The "Weekend" section, included in the Friday edition, has an annotated guide to everything from plays and galleries to concerts and nightclubs. The "Ticket" column of this section details the week's entertainment highlights. You can pick up the Herald's free weekly tabloid, *The Street,* at newsstands and bookstores for a list of local happenings. Providing even more detailed information is *Miami New Times* (⊕ www.miaminewtimes.com), the city's largest free alternative newspaper, published each Thursday. It lists nightclubs, concerts, and special events; reviews plays and movies; and provides in-depth coverage of the local music scene. "Night & Day" is a rundown of the week's cultural highlights.

Ocean Drive, Miami Beach's model-strewn, upscale fashion and lifestyle magazine, squeezes club, bar, restaurant, and events listings in with fashion spreads, reviews, and personality profiles. Paparazzi photos of local party people and celebrities give you a taste of Greater Miami nightlife before you even put on your black going-out ensemble.

The Spanish-language *El Nuevo Herald,* published by the *Miami Herald,* has extensive information on Spanish-language arts and entertainment, including dining reviews, concert previews, and nightclub highlights. *Spanish-language radio,* primarily on the AM dial, is also a good source of information about arts events. Tune in to WXDJ (95.7 FM), Amor (107.5 FM), or Radio Mambi (710 AM).

Much news of upcoming events is disseminated through flyers tucked onto windshields or left for pickup at restaurants, clubs, and stores. They're technically illegal to distribute, but they're mighty useful. And if you're a beachgoer, chances are that as you lie in the sun you'll be approached by kids handing out cards announcing the DJs and acts appearing in the clubs that night.

NIGHTLIFE

On weekend nights—and on weeknights in high season—the level of activity in popular Miami and Miami Beach neighborhoods can be exhilarating or maddening, depending on your perspective, as partiers spill into the streets and traffic grinds to a stop. Parking is a challenge in areas with lots of bars and clubs. If you do find a metered space on the street, you'll need plenty of quarters. Parking lots and garages (especially at complexes such as Bayside and CocoWalk) are an easier but potentially more expensive option than street parking. In South Beach, don't even think about driving from club to club; park in one of the municipal lots and take the Electrowave shuttle that makes a loop along key streets. Once you've found a place for your car, do your club crawling on foot: the major nightlife neighborhoods are safe and compact.

How to get past the velvet ropes at the hottest South Beach nightspots? First, if you're staying at a hotel, use the concierge. Decide which clubs you want to check out (consult *Ocean Drive* magazine celebrity pages if you want to be among the glitterati), and the concierge will fax your name to the clubs in order for you to be put on the guest list. This means much easier access and usually no cover charge (which can be $20 or so) if you arrive before midnight. Guest list or no guest list, follow these pointers: make sure there are more women than men in your group. Dress up—casual chic is the dress code. For men this means no sneakers, no shorts, no sleeveless vests, and no shirts unbuttoned past the top button. For women provocative and seductive is fine; overly revealing is not. Black is always right. At the door: don't name-drop—no one takes it seriously. Don't be pushy while trying to get the doorman's attention. Wait until you make eye contact, then be cool and easygoing. If you decide to tip him (which most bouncers don't expect), be discreet and pleasant, not big-bucks obnoxious—a $10 or $20 bill quietly passed will be appreciated, however. With the right dress and the right attitude, you'll be on the dance floor rubbing shoulders with South Beach's finest clubbers in no time.

Bars & Lounges

One of Greater Miami's most popular pursuits is bar hopping. Bars range from intimate enclaves to showy see-and-be-seen lounges to loud, raucous frat parties. There's a decidedly New York flair to some of the newer lounges, which are increasingly catering to the Manhattan party crowd who escape to South Beach for long weekends. If you're looking for a relatively unfrenetic evening, your best bet is one of the chic hotel bars on Collins Avenue.

South Beach

B.E.D. Innocently standing for beverages, entertainment, and dining, B.E.D. also offers king pillow-strewn beds in place of tables. ⊠ *929 Washington Ave., South Beach* ☎ *305/532–9070.*

Blue. Electric Blue is laid-back and chic and has been know to draw high-profile celebs such as Dennis Rodman. ⊠ *222 Espanola Way, at Collins Ave., South Beach* ☎ *305/534–1009.*

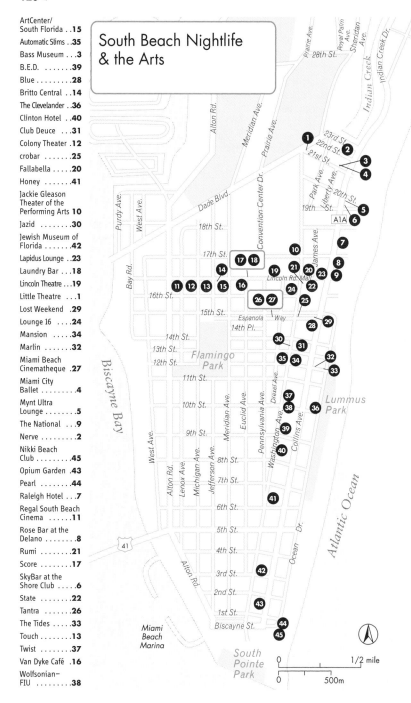

South Beach Nightlife
& the Arts

The Clevelander. Wanna meet other tourists? This always busy indoor sports bar and outdoor patio with live bands draws a college-style crowd that keeps its eye on the game or on the bikini-clad throng on Ocean Drive. It's the main draw at the hotel of the same name. ⊠ *1020 Ocean Dr., South Beach* ☎ *305/531–3485.*

Clinton Hotel. A stunning, lofty lobby with a cozy indoor bar and poolside lounge area provide a snug refuge from the louder nightspots along the avenue. Gourmet Chinese bar bites add to the appeal. ⊠ *825 Washington Ave., South Beach* ☎ *305/538–1471.*

Club Deuce. Although it's completely unglam, this pool hall attracts a colorful crowd of clubbers, locals, celebs—and just about anyone else. Locals consider it the best spot for a cheap drink. ⊠ *222 14th St., at Collins Ave., South Beach* ☎ *305/531–6200.*

Fallabella. Long and sleek with back-to-nature futuristic chic, the bar at the groovy Albion hotel is a serene getaway from mad Ocean Drive. ⊠ *1650 James Ave., between Washington and Collins Aves., South Beach* ☎ *305/913–1000.*

★ **Lapidus Lounge.** Named for the architect of the Fontainebleau Hilton, the DiLido Hotel (now the Ritz-Carlton South Beach), and other Miami Modernism classics, this elegant mezzanine-level lounge offers soothing decor, soft sounds and a view of the fabulous pool deck and cabana area—with the Atlantic Ocean as backdrop. ⊠ *1 Lincoln Road, South Beach* ☎ *786/276–4000.*

Laundry Bar. Do your laundry while listening to house music or quaffing a drink at the bar (you can leave your dry cleaning, too). It's mostly gay (with a ladies' night), but definitely straight-friendly. ⊠ *721 N. Lincoln La., 1 block north of Lincoln Rd., South Beach* ☎ *305/531–7700.*

Lost Weekend. Players at this pool hall are serious about their pastime, so it's hard to get a table on weekends. The full bar, which has 150 kinds of beers, draws an eclectic crowd, from yuppies to drag queens to slumming celebs like Lenny Kravitz and the guys in Hootie and the Blowfish. ⊠ *218 Espanola Way, at Collins Ave., South Beach* ☎ *305/672–1707.*

Marlin. It's the Austin Powers look here—fuchsia and orange pillows and cushions and mirrors everywhere. Deejays spin a different type of music every night for the 25-to-40 crowd. ⊠ *1200 Collins Ave., South Beach* ☎ *305/605–5000.*

Mynt Ultra Lounge. The name of this upscale lounge is meant to be taken literally—not only are the walls bathed in soft green shades, but an aromatherapy system pumps out different fresh scents, including mint. Celebs like Enrique Iglesias, Angie Everhart, and Queen Latifah have cooled down here. ⊠ *1921 Collins Ave., South Beach* ☎ *786/276–6132.*

★ **The National.** Don't miss a drink at the hotel's nifty wooden bar, one of many elements original to the 1939 building, which give it such a sense of its era that you'd expect to see Ginger Rogers and Fred Astaire hoofing it along the polished lobby floor. The adjoining Martini Room has a great collection of cigar and old airline stickers and vintage Bacardi ads on the walls. There's live jazz most nights. Don't forget to take a peek at the pool. ⊠ *1677 Collins Ave., South Beach* ☎ *305/532–2311.*

Nerve. This lounge is popular with locals who are avoiding attitude and celebs who are avoiding the spotlight. A sleek glass bar, soothing decor, and high-tech sound system are the draws here. DJs spin rock, retro rock, hip-hop, and house. ⊠ *247 23rd St., South Beach* ☎ *305/695–8697.*

Fodor'sChoice **Pearl.** An airy space lab of white and orange bathed in lavender light,
★ this restaurant-cum-nightclub overlooks the ocean and is next door to Nikki Beach Club. The food's not bad either. ⊠ *1 Ocean Dr., South Beach* ☎ *305/673–1575.*

Raleigh Hotel. In this art deco hotel there's a small, classy martini bar that's worth a visit. ⊠ *1775 Collins Ave., South Beach* ☎ *305/534–6300.*

Fodor'sChoice **Rose Bar at the Delano.** The airy lobby lounge at South Beach's trendiest
★ hotel manages to look dramatic but not cold, with long gauzy curtains and huge white pillars separating conversation nooks (this is where Ricky Martin shot the video for "La Vida Loca"). A pool table brings the austerity down to earth. There's also a poolside bar with intimate waterside cabanas. ⊠ *1685 Collins Ave., South Beach* ☎ *305/672–2000.*

Rumi. Named after the 13th-century Persian poet, this restaurant serves eclectic cuisine amid Moroccan furnishings and tapestries in rich chocolate, burgundy, and red, before shedding its Zen-like calm to become a club. ⊠ *330 Lincoln Rd., South Beach* ☎ *305/672–4353.*

Fodor'sChoice **SkyBar at the Shore Club.** Splendor-in-the-garden is the theme at this haute
★ spot by the sea, where multiple lounging areas are joined together. Daybeds, glowing Moroccan lanterns, and maximum atmosphere make a visit to this chic outdoor lounge worthwhile. Groove to dance music in the Red Room, or enjoy an aperitif and Japanese bar bites at Nobu Lounge. The Red Room, Nobu Restaurant and Lounge, and SkyBar all connect around the Shore Club's pool area. ⊠ *1901 Collins Ave., South Beach* ☎ *305/695–3100.*

Tantra. With its grass-floor lobby and aphrodisiacal dinner menu, this place takes sensory enhancement a step further when it transforms into a nightclub on Friday and Saturday and hosts its popular Goddess Party on Monday nights. ⊠ *1445 Pennsylvania Ave., South Beach* ☎ *305/672–4765.*

The Tides. For South Beach fabulousness, belly up to the glass-top bar for martinis and piano jazz in the cream-and-white lobby of this way-hip hotel. ⊠ *1220 Ocean Dr., South Beach* ☎ *305/604–5000.*

Touch. This tropical spot is so hip that even jaded New Yorkers will feel they're getting something new—a restaurant where lingering is not merely permissible, but *de rigueur.* And remember, you're in Miami—mojitos, martinis, and margaritas are the drinks of choice. ⊠ *910 Lincoln Rd., South Beach* ☎ *305/532–8003.*

Downtown Miami & Design District

Bahia. A 2-acre pool terrace high in the sky above bustling Brickell Avenue makes this an interesting stop for drinks and light snacks. The outdoor lounge area, just steps away from the pool bar, offers a relaxing place to grab a cool drink, sit back, and unwind. ⊠ *1435 Brickell Ave., Downtown* ☎ *305/358–3535.*

Bayside Marketplace. A shamelessly touristy retail and entertainment complex filled with stores and restaurants that you'll find in any big American city is somehow one of Florida's most-visited attractions. You can hop a disco boat for a midnight cruise, visit a daiquiri kiosk, or hang out at **Hard Rock Cafe** (☎ 305/377–3110), which you can locate by looking for the enormous guitar at the entrance. ⊠ *401 Biscayne Blvd., Downtown* ☎ *305/577–3344.*

Gordon Biersch. This financial district brew house is classier than most, with glass-enclosed copper pots cranking out tasty ales and lagers, an inspired menu, live music on Fridays, and a steady happy-hour crowd. ⊠ *1201 Brickell Ave., Downtown* ☎ *786/425–1130.*

★ **Grass.** Behind the iron gate (and finicky doormen) lies an open-air restaurant and lounge. Dine on gourmet, Asian-influenced cuisine on a thatched-roof patio and watch the bamboo (and the crowd) sway to tunes ranging from house to R&B. ⊠ *28 N.E. 40th St., Design District* ☎ *305/573–3355.*

M-Bar. At the lobby bar of the impeccably elegant Mandarin Oriental hotel you can choose from 250 martinis. Pick one and gaze out over Biscayne Bay. ⊠ *500 Brickell Key Dr., Brickell Key,* ☎ *305/913–8288.*

Fodor'sChoice **Tobacco Road.** Opened in 1912, this classic holds Miami's oldest liquor
★ license: No. 0001! Upstairs, in a space that was occupied by a speakeasy during Prohibition, local and national blues bands perform nightly. There's excellent bar food, a dinner menu, and a selection of single-malt Scotches, bourbons, and cigars. This is the hangout of grizzled journalists, bohemians en route to or from nowhere, and club kids seeking a way station before the real parties begin. ⊠ *626 S. Miami Ave., Downtown* ☎ *305/374–1198.*

Coconut Grove

CocoWalk. One of Miami's touristy shopping-and-eating complexes, CocoWalk is sweltering in the summertime and packed in the wintertime. In short, it's very popular. **Fat Tuesday** (☎ 305/441–2992) is a typical touristy place, serving sickly sweet concoctions like 190 Octane (190-proof alcohol), Swampwater (also 190 proof), Banana Banshees (banana liqueur, cream, and vodka), and Long Island Iced Tea. ⊠ *3015 Grand Ave., at McFarlane Rd., Coconut Grove* ☎ *305/444–0777.*

Monty's in the Grove. The outdoor bar here has Caribbean flair, thanks especially to live calypso and island music. It's very kid-friendly on weekends, when Mom and Dad can kick back and enjoy a beer and the raw bar while the youngsters dance to live music. Evenings bring a DJ and reggae music. ⊠ *2550 S. Bayshore Dr., at Aviation Ave., Coconut Grove* ☎ *305/858–1431.*

Orchid Lounge. The quirky furniture and such fanciful details as feathered lampshades characterize the bar. You can sip a fine cognac or choose from the extensive wine list and listen to live jazz, presented nightly. ⊠ *Mayfair House Hotel, 3000 Florida Ave., at Virginia St., Coconut Grove* ☎ *305/441–0000.*

Sandbar Grill. This rowdy sports bar comes complete with lots of varieties of beer and tequila, and plenty of TV sets. The kitchen serves Southern California–Mexican snacks, such as fish tacos, to 2 AM. ⊠ *3064 Grand Ave., at Main Hwy., Coconut Grove* ☎ *305/444–5270.*

Wyndham Grand Bay. With striped white pine and cherry floors, oversize bar stools, and pastel murals, this hotel bar serves up lots of European chic—and no wonder, it adjoins the elegant northern Italian Bice restaurant. There's live jazz Wednesday through Saturday and sushi or

Italian appetizers during happy hour (Wednesday at 5:30). ⊠ *2669 S. Bayshore Dr., at S.W. 27th Ave., Coconut Grove* ☎ *305/858–9600.*

Coral Gables

Stodgy Coral Gables? Not any more. This affluent suburb is undergoing a metamorphosis as its demographic changes from wealthy older folks to stylish younger professionals. Formerly uptight city officials are loosening the reins to allow street festivals and sidewalk dining and drinking venues, adding a spirited outdoor dimension to nightlife. The Gables will never have the sex appeal of South Beach or the high energy of the Grove, but it's increasingly popular with locals—young and old—who like its safe, tree-lined streets and easy parking.

Alcazaba. This dress-up nightclub at the Hyatt Regency has retro disco dancing, salsa, and merengue on Wednesday and Saturday nights. ⊠ *50 Alhambra Plaza, at Douglas Rd., Coral Gables* ☎ *305/569–4614.*

Bar at Ponce and Giralda. One of the oldest bars in South Florida, the old Hofbrau has been reincarnated and now serves up no-nonsense, live homegrown rock-and-roll and a nontouristy vibe. ⊠ *172 Giralda Ave., at Ponce de León Blvd., Coral Gables* ☎ *305/442–2730.*

Biltmore Hotel. This magnificent hotel's intimate and elegant bar attracts over-40 professionals and executives. ⊠ *1200 Anastasia Ave., at De Soto Blvd., Coral Gables* ☎ *305/445–1926.*

The Globe. The centerpiece of Coral Gables' emphasis on nightlife draws crowds of twentysomethings who spill into the street for live jazz Wednesday through Saturday and a bistro-style menu nightly. Outdoor tables and an art-heavy, upscale interior are comfortable, if you can find space to squeeze in. ⊠ *377 Alhambra Circle, at Le Jeune Rd., Coral Gables* ☎ *305/445–3555.*

JohnMartin's. The cozy upscale Irish pub hosts an Irish cabaret on Saturday nights, with live contemporary and traditional music—sometimes by an Irish band—storytelling, and dancers. ⊠ *253 Miracle Mile, at Ponce de León Blvd., Coral Gables* ☎ *305/445–3777.*

Pescado. This see-and-be-seen café and lounge has live jazz, a serious wine list, and gorgeous decor. A falling-water wall, low-lit sconces, and curvy leather banquettes soothe the after-work crowd inside, while comfy teak lounge chairs on the canopied, outdoor patio add to the relaxed yet elegant atmosphere. ⊠ *Village of Merrick Park, 320 San Lorenzo Ave., Coral Gables* ☎ *305/443–3474.*

Stuart's Bar-Lounge. Inside the charming 1926 Hotel Place St. Michel, this bar is favored by locals. Its style is beveled mirrors, mahogany paneling, French posters, pictures of old Coral Gables, and art nouveau lighting. ⊠ *162 Alcazar Ave., at Ponce de León Blvd., Coral Gables* ☎ *305/444–1666.*

Titanic Brewery & Restaurant. Noisy but cheerful, this campus nightspot attracts University of Miami students and upscale locals for live jazz and blues. ⊠ *5813 Ponce de León Blvd., at San Amaro Dr., Coral Gables* ☎ *305/667–2537.*

Toscana By Bice. At the Omni Colonnade Hotel, this Italian restaurant and bar (formerly Doc Dammer's) draws an older, sophisticated crowd for live jazz. ⊠ *180 Aragon Ave., at Ponce de León Blvd., Coral Gables* ☎ *305/441–2600.*

Cabaret, Comedy & Supper Clubs

If you're in the mood for scantily clad showgirls and feathered headdresses, you can still find the kind of song-and-dance extravaganzas that were produced by every major Miami Beach hotel in the 1950s. Modern-day offerings include flamenco shows, salsa dancing, and comedy clubs.

Casa Panza. The visionary Madrileñan owners of this Little Havana restaurant have energized the neighborhood with a twice-weekly tribute to *La Virgen del Rocío* (the patron saint of a province in Andalusia), in which the room is darkened and diners are handed lighted candles and sheet music. Everyone readily joins in the singing, making for a truly enjoyable evening. There is flamenco dancing on Tuesday, Thursday, Friday, and Saturday. ⊠ *1620 S.W. 8th St., Little Havana, Miami* ☎ *305/643–5343* ⊡ *Free.*

Club Tropigala. Once the La Ronde Room, where Frank Sinatra crooned for a crowd decked out in mink stoles and pinky rings, the Fontainebleau Hilton's nightspot is now a tropical jungle, with leaves dangling from the ceiling and orchids, banana leaves, and cascading waterfalls throughout. It's as close as you'll get to a Vegas-style revue. With such stars as Willy Chirino, Ricky Martin, and José Feliciano; Hispanic luminaries Albita and Julio Sabala; and a band that plays standards and Latin music for dancing, Club Tropigala brings back the old glamour of Miami Beach. Hotel guests receive complimentary admission, and reservations are suggested. ⊠ *4441 Collins Ave., Mid-Beach, Miami Beach* ☎ *305/672–7469* ⊡ *$20.*

★ **Hoy Como Ayer.** This tiny cabaret adorned with Cuban artwork is best known for Fuácata on Thursdays, where a DJ mixes old Cuban standards with hip-hop and is accompanied by a live drummer for a unique fusion experience. Other evenings include Spanish theater, live Latin salsa, and jazz. ⊠ *2212 S.W. 8th St., Little Havana, Miami* ☎ *305/541–2631.*

Improv Comedy Club. This long-standing comedy club hosts nationally touring comics nightly. Comedy club faithfuls will recognize Margaret Cho and George Wallace, and everyone knows Damon Wayans and Chris Rock, both of whom have taken the stage here. Urban Comedy Showcase is held Tuesdays and Wednesdays, with an open mike part of the evening on Wednesdays. A full menu is available. ⊠ *Streets of Mayfair, 3390 Mary St., at Grand Ave., Coconut Grove, Miami* ☎ *305/441–8200* ⊡ *$10–$32* ☉ *Shows Tues. 8 and 10:30, Wed.–Thurs. and Sun. 8:30, Fri. 8:30 and 10:45, Sat. 7:45, 10, and midnight.*

Lombardi's. You can shake it salsa-style or merengue until midnight to the music of three different bands on Friday, Saturday, and Sunday nights at this Downtown restaurant and bar. ⊠ *Bayside Marketplace, 401 Biscayne Blvd., Downtown, Miami* ☎ *305/381–9580.*

Dance Clubs

Mid-Beach & North

Bermuda Bar & Grille. The DJ here plays *loud* dance music into the wee hours of the morning. Male bartenders wear knee-length kilts, while female bartenders are in matching minis; however, the crowd dresses stylish island casual to match the atmosphere. In the big indoor tropi-

SALSA, MIAMI STYLE

WHILE MANY VISIT MIAMI to soak up some sun, others come here for something far hotter—the steamy salsa clubs. From Latin nights at hotel bars and spicy salsa-only nightclubs in Miami Beach to ranch-like settings inland that attract hordes of hard-core salseros (salsa dancers), Miami's vibrant salsa clubs are a terrific experience, if only to watch or be watched.

Miami's salsa, called Rueda or Casino-style salsa, is unique. Debbie Ohanian—a Miami transplant who started one of the city's foremost salsa clubs, Starfish—describes it as a sort of choreographed line dancing, like a Latin square dance, that started in Cuba's social clubs in the 1950s. Traditionally there are 180 different turns that people learn, and there's a caller. Unlike some other forms of salsa, there's not a lot of eye contact, and, also like a square dance, partners are exchanged. At many clubs, where a Casino Rueda typically begins the evening, the circles of dancers get so large, smaller circles form within. Having over 100 people in a Rueda is typical.

Beginners can get an overview of the salsa experience at ⊕ www.salsaweb.com. You'll find out about the differences in big-city styles, and anything else you want to know about salsa, from music to moves to movies.

Salsa novices should consider a salsa lesson, which are offered by several Miami nightclubs before the crowds turn out. Some lessons are free, while others are part of the cover charge. **Alcazaba** (⊠ 50 Alhambra Plaza, Coral Gables ☎ 305/569–4614), in the Hyatt Regency Coral Gables, has basic salsa lessons on Saturday. **Bermuda Bar & Grille** (⊠ 3509 N.E. 163rd St., North Miami Beach ☎ 305/945–0196) gives salsa lessons on Thursday night. Gloria and Emilio Estefan's restaurant, **Bongos Cuban Cafe** (⊠ 601 Biscayne Blvd., Downtown ☎ 786/777–2100), at the AmericanAirlines Arena, turns into a Latin-flavored dance club on Friday and Saturday nights, with lessons on Thursday. **Café Mystique** (⊠ 7250 N. W. 11th St., Miami ☎ 305/262–9500), at the Days Inn Miami International Airport Hotel, offers live Latin music four nights a week and Thursday-night salsa lessons. Other clubs may offer special salsa nights; check the weekly New Times.

Ready to try out your salsa skills? Get out on the floor and don't be shy to ask someone better than you to dance. (Just ask if they wouldn't mind showing you a couple of turns if you're still new at it.) In addition to the clubs with classes, there are other nightspots with salsa nights (call first). Perhaps the most authentic salsa experience in Miami can be had at **La Covacha** (⊠ 10730 N.W. 25th St., West Miami-Dade, Miami ☎ 305/594–3717), an open-air dance hall in West Miami-Dade County where you can hear not only salsa, but merengue, samba, soca, and Spanish-flavored rock. La Covacha attracts the young and old, Hispanics and Anglos, beginning dancers and seasoned salseros.**Quench** (⊠ 2801 Florida Ave., Coconut Grove, Miami ☎ 305/448–8150) is a hot spot for Saturday-night salseros, with two dance floors and plenty of space for trying out new moves. Saturday night is salsa night at **Paradis** (⊠ 7707 N.W. 103rd St., Hialeah Gardens ☎ 305/825–1000), the nightclub at the Howard Johnson Plaza Hotel–Miami Airport. **Señor Frog's** (⊠ 3480 Main Hwy., Coconut Grove, Miami ☎ 305/448–0999 ⊠ 616 Collins Ave., South Beach, Miami Beach ☎ 305/673–5262) sheds its Mexican restaurant mode on Saturday and becomes a hot Latin music nightspot.

cal forest there are booths you can hide in, seven bars, and three pool tables. Draft beer is served in yard glasses and frosted mugs. The place is closed Monday and Tuesday. ⊠ *3509 N.E. 163rd St., North Miami Beach* ☎ *305/945–0196.*

Jimmy'z at the Forge. Adjacent to the Forge steak house, this is as upscale a club as Miami Beach can offer—a VIP lounge indeed. That doesn't mean the party doesn't get bacchanalian at times, especially on Wednesdays. Any night, though, you'll see power suits with young things draped on either arm grooving to contemporary international music. ⊠ *432 41st St., at Pine Tree Dr., Mid-Beach, Miami Beach* ☎ *305/604–9798.*

South Beach

Automatic Slims. This locals' hangout has been called a cross between an I–40 truck-stop and a Motel 6. Neon signs, rowdy barmistresses, an occasional Lynyrd Skynyrd set, and the very popular Double-Wide Tuesday theme nights keep things from getting too serious. ⊠ *1216 Washington Ave., South Beach* ☎ *305/695–0795.*

Fodor'sChoice **crobar.** Sophisticated and fun, this South Beach branch of the popular
★ Chicago club combines sleek architecture in the form of massive sculptured monuments (think *Blade Runner*); performance art, such as angels swooping down on bungee cords; and state-of-the-art light and sound systems to dazzle the senses. Gwyneth Paltrow, Lennox Lewis, and Vanilla Ice have already checked it out. It's housed in the historic Cameo Theater, which is, unfortunately, carpeted. ⊠ *1445 Washington Ave., South Beach* ☎ *305/531–5027.*

Honey. The soft lighting, cozy couches and chaise longues, and low-down music go down as smoothly as the club's trademark honey-dipped apples. ⊠ *645 Washington Ave., South Beach* ☎ *305/604–8222.*

Lounge 16. This intimate laid-back lounge has hipster appeal and is hot with the locals. House music, room to dance, and a smaller-is-better attitude captures the vibe here. ⊠ *423 16th St., at Washington Ave., South Beach* ☎ *305/672–4472.*

Mansion. Savvy new ownership is bringing in a variety of mini-shows and special events in addition to the pulsating house beats and multilevel dance floors for which this capacious and always popular night club is known. ⊠ *1235 Washington Ave., South Beach* ☎ *305/532–1525.*

Nikki Beach Club. With its swell on-the-beach location, the full-service Nikki Beach Club has become a favorite pretty-people and celeb hangout. Teepees and hammocks on the sand, dance floors both under the stars and inside, and beach parties make this a true South Beach experience. ⊠ *1 Ocean Dr., South Beach* ☎ *305/538–1111.*

Opium Garden. Enter the Asian temple, and behold a lush waterfall, lots of candles, dragons, and tapestries. Casually chic twenty- and thirtysomethings go for the exotic intrigue of the popular nightspot and dance to house music and hip-hop. ⊠ *136 Collins Ave., South Beach* ☎ *305/531–5535.*

State. This upscale new club draws a fashion-conscious crowd. The current club trend of playing host to a variety of special events, including fashion shows and wrap parties, keeps things lively. ⊠ *320 Lincoln Rd., South Beach* ☎ *786/621–5225.*

Downtown

Bongos Cuban Café. Grab a mojito and hit the dance floor. It's hard to remain stationary at this lively Cuban restaurant and nightclub owned by Gloria and Emilio Estefan. Located behind AmericanAirlines Arena, the club has great views of Biscayne Bay and the Port of Miami. ☒ *601 Biscayne Blvd., Downtown* ☎ *786/777–2100.*

Space. Want 24-hour partying? Here's the place. Created from four Downtown warehouses, Space has three dance rooms, an outdoor patio, a New York industrial look, and a 24-hour liquor license. It's open on weekends only, and you'll need to look good to be allowed past the velvet ropes. ☒ *34 N.E. 11th St., Downtown* ☎ *305/375–0001.*

Coconut Grove

Flavour. Housed in a former Masonic temple on one of the Grove's main drags, this club offers something for everyone. A young, mostly local crowd enjoys shooting pool, dancing to pounding house music, '70s retro nights featuring old surf films, and Disco Inferno on Saturday nights. ☒ *2895 McFarlane Rd., Coconut Grove* ☎ *305/445–6511.*

★ **Oxygen Lounge.** Latin and dance sounds dominate at this sleek, below-ground lounge. Water cascades down a wall, while blue neon light casts a glow over the crowd of mainly young professionals out for a good time and a little dancing. ☒ *2911 Grand Ave., Coconut Grove* ☎ *305/ 476–0202.*

Quench. This bar, restaurant, and multilevel dance club offers plenty of space to move around, a tapas-style menu, and a pleasant lack of attitude. Music includes '80s retro, hip-hop, Top 40, and Latin beats. Saturday nights are popular for salsa and merengue dancing. ☒ *2801 Florida Ave., Coconut Grove* ☎ *305/448–8150.*

Gambling & Evening Cruises

Miami's waterfront location means there's no shortage of water-oriented activities, even at night. Several evening cruises depart from **Bayside Marketplace** in downtown Miami, offering different styles of entertainment to different crowds, and another cruise departs from **Dinner Key,** off Bayshore Drive in Coconut Grove. Gambling cruisers must be at least 21 years old. Get there in plenty of time to buy tickets and board. For gambling on land, head to **Miccosukee Resort & Gaming** (☒ 500 S.W. 177th Ave., West Miami-Dade, Miami ☎ 305/222–4600).

Casino Princesa. You can embark on a gambling cruise to nowhere from right next to the Hard Rock Cafe. ☒ *315 Biscayne Blvd., south of Bayside Marketplace, Downtown* ☎ *305/379–5825* ☜ *$9.95* ☉ *Daily 12:30 PM and 7:30 PM; late-night cruises weekends 1 AM–6 AM.*

Celebration. A sightseeing boat by day becomes a party boat by night, cruising the bay and blasting music. ☒ *401 Biscayne Blvd., at Bayside Marketplace, Downtown* ☎ *305/373–7001* ☜ *$10–$14* ☉ *Daily 11.*

Full Moon Cruise. If you're in town when the moon is full, make reservations for an evening on the Miami Sailing Club's 56-foot *Malu Kai.* The combination of a spectacular moonrise, dazzling skyline, and gentle sea breeze is unforgettable, making the drinks and snacks all the more enjoyable. ⊠ *Dinner Key Marina, 3400 Pan American Dr., at Bayshore Dr. and S.W. 27th Ave., Coconut Grove, Miami* ☎ *305/858–1130* 🖀 *$70 per person, $100 per couple* ⊙ *Call for dates and times.*

Heritage. This stately sailing vessel offers sedate sunset and skyline cruises. ⊠ *401 Biscayne Blvd., south of Bayside band stage, Downtown* ☎ *305/442–9697* 🖀 *$15–$20* ⊙ *Weekdays 6:30; weekends 6:30, 8, 9, 10, 11.*

Island Queen. When the sun goes down, this sightseeing boat lights up with neon and plies Biscayne Bay while you dance to the latest DJ mixes. There is a cash bar. ⊠ *401 Biscayne Blvd., at Bayside Marketplace, Downtown, Miami* ☎ *305/379–5119* 🖀 *$10* ⊙ *Mon.–Thurs. 7:30, 9; Fri.–Sun. 9, 10, 11, midnight.*

Gay Nightlife

Aside from a few bars and lounges on the mainland, Greater Miami's gay action centers on the dance clubs in South Beach. That tiny strip of sand rivals New York and San Francisco as a hub of gay nightlife—if not in the number of clubs then in the intensity of the partying. The neighborhood's large gay population and the generally tolerant attitudes of the hip straights who live and visit here encourage gay-friendliness at most South Beach venues that are not specifically gay. In addition, many mixed clubs, like crobar, have one or two gay nights. Laundry Bar has a mixed scene and also hosts a gay night, including one for the ladies. Generally, gay life in Miami is overwhelmingly male-oriented, and lesbians, although welcome everywhere, will find themselves in the minority. To find out what's going on, pick up the South Beach club rag *Hotspots,* widely available as the weekend approaches, or the alternative weeklies *TWN* (The Weekly News, ⊕ www.twnonline.org) and *The Express* (⊕ www.expressgaynews.com).

Bars & Lounges

Cactus Nightclub. In the northern reaches of Downtown, this is the place to head if you don't want to stay up to 4 AM to get some nightlife in. Special events include drag nights, male strippers, and a very popular Noche Latina on Saturdays. ⊠ *2041 Biscayne Blvd., Downtown* ☎ *305/438–0662.*

Dance Clubs

Fodor'sChoice ★ **crobar.** Steamy club windows on Monday nights are due to the fantastically popular Back Door Bamby night, with go-go girls and boys. Keep in mind the carpeted dance floor—your lug soles will resist movement. ⊠ *1445 Washington Ave., South Beach, Miami Beach* ☎ *305/531–5027.*

O'Zone. One of the most popular men's dance clubs on the mainland, this South Miami multilevel dance complex attracts Latin and Anglo patrons in their 20s and 30s. Pool tables and other games offer an alternative to elbow bending. ⊠ *6620 Red Rd., 1 block off U.S. 1, South Miami,* ☎ *305/667–2888.*

Score. This popular Lincoln Road hangout draws a good-looking, largely younger crowd. There's loud dance music and an outdoor patio perfect for people-watching. At the packed Sunday tea dance, a DJ spins old disco tunes and progressive music. ⊠ *727 Lincoln Rd., at Euclid Ave., South Beach, Miami Beach* ☎ *305/535–1111.*

Twist. This longtime hot spot and local favorite with two levels, an outdoor patio, and a game room is crowded from 8 PM on, especially on Monday, Thursday (2-for-1), and Friday nights. ⊠ *1057 Washington Ave., South Beach, Miami Beach* ☎ *305/538–9478.*

Live Music

Churchill's Hideaway. Never mind its off-the-beaten path location in Little Haiti—one of Miami's oldest rock clubs is the place for hard-driving live rock and, occasionally, national acts. ⊠ *5501 N.E. 2nd Ave. Little Haiti, Miami* ☎ *305/757–1807.*

I/O Lounge. This out-of-the-way spot attracts folks who come for the music. Groove to everything from live Latin funk to electro-pop outside on the grassy patio, or inside, where a long bar acts as a divider between the stage and DJ platform and a casual lounging area. ⊠ *30 N. E. 14th St., Downtown* ☎ *305/358–8007.*

★ **Jazid.** Thanks to a sleek interior design job in aqua tones, Jazid is an intimate, candlelighted standout on the strip. The music is jazz, with blues and R&B. Bands play downstairs in the cozy barroom and upstairs on an even tinier stage. Call ahead to reserve a table. ⊠ *1342 Washington Ave., South Beach, Miami Beach* ☎ *305/673–9372.*

La Covacha. This spot west of the airport has strayed a bit from its Latin roots by playing disco and non-Latin music. For the best in salsa, merengue, and Spanish pop, head here on a Friday night. ⊠ *10730 N. W. 25th St., West Miami-Dade, Miami* ☎ *305/594–3717.*

Luna Star Cafe. Yearning for the pre-electric '60s? Then head here to listen to acoustic music—folk, blues, and jazz—with a little storytelling thrown in. There's a full menu, plus exotic coffees, beers, ales, ciders, and fruit-and-spice beverages to complete the folksy experience. ⊠ *775 N.E. 125th St., North Miami* ☎ *305/892–8522.*

★ **One Ninety.** Locals come here for great food, including tapas served until 3 AM. Late at night the restaurant transforms into a music hot spot, where a multicultural mix of Miamians enjoys live music ranging from rock to rumba. ⊠ *190 N.E. 46th St., Design District, Miami.* ☎ *305/576–9779.*

SoHo Lounge. Four rooms of sound offer up everything from '80s rock to gothic and synth pop spun by DJs or performed live at this alternative-crowd hangout on the edge of the Design District. ⊠ *175 N.E. 36th St., Design District, Miami* ☎ *305/576–1988.*

Fodor'sChoice
★ **Tobacco Road.** Live blues, R&B, and jazz are on tap along with the food and drink at this Miami institution. ⊠ *626 S. Miami Ave., Downtown* ☎ *305/374–1198.*

Van Dyke Café. More restaurant than jazz club, this News Café spin-off hosts live jazz (or crooning Brazilian songstresses) on the second floor seven nights a week. Its location on South Beach's Lincoln Road Mall makes it a great spot to take a break during an evening shopping excursion or to stop for a drink after dinner. ⊠ *846 Lincoln Rd., at Euclid Ave., South Beach, Miami Beach* ☎ *305/534–3600.*

THE ARTS

If the arts are what make cities like New York, London, Tokyo, Buenos Aires, and Paris great, then Miami and Miami Beach are not great cities—not quite yet. But seeds of greatness, sown decades ago, have sprouted strong and true. Greater Miami, perceived by some as a comely lightweight in the arts, is undergoing a cultural renaissance about which other cities only dream.

Led by an expanding roster of up-and-coming collecting museums and performing groups, the arts scene in Greater Miami is coming into its own. Nonprofit cultural organizations have grown dramatically in number, from 110 to 750 in the last 20 years, including the internationally known Miami City Ballet and the New World Symphony. But to savor the area's vibrant cultural diversity, don't overlook the smaller, lesser-known arts groups. Performances from such innovative organizations as the Miami Light Project, which brings music, dance, film, and theater works to town in addition to commissioning local projects, and Momentum Dance Company, one of the area's oldest contemporary dance companies, are not to be missed.

Larger venues regularly attract international talent, such as classical ballet companies, Latin singing stars, and touring Broadway shows. The winter season especially brings traveling art exhibits to local museums and gallery walks to Coral Gables and to newer art districts in North Miami and Wynwood. Art and fashion events take place in the Design District, a cluster of galleries and interior-design showrooms just north of Downtown. And there are any number of cultural festivals on tap throughout the year. Tigertail Productions' biannual FLA/BRA Festival, for example, adds to the city's rich cultural mélange.

Thanks to the Art in Public Places program, you've probably already been exposed to large-scale installations: Rockne Krebs' *Miami Line,* a neon rainbow stretching across the Miami River, and Michele Oka Doner's bronze and mother-of-pearl marine life in the terrazzo walkway at Miami International Airport's Concourse A. You can't miss Roy Lichtenstein's outdoor mermaid, which graces the front lawn of the Jackie Gleason Theater in Miami Beach, or Claes Oldenburg and Coosje van Bruggen's *Dropped Bowl with Scattered Slices and Peels,* at Downtown's Government Center. Major new cultural projects include the restoration of the 1913 Lyric Theater in Overtown, home to famous jazz artists in the 1930s and '40s, and the Patricia & Phillip Frost Art Museum at Florida International University. On Miami Beach, the Cultural Campus is a two-square-block arts complex housing offices, performing space, rehearsal studios for the Miami City Ballet, and a library, all adjacent to the Bass Museum of Art. The new Performing Arts Center complex, due to open in 2006, promises to be a spectacular home for several of Miami's finest performing arts groups.

There have been missteps and setbacks: South Florida's regional symphony, the Florida Philharmonic, recently shut down operations, and funding squabbles occasionally threaten such venerable venues as the circa-1926

Coconut Grove Playhouse. But forward thinkers see enough in the works to envision a Miami that can fully express its multicultural uniqueness in limitless forms. So arts junkies, never fear—Miami is on its way.

Film

Greater Miami is a popular destination for filmmakers, who have used it as a location for movies ranging from the Elvis Presley classic *Clambake* to the 1983 crime flick *Scarface* to the gross-out comedy *There's Something About Mary*. It's also full of choices for filmgoers, who can see first-run foreign and independent films at an ever-expanding list of film festivals.

Those interested in moving images, including video and television work, should stop at the **Wolfson Media Center** (✉ 300 N.E. 2nd Ave., Downtown Miami ☎ 305/375–1505) on the Downtown campus of Miami Dade College. The center houses a collection of rare videos, including TV images of the Cuban Missile Crisis, John F. Kennedy's visit to Miami, and the 1968 Republican Convention, which it displays in special screening programs. The center also sponsors bus tours of Miami neighborhoods, during which you can watch video from earlier time periods to learn how development has changed the face of the city.

Film Festivals

Walk the red carpet in Miami. Although festival passes can cost plenty, most individual screenings are only $10. The most high profile of the lot is the **Miami International Film Festival** (☎ 305/348–5555 ⊕ www.miamifilmfestival.com), which unspools each January–February with 50 screenings of Hollywood and international biggies at Downtown's historic Gusman Center for the Performing Arts (174 E. Flagler St.), South Beach's Colony Theater (1040 Lincoln Rd.), the Regal South Beach Cinema (1100 Lincoln Rd.), and free big-screen showings right on the beach. In December the **Jewish Film Festival** (☎ 305/576–4030 ⊕ www.caje-miami.org/filmfestival) presents screenings of new work as well as workshops and panel discussions with filmmakers in several Miami locations. In March the **Miami Latin Film Festival** (☎ 305/279–1809 ⊕ www.hispanicfilm.com) presents French, Italian, and Portuguese movies along with Spanish and Latin American movies. During the last week of April and first week of May the **Miami Gay & Lesbian Film Festival** (☎ 305/534–9924 ⊕ www.mglff.com) hosts screenings and events at venues in South Beach and throughout Miami-Dade County. Each May, South Beach hosts the **Brazilian Film Festival** (☎ 305/899–8998 ⊕ www.brazilianfilmfestival.com), which unveils on a huge outdoor movie screen built on the beach especially for the occasion.

Film Houses & Cinemas

As in any major U.S. city, you can see Hollywood releases and some foreign and independent films at the many neighborhood multiplexes in Miami and Miami Beach. Most mainstream cinemas are in suburban shopping centers, such as Dolphin Mall in West Miami-Dade, Shops at Sunset Place in South Miami, and Loehmann's Fashion Island in Aventura. Out-of-the-ordinary venues include the striking glass-walled Regal South Beach Cinema on Lincoln Road and the historic Tower Theater.

AMC CocoWalk 16. Popular with teens on weekends, this theater at Coconut Grove's busy mall shows first-run movies and occasionally foreign films. ✉ *CocoWalk, 3015 Grand Ave., at Virginia St., Coconut Grove, Miami* ☎ *305/448–7075.*

Bill Cosford Cinema. Run by the School of Communication at the University of Miami, this first-run motion-picture theater has Florida premieres, film favorites, foreign and independent American films, presentations by visiting filmmakers, and mini-festivals. ✉ *University of Miami campus, Memorial Building, Coral Gables,* ☎ *305/284–4861* ⊕ *www.miami.edu.*

Miami Beach Cinematheque. Home to the Miami Beach Film Society, this cultural venue offers foreign-film picnic nights, first-run independent films, underground shorts and documentaries, and special film tributes. ✉ *512 Espanola Way, at Drexel Ave., South Beach, Miami Beach* ☎ *305/673–4567.*

Regal South Beach Cinema. Purists were not pleased when this huge glass-walled building went up at the end of Lincoln Road, but its mix of first-run movies and independent foreign films made it a welcome addition for South Beach movie lovers. You can order good food—sandwiches, salads, muffins—from the second floor café, and it will be delivered to your seat. ✉ *1100 Lincoln Rd., at Alton Rd., South Beach, Miami Beach* ☎ *305/674–6766.*

Tower Theater. Built in 1926, this was the first Miami cinema to show films with Spanish subtitles and became a cultural hub for newly arrived Cuban immigrants in the 1960s. Today Miami Dade College supports this historic venue with a lively mix of cultural offerings—from music, dance, and theater performances to film and art exhibitions. ✉ *1508 S.W. 8th St., Little Havana, Miami* ☎ *305/237–6180* ⊕ *www.culture.mdc.edu.*

Fine Arts

Art Galleries

Greater Miami's young visual arts community took a major leap in international status when the prestigious annual art fair Art Basel announced its debut in Miami Beach in December 2001. **Art Basel–Miami Beach** showcases artwork from 175 of the world's most respected art galleries, mixing renowned, established artists with cutting-edge newcomers. A host of crossover cultural events also take place during Art Basel–Miami Beach, including music, film, architecture, and design, further boosting the city's sense of pride and cultural cachet.

South Florida artists are enjoying unprecedented popularity, and local galleries, many of which showcase important Latin American artists, are also growing in recognition. One of the art-gallery hot spots is Lincoln Road, South Beach's colorful pedestrian mall, where you can stroll from gallery to gallery and enjoy food and wine along with the artwork. The Miami Beach community-at-large boasts a rich and diverse culture of contemporary artists and arts groups, which offer visitors eclectic and energizing experiences, both in traditional and nontraditional settings. In Coral Gables, stylish **Gallery Nights** are held the first Friday evening of every month, and a free shuttle bus takes you between galleries. North Miami offers **NoMi Gallery Nights** on the last Friday of the month, while the up-and-coming **Wynwood Art District** has begun offering gallery walks the second Saturday of the month. Another impressive collection of galleries is in Miami's Design District, north of Downtown. Check newspaper listings for events in this always-intriguing area.

If you like to watch artists at work, check out the Bakehouse Art Complex in the Design District, and ArtCenter/South Florida in three locations on Lincoln Road. During the week many area galleries are open by appointment only, so be sure to call ahead.

MIAMI BEACH **ArtCenter/South Florida.** More than a gallery, this 60,000-square-foot cam-
★ pus includes 52 artists' studios, exhibition galleries, and art education classrooms. The 800 Lincoln Road Gallery presents month-long exhibits by resident and outside artists. This is one of the galleries that ignited South Beach's resurrection, and it's a good place to see works in progress: the studios are open to the public. ⊠ *Main studio: 924 Lincoln Rd., South Beach* ☎ *305/674–8278* ⊕ *www.artcentersf.org* ☉ *Daily 11–11* ⊠ *gallery annexes* ⊠ *800 Lincoln Rd., South Beach* ☉ *Mon.–Thurs. 11–10, Fri.–Sun. 11–11* ⊠ *810 Lincoln Rd., South Beach* ☉ *Mon.–Thurs. 1–10, Fri.–Sun. 11–11.*

Bettcher Gallery. This contemporary art gallery promotes the achievement and evolution of emerging, mid-career, and established artists from around the world. ⊠ *Eden Roc Renaissance Resort and Spa, 4525 Collins Ave., Mid-Beach* ☎ *305/801–1047* ⊕ *www.bettchergallery. com* ⊠ *5582–3 N.E. 4th Ct., Miami* ☎ *305/758–7556* ☉ *Sun.–Thurs. noon–7, Fri.–Sat. noon–10.*

Britto Central. Romero Britto's colorful and playful pop art has become a ubiquitous part of the South Florida landscape, encompassing murals, billboards, sculpture, even neckties and scarves. ⊠ *818 Lincoln Rd., South Beach* ☎ *305/531–8821* ⊕ *www.britto.com* ☉ *Mon.–Thurs. 11–11, Fri.–Sun. 11–midnight.*

MIAMI **Bakehouse Art Complex.** You can watch visual and performance artists at work at this former 1920s bakery. In addition to the working studios, public galleries offer juried exhibitions, workshops, and classes; some of the artists work with the public schools. Renowned Miami outsider artist Purvis Young exhibits here, as do Caribbean artists. Free shows are hosted in the performance space. ⊠ *561 N.W. 32nd St., Design District* ☎ *305/576–2828.* ⊕ *www.bakehouseartcomplex.org* ☉ *Call for schedule weekdays 10–4.*

Barbara Gillman Gallery. A pioneer in discovering and exhibiting Florida artists, Barbara Gillman also shows other contemporary American and Latin American painting, sculpture, ceramics, works on paper, mixed media, and photography, including jazz photography and prints. ⊠ *3814 N.E. Miami Ct., Design District* ☎ *305/573–1920* ⊕ *www.artnet.com/ bgillman.html* ☉ *Thurs.–Sat. 11–6 and by appointment.*

Damien B. Art Center. Among the refreshing mix of art featured here are contemporary European artwork and art from Haiti, sculpture, photography, painting, and mixed media. Multimedia events are also a part of this lively studio and gallery scene. ⊠ *282 N.W. 36th St., Design District* ☎ *305/573–4949* ⊕ *www.damienb.com* ☉ *Mon.–Sat. 10–5.*

Haitian Art Factory. Here you'll find colorful paintings, sculpture, sequined ceremonial voodoo flags representing saints and deities, and other forms of folk art by Haitian artists. Check newspaper listings for special exhibitions. ✉ *835 N.E. 79th St., Little Haiti* ☎ *305/758–6939* ⊕ *www. haitianartfactory.com* ⊙ *Mon.–Thurs. 10–5, Fri. 10–4, Sat. 10–2.*

Wallflower Gallery. Sip green tea while perusing works by Miami artists in this unpretentious Downtown place—or come listen to Haitian dance and music performances, appearances by local bands, and poetry readings. ✉ *10 N.E. 3rd St., Downtown* ☎ *305/579–0069* ⊕ *www. wallflowergallery.com* ⊙ *Tues.–Fri. noon–8.*

CORAL GABLES & COCONUT GROVE **Artspace–Virginia Miller Galleries.** This venerable contemporary gallery, one of Greater Miami's oldest, has changing exhibits of paintings, drawings, and sculpture focusing on Latin American, Cuban, European, and American artists. ✉ *169 Madeira Ave., Coral Gables* ☎ *305/444–4493* ⊕ *www.virginiamiller.com* ⊙ *Weekdays 11–6.*

Fredric Snitzer Gallery. In a warehouse district, with a space that lends itself to large-scale installations, this gallery represents such contemporary artists from the United States and Latin America as Purvis Young and Naomi Fisher, along with Miami-based artists such as José Bedia. ✉ *3078 S.W. 38th Ct., Coral Gables* ☎ *305/448–8976* ⊕ *www.snitzer. com* ⊙ *Tues.–Sat. 11–5.*

Galerie D'Art Nader. This collection of fine Haitian art includes paintings by Haitian masters and contemporary artists in addition to sculpture, voodoo flags, and books on Haitian art. Custom framing is available. ✉ *1911 Ponce de León Blvd., Coral Gables* ☎ *305/444–1740* ⊕ *www.galeriedartnader.com* ⊙ *Weekdays 10–6, Sat. 11–4.*

Gary Nader Fine Art. Established by one of the world's top Latin American art dealers, this gallery exhibits works by such masters as Fernando Botero, Wifredo Lam, and Rufino Tamayo. ✉ *3306 Ponce de León Blvd., Coral Gables* ☎ *305/442–0256* ⊕ *www.garynader.com* ⊙ *Weekdays 10–6.*

One Ear Society. This gallery, located at the Streets of Mayfair shopping area, showcases affordable works of art created by talented amateurs and professional local artists. ✉ *2911 Grand Ave., Coconut Grove, Miami* ☎ *305/445–3864* ⊕ *www.oneearsociety.org* ⊙ *Tues.–Sun. 10–10.*

Art Museums & Collections

Greater Miami's art museums parallel the fast track that the area's cultural scene is moving on: they're growing, upgrading, and gaining national and international respect. Whether relative newcomers, like the Wolfsonian–FIU, or established venues that get a major makeover, like the Bass Museum of Art, these important facilities are attracting attention from locals and visitors alike. Add to that Greater Miami's ever-increasing art-related annual events, such as Art Deco Weekend, Art Miami, Miami Modernism, the Beaux Arts Festival, and, yes, even the Coconut Grove Arts Festival, and it's no wonder that Greater Miami is becoming a big-league member of the culture club.

Fodor'sChoice ★ **Bass Museum of Art.** This provocative and growing museum on the northern fringes of South Beach (on land given to the city by Miami Beach founder John Collins) has substantial exhibition space, a café, and a courtyard. Its expansion is part of a two-square-block Miami Beach Cultural Campus, which also houses the Miami City Ballet. Although its permanent collection includes an Albrecht Dürer and a Peter Paul Rubens, the Bass is most notable for visits by traveling exhibits of contemporary art, such as the recent *Haitian Spirit*, which featured selections from filmmaker Jonathan Demme's renowned Haitian art collection as well as photographer Bruce Weber's powerful series documenting Haitian life in Miami. ✉ *2121 Park Ave., South Beach, Miami Beach* ☎ *305/673–7530* ⊕ *www.bassmuseum.org* 🔗 *$6* ☉ *Tues.–Wed. and Fri.–Sat. 10–5, Thurs. 10–9, Sun. 11–5.*

Ⓒ **Historical Museum of Southern Florida.** Many kid-friendly exhibits here say "Please touch," including a player piano, an authentic trolley car from 1920s Miami, Victorian dress-up clothes, and living maps that let you "walk across the world" while experiencing the cultures that have influenced South Florida's history. Try a family overnight adventure— the museum calls them "camp-ins"—that's designed to let both parents and kids go behind the scenes. ✉ *Miami-Dade Cultural Center, 101 W. Flagler St., Downtown Miami* ☎ *305/375–1492* ⊕ *www.historical-museum.org* 🔗 *$5* ☉ *Mon.–Sat. 10–5, Thurs. 10–9, Sun. noon–5.*

Jewish Museum of Florida. The permanent exhibit in this restored art deco synagogue, entitled *MOSAIC: Jewish Life in Florida*, documents the long and rich history and culture of the Jewish residents of South Florida from 1763 until the present. Temporary exhibits focus on Jewish art and history. ✉ *301 Washington Ave., South Beach, Miami Beach* ☎ *305/672–5044* ⊕ *www.jewishmuseum.com* 🔗 *$5, Sat. free* ☉ *Tues.–Sun. 10–5.*

Latin American Art Museum. For a small storefront museum, it has an extensive collection of works by Cuban and Latin American artists, with an emphasis on emerging artists and a special dedication to women artists. The museum participates in Little Havana's Cultural Fridays on the last Friday of every month. ✉ *2206 S.W. 8th St., Little Havana, Miami* ☎ *305/644–1127* ⊕ *www.latinoweb.com/museo* 🔗 *Free* ☉ *Tues.–Fri. 11–5, Sat. 11–4.*

Fodor'sChoice ★ **Lowe Art Museum.** The county's first visual arts museum has a permanent collection that includes art from the European Renaissance and baroque periods; pre-Columbian pieces; Asian, African, and Native American art; and works by 20th-century Latin American and American artists, including Cundo Bermudez, Roy Lichtenstein, Deborah Butterfield, and Claes Oldenburg. Each January the Lowe sponsors the Beaux Arts Festival in Coral Gables, one of the area's largest outdoor art markets. ✉ *University of Miami, 1301 Stanford Dr., Coral Gables* ☎ *305/284–3603* ⊕ *www.lowemuseum.org* 🔗 *$5* ☉ *Tues.–Wed. and Fri.–Sat. 10–5, Thurs. noon–7, Sun. noon–5.*

Miami Art Central (MAC). This new not-for-profit organization showcases contemporary artists of Latin American and Hispanic descent in an elegant museum space and supports emerging talent through residency programs. Its inaugural exhibition featured works by José Bedia, Robert Chambers, Luis Gispert, Gean Moreno, and Jacin Giordano. ✉ *5960 Red Rd., South Miami* ☎ *305/455–3333* ⊕ *www.miamiartcentral.org* 🔗 *$5* ☉ *Thurs.–Fri. 4–7, weekends 11–6.*

★ Ⓒ **Miami Art Museum.** Along with the main library and the Historical Museum of Southern Florida, this component of downtown's Miami-Dade Cultural Center is one of the county's largest museums. It exhibits contemporary art of the western hemisphere with a focus on works from the 1940s to the present. In addition to the 189 works in the permanent collection, the museum has provocative works by artists including Frank Stella, James Rosenquist, and Robert Rauschenberg. This is no stuffy space: the second Saturday of the month is free for families. Interactive programs designed by the museum's education department make fine art fun for kids, and activities usually incorporate current work on display. ⊠ *Miami-Dade Cultural Center, 101 W. Flagler St., Downtown* ☎ *305/375–3000* ⊕ *www. miamiartmuseum.org* ⊠ *$5* ⊙ *Tues.–Fri. 10–5, weekends noon–5.*

★ **Museum of Contemporary Art (MOCA).** Its 1996 building and grounds designed by Charles Gwathmey, MOCA is known for provocative exhibitions (eight to 10 shows each year). Its collection of 20th-century American and European works reaches for the cutting edge. Permanent pieces include works from such artists as Louise Nevelson, Julian Schnabel, Dennis Oppenheim, and Anna Gaskell. Programs range from film and video to live jazz and lectures by contemporary artists. ⊠ *770 N.E. 125th St., North Miami* ☎ *305/893–6211* ⊕ *www.mocanomi.org* ⊠ *$5 Wed.–Sun., donations welcome Tues.* ⊙ *Tues.–Sat. 11–5, Sun. noon–5.*

Patricia & Phillip Frost Art Museum at Florida International University. Being affiliated with the Smithsonian means the FIU museum has access to that institution's huge collection of art and artifacts and is a major cultural institution. Known especially for its Latin American and 20th-century American art, it's also home to ArtPark at FIU, an outdoor sculpture park with works from the Martin Z. Margulies sculpture collection, including pieces by Alexander Calder and Isamu Noguchi. Permanent collections include paintings by such major 20th-century figures as Hans Hofmann, Rufino Tamayo, and Cundo Bermudez; an extensive collection of American prints from the 1960s, including works by Andy Warhol and Roy Lichtenstein; pieces by Haitian fine artists; and Haitian and Brazilian folk art. ⊠ *FIU campus, S.W. 107th Ave. at S.W. 8th St., West Miami-Dade, Miami* ☎ *305/348–2890* ⊕ *www.artmuseumatfiu. org* ⊠ *Free* ⊙ *Mon.–Tues. and Thurs.–Fri. 10–5, Wed. 10–9, Sat. 10–4, Sun. noon–4.*

Rubell Family Collection. In a huge warehouse near the Design District, the family that owns South Beach's Albion and Greenview hotels and Bal Harbour's Beach House displays their collection of conceptual art, photography, sculpture, and paintings by contemporary names such as Julian Schnabel, José Bedia, Cindy Sherman, Jean Michael Basquiat, Charles Ray, Takashi Murakami, and Jeff Koons. It's currently one of the country's leading private contemporary-art collections. ⊠ *95 N.W. 29th St., Downtown Miami* ☎ *305/573–6090* ⊠ *Free* ⊙ *Wed.–Sun. 10–6 or by appt.*

Spanish Cultural Center. Exhibitions here focus on works by Spanish and Latin American artists. The center also helps promote music, film, poetry, and other events highlighting the cultures of Spanish-speaking countries. ⊠ *800 Douglas Rd., Suite 170, Coral Gables* ☎ *305/448–9677* ⊕ *www.ccemiami.org* ⊠ *Free* ⊙ *Weekdays 10–3.*

Fodor'sChoice ★ **Vizcaya Museum and Gardens.** Once the winter residence of Miami pioneer James Deering, this Coconut Grove mansion on Biscayne Bay has 34 rooms decorated in rococo, baroque, neoclassical, and Italian Renaissance styles. In essence, Deering and his architect created a lavish 16th-century Italian country villa and complementary manicured grounds in Miami. A small café overlooks the swimming pool. ⊠ *3251 S. Miami Ave., Coconut Grove Miami* ☎ *305/250–9133* ⊕ *www.vizcayamuseum com* ⌨ *$12* ⊙ *House daily 9:30–5, gardens daily 9:30–5:30.*

FodorśChoice **Wolfsonian–Florida International University.** Thousands of artifacts of the
★ applied, decorative, and commercial arts of the 19th and 20th centuries are on display at this stylish museum of modern art and design. Collected from around the world by Wometco heir Mitchell Wolfson Jr. the pieces occupy an elegant former storage facility. The Wolfsonian's collection is concerned with the power of propaganda in art, and its exhibitions accentuate the ideological role of design in industrialization consumerism, and politics. It regularly mounts exhibitions on European and American art and design, including world's fairs and architecture British Arts and Crafts, and glorious German graphic design. The museum is administered by Florida International University. ⊠ *1001 Washington Ave., South Beach, Miami Beach* ☎ *305/531–1001* ⊕ *www wolfsonian.fiu.edu* ⌨ *$5* ⊙ *Mon.–Tues. and Fri.–Sat. 11–6, Thurs 11–9, Sun. noon–5.*

Performing Arts

In addition to the several large performing arts venues it already enjoys the City of Miami has plans to unite its most distinguished performing arts institutions in a permanent residence, the **Performing Arts Center o Greater Miami,** which is slated for completion in 2006. Incorporating the art deco Sears Tower, the monumental complex will house a symphony concert hall, ballet–opera house, and stageless black-box studio theater in a complex near the AmericanAirlines Arena, on Biscayne Boulevard Boosters hope it will transform the long-derelict Omni-Venetia Distric into a dazzling, pedestrian-friendly destination. And dazzle it will: Argentine architect Cesar Pelli's expansive plans will give patrons spectacular views of the nearby bay, the Downtown skyline, and the inland landscape.

GETTING TICKETS To order tickets for performing arts events by telephone, call **Ticketmaste** (☎ 305/358–5885) or contact the venue directly.

PERFORMING   **AmericanAirlines Arena.** Home to the NBA Miami Heat, this sleek
ARTS VENUES bayfront arena also hosts concerts, ice shows, circuses, and other events ⊠ *601 Biscayne Blvd., Downtown, Miami* ☎ *786/777–1000* ⊕ *www aaarena.com.*

Colony Theater. Once a commercial movie theater, the Colony has become a 465-seat city-owned performing arts center featuring dance, drama music, and experimental cinema. After a recent renovation it is welcoming back several of Miami's most innovative arts groups. ⊠ *1040 Lincoln Rd., South Beach, Miami Beach* ☎ *305/674–1026.*

Gusman Center for the Performing Arts. If you have the opportunity to attend a concert, ballet, movie, or touring stage production here, do so The colorful box-office kiosk and Olympia Theater marquee out front whet your appetite for what's inside this 1,739-seat downtown land mark—a stunningly beautiful and fanciful hall with twinkling stars and rolling clouds on the ceiling and Roman-style statues guarding the wings. The Gusman's showcase event is the annual Miami International Film Festival. ⊠ *174 E. Flagler St., Downtown* ☎ *305/374–2444* ⊕ *www.gusmancenter.org.*

Gusman Concert Hall. Not to be confused with the ornate Gusman Center, this modern, spacious 600-seat facility on the University of Miami campus is the site of concerts by Frost School of Music student groups, guest artists, and the annual Festival Miami concert series. ⊠ *University of Miami, 1314 Miller Dr., Coral Gables* ☎ *305/284–6477* ⊕ *www.music.miami.edu.*

Jackie Gleason Theater of the Performing Arts. With 2,700 seats, this is the premier auditorium on Miami Beach and the site from which the rotund comedian broadcast his popular TV shows in the 1960s. Named for Gleason after his death, it offers an assortment of professional, community, and student theater, with productions including all types of musicals, comedies, and dramas. Each year the auditorium hosts five or six major touring productions and the popular Broadway Series of avant-garde fare, familiar shows, and headliners. Performing artists such as B.B. King, the *Stomp* troupe, and Liza Minnelli perform here when they're in town, and the hall is the site of many classical and pop concerts. ⊠ *1700 Washington Ave., South Beach, Miami Beach* ☎ *305/673–7300* ⊕ *www.gleasontheater.com.*

James L. Knight Center. You can catch concerts (particularly popular Latin groups) and other musical events in this 5,000-seat riverfront venue. ⊠ *400 S.E. 2nd Ave., Downtown* ☎ *305/372–4633* ⊕ *www.jlknightcenter.com.*

Miami-Dade County Auditorium. Good sight lines, acceptable acoustics, and 2,498 comfortable seats satisfy patrons despite the auditorium's rather outdated design. Opera, concerts, and touring musicals are usually on the schedule, as well as the city's annual Christmas pageant, an imaginative mix of traditional and tropical elements. ⊠ *2901 W. Flagler St., Little Havana, Miami* ☎ *305/545–3395* ⊕ *www.co.miami-dade.fl.us/parks/Parks/mdc_auditorium.htm.*

Miccosukee Resort & Gaming. Nationally televised boxing, big-name entertainers, and late-night salsa and merengue dance parties are presented in the 2,000-seat Sports and Entertainment Dome at this resort and casino on the edge of the Everglades, west of Miami. ⊠ *500 S. W. 177th Ave., West Miami-Dade, Miami* ☎ *305/925–2555* ⊕ *www.miccosukee.com.*

Dance

You get a very clear picture of Greater Miami's very global nature by looking at its dance world: Cuba, Africa, Spain, India, Brazil, the Middle East, the Caribbean, and other cultures are all represented here, either through local dance groups or visiting performers. A good example of Miami's dance and diversity can be experienced at the annual **Florida Dance Festival** (⊠ New World School of the Arts, 25 N.E. 2nd St., Downtown ☎ 305/867–7111, ⊕ www.fldance.org), held two weeks in June. International modern dance is also a component of the **Tigertail FLA/BRA (Florida/Brazil) Festival** (⊠ 842 N.W. 9th Ct., Miami ☎ 305/324–4337 ⊕ www.tigertail.org). The showcase of performing and visual artists from Brazil, Mexico, Peru, and Miami is held in winter and spring.

National and international performers also regularly visit Miami Beach's Jackie Gleason Theater of the Performing Arts and Colony Theater as well as the Gusman Center in Downtown.

Black Door. South Florida's first contemporary African-American dance company brings together dancers from Jamaican, Haitian, Cuban, Trinidadian, Native American, and African-American heritages for performances at the Colony Theater and elsewhere. ☎ *305/380–6233* ⊕ *www.blackdoordance.org.*

Freddick Bratcher and Company. Catch this longtime company's modern, jazz, and spiritual moves at the Colony Theater. ☎ *305/667–1345.*

Giovanni Luquini and Dancers. The dance theater of Brazilian-born Giovanni Luquini has been lauded by critics for its innovation and excitement. Featured in local festivals and national tours outside of South Florida, the dancers perform at the Colony Theater and the Lincoln Theatre. ☎ *305/604–9765.*

Ifé-Ilé Afro-Cuban Dance and Music Ensemble. This organization presents traditional Afro-Cuban dance and music at various venues such as the Colony Theater and **Miami Dade College Wolfson Campus** (✉ 300 N. E. 2nd Ave., Downtown ☎ 305/237–3010). ✉ *Afro-Cuban Center, 4545 N.W. 7th St., Suite 13, Miami* ☎ *305/476–0388.*

Iroko Dance and Performance Center. The center presents Haitian and Afro-Cuban dance performances and workshops in an intimate studio space. Drumming classes are also available. ✉ *2100 Washington Ave., South Beach, Miami Beach* ☎ *305/604–9141.*

La Rosa Flamenco Theater. Spreading the art form of flamenco since 1985, this group presents company dancers and international guests at performances and workshops throughout the year, many at the Colony Theater. ☎ *305/672–0552,* ⊕ *www.larosaflamencotheatre.com.*

Maximum Dance Company. Pushing the boundaries of modern ballet, this troupe, with artistic directors Yanis Pikieris and David Palmer, makes its home at the historic Gusman Center for the Performing Arts. ✉ *174 E. Flagler St., Downtown, Miami* ☎ *305/259–9775* ⊕ *www.maximumdancecompany.com.*

Fodor'sChoice ★ **Miami City Ballet.** Miami's preeminent classical troupe and America's fastest-growing dance company has risen rapidly to international prominence in its relatively short existence. Since 1986, when one-time New York City Ballet principal Edward Villella became artist director, the ballet has become a world-class ensemble. As Florida's first major, fully professional, resident ballet company, the troupe re-creates the Balanchine repertoire and introduces works of its own during its September–March season. Villella also hosts children's works-in-progress programs. The ballet's home is in the two-square-block Miami Beach Cultural Campus. ✉ *2200 Liberty Ave., South Beach, Miami Beach* ☎ *305/929–7000* ⊕ *www.miamicityballet.org.*

Miami Dade College Cultural Affairs Office. Along with Miami Light Project, with whom it sometimes collaborates, this organization is one of two important presenters of dance in Miami. Operating out of its office at the college, the group brings in national and international dance troupes for performances at the Colony Theater and the Gusman Center in Downtown. ✉ *300 N.E. 2nd Ave., Suite 1467, Downtown* ☎ *305/ 237–3010* ⊕ *www.culture.mdc.edu.*

★ **Miami Light Project (MLP).** The MLP presents cutting-edge national and international dance and music groups, promotes local stage talent via the Mad Cat Theater performance space, and has introduced International Hip Hop Exchange/Miami, a festival celebrating the global influence of hip hop. Artists such as Laurie Anderson, Robert Wilson, Philip Glass, and longtime Cuban musicians Los Fakires have been on the bill. The MLP's annual Here and Now Festival, in February, showcases local talent through newly commissioned theater, music, dance, film, and video works—shown in the Light Box, the performance space adjacent to the MLP offices. ✉ *3000 Biscayne Blvd., Downtown* ☎ *305/576– 4350* ⊕ *www.miamilightproject.com.*

Momentum Dance Company. One of the oldest contemporary dance companies in the southeastern United States, this company gives more than 50 annual performances at various locations, including concert performances and children's programs. ☎ *305/858–7002* ⊕ *www. momentumdance.com.*

Performing Arts Network. A hub for multicultural arts activities, the network gives workshops and performances in various dance traditions, including Egyptian, Israeli, flamenco, salsa, jazz, ballet, and modern. ✉ *13126 W. Dixie Hwy., North Miami* ☎ *305/899–7730* ⊕ *www. panmiami.org.*

Music

Despite what you may hear blaring from boom boxes and car radios, Greater Miami is not all salsa and hip-hop. While South Florida mourns the recent loss of the Fort Lauderdale–based Florida Philharmonic, well-respected institutions like the New World Symphony and the Florida Grand Opera continue to thrive. Churches and synagogues also sponsor music series with internationally known performers. **Coral Gables Congregational Church** (☎ 305/448–7421 ⊕ www.coralgablescongregational.org) serves up jazz, blues, classical, and even barbershop quartets during its popular Summer Concert Series at this acoustically excellent church. The University of Miami's **Gusman Concert Hall** (☎ 305/271–7150, ⊕ www. sundaymusicals.org) offers Sunday Afternoons of Music, a classical concert series for adults, and Sunday Afternoons of Music for Children, with music, song, and dance for the younger set.

CLASSICAL MUSIC **Concert Association of Florida.** Directed by Judy Drucker, this not-for-profit organization founded in 1967 is the South's largest presenter of classical arts, music, and dance. Performers such as Luciano Pavarotti, José Carreras, Cecilia Bartoli, Isaac Stern, Yo-Yo Ma, Mikhail Baryshnikov, the Alvin Ailey American Dance Theater, Van Cliburn, and the New York Philharmonic have all come to various venues in Miami thanks to this group. ✉ *1470 Biscayne Blvd., Downtown* ☎ *305/808–7446 or 877/ 433–3200* ⊕ *www.concertfla.org.*

Friends of Chamber Music. At the acoustically great Gusman Concert Hall, on the University of Miami campus in Coral Gables, the Friends present an annual series of seven chamber concerts by internationally known guest ensembles, such as the Emerson, Guarneri, Tokyo, and Talich quartets. ⬤ *Penthouse, 1428 Brickell Ave., Miami* ☎ *305/372–2975,* ⬤ *www.miamichambermusic.org.*

Fodor'sChoice ★ **New World Symphony.** One of Miami's most valued cultural institutions, the New World is known as "America's training orchestra" because its musicians are recent graduates of the best music schools nationwide. They perform a largely modern repertory here for three years before going on to more established orchestras around the country. Under the direction of conductor Michael Tilson Thomas, the New World has become a widely acclaimed, artistically dazzling group that has toured extensively since its founding in 1988. From October through May, performances take place in its home venue, the landmark art deco **Lincoln Theatre.** Once a major movie palace, the theater was renovated in 1989 to become Miami Beach's loveliest and most acoustically superb auditorium. The symphony's concerts are broadcast live via speaker (and sometimes video) over the Lincoln Road Mall. Who would have thought you could rollerblade outdoors to live classical music? It's a beautiful way to spend a Saturday evening or Sunday afternoon. ✉ *555 Lincoln Rd., South Beach, Miami Beach* ☎ *305/673–3331 or 305/673–3330* ⬤ *www.nws.org.*

OPERA You may think of merengue more often than *Manon* when South Florida comes to mind, but Miami and Miami Beach have a burgeoning opera audience. The entire city turned out in 1995 to hear Pavarotti's open-air sundown performance on Miami Beach and again when the Three Tenors visited Pro Player stadium in 1997. And for purists, the city does have a reputable opera company.

Florida Grand Opera. The 13th-largest opera company in the United States, South Florida's leading opera company has been turning out world-class productions since 1941. It now presents five or six productions each year in the Miami-Dade County Auditorium. The series brings such luminaries as Placido Domingo and Luciano Pavarotti to Miami; in fact, Pavarotti made his American debut with the company in 1965, in *Lucia di Lammermoor.* The usually traditional European fare is sung in its original language, with English subtitles projected above the stage. ✉ *1200 Coral Way, The Roads, Miami* ☎ *305/854–1643* ⬤ *www.fgo.org.*

WORLD MUSIC As the gateway to the Americas, Miami is a natural locale for world music. Each spring Miami plays host to the annual Winter Music Conference (WMC), a five-day dance music–industry gathering that brings star DJs and dance-'til-dawn concerts to nightclubs and other venues throughout the city.

Rhythm Foundation. One of South Florida's largest presenters of world-music concerts attracts a devoted audience of international-minded music lovers. The Rhythm Foundation offers a lively mix of concerts featuring artists working in ancient styles as well as new artists creating music that blends electronic and traditional sounds. Major and emerging musicians from Latin America, the Caribbean, Africa, Asia, and Europe are showcased year-round at various venues. ⬤ *Box 398567, Miami Beach 33239* ☎ *305/672–5202* ⬤ *www.rhythmfoundation.com.*

Theater

British and American classics, original works by local playwrights, and Spanish-language plays are common to Miami's theater scene. A number of small avant-garde theater companies in South Beach and Coral Gables host original works. Children's theater also abounds, with regular series at the Actors' Playhouse at the Miracle Theatre, in Coral Gables.

Actors' Playhouse at the Miracle Theatre. This professional company presents musicals, comedies, and dramas year-round in Coral Gables' beautifully restored 600-seat Miracle Theatre. More intimate productions as well as musical theater for younger audiences take place in the 300-seat Balcony Theatre. ⊠ *280 Miracle Mile, Coral Gables* ☎ *305/444–9293* ⊕ *www.actorsplayhouse.org.*

City Theatre. Catch local talent at the City Theatre company's very popular Summer Shorts Festival—short plays, that is—held at the University of Miami in June. Locals are encouraged to wear their shorts, too. ⊠ *Jerry Herman Ring Theater, 1380 Miller Dr., Coral Gables* ☎ *305/365–5400* ⊕ *www.citytheatre.com.*

Coconut Grove Playhouse. Built in 1926 as a movie theater, the playhouse is now a serious regional theater owned by the state of Florida. It started presenting live theater in 1956, with the American debut of *Waiting for Godot,* starring Bert Lahr and Tom Ewell. In the main theater and cabaret-style Encore Room of the Spanish rococo–style Grove fixture, audiences enjoy tried-and-true Broadway plays and musicals as well as experimental productions. ⊠ *3500 Main Hwy., Coconut Grove, Miami* ☎ *305/442–4000 or 305/442–2662* ⊕ *www.cgplayhouse.com.*

GableStage. Professional performers stage modern classics and contemporary theater by American and British playwrights. ⊠ *Biltmore Hotel, 1200 Anastasia Ave., Coral Gables* ☎ *305/446–1116* ⊕ *www.gablestage.org.*

Jerry Herman Ring Theater. The University of Miami has a lively theater department with a program that's often just as ambitious as its professional counterparts (Broadway legend Jerry Herman is the drama school's most successful alumnus). The university's Department of Theatre Arts venue seats 311 and is where students stage four to six productions a year. ⊠ *1380 Miller Dr., Coral Gables* ☎ *305/284–3355* ⊕ *www.miami.edu/tha/ring.*

Little Theatre. Community and professional theater productions are staged at this unpretentious South Beach locale. ⊠ *2100 Washington Ave., South Beach, Miami Beach* ☎ *305/673–7784.*

Lyric Theater. Once one of the major centers of entertainment for the African-American community, the Lyric showcased more than 150 performers including Aretha Franklin, Count Basie, Sam Cooke, B.B. King, Ella Fitzgerald, and the Ink Spots. The restored theater is now the anchor site of the Historic Overtown Folklife Village. ⊠ *819 N.W. 2nd Ave., Overtown, Miami* ☎ *305/358–1146.*

New Theatre. In a 104-seat theater the company mounts contemporary and classical plays with an emphasis on new works and imaginative staging. *Anna in the Tropics,* the Pulitzer Prize–winning play by Nilo Cruz, was commissioned, developed, and produced by the theater during its

2002–03 season. ⊠ *4120 Laguna St., Coral Gables* ☎ *305/443–5909* ⊕ *www.new-theatre.org.*

Shores Performing Arts Theater. Once a Paramount movie palace, this building now houses a lively and talented theater organization whose productions include lost classics and rarely done gems from the past four decades. ⊠ *9806 N.E. 2nd Ave., Miami Shores* ☎ *305/751–0562* ⊕ *www.shorestheatre.org.*

SPANISH-
LANGUAGE
THEATER

At any given time about 20 Spanish theater companies are staging light comedy, puppetry, vaudeville, bawdy farces, and political satire. Some of the companies participate in annual festivals. To find out what's happening, read the Spanish newspapers or the *Miami Herald*'s "Weekend" section. When you call for tickets or information, be prepared for a conversation in Spanish—few box-office personnel speak English.

Las Mascaras. Cuban sex farces and Saturday comedies are on the bill at this lively Little Havana theater. ⊠ *2833 N.W. 7th St., Little Havana, Miami* ☎ *305/642–0358.*

Teatro Avante. The city's most successful crossover theater, with works that cater to the tastes of its mostly middle-aged Cuban-American audiences, provides supertitles for non-Spanish-speakers. Each summer Teatro Avante sponsors the Hispanic Theatre Festival, during which international directors, playwrights, and actors converge on Miami, often presenting the most provocative stagings around, all in Spanish, English, and Portuguese, and attracting a multicultural audience to various Greater Miami venues. ⊠ *235 Alcazar Ave., Coral Gables* ☎ *305/445–8877* ⊕ *www.teatroavante.com.*

Teatro de Bellas Artes. Audiences fill this 255-seat theater on Calle Ocho for Spanish plays and musicals staged throughout the year. Midnight musical follies, concerts, and female-impersonator acts are also part of the lineup. ⊠ *2173 S.W. 8th St., Little Havana, Miami* ☎ *305/325–0515.*

Theater & Music for Children

Actors' Playhouse Children's Theatre. After the show at this popular children's musical theater you can speak with the cast and pose with them for pictures. ⊠ *Miracle Theatre, 280 Miracle Mile, Coral Gables* ☎ *305/444–9293* ⊕ *www.actorsplayhouse.org.*

Concerts for Kids. Produced by the New World Symphony, this program puts a new twist on the petting-zoo concept: here kids can handle the musical instruments they've heard in performance. A recent concert featured "The Bernstein Beat," with guest narrator Jamie Bernstein, daughter of conductor Leonard Bernstein. ⊠ *541 Lincoln Rd., South Beach, Miami Beach* ☎ *305/673–3330* ⊕ *www.nws.org.*

Sunday Afternoons of Music for Children. This series presents child-friendly concerts at the University of Miami's Gusman Concert Hall. Concerts have included UM's Jazz Vocal Ensemble singing *Rhythm in My Nursery Rhymes* and the Miami City Ballet School performing *Come Dance with Us.* ⊠ *University of Miami, 1314 Miller Dr., Coral Gables* ☎ *305/667–6667* ⊕ *www.sundaymusicals.org.*

SPORTS &
THE OUTDOORS

5

By Kathy Foster **SUN, SAND, AND CRYSTAL-CLEAR WATER** mixed with an almost nonexistent winter and a cosmopolitan clientele make Miami and Miami Beach ideal for year-round sports and recreation. Though a considerable draw, water sports are hardly the whole picture. Greater Miami has championship golf courses and tennis courts, miles of bike trails along placid canals and through subtropical forests, and skater-friendly concrete paths under the elevated Metrorail.

And it's hard to find a city with as many championship teams. The Miami Dolphins, the only NFL team to have ever played a perfect season, regularly make the playoffs, as do the NBA Heat. In Major League Baseball, the Florida Marlins, written off as has-beens after a string of losing seasons, beat the Yankees to win the 2003 World Series in New York the first time in more than 50 years that another team has won it all in the House That Ruth Built. At the college level, the Miami Hurricanes, the alma mater of Warren Sapp, Edgerrin James, and Jeremy Shockey, are perennial top-10 contenders, with five national football championships since 1983.

Auto Racing

★ For NASCAR Winston Cup events, head south to the **Homestead–Miami Speedway,** which hosts the Ford 400 Winston Cup Series season finale. The highlight of the speedway schedule, it's held the second Sunday in November in conjunction with the NASCAR Craftsman Truck Series season finale and other races. The speedway, built in 1995 and improved with steeper banking in 2003, is also home to the Toyota Indy 300 IRL season opener each February and other Indy-car racing. ⊠ *1 Speedway Blvd., Exit 6 of Florida's Tpke. (Rte. 821) at S.W. 137th Ave., Homestead* ☎ *305/230–7223* ⊙ *Weekdays 9–5* ⊠ *Prices vary according to event.*

Ballooning

Balloonport of Coconut Grove offers an aerial view of Miami-Dade, from the Atlantic Ocean to the Everglades. Because of South Florida's unusual wind patterns, balloon flights take place in early morning. Owner Don Kaplan gives his passengers a 5:30 AM wake-up call, setting up a meeting spot along U.S. 1 south of Miami. From there the launch site is determined by the wind. Set aside three hours for the pre-launch set-up, flight, and champagne ceremony that celebrates the landing. Balloons hold from two to six passengers. ⊠ *Box 1211, Miami, 33233* ☎ *305/ 858–2719* ⊠ *$175 per person.*

Baseball

🕐 The **Florida Marlins** did what few thought possible; they came out of nowhere to beat the New York Yankees and win the 2003 World Series. This time owner Jeffrey Luria promises not to split up the team, as former owner Wayne Huizinga did after the team won in 1997. Now the only thing lacking is a baseball-only stadium with a retractable roof to use on rainy days; they currently play home games at Pro Player Stadium, April through early October. ⊠ *Pro Player Stadium, 2267 N.W.*

199th St., 16 mi northwest of Downtown, between I–95 and Florida's Tpke., Miami ☎ *305/626–7400 or 877/MARLINS* ⊕ *www.marlins.mlb. com* ⊡ *$4–$55, parking $10.*

You can catch the **University of Miami Hurricanes** at Mark Light Field. Coached by Jim Morris, the team has advanced to the NCAA College World Series in eight of his 10 years at Miami, and they won the 2001 national championship, a title they have captured four times. ⊠ *University of Miami campus, San Amaro Dr. and Ponce De León Blvd., Coral Gables* ☎ *305/284–2263 or 800/462–2637* ⊕ *www.hurricanesports.com* ⊡ *$5–$15, parking free.*

Basketball

The **Miami Heat,** four-time defending NBA Atlantic Division champs, play at the 19,600-seat, waterfront AmericanAirlines Arena. The state-of-the-art venue has indoor fireworks, restaurants, a wide patio overlooking Biscayne Bay, and a special-effects scoreboard that resembles a metallic sea anemone with tentacles holding wide-screen TVs. During Heat games, when the 1,100 underground parking spaces are reserved for season-ticket holders, you can park across the street at Miami's Bayside Marketplace ($10), at metered spaces along Biscayne Boulevard, or in lots on side streets, where prices range from $10 two blocks from the arena to $25 across the street (a limited number of disabled spaces are available on-site for non–season ticket holders for $25). Better yet, take the Metromover to the Park West or Freedom Tower station. Home games are held November through April. ⊠ *AmericanAirlines Arena, 601 Biscayne Blvd., Downtown* ☎ *786/777–4328, 800/462–2849 ticket hot line* ⊕ *www.nba.com/heat* ⊡ *$10–$180.*

After years of trying to gain recognition in a city accustomed to championship teams, the **University of Miami Hurricanes** basketball team has finally hit the big time. Reborn in the mid-'80s after a two-decade hiatus, the team won the Big East season title for 2000 and now competes in the Atlantic Coast Conference. Coached by Perry Clark, the Hurricanes regularly make NCAA tournament appearances. The new built-for-basketball Convocation Center, on the UM campus, seats 7,000 fans. ⊠ *Convocation Center, 1245 Walsh Ave., Coral Gables* ☎ *305/284–2263 or 800/462–2637* ⊕ *www.hurricanesports.com* ⊡ *$15–$30, parking free.*

Beaches

Almost every side street in Miami Beach dead-ends at the ocean. Sandy shores also stretch along the southern side of the Rickenbacker Causeway to Key Biscayne, where you'll find two more popular beaches. Greater Miami is best known for its ocean beaches, but there's freshwater swimming here, too, in pools and lakes. Below are just a few highlights for the get-wet set.

Mid-Beach & North

You'll find plenty of parking and plenty of people at **Haulover Beach Park,** a county park. Tunnels leading from the beach to the lots are less than pristine, but folks still head here for swimming under the watchful gaze of lifeguards. The beach is nice for those who want to get to the water without a long march across hot sand, and at the north end, a rare clothing-optional beach lures people who want to tan every nook and cranny. There are facilities for barbecues, tennis, or volleyball, plus showers for rinsing off after a day in the sun and surf. Or check out the kite rentals, charter fishing excursions, and a par-3, 9-hole golf course. ⊠ *10800 Collins Ave., north of Bal Harbour, North Miami-Dade, Miami Beach* ☎ *305/947–3525* 🖃 *$4 per vehicle* ☼ *Daily sunrise–sunset.*

A natural setting beckons at **North Shore Open Space Park,** from 79th to 87th streets on Collins Avenue, in Miami Beach. North Shore has a saltwater beach and plenty of picnic tables, rest rooms, and healthy dunes. An exercise trail, concrete walkways, a playground, and lifeguards compromise or enhance the otherwise natural scene, depending on your point of view. You can park at a meter or in one of the pay lots across Collins Avenue. ⊠ *7901 Collins Ave., south of Surfside, North Beach, Miami Beach,* ☎ *305/993–2032* 🖃 *$1 per person* ☼ *Daily 7–6.*

★ ☻ Across the Intracoastal Waterway from Haulover is **Oleta River State Park,** 1,000 acres of subtropical beauty along Biscayne Bay. Swim in the calm bay waters and bicycle, canoe, and bask among egrets, manatees, bald eagles, and fiddler crabs. Highlights include picnic pavilions, five on the Intracoastal and two adjacent to a man-made swimming beach; a playground for tots; a mangrove island accessible only by boat; mountain-bike trails; and primitive but air-conditioned cabins ($40 per night, reservations required) for those who wish to tackle the trails at night. ⊠ *3400 N.E. 163rd St., North Miami Beach* ☎ *305/919–1846* 🖃 *$1 per person on foot or bike; $5 per vehicle up to 8 people, $1 each additional* ☼ *Daily 8–sunset.*

Parlez-vous français? If you do, you'll feel quite comfortable at **Surfside Beach.** This stretch of beach is filled with the many French Canadians who spend the winter here. ⊠ *Collins Ave. between 88th and 96th Sts., Surfside.*

South Beach

The stretch of beach along **Ocean Drive**—primarily the 10-block stretch from 5th to 15th streets—is one of the most talked-about beachfronts in America. The beach is wide, white, and bathed by warm aquamarine waves. Separating the sand from the traffic of Ocean Drive is palm-fringed Lummus Park, with its volleyball nets and chickee huts for shade. The beach also plays host to some of the funkiest lifeguard stands you'll ever see, pop stars shooting music videos, and visitors from all over the world. The beach at 12th Street is popular with gays. Because much of South Beach has an adult flavor—women are often casually topless—many families prefer the beach's quieter southern reaches, especially 3rd Street Beach. Unless you're parking south of 3rd Street, metered spaces near the waterfront are rarely empty. Instead, opt for a public garage and walk; you'll have lots of fun people-watching, too. ⊠ *Ocean Dr. between 1st and 22nd Sts., South Beach, Miami Beach* ☎ *305/673–7714*

You can't swim at **South Pointe Park,** but you can walk or bicycle out on 50-yard Sunshine Pier, which adjoins the 1-mi-long jetty at the mouth of Government Cut. It's a great place to fish or watch huge cruise ships pass. No bait or tackle is available in the park. Facilities include two observation towers, rest rooms, and volleyball courts. ⊠ *1 Washington Ave., South Beach, Miami Beach.*

Key Biscayne & Virginia Key

Fodor's Choice
★

Beyond Key Biscayne's commercial district, at the southern tip of the island, is **Bill Baggs Cape Florida State Park,** a natural oasis with great beaches, sea grass–studded dunes, blue-green waters, and plenty of native plants and trees. The 410-acre park has a restored lighthouse, 18 picnic shelters, and two cafés, which serve beer and wine and meals that range from hot dogs to lobster. A stroll or bike ride along paths and boardwalks provides wonderful views of the bay and Miami's skyline. Also on site are bicycle, skate, kayak, and people-powered water-bike rentals, plus a playground and fishing platforms. ⊠ *1200 S. Crandon Blvd., Key Biscayne* ☎ *305/361–5811 or 305/361–8779* ⛽ *$1 per person on foot, bike, motorbike, or bus; $5 per vehicle up to 8 people* ☼ *Daily 8–sunset, lighthouse tours Thurs.–Mon. 9:30 and 12:30.*

★ ☾

The 3½-mi-long beach at **Crandon Park** has been rated among the top 10 in North America by the University of Maryland's esteemed Dr. Beach. The sand is soft, there's a great view of the Atlantic, and parking is inexpensive and plentiful. On busy days be prepared for a long hike from your car to the beach. There are bathrooms, outdoor showers, plenty of picnic tables and concession stands, and a restored carousel (open weekends 10–5, until 6 in summer, admission $1). Marine-theme play sculptures, a dolphin-shape spray fountain, and an old-fashioned outdoor roller rink draw kids to the beachfront playground. Skates rent for $5 an hour. Children enjoy the interactive exhibits at the $4 million **Marjory Stoneman Douglas Biscayne Nature Center** (☎ 305/361–6767 ☼ daily 9–4) at the park's north end. ⊠ *4000 Crandon Blvd., Key Biscayne* ☎ *305/361–5421* ⛽ *$4 per vehicle* ☼ *Daily 8–sunset.*

Just after crossing the causeway onto Virginia Key you'll see a long strip of bayfront popular with windsurfers and sailboaters, called **Hobie Beach** after the Hobie Cats that set sail from the shore. It's also the only Miami-area beach that allows dogs. Nearby rest rooms and a great view of the curving shoreline make this an ideal place to park and have your own tailgate party. ⊠ *South side of Rickenbacker Causeway, Virginia Key, Miami* ☎ *305/361–1281* ⛽ *Expressway toll $1 per vehicle* ☼ *Daily sunrise–sunset.*

Coral Gables

☾

Among the estates along historic Old Cutler Road, in an area few visitors realize is part of Coral Gables, is **Matheson Hammock Park.** Named for the type of characteristically Floridian ecosystem found here (not for a preponderance of hammocks swinging from trees), Miami-Dade County's oldest park is one of its most appealing. The bathing beach is separated from peaceful Biscayne Bay by a narrow walking path, and its slowly sloping shore is ideal for children. Even the parking lot is on the bay. The park has plenty of lush walking and bike trails, picnic tables under towering trees, changing facilities, showers and bathrooms, plus a seafood restaurant. ⊠ *9610 Old Cutler Rd., Coral Gables* ☎ *305/ 665–5475* 💬 *$4 per car* ◑ *Daily 6–sunset.*

South Miami-Dade

Larry and Penny Thompson Park, a Miami secret, is a laid-back and beautiful 243-acre county park with a 35-acre freshwater lake, white-sand beach, water slide, and concession stand. ⊠ *12451 S.W. 184th St., 1 mi west of Exit 13S of Florida's Tpke. (Rte. 821), South Miami-Dade, Miami* ☎ *305/232–1049* 💬 *$3 lake, $4 with water slide* ◑ *Memorial Day–Labor Day, daily 10–6.*

Bicycling

Perfect weather and flat terrain make Miami-Dade County a popular place for cyclists. Add a free color-coded map that points out streets best suited for bicycles, rated from best to worst, and it's even better. Also available are printouts listing parks with multiuse paths and information about local bike clubs. The map is available from bike shops and also from the **Miami-Dade County Bicycle Coordinator** (⊠ Metropolitan Planning Organization, 111 N.W. 1st St., Suite 910, Miami 33128 ☎ 305/375–1647), whose purpose is to share with you the glories of bicycling in South Florida. There's some especially good cycling to be had in South Miami-Dade.

Hook up with local riders and get details on dozens of monthly group rides from the **Everglades Bicycle Club** (☎ 305/598–3998 ⊕ www. everglades-bicycleclub.org). On Key Biscayne, **Mangrove Cycles** (⊠ 260 Crandon Blvd., Key Biscayne ☎ 305/361–5555) rents bikes for $9 for two hours or $12 per day. On Miami Beach the proximity of the **Miami Beach Bicycle Center** (⊠ 601 5th St., South Beach, Miami Beach ☎ 305/ 674–0150) to Ocean Drive and the ocean itself makes it worth the $20 per day (or $8 per hour).

★ Riders who want to take it easy can visit **Bill Baggs Cape Florida State Park,** where you can pedal into the park and follow the paved, speed-controlled road to the beach, picnic areas, or lighthouse. If you arrive by car, park near the lighthouse and catch the paved path that meanders for 2 mi along Biscayne Bay and through the tropical hardwoods. ⊠ *1200 S. Crandon Blvd., Key Biscayne* ☎ *305/361–5811 or 305/ 361–8779* 💬 *$1 per person on bike, $5 per vehicle up to 8 people* ◑ *Daily 8–sunset.*

The Old Cutler Trail, a popular leisurely bike ride, leads 2 mi south from Cocoplum Circle (at the end of Sunset Drive in Coral Gables) to Matheson Hammock Park and Fairchild Tropical Garden. You can turn into **Matheson Hammock Park** and take a bike path about 1 mi through the mangroves to Biscayne Bay. You'll feel as if you've discovered South Florida before the Spanish conquistadors arrived. ⊠ *9610 Old Cutler Rd., Coral Gables* ☎ *305/665–5475* 💬 *$4 per car, free on bike* ◑ *Daily 6–sunset.*

There aren't any mountains within 500 mi of Miami, but **Oleta River State Park** does have challenging dirt trails with hills and views of Biscayne Bay for experienced all-terrain bikers. Several miles of new trails for technical riding and speed have been added, and an elevated board-walk was built over an area that floods in the rainy season. ☒ *3400 N.E. 163rd St., North Miami Beach* ☎ *305/919–1846* ▭ *$1 per person on bike; $5 per vehicle up to 8 people, $1 each additional* ☉ *Daily 8–sunset.*

Boating & Sailing

Boating, whether on sailboats, powerboats, or luxury yachts, Wave Runners or windsurfers, is a passion in greater Miami. The Intracoastal Waterway, wide and sheltered Biscayne Bay, and the Atlantic Ocean provide ample opportunities for fun aboard all types of watercraft.

Windsurfing is particularly popular in Miami Beach. The best spots are at 1st Street (north of the Government Cut jetty) and at 21st Street; you can also windsurf around 3rd, 10th, and 14th streets. The safest and most popular windsurfing area in city waters is south of town at Hobie Beach (on the south side of the Rickenbacker Causeway, on Virginia Key).

Marinas

Named for an island where early settlers had picnics, **Dinner Key Marina** (☒ 3400 Pan American Dr., Coconut Grove,, Miami ☎ 305/579–6980) is Greater Miami's largest, with nearly 600 moorings slips at nine piers. There's space for transients and a boat ramp. **Haulover Marine Center** (☒ 15000 Collins Ave., north of Bal Harbour, North Miami-Dade, Miami Beach ☎ 305/945–3934), which has a bait-and-tackle shop and a 24-hour marine gas station, is low on glamour but high on service.

Near the Art Deco District, **Miami Beach Marina** (☒ MacArthur Causeway, 300 Alton Rd., South Beach, Miami Beach ☎ 305/673–6000) has about every marine facility imaginable—restaurants, charters, boat and vehicle rentals, a complete marine-hardware store, a dive shop, excursion vendors, a large grocery store, a fuel dock, concierge services, and 400 slips accommodating vessels of up to 250 ft. There's also a U.S. Customs clearing station and a charter service, Florida Yacht Charters.

One of the busiest marinas in Coconut Grove is **Monty's Marina** (☒ 2640 S. Bayshore Dr., Coconut Grove, Miami ☎305/854–7997), handy if you've brought your own vessel but otherwise of little interest to visitors.

Rentals & Charters

Castle Harbor (☒ Matheson Hammock Park, 9610 Old Cutler Rd., Coral Gables ☎ 305/665–4994), in operation since 1949, rents sailboats for those with U.S. Sailing certification and offers classes for those without. When you're ready to rent, take your pick between a 22-foot Capri ($190 per day) or a 23-foot Ensign ($25 an hour, $100 for half day).

You can rent 20- to 34-foot powerboats through **Club Nautico** (☒ 2560 Bayshore Dr., Coconut Grove, Miami ☎ 305/858–6258 ▭ 5420 Crandon Blvd., Key Biscayne ☎ 305/361–9217), a national powerboat rental company. Half- to full-day rentals range from $200 to $699. You may want to consider buying a club membership; it'll cost a bundle at first, but you'll save about 50% on all your future rentals.

Whether you're looking to be on the water for a few hours or a few days, **Cruzan Yacht Charters** (✉ 3375 Pan American Dr., Coconut Grove, Miami ☎ 305/858–2822 or 800/628–0785) is a good choice for renting manned or unmanned sailboats and motor yachts. If you plan to captain the boat yourself, expect a two- to three-hour checkout cruise and at least a $500 daily rate (three-day minimum).

The family-owned **Florida Yacht Charters** (✉ MacArthur Causeway, 300 Alton Rd., South Beach, Miami Beach ☎ 305/532–8600 or 800/537–0050), at the full-service Miami Beach Marina, will give you the requisite checkout cruise and paperwork. Then you can take off for the Keys or the Bahamas on a catamaran, sailboat, or motor yacht. Charts, lessons, and captains are available if needed.

Vendors on Miami Beach and Virginia Key rent gas-powered Wave Runners, also known as Jet Skis, by the hour (a minimum age of 18 or 19 often applies). Rates are $90 an hour. **Hector's Watersports** (☎ 305/318–9268), which operates by reservation only, can arrange Wave Runner excursions off Fisher Island, Key Biscayne, or Star Island. You can rent Wave Runners from **Key Biscayne Boat Rentals** (✉ 3301 Rickenbacker Causeway, Virginia Key, Miami ☎ 305/361–7368).

Playtime Watersports (✉ Collins Ave., Mid-Beach, Miami Beach ☎ 786/234–0184 ✉ Eden Roc, 4525 Collins Ave. ✉ Wyndham, 4833 Collins Ave. ✉ Alexander Hotel, 5225 Collins Ave.) sells and rents high-end water-sports equipment, including Wave Runners and wind-driven devices, from concessions at several Collins Avenue hotels.

In addition to renting equipment, the friendly folks at **Sailboards Miami** (✉ 1 Rickenbacker Causeway, ⅓ mi past toll plaza, Key Biscayne ☎ 305/361–7245) say they teach more windsurfers each year than anyone in the United States and promise to teach you to windsurf within two hours—for $69. Rentals average $25–$30 for one hour and $100 for four hours.

One-stop equipment shopping can be had at **Water Play** (✉ 2220 Coral Way, at S.W. 22nd Ave., Coral Gables ☎ 305/860–0888). The store sells gear for windsurfing, sailing, and waterskiing—and can direct you to vendors that organize excursions.

Canoeing & Kayaking

Looking at Miami's skyscrapers, it's hard to remember the outback is so close. Canoe-friendly canals crisscross the city, leading from urban areas to parks or to Biscayne Bay.

Paddling Spots

At **Bill Baggs Cape Florida State Park**, you can rent and launch a kayak on the Atlantic side. As you paddle along this 1½-mi stretch of ocean, you'll see the historic lighthouse, people playing in the surf or beach-combing on the bathing beach, and, after that, dunes covered with sea oats framed by pine trees and palms. Rentals are $10 an hour for a single, $15 an hour for a double kayak. *✉ 1200 S. Crandon Blvd., Key Biscayne ☎ 305/361–5811 or 305/361–8779 ☞ $1 per person on foot, bike, motorbike, or bus; $5 per vehicle up to 8 people.*

To get away from it all, take a canoe or kayak to **Black Point Park.** The put-in spot is past the picnic pavilion. Within 100 yards you'll come to a lagoon. Immediately to the east is Biscayne Bay; to the north is a waterway filled with mangrove hammocks to explore. An open-air restaurant with live music has varying hours. ⊠ *24775 S.W. 87th Ave., Cutler Ridge Miami* ☎ *305/258–4092* ⊠ *Free.*

Matheson Hammock Park has a launch site but no rentals. ⊠ *9610 Old Cutler Rd., Coral Gables* ☎ *305/665–5475* ⊠ *$4 per car.*

Canoes and kayaks are perfect for **Oleta River State Park,** an unexpected natural water source in the middle of a bustling commercial district, near Intercoastal Mall. Rentals come with a map showing the various mangrove channels splitting off the Intracoastal Waterway. Allow about an hour to paddle the canals, where you'll spot wading herons, crabs scuttling among the hairy mangrove roots, and maybe a lumbering manatee. Kayaks cost $8 per hour, $20 for a half day, $25 a day, and $35 overnight. You can rent paddleboats, too. ⊠ *3400 N.E. 163rd St., North Miami Beach* ☎ *305/919–1846 park, 305/947–0302 boat rentals* ⊠ *$1 on foot or bike; $4 per vehicle with up to 8 people, $1 each additional* ☉ *Daily 8–sunset.*

A favorite **South Miami put-in spot** for a bring-your-own canoe or kayak is just beyond the locks on the east side of Red Road, south of South Miami and near Pinecrest Gardens, site of the original Parrot Jungle & Gardens. From here it's an easy paddle to Biscayne Bay. ⊠ *11000 S.W. 57th Ave., at S.W. 112th St., Pinecrest.*

Rentals

On Key Biscayne—Windsurfer Beach, to be exact—**Sailboards Miami** (⊠ 1 Rickenbacker Causeway, ⅓ mi past toll plaza, Key Biscayne ☎ 305/361–7245) rents kayaks for $13 per hour for a single, $18 for a double. Right on the bay, **Shake-A-Leg** (⊠ 2600 S. Bayshore Dr., Coconut Grove, Miami ☎ 305/858–5550), a nonprofit organization for the physically and mentally disabled and for youth at risk, also rents kayaks to the general public. Singles cost $10 for an hour, $30 for four hours; doubles are $15 per hour, $45 for four hours.

Dog Racing

Flagler Greyhound Track has dog races during its June–November season and a poker room that's open when the track is running. Closed-circuit TV brings harness-racing action here as well. The track is five minutes east of Miami International Airport, off Dolphin Expressway (Route 836) and Douglas Road (N.W. 37th Avenue). ⊠ *401 N.W. 38th Ct., Little Havana, Miami* ☎ *305/649–3000* ⊠ *Free for grandstand and clubhouse, parking free–$3* ☉ *Racing daily 8:05 PM plus Tues., Thurs., and Sat. 1:05 PM.*

Fishing

In Greater Miami, before there was fashion, there was fishing. Deep-sea fishing is still a major draw, and anglers drop a line for sailfish, kingfish, dolphin, snapper, mahimahi, grouper, and tuna. Small charter boats cost $500 for a half day or $750–$800 for a full day and provide everything but food and drinks. If you're on a budget, you might be better off paying around $30 for passage on a larger fishing boat—rarely are they filled to capacity. Most charters have a 50–50 plan, which allows you to take (or sell) half your catch while they do the same. Just don't let anyone sell you an individual fishing license; a blanket license for the boat should cover all passengers. Charters operate out of Bayside Marketplace, Crandon Park Marina, Haulover Beach Park, Key Biscayne, and Miami Beach Marina.

Old Miami's original Pier 5 has been resurrected at Bayside Marketplace. Among a handful of charters docking behind Snapper's Restaurant, **Blue Waters Sportfishing Charters** (✉ Bayside Marketplace, 401 Biscayne Blvd., Downtown ☎ 305/373–5016) charges $800 for a full day, $500 for a half day (5 hours) on a six-passenger boat. Capt. Jimbo Thomas takes people fishing on the *Thomas Flyer* (✉ Bayside Marketplace, 401 Biscayne Blvd., Downtown ☎ 305/374–4133), a six-passenger boat that runs $750 for a full day, $500 for a half day.

Crandon Park Marina (✉ 4000 Crandon Blvd., Key Biscayne ☎ 305/361–1281) has earned an international reputation for its knowledgeable charter-boat captains and good catches. Heading out to the edge of the Gulf Stream (about 3 to 4 mi), you're sure to wind up with something on your line (sailfish are catch-and-release). A full day on a six-passenger boat costs $750, a half day (5 hours) $500.

The marina at Haulover Beach Park lays claim to the largest charter/drift-fishing fleet in South Florida. Among the ocean-fishing charters is the **Kelley Fleet** (✉ Haulover Beach Park, 10800 Collins Ave., north of Bal Harbour, North Miami-Dade, Miami Beach ☎ 305/945–3801), whose 65- or 85-ft party boat costs $30 per person. Going out on *Therapy IV* (✉ Haulover Beach Park, 10800 Collins Ave., north of Bal Harbour, North Miami-Dade, Miami Beach ☎ 305/945–1578), a six-passenger boat, is $100 per person.

For a boat to fish in the bay around Key Biscayne, try **Key Biscayne Boat Rentals** (✉ 3301 Rickenbacker Causeway, Virginia Key, Miami ☎ 305/361–7368), which carries six-passenger, 21-foot open Fisherman motorboats for $275–$315 for the full day, $195–$225 for a half day, and $160 for two hours.

Charters from Miami Beach Marina include the two-boat **Reward Fleet** (✉ MacArthur Causeway, 300 Alton Rd., South Beach, Miami Beach ☎ 305/372–9470). Rates run $30 per person including bait, rod, reel, and tackle, $15 for kids.

Fitness Classes & Gyms

Miami is like L.A. in the sense that gym culture is, well, culture, so you won't have a hard time finding a place to work out, especially in South Beach. **Club Body Tech** (✉ 1253 Washington Ave., between 12th and 13th Sts., South Beach, Miami Beach ☎ 305/674–8222) is for the already fit and buff. But what did you expect? You're in Miami. Day passes are $21, and the gym's equipment is worth it. **Crunch Fitness** (✉ 1259 Washington Ave., South Beach, Miami Beach ☎ 305/674–8222, 305/674–0247 for class schedule), the leader in forward-thinking classes and gym fashion, will sell you a day pass for about $21 or a three-day one for $50, which is good for most classes, equipment, and weights.

Football

Consistently ranked as one of the top teams in the NFL, the **Miami Dolphins,** under coach Dave Wannstedt, are continuing the winning tradition. Year in and year out, the Dolphins have one of the largest average attendance figures in the league. Fans may be secretly hoping to see a repeat of 1972's perfect season, when the team, led by legendary coach Don Shula, compiled a 17–0 record (a record that still stands). September through January, on home game days the Metro Miami-Dade Transit Agency runs buses to the stadium. ✉ *Pro Player Stadium, 2267 N. W. 199th St., 16 mi northwest of Downtown, between I–95 and Florida's Tpke., Miami* ☎ *305/620–2578* ⊕ *www.miamidolphins.com* 🖃 *$22–$175, parking $20.*

Now competing in the powerful Atlantic Coast Conference, the **University of Miami Hurricanes** are regular top-10 contenders and have won five national football championships since 1983. During the September–November season the home-team advantage is measured in decibels, as about 45,000 fans literally rock venerable Orange Bowl Stadium when the team is on a roll. ✉ *Orange Bowl Stadium, 1145 N.W. 11th St., Downtown* ☎ *305/284–2263 or 800/462–2637* ⊕ *www.hurricanesports.com* 🖃 *$20–$50, parking $20–$30.*

Golf

Greater Miami has more than 30 private and public courses. Costs at most courses are higher on weekends and in season, but you can save by playing on weekdays and after 1 or 3 PM, depending on the course— call ahead to find out when afternoon–twilight rates go into effect. To get a **"Golfer's Guide for South Florida,"** which includes information on most courses in Miami and surrounding areas, call 800/864–6101. The cost is $3.The 18-hole, par-71 championship **Biltmore Golf Course** (✉ 1210 Anastasia Ave., Coral Gables ☎ 305/460–5364), known for its scenic layout, has been restored to its original Donald Ross design, circa 1925. Greens fees range from $32 to $65 in season, and an optional cart is $22. The gorgeous hotel makes a great backdrop.

The **California Golf Club** (✉ 20898 San Simeon Way, North Miami Beach ☎ 305/651–3590) has an 18-hole, par-72 course, with a tight front nine and three of the area's toughest finishing holes. A round of 18 holes will set you back between $30 and $50, cart (required) included.

Overlooking the bay, the **Crandon Golf Course** (✉ 6700 Crandon Blvd., Key Biscayne ☎ 305/361–9129,) is a top-rated 18-hole, par-72 public course in a beautiful tropical setting. Expect to pay around $137 for a round in winter, $58 in summer, cart included. After 3, the winter rate drops to $37. The **Royal Caribbean Classic** (⊠ 4000 Crandon Blvd., Key Biscayne ☎ 305/374–6180) kicks off the Senior PGA tour here each year in early February.

Don Shula's Hotel & Golf Club (⊠ 7601 Miami Lakes Dr., 154th St. Exit off Rte. 826, Miami Lakes ☎ 305/820–8106), in northern Miami, has one of the longest championship courses in the area (7,055 yards, par-72), a lighted par-3 course, and a golf school. Weekdays you can play the championship course for $100, $140 on weekends; golf carts are included. The lighted par-3 course is $12 weekdays, $15 weekends, and $15 for an optional cart. The club hosts more than 75 tournaments a year.

Among its six courses and many annual tournaments, the **Doral Golf Resort and Spa** (⊠ 4400 N.W. 87th Ave., 36th St. Exit off Rte. 826, Doral, Miami ☎ 305/592–2000 or 800/713–6725), just west of Miami proper, is best known for the par-72 Blue Monster course and the PGA's annual Ford Championship. (The week of festivities planned around this tournament, which offers $1 million in prize money, brings hordes of pro-golf aficionados in late February and early March.) Fees range from $195 to $275. Carts are not required, but there's no discount for walking.

Fairmont Turnberry Isle Resort & Club (⊠ 19999 W. Country Club Dr., Aventura ☎ 305/933–6929) has 36 holes designed by Robert Trent Jones. The South Course's 18th hole is a killer. Greens fees, including a mandatory cart, range from $121 to $160, but since it's private you won't be able to play unless you're a hotel guest. Proper golf shoes are required.

For a casual family outing or for beginners, the 9-hole, par-3 **Haulover Golf Course** (⊠ Haulover Beach Park, 10800 Collins Ave. North Miami-Dade, Miami Beach ☎ 305/940–6719) is right on the Intracoastal Waterway at the north end of Miami Beach. The longest hole on this walking course is 120 yards; greens fees are only $6, less on weekdays for senior citizens.

Normandy Shores Golf Course (⊠ 2401 Biarritz Dr., Normandy Isle, Miami Beach ☎ 305/868–6502), on its own little bay-side island between South Beach and Surfside, is good for senior citizens. The par-71 course has some modest slopes and average distances, and the $55 per-person fee includes a cart.

Horse Racing

The glass-enclosed, air-conditioned **Calder Race Course** has an unusually extended season, from late May to early January. The high point of the season, the Tropical Park Derby for three-year-olds, comes in the final week, usually on January 1. The track is on the Miami-Dade–Broward County line, ¾ mi from Pro Player Stadium. ⊠ *21001 N.W. 27th Ave., Hallandale Beach Blvd. Exit off I–95, Miami ☎ 305/625–1311 ☜ $2, clubhouse $4, parking $1–$5 ⊙ Gates open at 11, racing 12:25–5.*

Gulfstream Park, north of the Miami-Dade County line, usually has racing January through March. The track's premiere race is the Florida Derby. ⊠ *21301 Biscayne Blvd. (U.S. 1), between Ives Dairy Rd. and Hallan-*

dale Beach Blvd., Hallandale ☎ *954/454–7000* 🖃 *$3, clubhouse $5, parking free* ⊙ *Wed.–Mon. post time 1* PM.

In-Line Skating

Miami Beach's ocean vistas, wide sidewalks, and flat terrain make it a perfect locale for in-line skating. And don't the locals know it. Very popular is the **Lincoln Road Mall** from Washington Avenue to Alton Road; many of the restaurants along this pedestrian mall have outdoor seating where you can eat without shedding your skates. For a great view of the Art Deco District and action on South Beach, skate along the sidewalk on the east side of **Ocean Drive** from 5th to 14th streets. In South Miami an often-traversed concrete path winds **under the elevated Metrorail** from Vizcaya Station (across U.S. 1 from the Miami Museum of Science) to Red Road at U.S. 1 (across from the Shops at Sunset Place). You don't have to bring your own; a number of in-line skate shops offer rentals that include protective gear.

Fritz's Skate and Bike Shop (🖃 730 Lincoln Rd., South Beach, Miami Beach ☎ 305/532–1954) charges $8 an hour or $24 for 24 hours. **Skate 2000** (🖃 9525 S. Dixie Hwy., Pinecrest ☎ 305/665–6770) is a bit of a drive from the popular tourist areas but has rates as low as $10 a day.

Jai Alai

Don't know what it is? Visit the **Miami Jai Alai Fronton** to learn about this game invented in the Basque region of northern Spain. Jai alai is perhaps the world's fastest game: jai alai balls, called *pelotas,* have been clocked at speeds exceeding 170 mph. The game is played in a 176-foot-long court, and players literally climb the walls to catch the ball in a *cesta* (a woven basket), which has an attached glove. You can place your wager on the team you think will win or on the order in which you think the teams will finish. The Miami fronton, built in 1926, is America's oldest. Sessions comprise 13 games (14 on Fridays and Saturdays)—some singles, some doubles. 🖃 *3500 N.W. 37th Ave., 1 mi east of the airport, north of Downtown* ☎ *305/633–6400* 🖃 *$1, reserved seats $2, Courtview Club $5* ⊙ *Mon. and Wed.–Sat. noon–5, plus Mon. and Fri.–Sat. 7–midnight, Sun. 1–6.*

Jogging

There are numerous places to run in Miami, but the routes recommended below are considered among the safest and most scenic. **Foot Works** (🖃 5724 Sunset Dr., South Miami ☎ 305/667–9322), a running-shoe store that sponsors races and organizes marathon training, is a great source of information. The **Miami Runners Club** (🖃 8720 N. Kendall Dr., Suite 206, Miami ☎ 305/227–1500) has information on running-related matters, such as routes and races.

The beachside **Bal Harbour** jogging path begins at the southern boundary of town, where it connects with the Surfside path. Mostly made of hard-packed sand and gravel at this point, the path turns into paved brick behind the Sheraton Bal Harbour. This jogging trail runs between the hotels and the ocean for about 2 mi, ending at the Haulover Cut passageway between the Intracoastal Waterway and the Atlantic Ocean, a popular fishing spot.

In **Coconut Grove,** follow the pedestrian-bicycle path on South Bayshore Drive, cutting over the causeway to Key Biscayne for a longer run and a chance to jog uphill on the two wide bridges linking the key to the mainland. **Coral Gables** has a jogging path around the Riviera Country Club golf course, south of the Biltmore Country Club. From the south shore of the Miami River in **downtown Miami** you can run south along the sidewalks of Brickell Avenue, turn left on 8th Street and right on Brickell Bay Drive, and continue along the bay to Southeast 15th Street.

In **South Beach** good running options are Bay Road, parallel to Alton Road, and the Ocean Drive sidewalk across the street from the art deco hotels and outdoor cafés. And, of course, you can run right along the Atlantic on the beach. One good route is to follow the ramp down to the beach at 21st Street, then jog south along the hard-packed sand all the way to South Pointe Park, at the southernmost tip of Miami Beach. There you can get a great view of Government Cut, the passageway that cargo and cruise ships take as they leave the Port of Miami and head out toward the Bahamas or the Caribbean. You also get a close-up view of the ultra-chic, multimillion-dollar condos on Fisher Island, on the far side of Government Cut.

Surfside, north of Miami Beach, has brilliant ocean vistas. You can park your car on any side street near 87th Street and Collins Avenue and walk onto the sand. Climb the rise to the path that looks like a levee. This elevated hard-packed, sand-and-gravel trail, which runs between the condos and hotels and the beach from 87th to 96th streets, gives you a clear view of the ocean. Another plus is that it's off-limits to skaters and bikers.

Pool

 ★ ☺   The 825,000-gallon **Venetian Pool,** fed by artesian wells, is so special that it's on the National Register of Historic Places. The picturesque pool design and lush landscaping place it head and shoulders above typical public pools, and a snack bar, lockers, showers, and free parking make an afternoon here pleasant and convenient. Children must be at least 38″ tall or three years old. ⊠ *2701 De Soto Blvd., Coral Gables,* ☎ *305/ 460–5356* ⊠ *$6–$9, free parking across De Soto Blvd.* ☺ *June–Aug., weekdays 11–7:30, weekends 10–4:30; Sept.–Oct. and Apr.–May, Tues.–Fri. 11–5:30, weekends 10–4:30; Nov.–Mar., Tues.–Sun. 10–4:30.*

Scuba Diving & Snorkeling

Diving and snorkeling on the off-shore coral wrecks and reefs on a calm day can be comparable to the Caribbean. Chances are excellent you'll come face to face with a flood of tropical fish. One option is to find Fowey, Triumph, Long, and Emerald reefs in 10- to 15-foot dives that are perfect for snorkelers and beginning divers. On the edge of the continental shelf a little more than 3 mi out, these reefs are just ¼ mi away from depths greater than 100 feet. Another option is to paddle around the tangled prop roots of the mangrove trees that line the coast, peering at the fish, crabs, and other creatures hiding there.

It's a bit of a drive, but the best diving and definitely the best snorkeling to be had in Miami-Dade is on the incredible living coral reefs in **Biscayne National Park** (⊠ 9710 S.W. 328th St., Exit 6 of Florida's Tpke., Homestead ☎ 305/230–1100 ⊕ www.nps.gov/bisc/), in the rural southeast corner of the county. With 95 percent of its 173,000 acres underwater, this is the national park system's largest marine park. The huge park includes the northernmost islands of the Florida Keys and the beginning of the world's third-longest coral reef. Guided snorkeling and scuba trips, offered from the visitor center, cost $36 for a three-hour snorkel trip (daily 1:30–4:30), including equipment, and $58 for a 4½-hour, two-tank dive trip (weekends 8:30–1), weather permitting. Scuba equipment is available for rent.

Perhaps the area's most unusual diving options are its **artificial reefs** (⊠ 1920 Meridian Ave., South Beach, Miami Beach ☎ 305/672–1270). Since 1981, Miami-Dade County's Department of Environmental Resources Management (DERM) has sunk tons of limestone boulders and a water tower, army tanks, a 727 jet, and almost 200 boats of all descriptions to create a "wreckreational" habitat where divers can swim with yellow tang, barracudas, nurse sharks, snapper, eels, and grouper. Most dive shops sell a book listing the locations of these wrecks. Information on wreck diving can be obtained from the Miami Beach Chamber of Commerce.

Divers Paradise of Key Biscayne (⊠ 4000 Crandon Blvd., Key Biscayne ☎ 305/361–3483) has a complete dive shop and diving-charter service next to the Crandon Park Marina, including equipment rental and scuba instruction with PADI affiliation. The PADI-affiliated **Diving Locker** (⊠ 223 Sunny Isles Blvd., Sunny Isles ☎ 305/947–6025) sells, services, and repairs scuba equipment. It offers four-day and three-week international certification courses as well as more advanced certifications. The individualized four-day program for beginners is $400. Wreck and reef sites are reached aboard fast and comfortable six-passenger dive boats. **South Beach Dive and Surf Center** (⊠ 850 Washington Ave., South Beach, Miami Beach ☎ 305/531–6110), an all-purpose dive shop with PADI affiliation, runs night and wreck dives right in the center of it all. Its boats depart from marinas in Miami Beach, Haulover, and Key Largo, in the Florida Keys.

Tennis

Miami-Dade has more than a dozen tennis centers and nearly 500 public courts open to visitors; nonresidents are charged an hourly fee. Some courts take reservations on weekdays.

Biltmore Tennis Center has 10 hard courts and a view of the beautiful Biltmore Hotel. ⊠ *1150 Anastasia Ave., Coral Gables* ☎ *305/460–5360* 🖾 *Day rate $5.25, night rate $7, per person per hr* ⊙ *Weekdays 7 AM–10 PM, weekends 7–8.*

Very popular with locals, **Flamingo Tennis Center** has 19 clay courts smack dab in the middle of Miami Beach. You can't get much closer to the action. ✉ *1000 12th St., South Beach, Miami Beach* ☎ *305/673–7761* ☞ *Day rate $8, night rate $9.50, per person per hr* ⊙ *Weekdays 8* AM*–9* PM*, weekends 8–8.*

Fodor'sChoice The 30-acre **Tennis Center at Crandon Park** is one of America's best. In-
★ cluded are two grass, eight clay, and 17 hard courts. Reservations are required for night play, when the clay and grass courts are closed. Otherwise courts are open to the public except during the 12 days of the NASDAQ-100 Open each spring. This pro tournament is the world's fifth largest in attendance, offers more than $6 million in prize money, and draws such players as Andre Agassi, Gustavo Kuerten, and Venus and Sabrina Williams to compete in the 14,000-seat stadium. ✉ *7300 Crandon Blvd., Key Biscayne* ☎ *305/365–2300, 305/442–3367 NAS-DAQ-100 Open* ☞ *Laykold courts: day rate $3, night rate $5, per person per hr; clay courts: $6 per person per hr; grass courts: $8 per person per hr. NASDAQ-100 Open: $10–$45* ⊙ *Daily 8* AM*–9* PM.

Yoga

Miami YogaShala (✉ 747 4th St., at Meridian Ave., South Beach, Miami Beach ☎ 305/538–4059 ⊕ www.miamiyoga.com ✉ 8701 Collins Ave., North Beach, Miami Beach ☎ 305/866–1650) has basic and ashtanga classes daily (guided ashtanga is recommended for all levels), many taught by yogi Paul Toliuszis ($16). **Synergy Center for Yoga and the Healing Arts** (✉ 435 Española Way, at Drexel Ave., South Beach, Miami Beach ☎ 305/538–7073 ☞ 305/538–1244 ⊕ www.synergyyoga.org) has a range of courses daily ($14) plus specialty workshops and body-work treatments. The center also offers yoga on the beach for only $5 (bring a towel).

SHOPPING

6

Updated by
Karen
Schlesinger

MIAMI TEEMS WITH SOPHISTICATED SHOPPING malls and the bustling avenues of commercial neighborhoods, which glitter with the storefronts of name-brand retailers from Armani to Zegna. Bal Harbour Shops, the ultimate shopping mall, is anchored by Neiman Marcus and Saks Fifth Avenue and overflows with high-end merchandise from Escada, Chanel, Prada, Cartier, Fendi, Gucci, and dozens of other exclusive shops. Collins Avenue in South Beach satisfies all kinds of fashion appetites, whether for Banana Republic, Urban Outfitters, or Barneys Co-op. One block over on Washington are a handful of trend-conscious shops like Versace Jeans Couture and Diesel and flashy club-wear stores. In the discriminating Design District, many top-name designers hold shop when they are not rehabbing the latest South Beach hotel.

But this is also a city of tiny boutiques tucked away on side streets—such as South Miami's Red, Bird, and Sunset roads intersection—and outdoor markets touting unusual and delicious wares. Bring your wallet and choose from a wide variety of merchandise, some of which is rare anywhere but here. Stroll through Spanish-speaking neighborhoods where shops sell clothing, cigars, and other goods from all over Latin America. At an open-air flea-market stall, score an antique glass shaped like a palm tree and fill it with some fresh Jamaican ginger beer from the table next door. Or stop by your hotel gift shop and snap up an alligator magnet for your refrigerator, an ashtray made of seashells, or a bag of gumballs shaped like Florida oranges. Who can resist?

Malls

People fly to Miami from all over the world just to shop, and the malls are high on their list of spending spots. Stop off at one or two of these climate-controlled temples to consumerism, many of which double as mega entertainment centers, and you'll understand what makes Miami such a vibrant shopping destination.

Aventura Mall. Thanks to more than 250 shops, you could spend a full day here meandering through Macy's, Lord & Taylor, JCPenney, Sears, Burdines, and Bloomingdale's and then spend your evening at the 24-screen multiplex with stadium seating. The mall's smaller stores—Anika for cutting-edge designer fashions, Coach for luxury leather goods—are alluring, too. ⊠ *19501 Biscayne Blvd., Aventura* ☎ *305/935–1110* ⊕ *www.shopaventuramall.com.*

FodorsChoice **Bal Harbour Shops.** Local and international shoppers flock to this swank
★ collection of 100 high-end shops, boutiques, and department stores, which include such names as Christian Dior, Gucci, Hermès, Salvatore Ferragamo, Tiffany, and Valentino. Many European designers open their first North American signature store at this outdoor, pedestrian-friendly mall, and many American designers open their first boutique outside of New York here. Restaurants and cafés, in tropical garden settings, overflow with style-conscious diners. ⊠ *9700 Collins Ave., Bal Harbour* ☎ *305/866–0311* ⊕ *www.balharbourshops.com.*

Bayside Marketplace. This 16-acre shopping complex overlooking Biscayne Bay has 100 specialty shops, a concert pavilion, tour-boat docks, a food court, outdoor cafés, Latin steak houses, seafood restaurants,

Treats for Your Feet

If you are footloose and ready for serious shoe shopping, slip into something comfortable and get walking. Start on the south end of South Beach at 6th Street and Collins Avenue, and work your way north. At **Intermix Giroux, Nicole Miller,** and **Banana Republic** you can find a mix of men's and women's shoes, sandals, boots, and loafers, from high-end designer styles to seasonal staples. When you get to 8th Street, head one block west to Washington Avenue to examine the extremes of the Miami shoe scene: flip-flops and fins at the **South Beach Surf & Dive Shop** and Lucite stilettos adorned with pink feathers at **Santini Mavardi.** Walk north to 15th Street, and go one block east to pick up beach sandals for the whole family at **Absolutely Suitable.** If your toes aren't too tired, take them west when you reach Lincoln Road. Pick a pair of vintage or resale shoes at **Sasparilla Vintage, Fly Boutique,** or **Consign of the Times,** or acquire a hip, new pair at **Neo Scarpa, Chroma,** or **Base** as you continue west on Lincoln Road.

6

Home Decor

Get your credit card ready, and save your quarters for the meters. The **Miami Design District** is where those who are interested in home decor do serious shopping. Although the district is officially open Monday–Saturday 10–5, most of the stores are really closed on the weekend. The Design District is walkable in a half day, even if you stop at most every furniture, fabric, tile, lighting, art, and antiques store. Start one building south of the yellow Buick Building and its painted cameos of Roman mythological figures, at N.E. 2nd Avenue and N.E. 39th Street. Here **Holly Hunt** showcases interior design at its best. Cross the street to enter the Buena Vista Building, where **Emporio San Firenze** has Italian chandeliers on display. Continue north on N.E. 2nd Avenue to N.E. 40th Street, where the Moore Building houses **Luminaire Contract.** Heading west on N.E. 40th Street, you'll find **Oriental Rugs International, Artisan Antiques Art Deco, World Resources,** and **Luxe Cable & Light.** You can finish the tour at the Living Room Building, at N.E. 40th Street and North Miami Avenue, but not in order to shop. Its exaggerated, Delano-esque outdoor living room, with large-scale participatory art as furnishings, is a good place to relax.

Outdoor Markets

Weekend markets are a great way to check out Miami's neighborhoods. Although many claim to be open from morning to evening, most are picked through by midday. On Saturdays, jump in your car early to check out two markets in adjacent (but not walkable) neighborhoods. Start at the earlier riser of the two, the **Coral Gables Farmers' Market,** located in a small park near City Hall. Here booths are filled with produce, plants, breads, prepared foods, and even art. Leave the Gables and head east into the Grove for the **Coconut Grove Farmers' Market.** In a large tented stand just outside the heart of the Grove, this market is all about feel-good fuel for body and soul. Tables of organic fruits, veggies, and freshly prepared raw foods draw hippies past and present and the trendy health-conscious crowd.

You can visit three markets in one Sunday as part of a walking tour that will take one to four hours, depending on how often you stop to contemplate the goods. Start on the west end of Lincoln Road (at Alton Road), and browse the **Lincoln Road Outdoor Antique and Collectibles Market,** loaded with art deco treasures and collectibles mixed in with garage sale–style junk. Stroll east on Lincoln Road; within a few blocks you'll reach the **Lincoln Road Farmers' Market.** Most stands are brimming with fresh fruits and veggies from Florida's rich farmland to the west, although the mangoes and avocados may have been plucked from a tree right here on South Beach. Travel two blocks south to scenic Española Way, and follow the sounds of live music to the **Española Way Market.** Here international flavors extend to both food and trinkets. Buy a Jamaican pattie from one stand and a batik-print sarong from another.

and a Hard Rock Cafe. It's open late (until 10 during the week and 11 on Friday and Saturday), and its restaurants stay open even later. ⊠ *401 Biscayne Blvd., Downtown* ☎ *305/577–3344* ⊕ *www.baysidemarketplace.com.*

CocoWalk. It's got three floors containing nearly 40 chain and specialty shops (Coco Paris, Victoria's Secret, and Express, among others), blending the bustle of a mall with the breathability of an open-air venue. Kiosks with cigars, beads, incense, herbs, and other small items are scattered around the ground level, while restaurants and nightlife (Hooters, Fat Tuesday, and a 16-screen AMC theater, to name a few) are upstairs. Hanging out and people-watching is somewhat of a pastime here. The stores stay open almost as late as the popular restaurants and clubs. ⊠ *3015 Grand Ave., Coconut Grove, Miami* ☎ *305/444–0777* ⊕ *www.cocowalk.com.*

Dadeland Mall. The oldest mall in the county also feels like the biggest and busiest. Retailers include Saks Fifth Avenue, JCPenney, Lord & Taylor, Florida's largest Burdines department store, Burdines Home Gallery, and more than 185 specialty stores. Plus there are 12 places to eat, which vary from counter service to server service. It's on the south side of town and close to a Metrorail station. ⊠ *7535 N. Kendall Dr., Kendall, Miami* ☎ *305/665–6226.*

Dolphin Mall. This mall has more than 200 outlet, dining, and entertainment venues, many of which are new to the area, including Hilo Hattie, Gap Maternity, Quicksilver, and the terrific knock-off store Forever 21. Major anchors include Linens 'n Things, Marshalls MegaStore, Off 5th Saks Fifth Avenue Outlet, and Old Navy. A 400,000-square-foot entertainment center includes Dave & Buster's and a 19-screen cinema. The mall also has an enormous 850-seat food court and daily tourist-only shuttle service. Need more? Miami International Mall is next door (1455 N.W. 107th Ave.). ⊠ *11401 N.W. 12th St., West Miami-Dade, Miami* ☎ *305/365–7446* ⊕ *www.shopdolphinmall.com.*

The Falls Shopping Center. Taking its name from the waterfalls and lagoons inside, this upscale, open-air mall on the city's south side has Macy's and Bloomingdale's, 100 specialty stores, restaurants, and a 12-theater multiplex. Shop highlights are Tupelo Honey, for casual cotton clothing; the Discovery Channel Store, with science and nature-theme merchandise; and Restoration Hardware, a source for retro chic housewares. ⊠ *8888 S.W. 136th St., at U.S. 1, South Miami* ☎ *305/255–4570* ⊕ *www.shopthefalls.com.*

Loehmann's Fashion Island. Although it's clearly anchored by Loehmann's, the nationwide retailer of off-price designer fashions, this specialty mall also has a few other biggies, including Rochester Big & Tall and a Barnes & Noble bookstore. You can also grab a bite at any of several restaurants, lounges, and snack shops, including celebrated chef Allen Susser's namesake restaurant, Chef Allen's. ☒ *18701 Biscayne Blvd., Aventura* ☎ *no phone.*

Main Street. From cobblestone sidewalks to fountains and vintage-looking street lamps, Main Street was designed to resemble a picturesque small town. This shopping and restaurant promenade is home to Purple Frog, Via Moda, and a number of other small boutiques, along with such eateries as Tony Roma's, Shula's Steak 2, and Buca Di Beppo, an Italian restaurant. Main Street also hosts a number of annual festivals and events. ☒ *6843 Main St., Miami Lakes* ☎ *305/817–4198.*

Sawgrass Mills. This massive outlet mall is actually well north of Miami in western Broward County, but it's definitely worth a trip. Almost 2 mi long, Sawgrass has more than 400 manufacturer and retail outlet stores, name-brand discounters, specialty stores, pushcarts, and kiosks. Choices include Off 5th Saks Fifth Avenue Outlet, the Clearance Center from Neiman Marcus, Spiegel Outlet Store, and Nordstrom Rack. Two huge food courts plus 11 restaurants and a 23-screen movie theater offer a break from shopping. ☒ *12801 W. Sunrise Blvd., Sunrise* ☎ *954/846– 2300* ⊕ *www.sawgrassmillsmall.com.*

Shops at Sunset Place. A huge banyan tree spreads its tendrils in front of an entrance to this giant pastel bunker, containing NikeTown, A/X Armani Exchange, Virgin Megastore, and four dozen others. Entertainment options include a 24-screen cinema, and a GameWorks arcade filled with electronic games. ☒ *5701 Sunset Dr., U.S. 1 and Red Rd., South Miami* ☎ *305/663–4222.*

Streets of Mayfair. This open-air complex of promenades, balconies, and sidewalk cafés bustles both day and night, thanks to its Coconut Grove setting and its popular tenants: an improv comedy club, martini lounge, and a few all-night dance clubs. Enzo Angiolini; Borders Books, Music, & Cafe; and a dozen other shops and restaurants are also here. ☒ *2911 Grand Ave., Coconut Grove, Miami* ☎ *305/448–1700.*

Fodor'sChoice ★ **Village of Merrick Park.** At this Mediterranean-style shopping and dining venue Neiman Marcus and Nordstrom anchor 115 specialty shops. Designers such as Etro, Jimmy Choo, Ted Baker, Burberry, Carolina Herrera, and Bottega Veneta fulfill most high-fashion needs, while luxury-linen purveyor Ann Gish and Brazilian contemporary-furniture designer Artefacto provide a taste of the haute-decor shopping options. International food venues and a day spa offer further indulgences. ☒ *358 San Lorenzo Ave., Coral Gables* ☎ *305/529–0200* ⊕ *www. villageofmerrickpark.com.*

Shopping Districts

If you're over the climate-controlled slickness of shopping malls and can't face one more food-court "meal," you've got choices in Miami. Head out into the sunshine and shop the streets of Miami, where you'll find big-name retailers and local boutiques alike. Take a break at a sidewalk café to power up on some Cuban coffee or fresh-squeezed OJ and enjoy the tropical breezes.

Downtown Miami

Nearly 1,000 stores, anchored by Burdines, Marshalls, Ross, and La Época (a Havana import), line the streets of downtown Miami. Sporting goods, cameras and electronics, beauty products, and housewares are among the goods for sale in this commercial hub. With the Seybold Building as its flagship, a large jewelry district is second in the United States only to New York City's Diamond District. Hourly parking lots are available, or you can get here via Metrorail or Metromover. ⊠ *Biscayne Blvd. to 3rd Ave. and S.E. 1st St. to N.E. 3rd St., Downtown* ☎ *305/379–7070* ⊕ *www.downtownmiami.com.*

Miami Design District

★ Miami is synonymous with good design, and this visitor-friendly shopping district is an unprecedented melding of public space and the exclusive world of design. Covering a few city blocks around N.E. 2nd Avenue and N.E. 40th Street, the Design District contains more than 200 showrooms and galleries, including Kartell, Marc Corbin, Ann Sacks, Poliform, and Adamar Fine Arts. Unlike most showrooms, which are typically the beat of decorators alone, the Miami Design District's showrooms are open to the public and occupy windowed, street-level spaces. Bring your quarters, as all of the parking is on the street and metered. Visitor-friendly touches include art galleries and cafés, and the neighborhood even has its own high school (of art and design, of course) and hosts street parties and gallery walks. Although in many cases you'll need a decorator to secure your purchases, browsers are encouraged to consider for themselves the array of rather exclusive furnishings, decorative objects, antiques, and art. ⊠ *N.E. 36th St. to N.E. 42nd St. between N.E. 2nd Ave. and N. Miami Ave., Design District, Miami* ⊕ *www.miamidesigndistrict.net.*

Miracle Mile–Downtown Coral Gables

Lined with trees and busy with strolling shoppers, Miracle Mile is the centerpiece of the downtown Coral Gables shopping district, which is home to men's and women's boutiques, jewelry and home furnishing stores, and a host of exclusive couturiers and bridal shops. More than 30 first-rate restaurants offer everything from French to Indian cuisine, while art galleries and the Actors' Playhouse give the area a cultural flair. ⊠ *Douglas Rd. to LeJeune Rd. and Aragon Ave. to Andalusia Ave., Coral Gables* ☎ *305/569–0311* ⊕ *www.shopcoralgables.com.*

South Beach–Collins Avenue

★ Give your plastic a workout in Gianni Versace's old stomping grounds just south of Lincoln Road. Among the high-profile tenants on this densely packed two-block stretch of Collins Avenue between 6th and 8th streets are Club Monaco, MAC, Kenneth Cole, Polo Sport, and A/X Armani Exchange. Sprinkled amid the upscale vendors are hair salons, spas, cafés, and such familiar stores as the Gap, Urban Outfitters, and Banana Republic. Be sure to head over one street east and west to catch the shopping on Ocean Drive and Washington Avenue. ✉ *Collins Ave. between 6th and 8th Sts., South Beach, Miami Beach* ☎ *305/672–1270.*

South Beach–Lincoln Road Mall

Fodor'sChoice ★ This eight-block-long pedestrian mall is home to more than 150 shops, 20-plus art galleries and nightclubs, about 50 restaurants and cafés, and the renovated Colony Theatre. Tiffany & Co. was one of the first of the exclusive boutiques here in the 1940s, when Lincoln Road was known as the Fifth Avenue of the South. Today an 18-screen movie theater anchors the west end of the street, which is where most of the worthwhile shops are; the far east end is mostly discount and electronic shops. Sure, there's a Pottery Barn, a Gap, and a Williams-Sonoma, but the emphasis is on emporiums with unique personalities, like En Avance, Neo Scarpa Accessories, and Sage. Do as the locals do, and meander along "the Road" day or night, stopping for a refreshment at one of the top-flight bistros or open-air eateries. ✉ *Lincoln Rd. between Alton Rd. and Washington Ave., South Beach, Miami Beach* ☎ *305/672–1270.*

Specialty Stores

Beyond the shopping malls and the big-name retailers, Greater Miami has all manner of merchandise to tempt even the casual browser. For consumers on a mission to find certain items—art deco antiques or cigars, for instance—the city streets burst with a rewarding collection of specialty shops.

Antiques

Alhambra Antiques (✉ 2850 Salzedo St., Coral Gables ☎ 305/446–1688) houses a collection of high-quality decorative pieces acquired on annual jaunts to Europe.

American Salvage (✉ 7001 N.W. 27th Ave., Opa-Locka ☎ 305/691–7001) may be off the beaten path, but it's a good place to rescue less-than-perfect art deco furniture, such as 1930s armoires, bookshelves, and kitchenware, at bargain prices.

★ **Architectural Antiques** (✉ 2500 S.W. 28th La., Coconut Grove, Miami ☎ 305/285–1330 ⊕ www.miamiantique.com) carries large and eclectic items—railroad crossing signs, statues, English roadsters—along with antique furniture, lighting, paintings, and silverware, all in a cluttered setting that makes shopping an adventure.

Artisan Antiques Art Deco (✉ 110 N.E. 40th St., Design District, Miami ☎ 305/573–5619) purveys china, crystal, mirrors, and armoires from the French art deco period, but an assortment of 1930s radiator covers, which can double as funky sideboards, are what's really neat here.

Morningside Antiques (✉ 6443 Biscayne Blvd., Morningside, Miami ☎ 305/751–2828) is an antiques market in a mall setting. This emerging antiques area includes vendors who specialize in English, French, and American furniture and collectibles.

★ **Senzatempo** (✉ 1655 Meridian Ave., South Beach, Miami Beach ☎ 305/534–5588 ⊕ www.senzatempo.com) offers up a collection of vintage home accessories by European and American designers of the 1930s through the 1970s, including electric fans, klieg lights, and chrome furniture.

Valerio Antiques (✉ 250 Valencia Ave., Coral Gables ☎ 305/448–6775 ⊕ www.valerioartdeco.com) carries fine French art deco furniture, bronze sculptures, shagreen boxes, and original art glass by Gallé and Loetz, among others.

Beauty

Avanti (✉ 932 Lincoln Rd., South Beach, Miami Beach ☎ 305/531–9580) is an Aveda lifestyle store and hair salon. It's a good place to stock up on Aveda's deliciously scented shampoos and conditioners as well as skin creams.

Fodor'sChoice
★ **Brownes & Co.** (✉ 841 Lincoln Rd., South Beach, Miami Beach ☎ 305/532–8703 ⊕ www.brownesbeauty.com) provides luxurious products to those who appreciate them the most. Cosmetics include Molton Brown, Body & Soul, Le Clerc, and others. It also sells herbal remedies and upscale hair and body products from Bumble and Bumble. Try to resist something from the immense collection of scented European soaps in all sizes and colors. A popular in-house salon, **Some Like It Hot** (☎ 305/538–7544), offers some of the best waxing in town.

The Fragrance Shop (✉ 612 Lincoln Rd., South Beach, Miami Beach ☎ 305/535–0037) carries more than 800 perfume oils, including those that mimic famous brands, in a setting that resembles an 18th century apothecary. The staff will customize a unique blend for you or sell you a hand-blown perfume bottle made by one of many international artisans.

GBS Beauty Supply (✉ 308 Miracle Mile, Coral Gables ☎ 305/446–6654 ⊕ www.gbsbeauty.com) has been selling discount beauty products in the Gables since the '70s and has since spread to other locations in Greater Miami, including Aventura, Pinecrest, and Miami Beach. This well-appointed retailer and in-house salon carries top brand-name personal products for men, women, and even babies.

Sephora (☎✉ 721 Collins Ave., South Beach, Miami Beach ☎ 305/532–0904 ⊕ www.sephora.com) is a makeup, skin-care, and fragrance emporium. Find Bliss, Calvin Klein, Clinique, Hardy Candy, Nars, Shu Uemura, and Stila among the masses of beauty products organized alphabetically.

Books

Afro-In Books and Things (✉ 5575 N.W. 7th Ave., Liberty City, Miami ☎ 305/756–6107) specializes in books by African-American writers for children and teen readers—although it has an impressive section of books for adults, too.

Barnes & Noble (✉ 152 Miracle Mile, Coral Gables ☎ 305/446–4152) like others in the superstore chain, encourages customers to pick a book off the shelf and lounge on a couch. A well-stocked magazine and international news rack and an espresso bar–café make it even easier to while away a rainy afternoon here or at the Kendall, North Miami Beach, or South Miami locations.

Fodor'sChoice
★ **Books & Books, Inc.** (✉ 265 Aragon Ave., Coral Gables ☎ 305/442–4408 ✉ 933 Lincoln Rd., South Beach, Miami Beach ☎ 305/532–3222). Greater Miami's only independent English-language bookshops, specialize in contemporary and classical literature as well as in books on the arts, architecture, Florida, and Cuba. At either location you can lounge at

the café, browse the photography gallery, or sit in the courtyard and flip through magazines. Both stores host regular poetry and other readings. **Borders** (✉ 3390 Mary St., Coconut Grove, Miami ☎ 305/447–1655) carries more than 2,000 periodicals in 10 languages from 15 countries, in addition to books, CDs, and videos. This national book retailer has six other locations throughout Miami.

Downtown Book Center (✉ 247 S.E. 1st St., Downtown ☎ 305/377–9939) sells novels by leading Central and South American authors, as well as Spanish-language maps and computer manuals.

Eutopia Books (✉ 1627 Jefferson Ave., South Beach, Miami Beach ☎ 305/ 532–8680) is the rare Miami area store that sells rare books. In addition to an impressive collection of vintage art books, you'll find early 20th-century children's classics.

★ **Kafka's** (✉ 1464 Washington Ave., South Beach, Miami Beach ☎ 305/ 673–9669), a bookstore and café with character, sells previously owned books, including a good selection of used art books and literature. In addition, the shop carries a terrific selection of obscure and familiar periodicals and offers the use of computers and Internet access for a fee.

La Moderna Poesia (✉ 5246 S.W. 8th St., Little Havana, Miami ☎ 305/ 446–9884 ✉ 3870 E. 4th Ave., Hialeah ☎ 305/556–7717), with more than 100,000 titles, is the region's largest and most complete source for *los libros en español*.

Libreria Distribuidora Universal (✉ 3090 S.W. 8th St., Little Havana, Miami ☎ 305/642–3234) is a favorite of book lovers who want Cuban flavor in their Spanish reading material. You'll also find Latin American and Caribbean reference books and literature here.

Pierre International Bookstore (✉ Biscayne Harbor Shops, 18185 Biscayne Blvd., Aventura ☎ 305/792–0766) is a pleasant place to browse for and buy books in Spanish, French, or Portuguese. This store happily accommodates special orders of foreign-language titles.

Super Heroes Unlimited (✉ 1788 N.E. 163rd St., North Miami Beach ☎ 305/940–9539) beckons to comic-book readers looking for monthly refills of *Spawn* and *X-Men* and tempts with an enviable selection of Japanese *animé*. Its odd strip-mall location doesn't keep *Justice League* fans from picking up statues, trading cards, T-shirts, and other collectibles of their favorite superheroes.

Children's Clothing & Toys

★ **Alexa & Jack** (✉ 635 Lincoln Rd., South Beach, Miami Beach ☎ 305/ 534–9300) is a designer children's boutique where you can indulge your favorite little person. Carrying pint-size fashions by D&G Junior, Moschino, and Sonia Rykiel; bathing suits by Vilebrequin; and baby clothes by Juicy Couture, the store also has oodles of small gifts, toys, and accessories, in case you are not sure of a child's size.

F.A.O. Schwarz (✉ Bal Harbour Shops, 9700 Collins Ave., Bal Harbour ☎ 305/865–2361 ✉ Aventura Mall, 19501 Biscayne Blvd., Aventura ☎ 305/692–9200), the ultimate toy store, has videos, books, action figures, and candy for kids of all ages.

Gap Kids (✉ Bayside Marketplace, 401 Biscayne Blvd., Downtown ☎ 305/539–9334) carries casual sportswear for the discriminating youngster, ages two years and up. (Baby Gap is for children up to 24

months.) With more than 10 Gap Kids in town, you can find one in mos
malls and shopping districts.

Peekaboo (⊠ 6807 Main St., Miami Lakes ☎ 305/556–6910) carrie
educational toys for kids and has an exceptional collection of Europea
clothing for infants to teens.

Sweetdreams Candies (⊠ 708 Lincoln Rd., South Beach, Miami Beac
☎ 305/538–8155) makes it great to be a kid in a candy store. Th
wild assortment of treats includes jelly beans, lollipops, cotton candy
bubblegum, rock candy, taffy, gummi bears, homemade chocolates, an
some toys.

Cigars

Bill's Pipe & Tobacco (⊠ 2309 Ponce de León Blvd., Coral Gables ☎ 30
444–1764) has everything for the smoker, including a wide selection c
pipes and pipe tobacco, cigars, accessories, and gifts.

Condal & Peñamil (⊠ 741 Lincoln Rd., South Beach, Miami Beac
☎ 305/673–3194) is a cigar, coffee, and cocktail bar where you can ge
boxes of cigars with personalized labels. Name a dozen after yoursel
or your new kid.

El Credito Cigars (⊠ 1106 S.W. 8th St., Little Havana, Miami ☎ 30
858–4162), in the heart of Little Havana, employs rows of workers a
wooden benches. They rip, cut, and wrap giant tobacco leaves, and pres
the cigars in vises. Dedicated smokers find their way here to pick up
$90 bundle or to peruse the *gigantes, supremos,* panatelas, and Churchil
available in natural or *maduro* wrappers.

Harriels Tobacco Shoppe (⊠ 11401 S. Dixie Hwy., Pinecrest ☎ 305/252
9010 ⊕ www.harriels.com) caters to the serious smoker with a vast se
lection of premium cigars, imported cigarettes, and decorative pipes.

Macabi Cigars (⊠ 3473 S.W. 8th St., Little Havana, Miami ☎ 305/446
2606) carries cigars, cigars, and more cigars, including premium an
house brands. Humidors and other accessories are also available.

Yucky's Tobacco & Emporium (⊠ 3418 Main Hwy., Coconut Grov
Miami ☎ 305/444–4997), a popular store with University of Miami stu
dents, stocks smoking paraphernalia, including water pipes, incense, an
things that glow in the dark.

Clothing for Men & Women

Banana Republic (⊠ 1100 Lincoln Rd., South Beach, Miami Beac
☎ 305/534–4706 ⊠ 800 Collins Ave., South Beach, Miami Beac
☎ 305/674–7079) showcases the season's latest dependable, work-o
play fashions for men and women, all with that slightly trendy yet so
phisticated Gap-enterprise touch. The two-story Lincoln Road store
in a former bank, with dressing rooms in the bank's old vault an
cashiers in the old teller stations.

★ **Base** (⊠ 939 Lincoln Rd., South Beach, Miami Beach ☎ 305/531
4982) is a constantly evolving shop with a cutting-edge magazine se
tion, an international CD station with DJ, and groovy home accessorie
Stop here for men's and women's eclectic clothing, shoes, and acce
sories that mix Japanese design with Caribbean-inspired material
The often-present house label designer may help select your wardrobe
newest addition.

Chroma (✉ 920 Lincoln Rd., South Beach, Miami Beach ☎ 305/695–8808) is where fashionistas go for Barbara Bui, Catherine Malandrino, and Mint, as well as up-and-coming designers.

Intermix (✉ 634 Collins Ave., South Beach, Miami Beach ☎ 305/531–5950) is a modern New York boutique with the variety of a department store. You'll find fancy dresses, stylish shoes, slinky accessories, and trendy looks by sassy and somewhat pricey designers like Chloé, Stella Mc-Cartney, Marc Jacobs, Moschino, and Diane von Furstenberg.

J. Bolado Clothiers (✉ 336 Miracle Mile, Coral Gables ☎ 305/448–2507) has been in the neighborhood since 1968. This family-owned men's store carries classic styles from imported and domestic designers. The house specialties are made-to-measure suits and custom shirts, and there are three generations of tailors on the premises.

Kristine Michael (✉ 7271 S.W. 57th Ave., South Miami ☎ 305/665–7717) is a local fashion institution with suburban moms and University of Miami students. The store's hip and up-to-the-minute selection of pieces from Theory, Alice & Olivia, Kors, and C & C California stands out from the national retailers across the street at the Shops at Sunset Place.

Nicole Miller (✉ 656 Collins Ave., South Beach, Miami Beach ☎ 305/535–2200) showcases the spunky New York designer's distinctive fashions, including boxers and ties for him and handbags and shoes for her.

Polo Ralph Lauren (✉ Bal Harbour Shops, 9700 Collins Ave., Bal Harbour ☎ 305/861–2059) has a complete selection of Polo for Men and Ralph Lauren for women, along with accessories and a few items from the Home Collection, including frames and fragrances.

Scoop (✉ Shore Club hotel, 1901 Collins Ave., South Beach, Miami Beach ☎ 305/695–3297), the New York shop for pretty young things, has a small but spaciously arranged Miami outpost, which carries all the Helmut Lang, Marc Jacobs, and hip-slung Earl and Seven Jeans that you'll need to make it through a club's velvet rope.

★ **Sylvia Tcherassi** (✉ 358 San Lorenzo Ave., Coral Gables ☎ 305/461–0009), the Colombian designer's signature boutique, in the Village of Merrick Park, features feminine and frilly dresses and separates accented with chiffon, tulle, and sequins.

SHOES **Giroux** (✉ 638 Collins Ave., South Beach, Miami Beach ☎ 305/672–3015) carries some men's and women's shoes by American, Spanish, and house-label designers. But the highlight of the selection is the Italian shoe company of brothers Goffredo Fantini and Enrico Fantini, who design independent men's lines and collaborate on their women's shoe collection, Materia Prima.

Koko & Palenki (✉ CocoWalk, 3015 Grand Ave., Coconut Grove, Miami ☎ 305/444–1772) is where Grovers go for a well-edited selection of trendy shoes by Calvin Klein, Casadei, Charles David, Stuart Weitzman, Via Spiga, and others. Handbags, belts, and men's shoes add to the selection. Koko & Palenki also has stores in the Aventura and Dadeland malls.

Neo Scarpa (✉ 817 Lincoln Rd., South Beach, Miami Beach ☎ 305/535–5633) carries each season's must-have men's and women's shoes—Dolce & Gabbana, Giuseppe Zanotti, Robert Clergerie, and Sigerson Morrison top the charts. If you're looking for Prada, the staff will send you across the road to their accessory store at 710 Lincoln Road.

Santini Mavardi (⌂ 935 Washington Ave., South Beach, Miami Beach ☏ 305/538–6229) is where celebs stop for custom-made shoes and a matching outfit. Platform sandals with feather accents, Lucite stilettos with rhinestones, and wood wedge heels with lace-up leather straps round out this ultra-sexy shoe selection.

SWIMWEAR **Absolutely Suitable** (⌂ 1560 Collins Ave., South Beach, Miami Beach ☏ 305/604–5281) carries women's and men's swimwear and accessories for lounging poolside. The salespeople will put you in a suit that fits just right and dress you from sunhat to flip-flop.

Everything but Water (⌂ Aventura Mall, 19501 Biscayne Blvd., Aventura ☏ 305/932–7207) lives up to its name, selling everything for the water (except the water itself). The complete line of women's and junior's swimwear includes one- and two-piece suits and tankinis (tank tops with bikini or high-top bottoms).

South Beach Surf & Dive Shop (⌂ 850 Washington Ave., South Beach, Miami Beach ☏ 305/531–6110 ⊕ www.southbeachdivers.com) is a one-stop shop for beach gear—from clothing and swimwear for guys and gals to wake-, surf-, and skateboards. The shop also offers multilingual surfing, scuba, snorkeling, and dive lessons and trips.

VINTAGE **Consign of the Times** (⌂ 3300 Rice St., Coconut Grove, Miami ☏ 305/
CLOTHING 443–4331 ✉ 1635 Jefferson Ave., South Beach, Miami Beach ☏ 305/535–0811) sells vintage and consignment items by top designers at pre-owned prices, including Chanel suits, Fendi bags, and Celine and Prada treasures.

★ **Fly Boutique** (⌂ 650 Lincoln Rd., South Beach, Miami Beach ☏ 305/604–8508) is where South Beach hipsters flock for the latest arrival of used clothing. At this resale boutique '80s glam designer pieces fly out at a premium price, but vintage camisoles and Levi's corduroys are still a resale deal. Be sure to look up—the eclectic lanterns are also for sale.

Fodor'sChoice **Miami Twice** (⌂ 6562 S.W. 40th St., South Miami ☏ 305/666–0127) has
★ fabulous vintage clothes and accessories from the last three decades. After all, everyone needs a leisure suit or platform shoes. Check out the vintage home collectibles and furniture, too.

Sasparilla Vintage (⌂ 1630 Pennsylvania Ave., South Beach, Miami Beach ☏ 305/532–6611), just off Lincoln Road, teems with a well-chosen selection of gotta-have-it vintage. Resale accessories in excellent condition from Gucci, Dolce, Dries, and Pucci are neatly organized among colorful party outfits like a vintage Missoni rainbow-color dress.

Essentials

Central Ace Hardware (⌂ 545 41st St., Mid-Beach, Miami Beach ☏ 305/531–0836) is less a hardware store than a place to outfit your apartment, efficiency, or hotel room with nondisposable items ranging from corkscrews to coolers.

Compass Market (⌂ 860 Ocean Dr., South Beach, Miami Beach ☏ 305/673–2906) crams wall-to-wall merchandise into a cute and cozy basement shop in the Waldorf Towers hotel. (The somewhat confusing entrance is on 9th Street.) The market stocks all the staples you'll need, from sandals, souvenirs, cigars, and deli items to umbrellas, newspapers, wine, and champagne.

Food

Fodor'sChoice **Epicure Market** (✉ 1656 Alton Rd., South Beach, Miami Beach ☎ 305/
★ 672–1861) is one of Miami's most cherished establishments. Pick up
jars of homemade chicken-noodle or green-pea soup or some of the
exquisite (if pricey) produce. The bakery has a scrumptious array of cook-
ies, cakes, and breads made daily, or you can wander down aisles full
of imported chocolate and local celebrities.

Oak Feed Natural Food Market (✉ 3155 Oak Ave., Coconut Grove,
Miami ☎ 305/448–7595) peddles more than grains and granola.
Nearly everything you'd need to live a preservative-free existence is here—
baking mixes, teas, environmentally friendly household products, and
a veggie-oriented café.

Gifts & Souvenirs

Art Deco District Welcome Center (✉ 1001 Ocean Dr., South Beach, Miami
Beach ☎ 305/531–3484) hawks the finest in Miami-inspired kitsch, from
flamingo salt-and-pepper shakers to alligator-shape ashtrays, along with
books and posters celebrating the Art Deco District and its revival.

Britto Central (✉ 818 Lincoln Rd., South Beach, Miami Beach ☎ 305/
531–8821) is both a gallery and working studio. Posters, prints, ties,
and other objects feature the vibrant graphic designs of Brazilian artist
and Miami resident Romero Britto.

Indies Company (✉ 101 W. Flagler St., Downtown ☎ 305/375–1492),
the gift shop of the Historical Museum of Southern Florida, is dedicated
to the proposition that Miami is more than just art deco. You'll find
books on South Florida as well as interesting artifacts of Miami's history, including some inexpensive reproductions.

Le Chocolatier (✉ 1840 N.E. 164th St., North Miami Beach ☎ 305/944–
3020 ⊕ www.lechocolatier.com) tempts the palate with hand-dipped and
molded chocolate creations, made into gift baskets and other gift items
or eaten on the spot. You can linger to watch chocolate being made
through a glass partition.

Pink Palm (✉ 737 Lincoln Rd., South Beach, Miami Beach ☎ 877/538–
8373 ⊕ www.pinkpalm.com) flaunts a sometimes racy, sometimes
funny, and sometimes beautiful selection of sophisticated greeting cards,
gifts, and souvenirs. There's another location at the Village of Merrick
Park in Coral Gables.

Wolfsonian Museum Gift Shop (✉ 1001 Washington Ave., South Beach,
Miami Beach ☎ 305/531–1001 or 305/535–2680) sells books on design and architecture, small objects from the world of Alessi and other
kitchenware geniuses, as well as posters and reproductions from the museum's collection of objects from the 1930s.

Home Furnishings

Addison House (✉ 5201 N.W. 77th Ave., Doral Miami ☎ 305/640–2400
⊕ www.addisonhouse.com) is an outlet for a wide variety of traditional name-brand furniture from North Carolina, a premier furniture-
producing region.

★ **Cookworks** (✉ Bal Harbour Shops, 9700 Collins Ave., Bal Harbour
☎ 305/861–5005) accesses your inner celebrity chef and entertainment
guru with a fabulous array of kitchen items, including table linens,

plates and utensils, small appliances and gadgets, gourmet foods and wines, cookbooks, and gift items. Most of the merchandise is direct from France or Italy.

★ **Design within Reach** (✉ 927 Lincoln Rd., South Beach, Miami Beach ☎ 305/604–0037 ⊕ www.dwr.com) caters to furniture junkies looking for reproductions of such modern masters as Eames, Starck, Saarinen, and Noguchi. Tucked in the Sterling Building, the studio is marked by an inviting patio displaying unusual outdoor furnishings.

★ **Details** (✉ 1711 Alton Rd., South Beach, Miami Beach ☎ 305/531–1325 ⊕ www.detailsathome.com) has beautiful home accessories, trendy knickknacks, and furniture from coffee tables to chairs. The sofas summon you to sit on them and consider just how good your home would look with one—or two.

Eclectic Elements (✉ 2227 Coral Way, Coral Gables ☎ 305/285–0899 ⊕ www.eemiami.net) carries a playful collection of very Miami modern and retro furniture, mirrors, and clocks that would have pleased the Jetsons.

Fodor'sChoice **Holly Hunt** (✉ 3833 N.E. 2nd Ave., Design District, Miami ☎ 305/571–
★ 2012 ⊕ www.hollyhunt.com) is a spectacular 40,000-square-foot showroom of custom indoor and outdoor furniture, lighting, and fabrics by Holly Hunt and other revered designers, such as Christian Liaigre, John Hutton, Rose Tarlow, and Mattaliano. If you're going to buy, bring a designer, but browsing to see how the best of the best do home decor is free and inspiring.

Inspiration by Scan Design (✉ 3025 N.E. 163rd St., North Miami Beach ☎ 305/944–8080 ⊕ www.inspirationfurniture.com) sells contemporary Scandinavian-design furniture that goes beyond the basics of blond veneered plywood.

Luminaire (✉ 2331 Ponce de León Blvd., Coral Gables ☎ 305/448–7367 ⊕ www.luminaire.com ✉ 4040 N.E. 2nd Ave., Design District, Miami ☎ 305/576–5788) is Miami's leading purveyor of contemporary furniture. Pieces from more than 100 manufacturers and 200 designers include European manufacturers such as Cassina and Interlubke. The Design District store focuses on home office and lobby design.

Oriental Rugs International (✉ 131 N.E. 40th St., Design District Miami ☎ 305/576–0880) sells mostly Iranian rugs from the 20th century but also carries antique and contemporary rugs from Turkey, France, and India.

Spiaggia (✉ 1624 Alton Rd., South Beach, Miami Beach ☎ 305/538–7949) may mean *beach* in Italian, but here it signifies a home furnishings store on the Beach. Candle addicts can pick up plenty of giant tabletop candles, tiny tapers, and novelty candles in soothing scents to light up their life.

World Resources (✉ 56 N.E. 40th St., Design District Miami ☎ 305/576–8799) carries a stock of global furniture and accessories, specializing in Indonesian, Indian, and Asian imports that include vases, tea chests, and ornate canopy beds.

Jewelry

Beverlee Kagan (✉ 5831 Sunset Dr., South Miami ☎ 305/663–1937) deals in vintage and antique jewelry, including art deco–era bangles, bracelets, and cuff links.

By Design (⊠ 297 Miracle Mile, Coral Gables ☎ 305/441–9696 ⊕ www.bydesignfinejewelry.com) designs fine jewelry from precious metals and stones. If you have a particular piece that you would like to create, this is the place to have it meticulously executed.

Bulgari (⊠ Bal Harbour Shops, 9700 Collins Ave., Bal Harbour ☎ 305/861–8898) jewelry, watches, silver, and luxury perfumes are known the world over. If you're looking for a gift that will impress, from a silk scarf or tie to a leather accessory, this is the place.

Gray & Sons Jewelers (⊠ 9595 Harding Ave., Surfside ☎ 305/865–0999 ⊕ www.grayandsons.com) offers fine new and pre-owned watches and estate jewelry, with more than 35 brands to choose from.

Holden (⊠ 608 Lincoln Rd., South Beach, Miami Beach ☎ 305/672–1527) carries reproductions of period timepieces, as well as funky retro-looking modern watches.

Me & Ro (⊠ Shore Club hotel, 1901 Collins Ave., South Beach, Miami Beach ☎ 305/672–3566 ⊕ www.meandrojewelry.com) is a trendy New York–based jewelry shop run by Michele Quan and Robin Renzi, with a celebrity clientele that reads like a who's who. Designs are crafted from silver, gold, and semi-precious stones.

Morays Jewelers (⊠ 50 N.E. 2nd Ave., Downtown ☎ 305/374–0739) has been a Downtown mainstay since 1944. An authorized dealer of more than 30 top-quality Swiss watch brands, the store also offers an array of jewelry and gift items.

Starck Design (⊠ 704 Lincoln Rd., South Beach, Miami Beach ☎ 305/674–7656) stocks German-designed jewelry and watches, including stainless steel and titanium pieces.

Lighting

Benson Lighting and Fans (⊠ 12955 S.W. 87th Ave., South Miami ☎ 305/235–5841) is the place to go if you're hoping to give your home a tropical makeover, complete with classic ceiling fans.

Emporio San Firenze (⊠ 180 N.E. 39th St., Design District, Miami ☎ 305/572–0990) is sure to have the Italian chandelier of your dreams. Classical to modern designs are hand-forged from wrought iron or brass and decorated with Murano glass and Venetian silk.

Farrey's (⊠ 1850 N.E. 146th St., North Miami ☎ 305/947–5451 ⊕ www.farreys.com ⊠ 3000 S.W. 28th La., Coconut Grove, Miami ☎ 305/445–2244) is a giant warehouse of lighting fixtures. Check out the selection of nautical-deco fixtures for inside and outside the house.

Luxe Cable & Light (⊠ 1 N.E. 40th St., Design District, Miami ☎ 305/576–6639 ⊠ 4023 Le Jeune Rd., Coral Gables ☎ 305/476–7778) lights up two locations in Miami with creative chandeliers, innovative wall sconces, and funky table lamps.

Music

Blue Note Records (⊠ 16401 N.E. 15th Ave., North Miami Beach ☎ 305/940–3394) is the place for rare oldies and vinyl rarities, as well as the latest discs from contemporary artists. A sister store, **Blue Note Jazz** (⊠ 2299 N.E. 164th St., North Miami Beach ☎ 305/354–4563), caters to jazz fans but also has a vinyl annex upstairs that caters to DJs.

Do-Re-Mi Music Center (✉ 1829 S.W. 8th St., Little Havana, Miami ☎ 305/541–3374) satisfies shoppers who want to go home with suitcases full of salsa, merengue, or other Latin dance music.

Sam Ash Music (✉ 5360 N.W. 167th St., West Miami-Dade, Miami ☎ 305/628–3510 ✉ Dolphin Mall, 11421 N.W. 12th St., West Miami-Dade, Miami ☎ 786/331–9688) stocks music supplies from guitar strings and drumsticks to amps and keyboards and has DJ-demo, drum, percussion, and keyboard rooms that let you sample the merchandise before buying. The 48,000-square-foot store also offers instrument repairs and international sales.

Spec's Music (✉ 501 Collins Ave., South Beach, Miami Beach ☎ 305/534–3667) has 10 stores, which can be found in most major malls throughout Greater Miami. The South Beach supermarket-size store has new releases of rock, hip-hop, jazz, R&B, Spanish-language titles, and world music.

New Age

Maya Hatcha (✉ 3058 Grand Ave., Coconut Grove, Miami ☎ 305/443–9040) is a long-standing Grove staple that highlights feng shui crystals, candles, Indian and Native American jewelry, and imported clothing.

Mystical Aamulet Network (✉ 7360 S.W. 24th St., Westchester, Miami ☎ 305/265–2228) serves Miami's Wiccan, pagan, and metaphysical communities from its location just west of Coral Gables. Visitors can pick up books on witchcraft, as well as amulets, tarot cards, crystals, and jewelry.

★ **9th Chakra** (✉ 530 Lincoln Rd., South Beach, Miami Beach ☎ 305/538–0671 ⊕ www.9thchakra.com) offers inspirational books (in English and Spanish), crystals, jewelry, feng shui products, candles, essential oils, and music to meditate by. In a new location, the store offers even more gifts for the soul. Tarot card readings are performed in English and Spanish on alternating days.

Odds & Ends

Condom USA (✉ 3066 Grand Ave., Coconut Grove, Miami ☎ 305/445–7729) sells condoms by the gross, sexually oriented games, and other titillating objects. If you're easily offended, stay away, but if you're easily aroused, stay the night (or at least until closing—2 AM on Friday and Saturday, midnight the rest of the week).

Gold Kiosk (✉ 1685 Collins Ave., South Beach, Miami Beach ☎ 305/674–6160) is not your typical hotel sundry shop. Located in the Delano, this small boutique carries a little bit of only the best—from designer towels and fancy sun lotions to international magazines and signature souvenirs to a limited but high-end selection of clothing.

Gotta Have It! Collectibles (✉ 4231 S.W. 71st Ave., South Miami ☎ 305/446–5757) caters to autograph hounds with its signed team jerseys, canceled checks from the estate of Marilyn Monroe, Beatles album jackets, and Jack Nicklaus scorecards. If they don't have the autograph you desire, they'll track one down.

La Casa de los Trucos (✉ 1343 S.W. 8th St., Little Havana, Miami ☎ 305/858–5029) is a popular magic store that first opened in Cuba in the 1930s; the exiled owners reopened it here in the 1970s. When they're in, the owners perform for you.

Oceans of Notions (✉ 10990 Biscayne Blvd., North Miami ☎ 305/893–3194) is a no-frills notions store with fabric, thread, leather cord, beads, and boas for do-it-yourself fashion projects.

Pop (✉ 1151 Washington Ave., South Beach, Miami Beach ☎ 305/604–3604 ⊕ www.popsouthbeach.com) is packed with costumelike club gear for eccentric party goers. Don't be scared off by the wacky window displays. Among the rainbow wigs are fun trinkets for normal folks, although the stuff may end up in your junk drawer back home.

Yarn Studio (✉ 3201 Collins Ave., South Beach, Miami Beach ☎ 786/488–8487), a subterranean shop in the Saxony Hotel, overflows with yarn for all your knitting needs. Lessons are available for the knitting-needle novice.

Only in Miami

ABC Costume Shop (✉ 3704 N.E. 2nd Ave., Design District, Miami ☎ 305/573–5657 ⊕ www.abccostumeshop.com) is a major costume source for TV, movie, and theatrical performances. Open to the public, it rents and sells outfits from Venetian kings and queens to Tarzan and Jane. Hundreds of costumes and accessories, such as wigs, masks, gloves, tights, and makeup, are available to buy off the rack, and thousands are available to rent.

Botanica Nena (✉ 902 N.W. 27th Ave., Downtown ☎ 305/649–8078) is the largest and most complete *botanica* (a store specializing in the occult) in Miami, stocking roots, herbs, seashells, candles, incense, and potions of all sorts. Its controversial subject matter and less-than-desirable location make this shop best left to the adventurous.

★ **Dog Bar** (✉ 723 N. Lincoln La., South Beach, Miami Beach ☎ 305/532–5654), just north of Lincoln Road's main drag, caters to enthusiastic animal owners who simply must have that perfect leopard-skin pet bed, gourmet treats, and organic food.

La Casa de las Guayaberas (✉ 5840 S.W. 8th St., Little Havana, Miami ☎ 305/266–9683) sells custom-made guayaberas, the natty four-pocket dress shirts favored by Latin men. Hundreds are also available off the rack.

Orchids (✉ 2662 S. Dixie Hwy., Coconut Grove, Miami ☎ 305/665–3278) will satisfy your yen for mysteriously beautiful varieties of orchids, bromeliads, and bonsai.

Sinbad's Bird House (✉ 7201 Bird Rd., South Miami ☎ 305/262–6077) has the perfect address for a purveyor of chirping, chattering, fluttering critters. Find everything you need to care for Polly, or choose a new pet from the vast selection of hand-raised baby birds.

Snakes at Sunset (✉ 9761 Sunset Dr., South Miami ☎ 305/757–6253) will sell you friendly snakes, spiders, lizards, and amphibians to bring that special touch of warmth to your home.

Sporting Goods

Bikes to Go (✉ 6600 S.W. 80th St., Miami ☎ 305/666–7702) sells wheels and products that protect you from the hazards of biking but does not rent equipment.

★ **Electric Rentals** (✉ 233 11th St., South Beach, Miami Beach ☎ 305/532–6700 ⊕ www.electricrentals.com) is a one-stop shop for Segways, the dynamic human transporter. Renting a Segway at this storefront between

Washington and Collins avenues includes hands-on training and in struction on the rules of the road. Tours are also available.

Miami Golf Discount Superstore (⊠ 111 N.E. 1st St., 2nd floor, Down town ☎ 800/718–8006 ⊕ www.miamigolfdiscount.com) has 10,000 square feet of golf equipment, including clubs, balls, shoes, and cloth ing. A practice net lets you test your swing.

Power Sports (⊠ 17777 N.W. 2nd Ave., North Miami Beach ☎ 305/651-4999) appeals to the oceangoing fast crowd with brand-name Jet Skis for sale.

Ride (⊠ 711 Washington Ave., South Beach, Miami Beach ☎ 305/673-3307) will help you zip around South Beach on your very own motorized Italjet, Aprillia, Kymco, or Moskito scooter. Buy one—along with accessories and apparel—or rent one while you're in town.

Outdoor Markets

Pass the mangos! Greater Miami's farmers markets and flea markets take advantage of the region's balmy weather and tropical delights to lure shoppers to open-air stalls filled with produce and collectibles.

★ **Coconut Grove Farmers' Market.** The most organic of Miami's outdoor markets specializes in a mouthwatering array of local produce as well as such ready-to-eat goodies as cashew butter, homemade salad dressings, and fruit pies. If you are looking for a downright granola crowd and experience, pack your Birkenstocks, because this is it. ⊠ *Grand Ave. and Margaret St., Coconut Grove, Miami* ☎ *305/238–7747* ۞ *Sat. 10–5:30.*

Coral Gables Farmers' Market. Some 25 local produce growers and plant vendors sell herbs, fruits, fresh-squeezed juices, chutneys, cakes, and muffins at this market located between Coral Gables' City Hall and Merrick Park. Artists also join in. Regular events include gardening workshops, children's activities, and cooking demonstrations offered by Coral Gables' master chefs. ⊠ *405 Biltmore Way, Coral Gables* ☎ *305/460–5311* ۞ *Jan.–Mar., Sat. 8–1.*

Española Way Market. This market has been a city favorite since its debut in the heart of South Beach in 1995. Along a two-block stretch of balconied Mediterranean-style storefronts, the road closes to traffic, and vendors set up tables on the wide sidewalks as street musicians beat out Latin rhythms. You might find silver jewelry, antique lanterns, orchids, leather jackets, cheap watches, imports from India and Guatemala, or antique Venetian painted beads. Scattered among the merchandise, food vendors sell tasty but inexpensive Latin snacks and drinks. Park along a side street. ⊠ *Española Way between Drexel and Washington Aves., South Beach, Miami Beach* ☎ *305/531–0038* ۞ *Sat. 9:30 AM–midnight, Sun. 10:30 AM–9 PM.*

Lincoln Road Farmers' Market. With all the familiar trappings of a farmers' market, this is quickly becoming a must-see event before or after visiting the Antique and Collectibles Market. It brings local produce and bakery vendors to the Lincoln Road Mall and often features plant workshops, art sales, and children's activities. This is a good place to pick up live orchids, too. ⊠ *Lincoln Rd. between Meridian and Euclid Aves., South Beach, Miami Beach* ☎ *305/673–4166* ۞ *Sun. 9–7.*

★ **Lincoln Road Outdoor Antique and Collectibles Market.** Interested in picking up samples of Miami's ever-present modern and Moderne furniture and accessories? This outdoor show offers eclectic goods that should satisfy post-Impressionists, deco-holics, Edwardians, Bauhausers, Goths, and '50s junkies. ✉ *Lincoln and Alton Rds., South Beach, Miami Beach* ☎ *305/673–4991* ⊕ *www.antiquecollectiblemarket.com* ☉ *Oct.–May, 2nd and 4th Sun. 9–6.*

Normandy Village Marketplace. Smaller, quieter, but building momentum, this farmers' market convenes at the Normandy Village Fountain, where a diverse mix of local vendors sells fruits and vegetables, herbs, plants and fresh-cut flowers, jams and breads, jewelry, and incense. ✉ *900 71st St., North Beach, Miami Beach* ☎ *305/531–0038* ☉ *Sat. 9–6.*

UNDERSTANDING MIAMI

SUN AND SAND, SALSA AND STYLE, Miami is distinctly different from any other city in America—or any city in Latin America, for that matter. This is no sleepy little beach outpost, no drowsy southern town. How could anyone nod off knowing a hurricane might blast through or swallow-size mosquitoes could attack at any moment? Seriously: how could anyone nap knowing there's so much excellent shopping, dining, and people-watching to be done?

Both logically and geologically, the city of Miami shouldn't even be here. Way back when, it was not much more than a swamp between the Everglades and the Atlantic Ocean. The first inhabitants were the Tequesta, who called this area home long before Spain's gold-hungry treasure ships sailed along the Gulf Stream a few miles offshore. They were followed by the Seminole, who learned how to prosper in the local ecosystem. Eventually the Seminole skedaddled, less likely because of the floods and hurricanes than because of Andrew Jackson. Today's residents don't have to worry about Old Hickory, and modern technology seems to be keeping the mosquitoes at bay, so why not head south for a little fun in the sun?

The end of the 20th century brought big changes to Miami. In the early 1980s Miami Beach was an oceanside geriatric ward. Today's South Beach residents have a hip that doesn't break. The average age of locals dropped from the mid-sixties in 1980 to a youthful early forties today. Toned young men outnumber svelte young women two to one, and hormones are as plentiful as cell phones. At night the revitalized Lincoln Road Mall gets into full swing as crowds descend on its restaurants, cafés, galleries, and theaters—but the Road also suffers from the vacancies that come with rapidly rising rents. And inevitably, those ever-present retail chains,

such as the Gap, Pottery Barn, Williams-Sonoma, and Banana Republic have set up shop on the Road. Those who have seen how high rents can crush a dream are heading to the northern beaches and to the southern reaches of South Beach, whose derelict buildings, once a flashback to the pre-renaissance days of the 1980s, are being refitted as affordable apartments and boutique hotels. This is where the new Miami Beach revival is taking place.

In Miami (as opposed to Miami Beach), boom times started in the 1970s for a small group of Latin American drug dealers. These "Cocaine Cowboys," as they were known, made and spent millions in Miami, investing in real estate and launching major construction projects. Their day ended in the 1980s, but by then economic development had its own—legal—momentum. Today, 150-plus U.S. and multinational companies have their Latin American headquarters here. Greater Miami is home to more than 40 foreign bank agencies, 11 Edge Act banks, 23 foreign trade offices, 31 binational chambers of commerce, and 53 foreign consulates.

As North America's gateway to the Southern Hemisphere and Latin America, Miami has become a multicultural metropolis that works and plays with vigor and that invites the world to celebrate its diversity. Miami is largely Cuban, as a result of two major waves of immigration, one in the early 1960s, then another in the 1980s. No matter where you spin your radio dial, virtually every announcer punctuates his harangue with an emphatic "COO-BAH!" Look around and you'll see Spanish on billboards, hear it in elevators, and pick it up on the streets. *Newsweek* called Miami "America's Casablanca," and the comparison may be apt. Many Cuban Americans straddle the Cuba–America divide, maintaining ties with their families back home and creating a culturally rich life in

Miami. Some, perhaps with less affluence or resources, are less successful: in 1999 both the United States and Cuba followed the plight of young Elián González, whose citizenship was hotly debated when his mother perished at sea in an illegal attempt to emigrate.

In addition to the Cuban population, there are also residents from Brazil, China, Colombia, El Salvador, Germany, Greece, Haiti, Iran, Israel, Italy, Jamaica, Lebanon, Malaysia, Nicaragua, Panama, Puerto Rico, Russia, Sweden, and Venezuela—all speaking in their own tongue and carrying on their own traditions. Miami seems to know it will remain a montage of nationalities, and it celebrates the cultural diversity at festivals, world-music performances, and a wealth of exotic restaurants. Annual film festivals—including Latin, gay, and Jewish—also reflect the local cultural landscape.

Miami has always attracted its fair share of hucksters, scammers, and fly-by-nighters and celebs, too. From the carpetbaggers to Al Capone, from the Colombian drug lords of the '80s to the Russian mafia in the '90s, this city opens its arms to anyone with flash and cash. Miami bid farewell to Madonna and Sylvester Stallone, who swept into town for a few years, and extended an uneasy greeting to O. J. Simpson and his children. High-profile hometown heroes Gloria and Emilio Estefan lead the list of Latin artists who spend much of their time here, along with Jon Secada, Julio Iglesias, Albita, and Andy Garcia. Thanks to a booming film industry and Miami's appeal to fashion magazines, year-round movie and photo shoots attract squadrons of beautiful people, filling up chic restaurants and VIP lounges of SoBe clubs.

Although you might not think it to look around, Miami's restaurant scene isn't mere glam without culinary gusto. The city is teeming with celebrity chefs, and most have an inventive flair derived from flavors found in kitchens around the globe.

Miami's New World Cuisine was formed over a decade ago, when a group of master chefs dubbed the "Mango Gang" created a new genre that makes splendid use of fresh native fruits and vegetables and local seafood, spiced up with Caribbean and Latin influences. Tropical treats such as mango, star fruit, avocado, papaya, cilantro, yuca, guava, and plantains are used lavishly, and stone crabs, conch, grouper, and Florida lobster make frequent mouthwatering appearances, sometimes along with more contemporary or Continental items. Do try the obvious: Cuban *medianoche* sandwiches, Brazilian barbecue, Nicaraguan grilled steaks, Jamaican jerk chicken. Then seek out Peruvian ceviche, Haitian *griots* (seasoned, fried cubes of pork), and some of the innovative Pan-Asian combinations that are born not of fad, but bona fide cultural fusion.

With an emphasis on its cultural heritage, many old neighborhoods are being rediscovered and revivified through special monthly events, such as Little Havana's Cultural Fridays, Homestead's Friday Fests, and Coral Gables's Gallery Nights. Other up-and-coming areas are emerging—lively Brickell Village in the financial district, the trendy Miami Design District, and the residential Morningside and Belle Meade districts north of Downtown, where gracious homes are being restored and antiques shops are replacing blighted storefronts along Biscayne Boulevard. Equally impressive are efforts to shed, for once and for all, Miami's image as a cultural backwater. The long-delayed Performing Arts Center, with a concert hall, ballet and opera house, and black box theater, has finally secured funding and is expected to revitalize the Omni area, just north of Downtown. In Miami Beach, the Collins Park Cultural Center will eventually be returned to a park with an ocean view—as it incorporates the renovated Bass Museum and the new Miami City Ballet.

You can easily have the kind of fun here that will drain your wallet. But look for less flashy ways to explore Miami, too. Skip the chichi restaurant and go for an ethnic eatery. Tour Lincoln Road Mall, downtown Coral Gables, or Coconut Grove on foot. Or take South Beach's colorful Electrowave shuttle, Florida's first electric transportation system, which really works for getting around traffic-clogged SoBe. Coral Gables, too, has an electric-hybrid trolley that ferries people around the downtown area. Winter *is* the best time to visit, but if money is an issue, come in the off-season—after Easter and before October. You'll find plenty to do,

and room rates can come down considerably. Summer brings many European and Latin American vacationers who find Miami congenial despite the heat, humidity, and intense afternoon thunderstorms. Like millions of others, they've discovered the many natural and unnatural pleasures to be had year-round in America's southernmost metropolis.

So whaddya waitin' for? Grab your lotion and head to the ocean.

— Gary McKechnie;
updated by Patty Shillington

MAGIC CITY

AGIC CITY. CITY OF THE FUTURE. CITY OF DREAMS. Gateway to the Caribbean. Capital of South America. The New New York. These names and scores more have been coined for a city that clings to a strip of ancient coral sea-bottom heaved up eons ago between the Gulf Stream and the Everglades. Known on the map and in the news as Miami, it was originally an Indian settlement, then an agricultural community purveying some odd root called "coontie," a backwater and a port for pirates and ship-scuttlers. Later, the 1920s boomtown was erased by a scourge called hurricane and entered a period of sleepy tourism. Those "Moon over Miami" days gave rise by the 1950s to an East Coast version of Las Vegas.

Things picked up some more in the 1960s, when Miami became a second home for thousands of Cubans fleeing Fidel, and the city served as the staging area for the ill-fated Bay of Pigs invasion. That stormy decade went out with a bang, with protests in Miami Beach and race riots in Liberty City sparked by the presidential nomination of Richard Nixon at the 1968 Republican National Convention. The 1970s were the glory days of the hometown football team, the Dolphins, and then the 1980s kicked off with the Mariel boatlift of political refugees and purged prisoners from Cuba to South Florida. An explosion of immigration from South America, Latin America, and the Caribbean and, of course, the explosion of *Miami Vice* on television rounded out the decade. Enter the 1990s and more home teams—the Heat and Marlins and Panthers. South Beach was reborn as "SoBe," crammed with more models, more movie and fashion shoots, more art deco hotels, more outdoor cafés, and more retro fashion per square foot than anyplace else on Earth.

In a little more than 100 years of boom and bust, crime and punishment, high times and low, Miami has endured it all. Here, human cycles wax and wane like the tides that have lapped the shores of Biscayne Bay from the days long before time was invented.

Which brings us to the true source of the world's endless fascination with Miami: its natural beauty. Flora and fauna in exotic profusion, and beaches brushed by temperate breezes from an Atlantic riding high outside a sheltering reef, make it a paradise and a wellspring of living poetry: palm, hibiscus, bougainvillea. Anhinga, osprey, gull. Manatee, snapper, bonefish, grouper. Coral reef and hardwood hammock. Mangrove, banyan, and the fabled Dade County pine, so dense, the story goes, it takes two men to carry those two-by-fours. Mango, guava, litchi nut, grapefruit. Alligator and flamingo. Orange, lemon, lime.

Miami is a pleasure dome, but it is also a working city, a place of constant beginnings and renewal, a place where anything can happen—and often does. It is, as it always has been, a city of dreams. The late poet Richard Hugo once told a gathering of students that he had always lived on the edge in his profession and lifestyle, just as he had always lived on the edge of the continent, on one coast or another. "It's the perfect place for the writer," he said. "Out there on the edge, looking in, where you're able to observe things more clearly."

Hugo would have loved Miami, city on the edge, on the frontier; gateway between North and South, portal to the Caribbean, entry point for seekers of the American Dream. Contemporary commentators as diverse as Joan Didion (*Miami*), David Rieff (*Going to Miami*), and T. D. Allman (*Miami: City of the Future*) have agreed that the very future of the nation can be glimpsed from the vantage point of this city. As New York served as bellwether for a changing America at the beginning of the 20th century and Los Angeles did at mid-century, so Miami serves at the end of one century and the beginning of the next. Hugo would have loved the intellectual energy of it all, as wave after wave of new, revitalizing culture sweeps ashore. Miami is not a melting pot, but rather a rich stew, dizzying in its complexity.

A Miami commuter, stalled in an unaccountable traffic jam, stares in wonder as a young, bare-chested man races down the center line of a busy multilane boulevard, holding aloft a Nicaraguan flag the size of a small billboard. Buoyant strains of music trail in the young man's wake. There's a flatbed truck stopped in the intersection ahead, a troupe of musicians up there, blaring Latin rhythms at maximum volume, a cheering crowd gathered around. Nicaragua has just defeated Colombia in soccer, someone explains to the stalled commuter. Just an exhibition match in the Orange Bowl, a few miles away, but it's a big victory anyway, and normal life will have to wait a few minutes here in Miami. The stalled commuter reflects that, as reasons for being stuck in traffic go, this one is, at the very least, remarkable.

There's a certain chaos to life in a city of some 2 million that contains a full-blown colony of so many Latin American and Caribbean expatriates. But what a panoply of variety comes with the chaos: shops, markets, restaurants, consulates, and even ethnic driving schools devoted to serving a newly arrived populace. Within a 20-minute driving radius, places like these offer the old-timer (someone who's lived in Miami for more than a decade) a taste of another, and then another, culture. Some people might pick a place to live or to visit because it's all of a piece—no surprises, every warp and weave of the cultural fabric an indistinguishable part of the whole. Comfortable perhaps, and reassuring, but they won't find it in Miami.

Hugo would have treasured Miami's everyday poetry: the sights, sounds, smells, and tastes—and the touch of the Gulf Stream breeze. There might be millions of bodies milling about the metropolis, but there's always an avenue of escape. Live a lifetime in Miami, and the possibilities only multiply. Calm bay waters for sailing or for puttering about the shallows in a john boat with a pole and some bait shrimp, prospecting for mangrove snapper. Find a friend or a willing captain for a high-powered cruise to Hemingway's beloved great blue Gulf Stream, where the fins and the swords of the great game fish still cross—all just a half hour out.

Say you're a country kid at heart, yearning for a fix of rustic—if that's the case, you head south. Fortify yourself with a breakfast of *huevos rancheros* at a modest South Miami-Dade storefront run by a Mexican family that came over to work the sprawling vegetable fields covering that part of Miami-Dade County. Another few miles south, you find yourself covering terrain as vast, unspoiled, and awesome as the African veldt. No lions lurking in the unpopulated "river of grass" that is Everglades National Park, of course, but don't tell your imagination that. Besides, once you get to Flamingo—the end of the road—and stare out over those boundless tidal flats at the thousands of meandering pink creatures that give the place its name, you'll forget about the lions anyway.

Locals like to make this trip in winter. For one thing, the mosquitoes are in hibernation. For another, you can stop off on the way home for a fresh-picked-strawberry shake and some home-baked goods at the stand an enterprising Amish family maintains every season, a place tucked alongside a country road as remote and Rockwellian as a Pennsylvania lane.

Another mood might send a person into Miami's heart, say, for lunch on bustling Calle Ocho—Southwest 8th Street—the main thoroughfare of Little Havana. Although Little Havana might now be more properly called Little Latin America, there are still any number of Cuban restaurants where veteran waitresses will guide the uninitiated toward *ropa vieja,* fried pork or grouper chunks, a chicken breast braised in lime juice, and some black beans and rice and diced onion to go with that, of course. To wash it down, maybe have a Hautey cerveza or two, now that the once-celebrated Cuban beer is again being produced, now stateside. Come to Little Havana in the evening and you can combine dinner with a visit to a club for a Rio-style revue or a knockout solo performance. Whether you watch Cuban chanteuse Albita belting out a tune or high-kicking beauties in Carmen Miranda getups, you'll swear you've slipped through a warp into another life and time. But it's really Miami, and there are still another three dozen cuisines and cultures to go.

No misunderstanding why Miami has been called America's Casablanca. In the same way bits of every Mediterranean culture found their way to that North African port, so has every Latin and Caribbean culture left its mark on modern-day Miami. Much as Casablanca did, Miami mixes the elegant and the raffish, the sophisticated and the casual. At one of the scores of sidewalk cafés in South Beach, a pair of leggy models in bikini tops and cutoffs rollerblade up to a table, chatting in German. They plop down next to a group of suited businessmen hammering out the possibilities—in rapid-fire Spanish—of a convention hotel on the vacant property just over there, at the end of Ocean Drive, where barely a decade ago one might have snapped up a run-down pensioner's hostel for the price of an upscale automobile.

* * *

A T THE EDGE, there is always action, and there is the heat that comes with it. Where less than two decades ago there was only one professional sports team in South Florida, suddenly there are four, and it's

no accident that the basketball club is named for that amalgam of climatological factors and plain old frictional force known as heat.

Of course, to some, being "on the edge" leads to edginess, what with all those cultures colliding and sometimes sending off sparks. Nothing like a session of the Miami-Dade County government for a lesson in pluralism, for example. This friction has captured the attention of a certain group of artists.

In the 1920s, the writers went off to Paris. In the late 1950s, the poets hung out in North Beach and Berkeley, the novelists took New York, and the most interesting among them were known as the Beats. Now, as a new century begins—apparently these things cycle every 40 years or so—there's another literary center and another group of writers scribbling away there: genus, *Miami;* species, *mystery writer.*

There's little doubt that Miami supports more crime, thriller, and mystery writers per capita than just about any other city in the country. There's Carl Hiaasen, James W. Hall, Edna Buchanan, Paul Levine, Barbara Parker, James Grippando, Carolina Garcia Aguilera, Vicki Hendricks, and Cherokee Paul MacDonald, not to mention yours truly. Elmore Leonard spends half the year down this way and sets about the same amount of his work in these parts. Although, sadly, John D. MacDonald, who gave us Travis McGee, and Charley Willeford, who gave us Hoke Moseley, have left us, and Doug Fairbairn (*Shoot, Street Eight*) is no longer writing, their work is still in print and swells the oeuvre significantly.

Not too long ago, *Tropic* magazine commissioned a spoof, a serialized mystery novel jestingly titled *Naked Came the Manatee,* to be penned in weekly installments by members of the Miami mystery crew. Within days, and long before the first word saw newsprint, three major publishing houses heard of the venture and enered into a bidding war that escalated well into the six figures, this for the rights to reprint within hard covers what is essentially an extended joke.

How to explain it? As James W. Hall likes to say, Miami history can be divided into three periods: 1) before *Miami Vice,* 2) during *Miami Vice,* and 3) after *Miami Vice.* It's not only a good joke, it is incisive commentary on what is going on here. The 1980s television series ("*Saturday Night Fever* on a Donzi ," as one wag dubbed it) not only revolutionized American television, it's ingrained in our consciousness, worldwide and forevermore, the idea that danger, double-dealing, and flash flourish in Miami. The impact of *Miami Vice* is more than an accident of television programming. Viewers and readers are captivated by the beauty here, to be sure, as they are by the irony and the tragedy of violence in such paradise. And the attraction of Miami crime fiction, whether in print, on film, or on television, goes deeper.

Miami has become the American city of the future, the focal frontier town where immigrants stream in to settle, clash, and clamor up against all the interests that have been established before them. It is, above all, a city on the edge, where everything is up for grabs, where nothing has yet been decided, where the conflicts and the comminglings presage that which is to come for America as a whole.

South Florida's beauty represents paradise. Its open portals signify promise. The attendant and seemingly inescapable violence portends the difficulties faced by a nation that has been living on the quick since the first days of the republic. But the flip side is the sense of possibility that's palpable in the Miami air. There's a freshness here, a sense that no group's firmly in charge, that one person's dreams are as good as anyone else's, and just as likely to come true. In Miami. On the edge.

— *Les Standiford*

Les Standiford, one of Miami's crew of crime novelists, is the author of nine books, including Presidential Deal, Black Mountain, *and* Miami: City of Dreams.

MIAMI AT A GLANCE

Fast Facts

Nickname: Little Cuba, Magic City
Type of government: The Miami-Dade metro area comprises a large unincorporated area and 32 municipalities, one of which is the City of Miami, which is also the county seat. Each municipality has its own government and provides city-type services such as police and zoning protection. A mayor and the 13-member Miami-Dade Board of County Commissioners govern the entire county.
Population: City 328,472, metro area (Miami-Dade County) 2.3 million

Population Density: 1,176.4 people per square mi
Median age: 36.9
Crime rate: Down 3.7%
Language: Seventy precent of Miami-Dade residents report that they speak a language other than English at home. Fifty percent report that they did not speak English "very well."
Ethnic groups: Latino 60%; black 19%, white 18%; other non-Asian 2%; Asian 1%

Miami Beach is where neon goes to die.

—Lenny Bruce

Geography & Environment

Longitude: 80° W (same as Panama City, Panama; Toronto, Canada
Latitude: 25° N (same as Karachi, Pakistan; Monterrey, Mexico; Riyadh, Saudi Arabia; Taipei, China)
Elevation: Sea level
Land area: 1,955 square mi
Terrain: Coastal, islands
Natural hazards: Fires, flooding, hurricanes, tornados

Environmental issues: Air quality, which improved in the 1990s, but remains an issue due to a combination of heat, traffic, and industry; canal management in Coral Gables and elsewhere with dams, damage to beaches and reefs from heavy boat traffic; effects of limerock mining along eastern edge of Everglades; wetlands preservation

Economy

Per capita income: $26,898
Unemployment: 6.5%
Work force: 1,093,800 (metro area)
Major industries: Aircraft repair, aluminum products, Caribbean shipping, cement, clothing, electronic components, fishing, furniture, machinery, plastics, publishing, shellfishing, tourism, transportation equipment

Did You Know?

• Miami's port is among the world's busiest. In 2002, 3.6 million people boarded cruise ships and 8.7 million tons of cargo set sail for other ports. The entire endeavor supports more than 45,000 workers.

• Miami's geography is the basis for one of the world's most popular video games: "Grand Theft Auto: Vice City" allows the player to drive through the streets, bridges, and seaport on missions.

• According to the 2000 Census, 135,810 Miami residents leave home for work between 7 AM and 7:29 AM, the most of any time period. It takes them, on average, 29 minutes to get to work, and 78% drive to work alone.

• The world's longest conga line was held in Miami, back in 1988. The "Miami Super Conga" was made up of just under 120 thousand people.

• The Carnaval Miami of 1990 saw the largest piñata on record, weighing in at 10,000 pounds and reaching 27 feet high.

• On the popular 1980s television show *Miami Vice,* it's no accident Sonny had a pet alligator. He and his partner, Tubbs, played for the University of Florida Gators in college. Elvis the alligator, as he was called on the show, was technically police property and the Vice Squad's mascot.

BOOKS & MOVIES

Books

Fiction. Steamy nights, sultry breezes, palm-dotted beaches, the heady whiff of frangipani in the air—all this idyllic setting needs is some seedy characters, a femme (or homme) fatale and a hard-boiled detective. South Florida's colorful scenery, both natural and human, is the canvas used by a whole posse of detective, mystery, and crime writers.

Interestingly, some of the finest fiction writers come from the *Miami Herald,* the city's top-notch daily newspaper. At the top of the list is Carl Hiaasen, who brilliantly skewers the pack of corrupt politicians, big-business phonies, land developers, and tourism interests every week in his *Herald* column. But it is his satirical fiction that manages to encompass everything that makes up Florida, for better and for worse. Populated by con artists, plastic surgeons, crooked cops, rednecks, bass fishermen, strippers, the Mafia, theme-park developers, backwoods hermits, and lottery winners, Hiaasen's hilarious novels will tell you all you need to know about South Florida. Read *Lucky You, Stormy Weather, Tourist Season, Skin Tight, Double Whammy, Native Tongue, Sick Puppy,* and *Strip Tease,* and you will be educated and entertained.

Pulitzer Prize–winner Edna Buchanan's two nonfiction books, *The Corpse Had a Familiar Face* and *Never Let Them See You Cry,* related the unbelievable and absolutely true crime stories she covered as a *Miami Herald* reporter. She later turned to fiction with a series of mysteries featuring Britt Montero, a Cuban-American reporter, including *Margin of Error*; *Contents Under Pressure*; *Miami, It's Murder*; and *Suitable for Framing.*

Other Miami-based mysteries are Paul Levine's Jake Lassiter series, featuring a pro football player turned lawyer, including *Night Vision* and *False Dawn*; Elmore Leonard's Palm Beach–based *Maximum Bob*; Les Standiford's *Deal on Ice,* featuring contractor-sleuth John Deal; and Charles Willeford's *Miami Blues,* with his lead character, Miami cop Hoke Mosely. James W. Hall's *Body Language* is a thriller set in Miami about a police photographer. Also located in Miami is *The Informant,* James M. Grippando's thriller about an FBI hunt for a serial killer. Author Peter Matthiessen's *Killing Mister Watson* is a novel about a real-life entrepreneur in the turn-of-the-20th-century Everglades.

Nonfiction. The country's most gleefully sophomoric humor columnist, Dave Barry, is on staff at the *Miami Herald,* and his many weekly columns and books deal with living in South Florida, one of which is *Dave Barry Turns 50.*

For a peek into Cuban-American society, check out Christina Garcia's *The Agüero Sisters,* the story of two long-estranged Cuban sisters, one in Cuba, the other in Florida. *Miami Herald* columnist Ana Veciana-Suarez chronicles the lives of three generations of Cuban-American women in *The Chin Kiss King.* Although they are not set in South Florida, the novels of young Haitian author Edwidge Danticat—*Breath, Eyes, Memory*; *The Farming of Bones: A Novel*; and *Krik? Krak!*—offer insight into Haitian life and culture.

A good introduction to Greater Miami is *Miami, the Magic City,* by historian Arva Moore Parks, one of the best-known chroniclers of local lore. Full of photographs and illustrations, this coffee-table book provides a fact-filled overview of the city's history from the time it was inhabited by human beings thousands of years ago. Also check out the well-documented *Miami Beach: A History,* by Howard Kleinberg. *The Life and Times of a Deco Dowager: The Edison Hotel* relays the art deco past of one of Ocean Drive's grande dames.

Pictures tell photogenic greater Miami's story well. With 400 color photos, *Miami:*

Hot and Cool, by Laura Cerwinske, takes a sophisticated look at Miami as the capital of American chic. *Miami,* by Santi Visalli, is one of a series of large-format photographic books on great American cities. Another good coffee-table book is *Miami: City of Dreams,* by Les Standiford and photographer Alan S. Maltz.

As an environmental hero, the late environmentalist Marjory Stoneman Douglas's name adorns Miami-Dade County streets, a school, and a nature center. Her classic *The Everglades: River of Grass* is a must-read for those interested in capturing the essence of those unique wetlands. Landscape photographer Clyde Butcher, whose Big Cypress Gallery is on Tamiami Trail in Ochopee, shows breathtaking Florida scenes from deep in the wilderness in *Clyde Butcher, Portfolio I: Florida Landscapes.*

How Miami deals with its unique cultural diversity and influx of immigrants has been a hot topic for social observation, leading to a number of thoughtful books on the topic. *City on the Edge: The Transformation of Miami,* by Alejandro Portes documents the development of Miami's ethnic communities. Other titles include T. D. Allman's *Miami, City of the Future*; David Rieff's *Going to Miami: Exiles, Tourists and Refugees in the New America*; and Joan Didion's *Miami,* an exploration of the influential Cuban community.

The chronicles of South Beach's Art Deco District are told by one of the key players in the preservation movement, the late Barbara Baer Capitman, in *Deco Delights: Preserving the Beauty* and *Joy of Miami Beach Architecture.* For more deco pick up *Tropical Deco: The Architecture and Design of Old Miami Beach,* by Laura Cerwinske and David Kaminsky, photographer.

A good way to whet your appetite for South Florida's distinctive cuisine—dubbed Floribbean or New World by foodies—is to check out *Mmmmiami: Tempting Tropical Tastes for Home Cooks Everywhere,* by cooking teacher Carole Kotkin and *Miami Herald* food editor Kathy Martin. Their recipes reflect Miami's tropical cuisine with strong Caribbean influences. Another good choice is Steven Raichlen's *Miami Spice: The New Florida Cuisine,* with 200 recipes that use native ingredients to capture the convergence of Latin, Caribbean, and Cuban cultures.

Film & Video

Greater Miami's ever-growing film business is visible as movie, fashion, and music video shoots take over the streets of South Beach, locations such as the Venetian Pool, or lush lots in Coconut Grove. Locals have come to take the street closings and detours in stride, but celebrity sightings are duly reported the next day in the *Miami Herald.*

Certainly Greater Miami's moviemaking industry has increased in stature since 1967, when Elvis Presley's *Clambake* was shot here (despite the appearance of mountains in some of the Miami scenes), and 1972, when Linda Lovelace's infamous *Deep Throat* gained notoriety. Movies at least partially filmed in South Florida include *Random Hearts,* with Harrison Ford; *Primary Colors,* with John Travolta and Emma Thompson; *Donnie Brasco,* with Johnny Depp and Anne Heche; *The Birdcage,* with Robin Williams and Nathan Lane; *Up Close and Personal,* with Robert Redford and Michelle Pfeiffer; and *Wrestling Ernest Hemingway,* with Robert Duvall and Shirley MacLaine.

The blockbuster gross-out comedy *There's Something About Mary,* with Cameron Diaz and Ben Stiller, was filmed at several South Florida locations. So was Jim Carrey's popular *Ace Ventura: Pet Detective. True Lies,* one of James Cameron's pre-*Titanic* megaeffects extravaganzas, captivated downtown Miami for days during filming of a helicopter mounted on a high-rise. Key scenes for critical dud *The Specialist,* with sometime Miami resident Sylvester Stallone and Sharon Stone, were shot at the Biltmore Hotel in Coral Gables. The dramatic car stunts in *Bad Boys II,* starring Will Smith, were filmed on the scenic MacArthur

Causeway that links Miami and South Beach. *2 Fast 2 Furious* and *Out of Time*, with Denzel Washington, also made Greater Miami their backdrop.

Other films—panned by critics but sometimes providing escapist fun—include *Wild Things*, with Kevin Bacon and Neve Campbell; *Big City Blues*, with Burt Reynolds and Vivian Wu; *Fair Game*, with William Baldwin and Cindy Crawford; *Blood and Wine*, with Jack Nicholson and Jennifer Lopez; and the unfortunate film version of Carl Hiaasen's very funny novel *Strip Tease*, starring Demi Moore and Burt Reynolds.

INDEX

NOTES

NOTES

FODOR'S KEY TO THE GUIDES

America's guidebook leader publishes guides for every kind of traveler. Check out our many series and find your perfect match.

FODOR'S GOLD GUIDES

America's favorite travel-guide series offers the most detailed insider reviews of hotels, restaurants, and attractions in all price ranges, plus great background information, smart tips, and useful maps.

COMPASS AMERICAN GUIDES

Stunning guides from top local writers and photographers, with gorgeous photos, literary excerpts, and colorful anecdotes. A must-have for culture mavens, history buffs, and new residents.

FODOR'S CITYPACKS

Concise city coverage in a guide plus a foldout map. The right choice for urban travelers who want everything under one cover.

FODOR'S EXPLORING GUIDES

Hundreds of color photos bring your destination to life. Lively stories lend insight into the culture, history, and people.

FODOR'S TRAVEL HISTORIC AMERICA

For travelers who want to experience history firsthand, this series gives in-depth coverage of historic sights, plus nearby restaurants and hotels. Themes include the Thirteen Colonies, the Old West, and the Lewis and Clark Trail.

FODOR'S POCKET GUIDES

For travelers who need only the essentials. The best of Fodor's in pocket-size packages for just $9.95.

FODOR'S FLASHMAPS

Every resident's map guide, with dozens of easy-to-follow maps of public transit, restaurants, shopping, museums, and more.

FODOR'S CITYGUIDES

Sourcebooks for living in the city: thousands of in-the-know listings for restaurants, shops, sports, nightlife, and other city resources.

FODOR'S AROUND THE CITY WITH KIDS

Up to 68 great ideas for family days, recommended by resident parents. Perfect for exploring in your own backyard or on the road.

FODOR'S HOW TO GUIDES

Get tips from the pros on planning the perfect trip. Learn how to pack, fly hassle-free, plan a honeymoon or cruise, stay healthy on the road, and travel with your baby.

FODOR'S LANGUAGES FOR TRAVELERS

Practice the local language before you hit the road. Available in phrase books, cassette sets, and CD sets.

KAREN BROWN'S GUIDES

Engaging guides—many with easy-to-follow inn-to-inn itineraries—to the most charming inns and B&Bs in the U.S.A. and Europe.

OTHER GREAT TITLES FROM FODOR'S

Baseball Vacations, The Complete Guide to the National Parks, Family Vacations, Golf Digest's Places to Play, Great American Drives of the East, Great American Drives of the West, Great American Vacations, Healthy Escapes, National Parks of the West, Skiing USA.